"In ReJesus, Alan and Michael successfully reinstate Jesus at the center of the spiritual life and mission of God's people. In an era overly focused on how to 'do church,' their message is clear; we must take a closer look at the life of Jesus. If you want to jump back into authentic, New Testament discipleship, then take their challenge to recalibrate the mission and work of the church around the story of Jesus. As only true practitioners can, they provide an abundance of practical insights and inspiration."

—Matt Smay, Missio Director of the Missional Church
Apprenticeship Practicum, co-author, *The Tangible Kingdom*

"Frost and Hirsch excavate the ruins of Western Christianity, digging through the accumulation of 2,000 years of dust in order to return the church to the sure foundation of Jesus Christ. This book is a challenging and helpful addition to the task of re-centering, re-founding, or, in their words, 're-Jesusing' Christianity. The Jesus-shaped church will look quite different from many of the modern variety, and Frost and Hirsch skillfully articulate both the need and the means to align the way of Jesus with the religion that bears his name."

—Mike Erre, Teaching Pastor at Rock Harbor Church in
Costa Mesa, California, author, *The Jesus of Suburbia*

"THIS is THE conversation to be had! While everyone is obsessed with reinventing the church—this puts not just the conversation, but the focus squarely back on where it belongs: Jesus! It's not the forms, the structures, the styles, the venues—it's the person of Jesus. I devoured every page of this book; I was completely engrossed in it. All true missional living starts and finishes with Jesus. When Jesus is at the core, not just of telling others about him but of creating a new life within us, we will be transformed and the church will be redefined. It will come not from ideas from without but from a person from within—Jesus! When Jesus is at the core, our faith and the church will always be alive to anyone, any time, any culture, and any place in the world. What Alan and Mike have done is write a book that answers the 'so what' of Jesus to his followers. The book is profound."

—Bob Roberts Jr., Senior Pastor of NorthWood Church
in Keller, Texas, author, *The Multiplying Church*

" 'The times, they are a-changing,' observed and sung by Dylan decades ago, continues to be the reality facing the church at the beginning of the 21st century. In response to our present challenges, Frost and Hirsch offer a fresh and provocative reading of the person of Jesus as the key for Christians to draw upon in living as contemporary disciples. They dig deep into the Jesus narrative for clues in understanding a wild Messiah—a ReJesus—and they discover key resources that are used to reclaim a radical call to discipleship. The reader will find their proposal to be openly invitational but should be prepared to be quite challenged."

—Craig Van Gelder, Professor of Congregational Mission,
Luther Seminary, author, *The Ministry of the Missional Church*

"Is the religion of Christianity the religion of Jesus? Is Jesus to be a model for our lives, or is he just a God-shaped security deposit? Frost and Hirsch recover God's call to become more like His Son and dare to place an earthy, narrative Christology at the center of all things missional."

—Sally Morgenthaler, author, *Worship Evangelism*,
contributor, *An Emergent Manifesto of Hope*

"As Christendom dies a slow death, people scour the landscape of literature to find answers for how to redo church, re-engage faith, or reposition so that we can maintain our present status quo of reputation, resources, and rest. In *ReJesus*, Hirsch and Frost call us past these pathetic pursuits to a new world, or old world, in which leaders follow Jesus and let Jesus reform the church. Read, only if you're willing to rethink everything."

—Hugh Halter, Missio Director, Pastor of Adullam in
Denver, Colorado, co-author of *The Tangible Kingdom*

"The themes of mission and personal and corporate renewal can be approached from a variety of perspectives. Many books on mission take a pragmatic approach, focusing on strategies; while those addressing renewal tend towards a nostalgic spiritualizing, drawing inspiration from previous revivalism the church. *ReJesus: A Wild Messiah for a Missional Church* represents a different approach. It draws together three key themes that are all too often compartmentalized: Christology, Missiology, and Ecclesiology. So many churches in the West are suffering from amnesia with regard to the Biblical narrative, or at best are guilty of a selective reading, resulting in a misrepresentation of Jesus to conform to our cultural assumptions and boundaries. Frost and Hirsch present us with a faithful portrayal of Jesus as fully human, as God intended us to be, by showing us what the God who dared to make us in his own image is really like. The authors present an untamed Jesus who makes scary, radical demands, while at the same time giving of himself to empower his followers with the courage and resources necessary to follow his leading. *ReJesus* reveals abundant evidence of extensive research, and dropped into the text are brief descriptions of individuals who embodied the challenges Frost and Hirsch present to the reader. In confronting such a gospel every seeker will find more than they bargained for! But the gospel was never a bargain, it is always a gracious gift—far too great and glorious for us to ever fully comprehend or exhaust its potential. In reading this book be prepared for a wild ride!"

—Eddie Gibbs, Senior Professor at Fuller
Theological Seminary, author, *LeadershipNext*

"Frost and Hirsch have done it again. Reading *ReJesus* provoked, frustrated, and ultimately convicted me of my need to live more deeply in the way of Jesus. If you are looking for another book on simply bolstering church *as-we-know-it*, this is not for you. If you and your church want to be challenged to walk in the Way of Jesus, this book delivers."

—Ed Stetzer, blogger (www.edstetzer.com),
author, *Planting Missional Churches*

"Alan Hirsch and Michael Frost continue to push the church into the future with their latest project, ReJesus. Herein they focus on what every Christian church must focus on—Jesus Christ—and they develop a Christ-centered strategy for missional ecclesiology. This is a timely and relevant book and deserves a wide readership."

—Tony Jones, national coordinator of Emergent Village, doctoral fellow in practical theology at Princeton Theological Seminary, author, *The New Christians: Dispatches from the Emergent Frontier*

"ReJesus calls to mind Jaroslav Pelikan's *Jesus Through the Centuries* and the stubborn fact we can never get outside our own culture(s) to a pure Jesus. That way is not open to those who confess the Incarnate One. In every age Christians are compelled to wrestle with the meaning of Jesus again. Colin Greene's *Christology in Cultural Perspective* reminds us of how we must continually wrestle with how to be faithful to Jesus in our day. Neibuhr's *Christ and Culture* shows how we continually shape Jesus out of our cultural imaginations. Yet, in all its eradicable shortcomings, the church is still the location where we're shaped by the revelation of God in Jesus Christ. We always wrestle with how to re-Jesus because we have no choice. May we do it with humility and a deep love for these clay vessels of history we call the church, for there is no other place in which Jesus is made present. This book is a contribution to that wrestling; like all such wrestling it is itself enmeshed in culture. I trust it encourages others to wrestle that we might all be more faithful followers of Jesus."

—Al Roxburgh, Vice President, Allelon Canada, co-author, *The Missional Leader*

"It is with such ease that the church veers off course. ReJesus draws us back to Jesus in all of his radical, passionate, and transformative beauty. Frost and Hirsch demonstrate by word and example that to be the church demands a fearless, intimate, and constant encounter with Christ. As individuals and as a community, we have no option but to heed their wisdom."

—Daniel M. Harrell, Associate Minister at Park Street Church in Boston, author, *Nature's Witness: How Evolution Can Inspire Faith*

"At this moment in history we are in the middle of an ecclesial and theological reformation that is at least as radical as, and likely more significant than, the Protestant Reformation of the 16th and 17th centuries. In this bold, compelling, and prophetic masterpiece, Hirsch and Frost articulate the beautiful vision of the Jesus-centered Kingdom that is driving this new Reformation. Hirsch and Frost brilliantly weave together insightful biblical exegesis, critical historical reflection, transforming spiritual discipleship, probing cultural analysis, and even a good bit of humor in ways that help readers get free from the deadening yoke of the Christian religion and rediscover the wild, untamed, life-giving Jesus of the Gospels. I hope everyone who professes faith in Christ will dare to read this book. They will not put it down unchanged."

—Greg Boyd, Senior Pastor of Woodland Hills Church in St. Paul, Minnesota, co-author, *The Jesus Legend*

"Calls for a fresh, radical following of Jesus Christ are not new. Reformers from Francis of Assisi to Mother Teresa have sounded the call; already in the New Testament the Apostle John says true Christians must 'walk as [Jesus] walked,' and Peter insists we must follow in Jesus' steps. What is new about the message of ReJesus is the creative interweaving of the themes of Jesus' example, God's mission, and the kingdom mission of the church—the 'reintegration,' as the authors put it, 'of the theological concepts of missio Dei, participatio Christi, and imago Dei.'

"The book is filled with images—visual, imaginative, conceptual, biographical— that evoke Jesus Christ and Jesus-like discipleship. The authors' eclectic mining of secondary sources also helps free Jesus from well-rooted stereotypes. I view this book as an enlargement of the foundation of the authors' provocative and prophetic earlier works, rather than a sequel to or restatement of them. I think the authors are correct: 'Christianity minus Christ equals Religion'—not authentic discipleship."

—Howard A. Snyder, Professor of Wesley Studies, Tyndale Seminary, Toronto, author, *Radical Renewal*

"How horrific it is to think that we could be so passionately missional, but subtly drift from being entirely Jesus-centric in the process. Anyone in the missional conversation must never, ever forget about this subtle drift. ReJesus challenges us all in very theological, hopeful, and practical ways to never let that happen."

—Dan Kimball, Pastor of Vintage Faith Church in Santa Cruz, California, author, *They Like Jesus But Not The Church*

"This books reads you; you don't read it. Over and over you will find yourself wrestling with yourself and with God. In the end you have more than a decision to make; you have a quest to pursue. What you do about that will define your life."

—Reggie McNeal, Leadership Network, author, *Missional Renaissance*

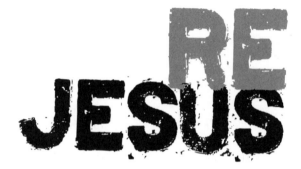

MICHAEL FROST
& ALAN HIRSCH

A WILD Messiah
for a Missional Church

HENDRICKSON
PUBLISHERS

STRAND PUBLISHING
Sydney

ReJesus: A Wild Messiah for a Missional Church
© 2009 by Michael Frost and Alan Hirsch

Published by Hendrickson Publishers, Inc., P.O. Box 3473, Peabody, Massachusetts 01961-3473.

Published in Australia and New Zealand by Strand Publishing, Suites 12–13, Fountain Plaza Business Centre, 148 The Entrance Road, Erina NSW 2250.

United States ISBN 978-1-59856-228-6
Australia ISBN 978-192-120-2919

Printed in the United States of America

Third Printing — September 2009

Hendrickson Publishers is strongly committed to environmentally responsible printing practices. The pages of this book were printed on 30% postconsumer waste recycled stock using only soy or vegetable content inks.

Library of Congress Cataloging-in-Publication Data

Frost, Michael, 1961–
   ReJesus : a wild Messiah for a missional church / Michael Frost and
Alan Hirsch.
      p. cm.
   Includes bibliographical references and index.
   ISBN 978-1-59856-228-6 (alk. paper)
      1. Mission of the church. 2. Jesus Christ. 3. Christianity—21st century.
   4. Postmodernism—Religious aspects—Christianity. I. Hirsch, Alan, 1959–
   II. Title.
   BV601.8.F76 2009
   270.8′3—dc22
                                                          2008034100

DEDICATIONS

Alan

To my various partners in the missional enterprise: Forge,
Church Resource Ministries (especially Sam Metcalf), *Missio*,
Shapevine, Church Planting Network (Exponential), and Christian
Associates. Also to Bob Roberts Jr. for his loving sponsorship,
and to my great friend and co-conspirator, Michael Frost.

Michael

For Peter Horsley in gratitude for his partnership
in life, leadership, and the gospel.

Contents

Introduction: Read This Bit First

Jesus is the center of all, the object of all, whoever does not know him, knows nothing aright, either of the world or of himself.
—Blaise Pascal

> *The means to know God is Christ, whom no one may know unless they follow after him with their life.*
> —Hans Denck

On the morning of June 7, 1964, the recently consecrated wing of the Ku Klux Klan known as the White Knights gathered solemnly in the Boykin Methodist Church in the pine woods near Raleigh, Mississippi. Concerned about what they saw as a wave of blacks and communists hitting the streets of Mississippi, the Klan had marshaled their forces to plan a so-called counter-attack against the civil rights movement. Armed with rifles, pistols, and shotguns and protected by men riding on horseback through the woods and by two Piper Cubs circling the property overhead, they bowed their heads as their Grand Chaplain ascended to the pulpit to read the following prayer:

> Oh God, our Heavenly Guide, as finite creatures of time and as dependent creatures of Thine, we acknowledge Thee as our sovereign Lord. Permit freedom and the joys thereof to forever reign throughout our land. May we as klansmen forever have the courage of our convictions that we may always stand for Thee and our great nation. May the sweet cup of brotherly fraternity ever be ours to enjoy and build within us that kindred spirit which will keep us unified and strong. Engender within us that wisdom kindred to honorable decisions and the Godly work. By the power of Thy infinite spirit and the energizing virtue therein, ever keep before us our oaths of secrecy and pledges of righteousness. Bless us now in this assembly that we may honor Thee in all things, we pray in the name of Christ, our blessed Savior. Amen.[1]

The congregation said their amens softly under their breaths. Later, Sam Bowers, the Imperial Wizard of the Ku Klux Klan of Mississippi, took to the pulpit and in overtly religious language declared what amounted to a holy war against the civil rights leadership, detailing a formal protocol for all Klan attacks on the "nigger-communist invasion of Mississippi."[2] Within the month, three civil rights workers were murdered execution-style in nearby Neshoba County.

The overtly Christian character of the Ku Klux Klan, its symbolism, and its language, will not be news to anyone—who can forget those burning crosses? But it's the specifically Christ-focused aspect of the Klan philosophy that continues to shock nearly half a century later. Praying in the name of Christ at the inauguration of what was effectively a racist death squad still jars, but there can be no denying that the KKK routinely called on Jesus to strengthen them in their quest. The devotion to Jesus of the Imperial Wizard, Sam Bowers, is well known. Ken Dean, the director of the Council of Human Relations in Mississippi in 1964, said of him, "The Imperial Wizard, in the most radical sense possible, is a believer in the sovereignty of God."[3] Indeed, more than that, Bowers believed that God's sovereignty is most supremely demonstrated in his raising of Jesus from the dead:

> There is one simple, and central, Empirical Fact, of manifested human history. That Empirical Fact, of course, is the Physical Resurrection of The Galilean . . . The genuineness of Faith is in the Omnipotent Power of God to perform the Miracle: The certainty of rational human knowledge is that the Resurrection did occur: As an Empirically manifested Fact.[4]

Charles Marsh, who in researching the civil rights movement in Mississippi began a correspondence with Bowers later in life, says of him: "Bowers as theologian is, in a most radical, perplexing, and bizarre sense, a believer in the Christ-centered shape of all reality."[5]

How distressing, then, to those of us who likewise seek to trust in the "Christ-centered shape of all reality," that we share such a faith with so reprehensible a set of characters as Sam Bowers and the KKK. How did followers of Jesus end up so far from the teaching and example of Jesus? How did Jesus followers like members of the Lutheran Church in Nazi Germany quote Jesus in one breath and incite racial vilification in the next? The same could be asked of the Crusaders or the Conquistadors or even the Rwandan death squads.

The KKK is, of course, an extreme example of a group adopting the image of Jesus in a way that seems foreign to us. But there are milder examples of this even within our own broad community of people who identify themselves as Christians. In 2005, while en route to a speaking tour of the United Kingdom, we decided to treat ourselves to a stopover in Rome. As one does when in the eternal city, we visited the Vatican and St. Peter's Basilica. It was every bit as beautiful as we had imagined. Everyone who sees St. Peter's agrees that it is a truly remarkable feat of human ingenuity, with perfectly designed shafts of natural light highlighting its artistic treasures, built on a scale designed to foster a feeling of spiritual awe. Like all tourists we wandered, mesmerized, our necks craned upwards to take in the sheer grandeur of the cathedral. Not looking where we were going, we accidentally bumped into each other, and there in the middle of the room that represented the heart of global Christianity for centuries, we reflected on what we were seeing and asked each other where Jesus was to be found in this place. Certainly, we agreed, the architecture of the basilica was stunning, and the sculpture, windows, and ceiling were beautiful. But both of us had the same nagging question bubbling around in our minds: Where is the poor, itinerant rabbi from Nazareth?

Similarly, on a recent speaking assignment in Moscow, Michael had the opportunity to wander through the Orthodox Cathedral of Christ the Savior. Constructed as recently as the 1990s, it is an astonishing feat of religious architecture. Situated on the banks of the Moskva River, a few blocks from the Kremlin, it replaced the original cathedral that had been destroyed by Stalin in 1931. It is constructed almost entirely of marble, and its gleaming golden domes or cupolas make it the tallest Orthodox church in the world. The white marble exterior is completely ringed by astonishing bronze relief statues of various saints and Christian heroes. Inside, the chapels are configured as an equal-sided cross measuring 85 meters wide, each replete with hundreds of gilt icons and frescoes. Wandering around the cavernous main chapel, which can hold up to ten thousand people, it is hard not to be amazed by the beauty of this house of worship. But if you look more closely, some disquieting features begin to emerge.

The original cathedral commemorated the so-called divine intercession that led to the Russian victory over Napoleon in 1812. In fact, Tchaikovsky's 1812 *Overture* debuted in the Cathedral of Christ the Savior in 1882. When Boris Yeltsin approved the rebuilding of the cathedral, it was designed to be as close a replica of the original as possible, including its deeply patriotic Russian themes. So, this great building manages to be both a religious space and a historical monument to the militaristic might of Russia. There are frescoes that deify historical figures and events. The two-story galleries surrounding the main church are devoted to the history of Russia and the war of 1812 specifically. In fact, the marble boards on the first floor commemorate the participants of that bloody war. The frescoes in the second-story gallery depict various historical events and personages that played a decisive role in the Orthodox church or in Russian history. Below the new church is a large hall for church assemblies, where the last Russian tsar and his family were glorified as saints in 2000. The face of Jesus therefore sits alongside an image of the incompetent Tsar Nicholas II, who oversaw the vicious Bloody Sunday massacre of unarmed, peaceful demonstrators in 1905.

As Michael left the cathedral and headed through the snow to the nearby Metro station he encountered an elderly woman kneeling on the frozen pavement, begging for loose change from disinterested passersby. While it was difficult to see the real Jesus in the cathedral frescoes, it wasn't hard to recall Jesus' words about what we do for the "least of these" being done as if for him. According to Jesus' own words, he should be identifiable in the ragged image of the suppliant pauper outside the cathedral far more than in the astonishing gilt iconography inside.

We open this book with these three vastly different stories—the 1964 massacre in Neshoba County, and our visits to the Vatican and the Russian Orthodox cathedral—to illustrate our concern with what has been promulgated in Jesus' name throughout history. In Mississippi, Rome, and Moscow, the name of Jesus has been invoked as central to movements that do not seem to be in accord with the Jesus we find in the pages of the Gospels. In the descriptions of the KKK's Bible-thumping reign of terror in Mississippi we are aghast that men could attempt to sanctify their actions with prayers to Jesus. In the Vatican, one of the archetypal buildings dedicated to the religion that was founded on Jesus Christ, we cannot locate the simple, hardy, revolutionary carpenter who is compellingly portrayed in the Gospels. At the Cathedral of Christ the Savior, the Jesus of the Gospels competes with tsars and generals for the affections of the devoted. All of these are unsettling insights that speak directly to the purpose of this book because they raise disturbing questions about the continuity between Jesus and the subsequent religion established in his name.

In saying this, we don't mean to equate the Catholic or Orthodox churches with the Ku Klux Klan. We simply mean to identify instances in which a group's depiction of the person of Jesus is incongruous to us. Indeed, the discontinuity between Jesus and the religion that bears his name that we found in Rome and Moscow is by no means limited to those churches or denominations. Both Catholic and Protestant groups, right up to our present time and including even the newer Christian church movements, have traded in the radical way of Jesus for the seemingly greater grandeur of such religious expressions.

These examples suggest questions that can be, indeed, should be, asked of all believers, churches, and denominations in any time and place:

- ↪ What ongoing role does Jesus the Messiah play in shaping the ethos and self-understanding of the movement that originated in him?

- ↪ How is the Christian religion, if we could legitimately call it that, informed and shaped by the Jesus that we meet in the Gospels?

- ↪ How do we assess the continuity required between the life and example of Jesus and the subsequent religion called Christianity?

- ↪ In how many ways do we domesticate the radical Revolutionary in order to sustain our religion and religiosity?

- ↪ And perhaps most important of all, how can a rediscovery of Jesus renew our discipleship, the Christian community, and the ongoing mission of the church?

These are not insignificant questions because they take us to the core of what the church is all about. They take us to the defining center of the movement that takes its cue from Jesus. Rather than call this reformation, we will call this task refounding the church because it raises the issue of the church's true founder or foundation. And in our opinion, nothing is more important for the church in our day than the question of refounding Christianity. It has a distinct poignancy at the dawn of the twenty-first century as we collectively attempt to address Christianity's endemic and long-trended decline in the West. We seem a little lost, if truth be told, and no quick-fix church-growth solution can be found that can stop the hemorrhage. There is no doubt that we face a spiritual, theological, missional, and existential crisis in the West.

We must admit that both of us are somewhat obsessed with mission and what it means to be a missional people. But we both remain convinced that it is Christology that remains even more foundational and therefore the primary issue. We have elsewhere asserted that it is Christology (the exploration of the person, teachings, and impact of Jesus Christ) that determines missiology (our purpose and function in the world), which in turn determines our ecclesiology (the forms and functions of the church).[6] We have found

Follow Me—Becoming a Little Jesus

Following Jesus involves more than simply accepting him as your Savior via some prayer of commitment, no matter how sincere that prayer might be. In order to follow Jesus you must also emulate him, using his life as a pattern for your own. We call this emulation becoming a "little Jesus."

When we call ourselves little Jesuses, we aren't claiming to be able to walk on water or die for the sins of the world. No, being a little Jesus means that we adopt the values embodied in Jesus' life and teaching. Only Jesus was able to feed thousands with small amounts of bread and fish, but as little Jesuses we can embrace the values of hospitality and generosity. We might not be able to preach to the multitudes, but we can commit to speaking truth to lies. We can't die for anyone's sins, but we can embrace selflessness, sacrifice, and suffering.

We hope to see a conspiracy of little Jesuses unleashed all over the world, transforming their communities the way Jesus transformed his. To give concrete examples of what it means to emulate Jesus, throughout this book we will be giving thumbnail portraits of the little Jesuses who have inspired us.

no reason to revise our opinion on this, but over time we have only become even more convinced of the primacy of this formula. Both of us (together and apart) have written books about a distinctly missional form of discipleship and ecclesiology.[7] In writing this book, we feel we are now getting to the nub of the matter. We are going back to the founder and recalibrating the entire enterprise along christological lines.

The core task of this book therefore will be to explore the connection between the way of Jesus and the religion of Christianity. We will attempt to assess the Christian movement in the light of the biblical revelation of Jesus and to propose ways in which the church might reconfigure itself, indeed, recalibrate its mission, around the example and teaching of the radical rabbi from Nazareth. Where is the continuity? Why is what we experience as Christianity discontinuous with the way of Jesus? How consistent is our witness with his life and teachings? And can we move away from his prototypal spirituality without doing irreparable damage to the integrity of the faith? How far is too far?

Similarly, Jacques Ellul, the French theologian and philosopher, raises a disturbing historical problem for us to solve, a problem that he calls "the subversion of Christianity."

> The question that I want to sketch in this work is one that troubles me most deeply. As I now see it, it seems to be insoluble and assumes a serious character of historical oddness. It may be put very simply: How has it come about that the development of Christianity and the church has given birth to a society, a civilization, a culture that are completely opposite to what we read in the Bible, to what is indisputably the text of the law, the prophets, Jesus, and Paul? I say advisedly "completely opposite." There is not just contradiction on one point but on all points. On the one hand, Christianity has been accused of a whole list of faults, crimes, and deceptions that are nowhere to be found in the original text and inspiration. On the other hand, revelation has been progressively modeled and reinterpreted according to the practice of Christianity and the church. . . . This is not just deviation but radical and essential contradiction, or real subversion.[8]

And while this might seem to be an overstatement, Ellul proceeds to back up his conclusions with some unnerving scholarship. To our thinking, no one has yet answered his questions in a satisfactory way. Yet they cannot be avoided if we are to re-establish ourselves as an authentic church in the twenty-first century. Therefore, among other things, we have taken it upon ourselves to further develop his concerns and to continue to raise the questions first posed by Ellul.

But this quest is not limited to the realm of scholarship and philosophy. For example, at a more popular level, Erwin McManus takes up a similar theme in *The Barbarian Way*, in which he rails against the transformation of Christianity from a dangerous and revolutionary spiritual force into a "religious civilization." And rightly so. Is such a civilization, with its associated civil religion, what Jesus intended for the movement he started? Was it his intention to produce a domesticated religion with a fully fledged mediating priesthood, cumbersome rituals, and dense theologies, along with all the other trappings of religions with ambiguous connections to the surrounding society and culture? Is this what Jesus meant when he came pronouncing the arrival of the kingdom of God or the tearing of the veil in the temple at his death?[9]

So what's this book all about? It's all about Jesus, with direct implications for our discipleship, some radical challenges for our churches, and some suggested reformulations for our spirituality. In short, it's about re-Jesusing the church.[10]

It's All About Jesus

From the beginning, let us say that we believe that the only way we can truly authenticate ourselves as an expression of Christianity is to somehow measure ourselves against the life and teachings of Jesus Christ, our Lord. And it is to him that we must now return if we are going to faithfully negotiate the profound challenges of the twenty-first century. But surely this is what the church tries to do in every age and context? Surely all expressions of Christianity seek to call Jesus Lord and have a special place reserved for him in their life and theology. We would argue that while confessionally this might be true, the church throughout history struggles to concretely conform its life to the radical life and teachings of Jesus. We don't say this judgmentally, as we are well aware how difficult it is to live a life based fully on Jesus. It is no easy thing, because the way that Jesus sets for us to follow is inherently subversive against all attempts to control, and thus institutionalize, the revelation that he so powerfully ushers in. In other words, it's just plain hard to create a religion out of the way of Jesus.

So this book is dedicated to the recovery of the absolute centrality of the person of Jesus in defining who we are as well as what we do. As hard as it is to truly follow him, we assert that we must constantly return to Jesus to authenticate as well as legitimize ourselves as his people. We have no other Archimedean point by which to set our coordinates or any other touchstone by which we can assess the abiding validity of our faith and to see if we are authentically Christian. The love of Jesus, and our commitment to live in conformity to him, is in effect an inbuilt spiritual mechanism at the heart of the church's theology and experience that provides an instrument for our ongoing renewal. It seems to us that a constant, and continual, return to Jesus is absolutely essential for any movement that wishes to call itself by his name.

But it is hard to keep a clear vision of the true way of Jesus, particularly when you live within a culture that is far askew from that way. Missiologist David Bosch grew up as a proud racist Afrikaner near Kuruman in South Africa. Looking back with shame, he recounts how in 1948, the same year he entered teacher's college, the pro-apartheid National Party was swept into power. For Afrikaners like Bosch, "it was to us like a dream come true when the Nationalist Party won that victory. We had no reservations whatsoever."[1] It was during this very time that young David Bosch was sensing a strong call into the Christian ministry, seeing no conflict between his support for apartheid and his belief in the teaching of Jesus.

But Bosch is not the only well-meaning theologian to have been guilty of such dissonance. Early last century, the well-known historian Adolf von Harnack remarked, "There is something touching in the striving of every individual to approach this Jesus Christ from the perspective of his personality and individual interests and to find in Him none other than himself, or to receive at the very least a small part of Him."[12] By "something touching" Harnack means something sad or pathetic or pitiful. As a historian of dogma, he had seen too many agendas take Jesus captive, quoting him to justify all manner of beliefs and practices. He became convinced that the kernel of the gospel had been overlaid by the husks of metaphysical concepts alien to the teachings of Jesus. The primitive stories of Jesus had been corrupted by official church dogma, claimed Harnack.

Indeed, it's not hard to find examples to support his view. Those who want to find in Jesus merely a reformer of Judaism, or the last of the prophets, have managed to do so quite readily. Supporters of violence have characterized him as a revolutionary, while Tolstoy and his disciples saw him as a teacher of nonresistance. To New Age scholars, Jesus is the holy one of an esoteric order. To the enemies of the traditional social order, he was a warrior against the routine. And to racists, Jesus was an Aryan Galilean. In fact, after ten years in prison for his involvement in the deaths of the three civil rights workers, Sam Bowers returned to Mississippi to devote himself to a study of the life of Christ and was never, in forty years of research, convinced that Jesus was anything other than Bowers believed him to be when he ascended that pulpit in 1964.

Harnack believed that the only answer to the problem of losing the kernel of the gospel under the husks of foreign ideas was to emancipate the gospel by returning to its primitive form, freeing it from centuries of superstitious Catholicism. And in this he was right. Setting Jesus free from Nazis, racist Afrikaners, Klansmen, and the dogma of the church is essential, but even Harnack wasn't able to let Jesus be Jesus. As a leading Protestant liberal, he launched what would famously be called the "quest for the historical Jesus," believing sincerely that if only the real Jesus could be recovered, he would be the inspiration for a renewed Christianity. Today, twentieth-century German liberals like Harnack are often seen as falling into the very trap in which they accused others of being snared. Besotted by the liberal humanism of their time and unable to escape the rigors of the new science, history, they limited their rediscovery of Jesus to that of a purely human figure. Harnack's quest for an emancipated Jesus led him to one without such concepts as revelation, incarnation, miracle, and resurrection, which he considered unscientific. In the much-quoted judgment of the Catholic George Tyrrell, "The Christ that Harnack sees, looking back through nine centuries of Catholic darkness, is only the reflection of a liberal Protestant face, seen at the bottom of a deep well."[13]

Suffering Prophet

Martin Luther King Jr.

Like Jesus announcing the kingdom of God, Dr. Martin Luther King Jr. prophetically spoke to the possibility of a new American society—a society without racism, oppression, and violence. His iconic "I Have a Dream" speech, singing out his hope for America's future, echoes Isaiah 40, "I have a dream that every valley will be exalted . . ." and Amos 5:24, "No, no we are not satisfied, and we will not be satisfied until justice rolls down like waters and righteousness like a mighty stream. . . ." His uncompromising stance on non-violence even in the face of extreme provocation was influenced by the non-violent activism of Mahatma Gandi in India, and deliberately embodied the explicit teachings of Jesus to turn the other cheek and to love one's enemies. King's message of hope and justice inspired African-Americans to claim their place at America's table, rather like Jesus' message gave hope to the poor of his day. As a little Jesus, King transformed society, and his assassination in 1968 mirrors the sacrificial death of Jesus. King is one of the ten twentieth-century martyrs from around the world who are depicted in statues above the Great West Door in London's Westminster Abbey.

Surely the challenge for the church today is to be taken captive by the agenda of Jesus, rather than seeking to mold him to fit our agendas, no matter how noble they might be. We acknowledge that we can never truly claim to know him completely. We all bring our biases to the task. But we believe it is inherent in the faith to keep trying and to never give up on this holy quest. The challenge before us is to let Jesus be Jesus and to allow ourselves to be caught up in his extraordinary mission for the world.

Whether it is the grand ecclesiastical project of the institutional churches, epitomized by the ostentatious excess of the Vatican, or the tawdry grab for the hearts and minds of the aspirational middle class by prosperity-style Pentecostalism, the Christian movement has been subverted. Like a forgotten nativity scene in a shopping mall dominated by Santa Claus, reindeer, elves, Disney characters, tinsel, baubles, and fake snow, the biblical Jesus is hard to find. But Jesus is still calling us to come and join him in a far more reckless and exciting adventure than that of mere church attendance. When allowed to be as he appears in the pages of Scripture, Jesus will not lead us to hatred, violence, greed, excess, earthly power, or material wealth. Instead, he will call us to a genuinely biblical and existential faith that believes in him, not simply believing in belief, as in many expressions of evangelicalism. It requires an ongoing encounter with Jesus. This will raise issues in the *ways of knowing* that bring about true spiritual transformation, which we will explore later in this book.

And so it is all about Jesus for us, with some direct implications for our lives as followers of Jesus.

✐ Direct Implications for Our Discipleship

Because this is a book about Jesus, it must also be a book that explores our living relationship with him. Therefore it should also be about discipleship— our experiencing the redemption he brings, being incorporated into his body, following in his way, becoming like him, and taking up his cause. And so any attempt to reJesus the church must also recover a real sense of the radical and revolutionary nature of what it means to follow Jesus in the current Western context. To be free in Jesus must somehow mean that the idols of our time come under some serious questioning. For instance, to be free in Jesus surely will mean liberation from the shackles of a predominant and omnipresent middle-class consumerism that weighs heavily on us. To be free in Jesus means allowing Jesus to be Jesus, and in doing so, allowing Jesus to challenge our religiosity or our self-righteousness or our greed or worse.

✐ Radical Challenges for Our Churches

Following Jesus will also have implications for a religion constrained by degenerating institutional forms and expressions. And so this is also a book that will have direct implications for missional ecclesiology (our understanding and practice of church). We will explore the implications of the love and following of Jesus for the missional church at the dawn of what might prove to be the most missionally challenging century ever. And given that we are mainly concerned with how Jesus shapes our mission and our experience of church, we believe that if we don't deal with Christology, how can we ever get mission, or even, and perhaps especially, a right view of ecclesiology? How many so-called new movements has the Protestant church seen in recent memory? Whether it is Pentecostalism, church growth theory, the third-wave charismatic movement, the parachurch movement, rapid church multiplication, emerging church, simple church, or the passion movement, so many of them have been presented as new ways of doing church. From our perspective, this is putting the cart before the horse. Let's get our Christology right and then dare to place all our deeply held desires for how to do church at its service. Not vice versa.

Are we fundamentally aligned with Jesus' purposes and will for his community on earth? It's a good question, and one we must ask at this critical time in history. When we direct that question to our founder, we find the answer somewhat disturbing. The only means we have of proposing a viable answer is to compare the 'religion' of Jesus with the religion of Christianity to see if these coincide. How else are we to assess our authenticity? If we are to take him as the prototypal Christian, and if, apart from the uniquely messianic aspects of his work, we are to take his words and actions as exemplary and authoritative for all of his followers everywhere, then we are left no option but to make this dangerous comparison. In fact, it's dangerous because we believe such a comparison will reveal the church to be on the wrong side of Jesus' type of barbarian spirituality and religion, precisely because his form of spirituality can hardly be considered to be civil. It must be called subversive by all that is called civilized. It is what Ellul called "antireligion." Jesus undermines any status quo that is not built on the all-encompassing demands of the kingdom, and this must call into question much of our religious codes, institutions, and behavior.

⟵Some Suggested Reformulations of Our Spirituality

And because this is a book about Jesus, it is also therefore a book exploring the nature of Christian spirituality and worship in our context. If Jesus is our center point, our guide, and the mediator between humanity and God, then we cannot bypass the implications that this will have for our spirituality.

It is true that Jesus is like God, but the greater truth, one closer to the revelation of God that Jesus ushers in, is that God is like Christ. As A. Michael Ramsey, the former Anglican archbishop, noted, "God is Christlike and in him is no unChristlikeness at all."[14] Or in the words of Jesus, "If you have seen me, you have seen the Father, I and the Father are one" (John 14:9, 1:14, 18). This has massive implications for us, especially for our understanding of God, but it does not exhaust the extent of the revelation we find in Jesus, because not only does Jesus redefine our concept of God but also he shows us the perfect expression of humanity as God intended it. In other words, he models for us what a true human being should be like. Therefore, focusing our discipleship on Jesus forces us to take seriously the implications of following him, of becoming like him. It sets the agenda for our spirituality. It acknowledges that Jesus as our model, our teacher, and our guide is normative for the Christian life. He is the standard by which we measure ourselves, the quality of our discipleship, and therefore our spirituality.

If the heart of Christian spirituality is to increasingly become like our founder, then an authentic comprehension of Jesus becomes critical. All too often the focal point of our corporate and individual life shifts from its true center in Jesus, resulting in various anomalies in our spirituality. A true Christian expression models itself on Jesus, and it is God's unambiguous aim to make us to be more like his Son. In fact, this is our eternal destiny: "to be conformed to the likeness of his Son" (Rom 8:29). In *The Forgotten Ways*, Alan calls this the "conspiracy of little Jesuses," and we believe it is fundamental to God's plan and purposes for his world.

If this worries us, if we think this would somehow upset the finely balanced ecology of our spirituality, then we can perhaps reframe the issue by posing it as a question: If Jesus is perfected humanity—the human image of God—how bad can we become if we became more like him? Would the world not be a better place if there were more little Jesuses around? It strikes us therefore as a matter of fundamental importance to our humanity, our spirituality, and our witness that we regularly get a truer perspective on the focal point and the defining center of our faith.

Finally, in doing this we hope that we can in some way restore Christology to the church at large, to make it applicable to the whole people of God. For far too long Christology has been the province of academic and professional Christians, who seem far more concerned with an examination of how the divine and human are related in Jesus' person than they are in the details of his life or the content of his teaching and vision. As theologians attempted to use speculative philosophy and ontology to explore the two natures of Christ, Christology became something of a complex science that in effect excludes the theologically uninitiated person. When the study of the remarkable life and teachings of Jesus becomes the sole province of theologians and religious professionals, when it is done in abstract and divorced from our daily concerns and from the missional context of the church, it will tend to degrade the vitality of our Christianity. The system we have historically constructed to try to probe the nature of Christ reaches Gnostic proportions and takes years to comprehend in a meaningful way. Only few very smart people can do that,

Righteous Forgiveness

Fannie Lou Hamer

Born to sharecroppers in rural Mississippi, Fannie Lou Hamer rose to prominence as an African-American woman in the Civil Rights movement of the 1960s. Like others in the movement, Hamer was deeply spiritual, and as a little Jesus, she stood up for the disenfranchised and forgave those who persecuted her. In 1962, the forty-four-year-old Hamer attended a rally sponsored by the Student Nonviolent Coordinating Committee (SNCC, an organization dedicated to fighting for civil rights through civil disobedience) and, inspired, she and her husband went to register to vote. Along the way, Hamer sang hymns, including "Go Tell It on the Mountain" and "This Little Light of Mine." For this, she and her husband were kicked out of their home, and Hamer lost her job. However, her tenacity also attracted the attention of SNCC, and the organization recruited her to be a field secretary. The following year, she was arrested with three other activists on trumped-up charges, and she sustained a near fatal beating at the hands of the police. Hamer, however, sang spirituals and refused to hate her tormenters. "It wouldn't solve any problem for me to hate whites just because they hate me," she explained. For the next fifteen years until her death, Hamer continued her work in the Civil Rights movement, including an organizational role in the 1964 Mississippi Freedom Summer and as a seated delegate at the 1964 and 1968 Democratic National Conventions, always applying her belief in the biblical righteousness of the cause. She was known for saying "I'm sick and tired of being sick and tired." She maintained that it wasn't enough just to claim to be a Christian. "If you are not putting that claim to the test, where the rubber meets the road, then it's high time to stop talking about being a Christian."

and the net effect is devastating for the church as an agency of Christ's kingdom. This is our concern, because the living link between Jesus and his people must never be dissolved or placed beyond the reach of the average Christian. To do this is to sever the church from its true source of life (John 7:38). Surely any loss of a direct, grassroots comprehension of Jesus must be a major cause in the degeneration of Christianity in any time and any place?

Therefore, we propose a rediscovery of Christology that includes a preoccupation with the example and teaching of Jesus for the purposes of emulation by his followers. Some will say that such emulation is arduous to achieve in general and impossible when it comes to the specifics of his redeeming death and resurrection, the miracles, and his judgment of the unrighteous. Surely, they argue, we cannot die for the sins of others or judge their deeds. And here's where we need a far richer Christology than we've been offered in the past. For us, Christology is the study and examination of the entire phenomenon of Jesus, including his person and work and teachings, for the purpose of determining in what ways the various elements of his life and activity can be emulated by sinful human beings. For example, we can't die for others, as Jesus did, but we can offer ourselves sacrificially in service of others. Paul compares husbands loving their wives with Jesus dying for our sins. A working Christology would help us understand Jesus better and provide the tools for appropriating his example into our lives.

So this is not primarily a book about renewal for its own sake, nor is it a book about Christology as a strictly theological discipline. Rather, it is an attempt to reinstate the central role of Jesus in the ongoing spiritual life of the faith and in the life and mission of God's people. More specifically, it is an attempt to recalibrate the mission of the church around the person and work of Jesus. This book then is a work of missional Christology, if there is such a thing. It is an attempt to revision and revitalize our vision of Jesus as master of history and Lord of the church against which, we are reminded, the gates of hell will not prevail (Matt 16:18). In short, it is about nothing less than reJesusing the church.

⌇Notes

1. Don Whitehead, *Attack on Terror: The* FBI *against the Ku Klux Klan in Mississippi* (New York: Funk & Wagnalls, 1970), 4, cited in Charles Marsh, *God's Long Summer: Stories of Faith and Civil Rights* (Princeton, N.J.: Princeton University Press, 1997), 64.

2. Marsh, *God's Long Summer,* 65.

3. Ibid., 62.

4. Letters to Charles Marsh, cited in ibid., 62–63. Note Bowers's reference to Jesus as "The Galilean." Bowers used this term to distinguish Jesus as a non-Jewish descendent of Aryan colonists in ancient Galilee.

5. Ibid., 63.

6. Most recently, Alan Hirsch, *The Forgotten Ways: Reactivating the Missional Church* (Grand Rapids, Mich.: Brazos, 2006), 143ff.; Michael Frost and Alan Hirsch, *The Shaping of Things to Come: Innovation and Mission for the 21st-Century Church* (Peabody, Mass.: Hendrickson, 2003), 16ff.

7. Michael Frost, *Exiles* (Peabody, Mass.: Hendrickson, 2006). See also Alan Hirsch, Neil Cole, and Wolfgang Simson, *Igniting Primal Fires*, which explores Ephesians 4:11 ministry (forthcoming).

8. Jacques Ellul, *The Subversion of Christianity* (Grand Rapids, Mich.: Eerdmans, 1986), 3.

9. We think not. The idea of "one nation under God" is the calling of Israel, not that of the church. One church under God is more like it. And the church is called to live among the nations, bearing witness, influencing, but never dominating.

10. The Christian organization in England called rejesus has a wonderful interactive website (ReJesus.co.uk) exploring Jesus' "life, character, teachings, and followers." We recommend it as a great place to spend some time.

11. J. Kevin Livingston, "David Jacobus Bosch," *The International Bulletin of Missionary Research* 23/1 (January 1999): 26–32.

12. Adolf von Harnack, *The Essence of Christianity*, quoted in Alexander Mens, *Son of Man* (Torrance, Calif.: Oakwood, 1992), 5.

13. George Tyrrell, *Christianity at the Cross-Roads* (London: Allen & Unwin, 1963), 49.

14. A. Michael Ramsey, *God, Christ and the World: A Study in Contemporary Theology* (London: SCM, 1969), 99.

Chapter One

How Jesus Changes Everything

"Jesus is Lord" is a radical claim, one that is ultimately
rooted in questions of allegiance, of ultimate authority,
of the ultimate norm and standard for human life.
Instead, Christianity has often sought to ally itself
comfortably with allegiance to other authorities,
be they political, economic, cultural, or ethnic.
—Lee Camp

In the same way the Church exists for nothing else but
to draw men into Christ, to make them little Christs.
If they are not doing that, all the cathedrals, clergy,
missions, sermons, even the Bible itself, are simply a
waste of time. God became man for no other purpose.
It is even doubtful, you know, whether the whole
universe was created for any other purpose. It says in
the Bible that the whole universe was made for Christ
and that everything is to be gathered together in Him.
—C. S. Lewis

K ey to encountering the biblical Jesus is a step that many Christians seem
to find painful, that is, our preparedness to read the Gospels in order to
emulate Jesus. It appears that a good church upbringing will do many marvelous things for you, but one of the unfortunate things it also does is convince
you that Jesus is to be worshipped but not followed. In his previous work, *Ex-*
iles, Michael argued that the traditional Christian depiction of the porcelain-
skinned Jesus has hindered our ability, indeed our desire, to actually be like
him.[1] We readily acknowledge that none of us have within us the fortitude, the
grace, the courage, and the imagination to actually be like Jesus. It is a lost

cause. But it's a lost cause made worth it by the forgiveness and grace shown us in Jesus' death on our behalf. By dying for us to set us free from the penalty for our sinfulness, he doesn't nullify the call to good works and godly living. Rather, he elevates from an endless and hopeless attempt to impress God to a joyful adventure of enjoying Christ's presence by imitating him. The quest to emulate Jesus isn't folly. When it's embraced by those who know they are forgiven for all the ways they will fall short, it is a daring exploit!

Making this very point, M. Scott Peck in *Further Along the Road Less Traveled* recounted the episode when Baptist theologian Harvey Cox was addressing a convention of Christian healers—pastors, therapists, nurses, doctors— that Peck was attending. During his presentation, Cox retold the story from Luke 8 of Jesus raising Jairus's daughter from the dead. In the well-known story, as Jesus and his companions are heading for the home of Jairus's dying girl, a woman who has been hemorrhaging for years breaks from the crowd and touches Jesus' robe in the hope that she too will be healed. Jesus reels around and demands to know who touched him. The cowering woman sheep-ishly owns up, and Jesus, feeling compassionate for her having endured years of unspeakable suffering, heals her and continues on his way to the house where the young girl has since died. Thereupon Jesus promptly brings the child back to life.

Having related the story (no doubt in greater detail than we just did), Cox asked his audience of six hundred Christian healers and therapists to in-dicate which of the characters in the story they most strongly identified with. The bleeding woman? The anxious father? The curious crowd? Or Jesus? What Cox found was that around a hundred felt they could relate to the desperate woman; several hundred identified with Jairus, whose daughter was dying; the majority identified with the perplexed group standing by. And six—yes, six—people felt they could identify with Jesus.

Peck's point in recounting this experience was to point out that there is something seriously wrong with Christianity when only one in every hundred Christians can identify with Jesus. Here was a story about Jesus the healer, told to healers, but none of them identified with Jesus. Have we made him so divine, so otherworldly, that we cannot connect with him anymore? Peck sug-gests that this leads to the excuse that we can't really be expected to follow Jesus because we perceive ourselves way down here and Jesus way up there, beyond identification. Says Peck, "That is exactly what we're supposed to do! We're supposed to identify with Jesus, act like Jesus, be like Jesus. That is what Christianity is supposed to be about: the imitation of Christ."[2]

By making Christ seem otherworldly, even ethereal, the church has inadvertently put him out of reach to us as an example or a guide. Even though Jesus routinely called people to follow him, the church has often represented this following in purely metaphysical or mystical terms. We can follow Jesus "in our heart" but not necessarily with our actions. Even after the phenomenally successful *What Would Jesus Do* campaign, in which Christians were encouraged to ask themselves this question before every action, it seemed that Christians were more interested in asking the question than in doing what Jesus would do. We have sanitized and tamed Jesus by encasing him in abstract theology, and in doing so we have removed our motivation for discipleship. When Jesus is just true light of true light, and not flesh and blood, we are only ever called to adore him, not follow him.

In Charles Sheldon's popular novel *In His Steps*, one of the characters, Rev. Henry Maxwell, encounters a homeless man who challenges him to take seriously the imitation of Christ. The homeless man has difficulty understanding why, in his view, so many Christians ignore the poor:

I heard some people singing at a church prayer meeting the other night,

All for Jesus, all for Jesus,
All my being's ransomed powers,
All my thoughts, and all my doings,
All my days, and all my hours.

and I kept wondering as I sat on the steps outside just what they meant by it. It seems to me there's an awful lot of trouble in the world that somehow wouldn't exist if all the people who sing such songs went and lived them out. I suppose I don't understand. But what would Jesus do? Is that what you mean by following his steps? It seems to me sometimes as if the people in the big churches had good clothes and nice houses to live in, and money to spend for luxuries, and could go away on summer vacations and all that, while the people outside the churches, thousands of them, I mean, die in tenements, and walk the streets for jobs, and never have a piano or a picture in the house, and grow up in misery and drunkenness and sin.[3]

This leads to many of the novel's characters asking, "What would Jesus do?" when faced with decisions of some importance. This has the effect of making the characters embrace more seriously the fact that Jesus lies at Christianity's core consciousness.

The difficulty for the church today is not in encouraging people to ask what Jesus would do, but in getting them to break out of their domesticated and sanitized ideas about Jesus in order to answer that question. Jesus was a wild man. He was a threat to the security of the religious establishment. He was baptized by a wild man. He inaugurated his ministry by spending time with

Practicing Dangerous Mercy

Sheila Cassidy

A single act of compassion altered the course of Sheila Cassidy's life. In 1975 while practicing medicine in Chile during the oppressive Pinochet regime, the young Australian provided medical care to one of the dictator's political opponents. Arrested and imprisoned by the Chilean secret police, Cassidy was tortured severely for information about anti-government forces. Her terrifying experience did not break the Roman Catholic, but instead proved to be the catalyst for a lifetime of human rights activism. Upon her release, Cassidy moved to the U.K., where she drew attention to human rights abuses in Chile by publicizing her story and writing a book, *Audacity to Believe*. She also spent a period of religious retreat in both a monastery and a convent before returning to her vocation as a doctor in 1980. Cassidy continued her human rights work to increase international opposition to the torture of political prisoners and also became active in the hospice movement, serving as the Medical Director of St. Luke's Hospice in Plymouth, England, for fifteen years. A true little Jesus, Sheila Cassidy emerged from her torture and imprisonment to a ministry deeply committed to life and peace.

the wild beasts of the wilderness. He was unfazed by a wild storm that lashed his boat on an excursion across a lake and with the wildness of the demoniacs of the Gaderenes. And while he ultimately brought peace to both those situations, in neither instance did Jesus appear overwhelmed or frightened by the circumstances. There was an untamed power within him. Even his storytelling, so often characterized by the church today as warm morality tales, was dangerous and subversive and mysterious. If your answer to the question "What would Jesus do?" is that he would be conventional, safe, respectable and refined, then we suspect you didn't find that answer in the Gospels.

As Terry Eagleton says, "[Jesus] is presented [in the Gospels] as homeless, propertyless, peripatetic, socially marginal, disdainful of kinfolk, without a trade or occupation, a friend of outcasts and pariahs, averse to material possessions, without fear for his own safety, a thorn in the side of the Establishment and a scourge of the rich and powerful."[4]

The process of reJesusing the church will begin with a rediscovery of the fierce and outrageous life of Jesus. Too many people have become turned off to the church because the object of our faith seems bland and insipid. It reminds us of the quip made by the archbishop who is reported to have said, "Everywhere Jesus went there was a riot. Everywhere I go they make me cups of tea!"

This was the experience of punk rocker, screenwriter, and novelist Nick Cave. Writing in an introduction to Mark's gospel, Cave talks about how as a younger man he found the Jesus presented to him in church as anemic and uninteresting. When he became interested in the Bible, he concentrated virtually all his attention on the Old Testament, drawn as he was to its violence and pervading sense of vengeance, perhaps not unsurprising for a punk. Later, an Anglican vicar in London suggested he read Mark instead, and Cave was astonished by the Jesus he discovered between its pages:

> The Christ that the church offers us, the bloodless, placid "Savior"—the man smiling benignly at a group of children, or calmly, serenely hanging from the cross—denies Christ his potent, creative sorrow or his boiling anger that confronts us so forcefully in Mark. Thus the church denies Christ his humanity, offering up a figure that we can perhaps "praise," but never relate to.[5]

Cave's introduction to Mark is beautifully written and deeply heartfelt. He writes about "that part of me that railed and hissed and spat at the world" initially taking pleasure in the "wonderful, terrible book," the Old Testament, before mellowing out in later life. "You no longer find comfort watching a whacked-out God tormenting a wretched humanity as you learn to forgive yourself and the world," he says somewhat unfairly of the Old Testament. Nonetheless, after all those blood-curdling stories he was well and truly ready to meet Jesus. And meet him he did, seeing Jesus in Mark with a fresh perspective many seasoned Christians often miss:

> The essential humanness of Mark's Christ provides us with a blueprint for our own lives, so that we have something we can aspire to, rather than revere, that can lift us free of the mundanity of our existences, rather than affirming the notion that we are lowly and unworthy. Merely to praise Jesus in his Perfectness, keeps us on our knees, with our heads pitifully bent. Clearly, this is not what Christ had in mind. Christ came as liberator. Christ understood that we as humans were for ever held to the ground by the pull of gravity—our ordinariness, our mundanity—and it was through his example that he gave our imaginations the freedom to rise and to fly. In short, to be Christ-like.[6]

Cave is no theologian and doesn't pretend to be, but he's on to something. Look at what happens to those Jesus encounters in the Gospels—the hemorrhaging woman, Jairus, the woman at the well, Mary Magdalene, Peter, Thomas—they are lifted up by him, transformed, strengthened, renewed. Jesus teaches them how to live, not just how to worship. Today, we need to accept Jesus as our guide, as well as our Savior. And only a Savior as human as the one portrayed in the Gospels could ever be our guide.

Long before Cave was writing this, another novelist was exploring the essential *humanity* of Jesus. The prodigious talent of Dorothy L. Sayers found in the story of Christ more than enough material to occupy her attention. Sayers, originally an advertising executive, is probably best remembered for her detective novels, set between the wars and featuring English aristocrat and amateur sleuth, Lord Peter Wimsey. While she might have preferred to be known for her magisterial translation of Dante's *Divine Comedy*, Christians seem to know her only for her 1941 radio play *The Man Born to Be King*, a dramatization of the life of Jesus. But the writing of that play was not the only time she turned her attention to Jesus. Her personal correspondence is littered with references to him, so much so, in fact, that it's not difficult to conclude that she was obsessed by Jesus. Her self-confessed quest was for a deep and proper understanding of his essence, his character and his mission, claiming as she did that such an understanding was "the difference between pseudo-Christianity and Christianity."[7]

For Sayers, an appreciation of the stained-glass Jesus was not enough to satisfy her. She needed to encounter the real Jesus. The "bloodless, placid Savior" that Nick Cave rebelled against repelled her every bit as much. In the introduction to the published version of *The Man Born to Be King* she discussed the importance of connecting with a flesh-and-blood Messiah:

> The writer of realistic Gospel plays . . . is brought up face to face with the "scandal of particularity." *Ecco homo*—not only Man-in-general and God-in-His-thusness, but also God-in-His-thisness, and *this* Man, *this* person, of a reasonable soul and human flesh subsisting, who walked and talked *then* and *there*, surrounded, not by human types, but by *those* individual people. The story of the life and murder and resurrection of God-in-Man is not only the symbol and epitome of the relations of God and man throughout time; it is also a series of events that took place at a particular point in time.[8]

While people like C. S. Lewis, who read *The Man Born to Be King* every Easter, appreciated Sayers's attempt to describe God in his *thisness*, not in his *thusness* (a great line), a good many churchgoers found her portrayal of

Jesus to be vulgar and unbecoming. Sayers's response to one caller, who telephoned to criticize her after the broadcast of her 1939 Advent play, *He That Should Come*, summed up her approach:

> If you mixed as much as I do with people to whom the Gospel story seems to be nothing but a pretty fairytale, you would know how much of their contemptuous indifference is due to one fact: that never for one moment have they seen it as a real thing, happening to a living people. Nor, indeed, are they fully convinced that Christians believe in its reality.[9]

You didn't want to cross Sayers when she was in full flight! But her assumption holds water. Until Martin Scorsese's *The Last Temptation of Christ* and Mel Gibson's gory *The Passion of the Christ*, all film versions of the life of Jesus portrayed him as unflappable and dignified. The crucified Christ was given a few spots of blood on his brow, his underarms were shaved, and his loincloth was fixed firmly in place. It seems that this was the church's favored version. Sayers's argument was that while the world saw a church that preferred a sanitized Savior, they had no choice but to conclude that the stories about him were myths and legends, not references to the historical incarnation of God in humankind. And while the central Christian story was merely a myth, it never laid any claim on the lives of believers or unbelievers alike. Like Robin Hood or the Knights of the Round Table, the Gospels might have taught a moral ethical code, but they didn't introduce us to *this* man, *this* person, who demanded to be the guide of *my* life. This Sayers called the "scandal of particularity," and it remains a scandal to this day.

But where is the scandalous Jesus in our churches today? Where is the Jesus who taunted the religious elite (Luke 20:32–36), who teased a Canaanite woman (Matt 15:21–28), who evaded arrest (John 7:32–36), who commended the faith of a pagan (Matt 8:5ff), who waited four days to resurrect Lazarus (John 9), who promised not peace but a sword (Matt 10:34ff)? To re*Jesus* the church, we need to take Christians along on a journey of rediscovery, a pilgrimage toward Jesus, to see as Jesus saw. It will involve an embracing of this scandal of particularity.

⟵ Taken Captive by Jesus

So what does it mean, then, to be taken captive by the agenda of the flesh-and-blood Jesus? We will argue that a rediscovery of the biblical Jesus will radically reshape our view of God, the church, and the world. And further, we believe that by allowing Jesus to shape us in these three areas we are better equipped to reJesus the church communities of which we are part. Obviously, this will involve a preparedness on our parts to resist capturing Jesus for our ends or molding him to our theological or political agendas. And it will involve a thoroughgoing attempt to view reality as Jesus does; in effect, to see through his eyes.

Through the eyes of Jesus, we will see God differently, no longer as a distant father figure, but through the paradigm of the *missio Dei* to find the sent and sending God. Second, we will see the church differently, no longer as a religious institution but as a community of Jesus followers devoted to participating in his mission. We call this the *participatio Christi*. And third, through Jesus' eyes we will see the world afresh, not simply as fallen or depraved but as bearing the mark of the *imago Dei*—the image of God.

Those taken captive by the sight of Christ must be prepared for a reintegration of the theological concepts of *missio Dei*, *participatio Christi*, and *imago Dei*. These three concepts are foundational for a rediscovery of missional practice in our time. They are also foundational for us to reJesus the church in the West.

You Will See God Differently

When our imaginations are taken captive by Jesus, we will see God differently. Rather than seeing God as a loving but distant Father who calls us to himself and directs the affairs of history from on high, we will begin to see God as near, as integrally involved in our lives; in effect, as one who sends himself to us rather than waiting for us to come to him. The Latin phrase *missio Dei* is used to describe more the divine nature of God than simply the practical nature of Christian mission. In this respect the term is better translated as "the God of mission" rather than "the mission of God." First coined by Karl Hartenstein in the 1950s, the term gained real currency because it located the idea of mission with the doctrine of God, not with the doctrine of the church. We often speak of mission being a function of the church's work in this world, but Hartenstein was anxious that the church understand that mission belongs to and describes God's work. We, the church, become partners in what God is doing, but it is never our initiative alone. Those who are taken captive by Jesus see mission not merely as a practice preferred by God but as an aspect of his very character. He *is* mission. Core to understanding God's nature is the realization that God cannot *not* be about the business of mission. He inhabits mission as part of the very stuff of his personality. In effect, he is both the sent and sending God.

In John 5, Jesus heals a lame man on the Sabbath and incurs the wrath of the Jewish leaders for, as they saw it, flouting the law of Moses. In his own defense, Jesus appeals to an even higher law than that of Moses. In effect, he appeals to the doctrine of *missio Dei*, even though he never uses such a term, when he says, "My Father is still working, and I also am working" (John 5:17). In other words, you Pharisees might refuse to work on the Sabbath, but God is unceasing in his redemptive activity, no matter the day or the date. Naturally, the Pharisees are outraged, not only because he is apparently disregarding the Sabbath but because he is equating himself with Yahweh's missional work. But Jesus presses on, making an even more provocative claim: "Very truly I tell you, the Son can do nothing on his own, but only what he sees the Father doing; for whatever the Father does, the Son does likewise" (John 5:19).

Nothing could be more scandalous! Effectively, Jesus is claiming to be captive to the *missio Dei*, attending only to his Father's missional activity, irrespective of narrow interpretations of Hebrew law. This stunning claim, that he is not operating under his own steam or on the basis of his own strategy but entirely at the impulse of the sent and sending Father, is a challenge to us. If we claim to be Jesus followers, we ought to be committed to being similarly (if imperfectly) in league with the *missio Dei*.

Later, in John 8, after a lengthy discussion about his oneness with the Father and the meaning of his death, Jesus concludes, "The one who sent me is with me; he has not left me alone, for I always do what is pleasing to him" (John 8:29). Earlier he had referred to his being sent by the Father (John 8:16), but that could have been interpreted as him saying that he has the Father's backing in his dealings with people. By verse 29 he reiterates that he is not alone, but here he makes it clear that he is talking about the Father's personal presence with him at all times, including at that moment. Even though his followers might desert him, as many had done (John 6), he is claiming that he will never be deserted by his Father. Here we get a glimpse into the mystery of the relations between the Father and the Son, for the Father sends the Son and yet is present with the Son. The sending refers to the incarnation and the presence to the eternal relations. In other words, the Father is both sending and sent.[10]

But note how Jesus points out that the Father's presence relies on the Son's commitment to always do what is pleasing to the Father. In this way, Jesus reveals the primacy of the *missio Dei*—the missionary Father. All that exists, even the Son and the Spirit in their eternal, uncreated being, are dependent upon the Father as the source of all life. All life is an expression of the Father's life. To do what pleases God is not simply a matter of morality but of sharing in God's life and mission. It is another way of saying that Christ does

Imitatio Christi

Janani Luwum

Janani Luwum embraced his vocation as a little Jesus, imitating his Lord even to the point of death. The Anglican Church appointed him to be the archbishop of Uganda, Rwanda, Burundi, and Boga-Zaire in 1974, during the murderous regime of Idi Amin in Uganda. Seizing power in a 1971 coup, Amin and his squads were responsible for over 300,000 deaths. Amin destroyed the economy, while bestowing riches on himself and his friends. In 1976 Luwum convened a meeting with Catholic and Muslim leaders at which they passed a resolution deploring Amin's attrocities. In so doing, Luwum knew he had marked himself for death. He had consciously begun his *imitatio Christi*. Four days before his arrest, Luwum met with his bishops for the last time and shared with them the gospel passage in which Jesus calms the storm, comparing it with the political storm they were enduring and calling on them to rely on Jesus' calming presence. "They are going to kill me. I am not afraid," he confided. After an atrocious beating, including rape, the archbishop was shot dead. It was rumored that it was Amin himself who fired the fatal shots. His death was reported as a car accident. Luwum's humiliation and suffering embody the passion of Jesus. Like Martin Luther King Jr., Luwum is memorialized as a twentieth-century martyr at Westminster Abbey.

what he sees the Father doing and speaks what he hears from the Father. He is devoted to the mission of God. As such he is the model of all discipleship. The life Jesus is offering involves being taken up into the mission of the Father.

No one has helped us understand this concept more than the missiologist David Bosch. This is the same David Bosch who celebrated the election of the architects of apartheid to the South African parliament in the late 1940s and went on to become one of the most celebrated missiologists in the world. During that time, he underwent a series of experiences that transformed him from a bigoted Afrikaner to a deeply compassionate missionary who worked in a poor black community in the Transkei region of South Africa. Exhausted from the back-breaking labors of working with the poor, he eventually accepted a position in 1975 as the professor of missiology at UNISA (University of South Africa) Pretoria, where he served until his untimely death in a car accident in 1992. What he discovered about the mission of Jesus can be summed up in the following statement:

> Mission [is] understood as being derived from the very nature of God. It [is] thus put in the context of the doctrine of the Trinity, not of ecclesiology or soteriology. The classical doctrine of the missio Dei as God the Father sending the Son, and God the Father and the Son sending the Spirit [is] expanded to include yet another "movement": Father, Son, and Holy Spirit sending the church into the world.[11]

This triune element to the *missio Dei* is not unique to the thinking of Bosch. In the 1930s, thinkers like Karl Barth and Karl Hartenstein were advocating a trinitarian base for a missional doctrine of God. When we see God as Jesus understood him, we see a God so devoted to his broken planet that he issues himself forth to redeem it. In the incarnation of Jesus, we hear the *missio Dei* presented to us in his teaching and embodied in his flesh. But further than that, the ministry of the Spirit continues to testify to God's character and his core missional orientation. Jacques Matthey writes in summary of those committed to the idea of *missio Dei*, "We have not separated the Father from the Son and the Spirit. This has consequences: we cannot limit the scope of Christ or the Spirit to inner-church circles."[12] In effect, you can't keep the Trinity locked up in church. God escapes the stained-glass crypt and sends himself out throughout the world: Father, Son, and Spirit.

But this doesn't mean that the church is not involved. Far from it. As Bosch said earlier, the cycle continues with the triune God sending the church into the world. It is essential that we recapture the importance and role of the church within the overall frame of *missio Dei*, without reverting to an old ecclesiocentric approach. We will return to this discussion soon.

Nonetheless, part of the process to reJesus the church will involve a dismantling of its much-loved temple theology. While Jesus embodies the fact that the Trinity is both sent and sending, his followers very often seem to prefer a deity who reveals himself in sacred buildings, liturgies, and sacramental practices. So-called temple theology locates God as a withdrawn deity calling recalcitrants back to his temple/church/cathedral to be reunited with him. But an encounter with the Jesus of the Gospels flies in the face of this idea. While we do find Jesus revering the Jerusalem temple as "my Father's house" (Luke 2:49), we don't think he is saying that his Father lives in that building. Rather, he is acknowledging that within the Jewish system of his time, the temple was seen as a physical embodiment of God's presence in Israel. What he then does is to equate his own person as such an embodiment by saying, "I am able to destroy the temple of God and to build it in three days" (Matt 26:61). We know he was speaking of his own body and its impending death and resurrection. But this is not only a comment on his certainty of being resurrected. It is a comment on where the physical presence of God is located. Rather than being seen in the temple, Jesus sees it in himself. He is the temple. He is the physical embodiment of God.

The instance of Jesus' physical death is depicted as a moment of great wildness. In contrast to being a solemn moment in which Jesus tenderly resigns himself to death, Matthew describes it as a time of great horror! An earthquake is unleashed beneath the city. The curtain of the temple is vandalized by God, torn in two from top to bottom. Graves burst open and the dead rise to wander through the city as a foretaste of the final resurrection yet to come. It's like a scene from *The Night of the Living Dead*! Everything about Jesus is wild, even his death. And the symbolism is unmistakable. Something has shifted in the spiritual realm. A cosmic tsunami has been unleashed. Through Jesus' death God has entered into our world for good. God will now no longer dwell in temples, but in the hearts of those who serve God.

This is picked up again by Paul, when he refers to the church as the body of Christ. The triune God doesn't reside in a temple or any other building. Rather, the physical embodiment of the Trinity is in the people of God, the followers of Christ. The *missio Dei* describes the impulse that saw the Father send his Son into the world to enflesh him. It is also the impulse that sees the Father, the Son, and Spirit send us into the world as his ambassadors, his representatives, enfleshing him here on earth. This leads us to our second aspect of being shaped by Jesus.

You Will See the Church Differently

Through Jesus' eyes, the church is the sent people of God. A church is not a building or an organization. It is an organic collective of believers, centered on Jesus and sent out into the world to serve others in his name. When we are taken captive by the Nazarene carpenter, we can no longer see ourselves as participants in a similar system to the one he came to subvert. Not only does Jesus undermine temple theology by becoming the temple himself, but also he undermines the sacrificial system by dispensing with sin without reference to ceremonial washings, rituals, or liturgies ("Go in peace, your sins are forgiven"). As noted earlier, he also plays fast and loose with the legalism of Sabbath keeping. In fact, he subverts the whole religious system. So why would he do that simply to replace it with a Christian religious system? He doesn't! He is antireligious, offering his followers direct access to the Father, forgiveness in his name, and the indwelling of the Holy Spirit. Therefore, to be reJesused is to come to the recognition that the church as the New Testament defines it is not a religious institution but rather a dynamic community of believers who participate in the way of Jesus and his work in this world.

As we said earlier, God's mission in this world is his and his alone. The glory of God, not the church, is the ultimate goal of mission. Our role as the church, however, is a humble participation in his grand scheme—the kingdom of God. We neither determine our own agenda nor merely imitate his but rather participate in the marvelous plan of God according to his call and guidance. Again, Bosch addresses this superbly:

> Mission takes place where the church, in its total involvement with the world, bears its testimony in the form of a servant, with reference to unbelief, exploitation, discrimination and violence, but also with reference to salvation, healing, liberation, reconciliation and righteousness . . . Looked at from this perspective mission is, quite simply, the participation of Christians in the liberating mission of Jesus, wagering on a future that verifiable experience seems to belie. It is the good news of God's love, incarnated in the witness of a community, for the sake of the world.[13]

The participation of Christians in the liberating mission of Jesus is referred to by the Latin term *participati Christi*. As Bosch suggests, this can never be boiled down simply to evangelistic preaching or social justice. As soon as someone can tell you the one thing you need to be doing in order to participate in the mission of Jesus, you can be sure they're not telling you the whole story. Mission involves everything Jesus is about in the world. And this cannot be limited to merely religious concerns. The liberating mission of Jesus is unfolding all around us. As Robert McAfee Brown once said about the meaning of life, it is "our task to create foretastes of [the Kingdom of God] on this planet—living glimpses of what life is meant to be, which include art and music and poetry and shared laughter and picnics and politics and moral outrage and special privileges for children only and wonder and humor and endless love."[14]

In both Luke and Mark's gospels we find the report of an incident where the disciple John notifies Jesus of a stranger who is performing exorcisms in his name: "We saw someone casting out demons in your name, and we tried to stop him, because he does not follow with us" (Luke 9:49). At that time there were many charlatans and magicians willing to perform various acts of sorcery for a fee. For example, when Philip, Peter, and John visit Samaria (Acts 8), they encounter one of Scripture's most beguiling characters, Simon the sorcerer, who had held all of Samaria in his sway with his magical powers. Even after his conversion and baptism, he still offers the disciples cash in return for the even greater magic they can perform. Back in Luke 9, John has discovered an un-known exorcist, using the name of Jesus to perform the miraculous, and he has asked him to cease and desist. But Jesus' response is staggering: "Do not stop him; for whoever is not against you is for you" (Luke 9:50). Jesus is suggesting that rather than running around drawing lines of demarcation between those who are in the community of Christ and those who are not, we are simply to bless all those who participate with us in the work of Jesus. This is how robust Jesus' view of the kingdom was. It couldn't be contained within borders. It was a living thing, a wild thing, and it was bursting out everywhere. It is one of our greatest mistakes to equate the church with the kingdom of God. The kingdom is much broader than the church—it is cosmic in scope. The church is perhaps the primary agent of the kingdom but must not be equated fully with it. We need to be able to see the kingdom activity wherever it expresses itself and join with God in it. Jesus shows us how to see God working in the strangest of places.

In Matthew 13:24–30, Jesus offers us an illustration or metaphor to make better sense of this:

> "The kingdom of heaven may be compared to someone who sowed good seed in his field; but while everyone was asleep, an enemy came and sowed weeds among the wheat, and then went away. So when the plants came up and bore grain, then the weeds appeared as well. And the slaves of the householder came and said to him, 'Master, did you not sow good seed in your field? Where, then, did the weeds come from?' He answered, 'An enemy has done this.' The slaves said to him, 'Then do you want us to go and gather them?'

> But he replied, 'No; for in gathering the weeds you would uproot the wheat along with them. Let both of them grow together until the harvest; and at harvest time I will tell the reapers, Collect the weeds first and bind them in bundles to be burned, but gather the wheat into my barn.'"

It will be impossible to separate the wheat from the weeds, so allow them to grow up together and leave it to God to sort out in the end. In other words, John, if some guy you don't know is driving out demons in my name, don't stop him. My kingdom is no respecter of our arbitrary lines of distinction.

How much does the church today need to be reJesused in order to appreciate this! Conservative Christians won't even acknowledge that the rock star, Bono, is on the side of the angels in his fight against global poverty. Certain denominations have demonized others. Some churches won't work with certain other churches as a matter of principle. And yet whoever is not against you is for you, says Jesus. He is teaching John to appreciate all others who serve in Christ's name. In effect, he demands that we abandon our painstaking attempts to weed the field, pulling out each wild plant by hand. Instead, he says, tend to the wheat. Participate in the growth of the kingdom—the wheat—and leave the business of weeding the field to God and his angels.

This isn't to say that such participation is a solo venture for individual Christians. Rather, it ought to be seen as a communal commitment. In this respect, the doctrine of *corpus Christi* (the body of Christ) should be acknowledged. God calls together bodies of believers to participate in his mission. Or, as John Eldridge puts it,

> God is calling together little communities of the heart, to fight for one another and for the hearts of those who have not yet been set free. The camaraderie, that intimacy, that incredible impact by a few stout-hearted souls—that *is* available. It is the Christian life as Jesus gave it to us. It is completely normal.[15]

Interestingly, the term Jesus, and more often Paul, employed to describe a gathering of Christians (since there was literally no such collective noun at the time) was the Greek term *ecclesia*. Today we translate it into the old Anglo-Saxon term "church." But that term today has come to refer more to places of Christian worship or to the institutional aspect of the Christian community. It has strayed a long way from Paul's original usage. Remember, Paul didn't invent the term *ecclesia*. It was already part of the vernacular of his time. He takes this pre-existing term and invests it with a new, distinctly Christian meaning. But it would be helpful to recall in what ways the term *ecclesia* was employed by Paul's non-Christian contemporaries in order to get closer to the original raw material Paul uses in developing his unique ecclesiology.

Most dictionaries will tell you that *ecclesia* literally means "the gathering of the called-out ones." It comes from two words, *ek*, meaning "out," and *kaleo*, meaning "to call." But in its original usage an *ecclesia* was not just an assembly or a gathering, as many suppose. If that's all Paul wanted to convey, he could have used *agora* and *panegyris* as well as *heorte*, *koinon*, *thiasos*, *synagoge*, and *synago*, all of which refer to an assembly. The word *ecclesia* had a political aspect to it. In fact, it wasn't a religious term, and neither was its use limited to a religious gathering. In Paul's time, an *ecclesia* was a gathering of the elders of a community. In smaller villages and towns across Judea, local elders would gather regularly to discuss and deliberate over a variety of social and political dilemmas facing the community. Neighborhood disputes, arguments over estates of deceased persons, communal responses to natural disasters—these were the kinds of things the council of elders would consider. Today, this might be similar to a meeting in the local town hall of a group of community leaders. In other words, an *ecclesia* was a gathering of wise community leaders, brought together by their common vision for the harmony and well-being of the wider community.

It was more than a body of unseen lawmakers who exercised authority and ran the offices of government through a vast bureaucratic system. It was a community within a community whose function was to add value to that community. It brought wisdom to the village. It helped the village be a better village. And of course, being the elders of that village meant that the leaders were required to live with the ramifications of their decisions. They were in the village, and their destiny was as connected to the prosperity and peace of that community as anyone. How interesting that Paul takes this term and Christianizes it for his fledgling communities. Of course, he adds to it the idea of the *ecclesia* being a body, striving for unity and diversity (1 Cor 12:12–31). He calls us a family, a household, with all the attendant expectations of an ancient Hebrew family—devotion, loyalty, affection (Gal 6:9–11). He refers to the *ecclesia* as a bride, emphasizing our duty to holiness and fidelity (Eph 5:22–32), and as an army, presupposing discipline and focus (Eph 6:10–13). There's more to Paul's idea of the church than just a gathering. But isn't it interesting that the base, raw material he uses to develop his vision for us is that of a group of elders adding value to the village, bringing wisdom, and connecting our destiny with that of the community? We think that to be the sent people of God implies that we will have our neighborhood's best interests at heart. We think Christians should see themselves as sent by Jesus into the villages of which they're part, to add value, to bring wisdom, to foster a better village. In short, to participate with the work of Christ all around us.

When Michael was planting the faith community of which he is currently part, smallboatbigsea, he was given a prophetic word from a woman at a meeting he was attending. She told him that a day would come when, if smallboatbigsea was taken away from its neighborhood, the whole community would grieve for its loss. For him, it's a cherished word. Those ancient villages in Judea would have grieved had all their wise, godly elders been suddenly taken away. They wouldn't have known how to be good, true, noble, and peaceful without their input. Is it not possible that Paul imagined a similar appreciation toward his churches? Did he choose *ecclesia*, of all the terms he might have used, because it contained this element of community service and value adding? If so then, to be sent to participate in the unfurling of the kingdom in our communities will necessarily mean the bringing of wisdom, peace, and grace to our villages.

You Will See the World Differently

We recognize that each person is created in the image of God and thus possesses the inherent dignity and value that accompanies it. We recognize also that God has been, and continues to be, at work within them, leading them on a unique and sacred journey. In our previous book together, *The Shaping of Things to Come*, we wrote about the importance of prevenient grace, the confidence that God goes before us, prevening (preparing) our participation in his work. More than that, though, God has already touched every person, leaving his unique fingerprints on that person's soul. The Latin term for this is *imago Dei*, the image of God.

To say that we are all made in the image of God is to acknowledge that there are certain, special qualities of human nature that allow God to be made manifest in us. It is a statement about God's love for humans but also a statement about the uniqueness and beauty of humans. A belief in the *imago Dei* is not a denial of the inherent sinfulness of all people. To deny such is not only heretical, it's just plain ignorant. The human race continues to give myriad examples of our depravity and potential for evil. Rather, it recognizes that God's image is so indelibly stamped on our nature that not even the fall can completely erase it. We, of all creation, are the creatures through whom God's plans and purposes can be made known. In other words, when Christians acknowledge the image of God in us, we can see ourselves as participants or partners with God.

But further, we can see even the unbeliever as bearing the mark of God, and such a mark in even the so-called lowest person must be respected and acknowledged. In other words, if humans are to love God, then humans must love other humans, as each is an expression of God. Jesus pointed this out with his parable of the sheep and the goats (Matt 25:31–46). The regular refrain from the king in the story, "I tell you the truth, whatever you did/did not do for one of the least of these, you did/did not do for me" powerfully illustrates the doctrine of *imago Dei*. Why feed the hungry or clothe the naked or visit the imprisoned or tend to the sick? Because even these, the least of these in fact, bear the image of the king.

The Bible does not claim that animals, though created by God, bear his image in the same way humans do. Humans are self-conscious, with the capacity for spiritual and moral reflection and growth. We differ from all other creatures because of our rational structure—our capacity for deliberation and free decision making. This freedom gives the human a centeredness and completeness that allows the possibility for self-actualization and participation in a sacred reality. However, as previously noted, the freedom that marks the *imago Dei* in human nature is the same freedom that manifests itself in estrangement from God, as the story of the fall exemplifies. According to this story, humans can, in their freedom, choose to deny or repress their spiritual and moral likeness to God. The ability and desire to love one's self and others, and therefore God, can be neglected, even resisted.

The vision Jesus brings is one where the believer learns to identify and tease out that image in others. When Jesus acknowledges the serene faith of a pagan centurion (Matt 8:10), the persistent faith of a Canaanite woman (Matt 15:28), and the desperate faith of the thief on the cross (Luke 23:43), he is finding the *imago Dei* in the least likely people—foreigners and criminals. Romans, Canaanites, thieves, adulteresses (John 8), and Samaritans (John 4) were seen by the Jewish establishment as being on a par with dogs. As we mentioned, animals are not seen in Scripture as bearing the image of God, so to disregard the *imago Dei* in certain peoples is to treat them like animals. You never see Jesus doing that. Lepers, prostitutes, tax collectors, children, demoniacs—they were treated with great grace and respect by him. Even the hemorrhaging woman whose issue of blood made her perennially unclean is paraded by Jesus before the ogling crowd, her faith acknowledged by the Savior of the world for all to see. This was the scandalous Jesus at his most untamed.

If we reJesus the church, we will lead it toward a greater respect for the unbeliever, a greater grace for those who, though they don't attend church services, are nonetheless marked by God's image. It will lead to a greater respect for people in general. This is illustrated in Willa Cather's marvelous novel about Christian mission, *Death Comes for the Archbishop*. Set in the wild Arizona territories at the turn of the twentieth century, the book portrays the life stories of two Catholic missionaries, bringing the gospel to a melting pot of frontier families, Mexican settlers, and Native Americans. At one point, one of the priests, Father Vaillant, describes an experience that encapsulates his missionary call. It is one of the best descriptions of the missionary vocation:

Down near Tucson, a Pima Indian convert once asked me to go off into the desert with him, as he had something to show me. He took me into a place so wild that a man less accustomed to these things might have mistrusted and feared for his life. We descended into a terrifying canyon of black rock, and there in the depths of a cave, he showed me a golden chalice, vestments and cruets, all the paraphernalia for celebrating Mass. His ancestors had hidden these sacred objects there when the mission was sacked by Apaches, he did not know how many generations ago. The secret had been handed down in his family, and I was the first priest who had ever come to restore to God his own. To me, that is the situation in a parable. The Faith, in that wild frontier, is like a buried treasure; they guard it, but they do not know how to use it to their soul's salvation. A word, a prayer, a service, is all that is needed to free these souls in bondage. I confess I am covetous of that mission. I desire to be the man who restores these lost children to God. It will be the greatest happiness of my life.[16]

Father Vaillant's testimony is anchored in a belief in the *imago Dei*. The buried church supplies are symbolic of the image of God buried deep in the souls of all people. The missionary task is not to bring God to them but to uncover the *imago Dei* and assist people to use this knowledge for the salvation of their souls. Vaillant assumes that the gospel is buried deep in the soil of all people and it is his job, through "a word, a prayer, a service" to unearth this treasure and "restore to God his own."

⟿ Marked by Jesus

Put simply, to undertake the reJesus project one must first be committed to being marked by Jesus, to submit oneself to being shaped and changed to reflect more and more the lifestyle and teaching of Jesus. This idea is wonderfully portrayed by the much-loved novelist and short-story writer Flannery O'Connor. This devout Christian saw her function as a writer in part to shake the spiritual cataracts from her secular readers' eyes and open their vision to an incarnational faith and an awareness of the operation of grace in the everyday world. Within virtually every story she wrote was embedded the presence of grace, waiting to be accepted or rejected by her characters and her readers. She died before the age of forty, having spent the last decade of her short life suffering from the effects of lupus, the debilitating disease that was to claim her. One of the last stories she wrote was completed in a hospital bed in defiance of her doctor's orders not to push her failing body any further. "Parker's Back" is considered to be the crowning achievement of her

Christian vision as a writer because it marvelously illustrates the fact that the complete, most fulfilled human being is the one who incarnates Jesus in his or her life. It seems somehow fitting that O'Connor died writing it.

Obadiah Elihue Parker (that name is foreboding in itself) is a tragicomic country hick, a good-for-nothing who drifts from job to job and place to place. His only overriding interest seems to be the collection of tattoos that adorn nearly every inch of his skin, with the exception of his back. Inspired by a tattooed man he saw at a county fair when he was fourteen, OE has spent more than a decade covering the front of his body with a variety of images, trying to emulate what he remembered as the symphony of colorful images on that tattooed man. And yet with each new tattoo, his dissatisfaction grows. Whereas his hero's pictures looked harmonized and integrated, OE saw his own designs as haphazard and messy. In OE Parker, O'Connor has created the typical human, striving for redemption and yearning to be something beautiful. And yet each new attempt to correct the overall effect of his tattoos leads to even greater disappointment.

When we meet Parker, he has married the daughter of a fundamentalist preacher, a dour young woman named Sarah Ruth who would only marry him in the county clerk's office because she believed church buildings to be idolatrous. Sarah Ruth, outwardly religious and deeply pious, becomes the ironic foil for her heathen husband's search for redemption. She represents that kind of Christian that Dorothy L. Sayers identified as preferring to take Jesus in fairytale form, not straight from the Gospels. She has rules for everything, having learned all her life how to judge and find wanting every experience and every person.

Sarah Ruth, as one might imagine, despises Parker's tattoos. But more than that, she seems displeased with everything he does. In voicing her dissatisfaction as clearly and as often as she does, she reinforces Parker's disappointment with himself. He desires more than anything to do just one thing that would please her. In a sense, his quest for redemption becomes located in his focus on pleasing the unpleasable Sarah Ruth. For a man who has only ever performed menial jobs, who has no money and very few prospects, it's not surprising that in his simplistic way, he decides that the only thing he could do to please her is to get the right tattoo in the middle of his back.

He visualized having a tattoo put there that Sarah Ruth would not be able to resist—a religious subject. He thought of an open book with "HOLY BIBLE" tattooed under it and an actual verse printed on the page. This seemed just the thing for a while; then he began to hear her say, "Ain't I got a real Bible? What you think I want to read the same verse over and over for when I can read all of it?" He needed something better.[17]

Brow-beaten and anxious about choosing wrongly, he ends up in a tattooist's parlor leafing through a catalogue of religious images before being stopped by the piercing gaze of a Byzantine icon of the face of Christ. O'Connor describes how Parker felt he "were being brought back to life by a subtle power" as the image of Jesus takes hold of him. He decides there and then that the most pleasing thing he could do was to have his whole back tattooed with this face of Christ. The symbolism of "Parker's Back" isn't restrained. O'Connor is obviously depicting a man being marked by Jesus, inscribed with the express image of God. Albeit in a secular way, she is none-theless describing Parker's baptism, his initiation into the family of Jesus. As surely as any catechumen is being marked by Jesus at baptism, OE Parker is equally denoted as belonging to him. Where none of the other of his slapdash collection of tattoos can satisfy him, his whole back now bears the unified, single image of God.

But as you might expect, not even this painful act of sacrifice can win Sarah Ruth's approval. When he returns home and reveals the Byzantine Christ across his back, she is initially confused. "It ain't nobody I know," she says tellingly. The irony is bitter. The devout Christian woman cannot recog-nize the face of Jesus, while the recalcitrant heathen is stained by it forever.

"It's him," Parker said.

"Him who?"

"God!" Parker cried.

"God? God don't look like that!"

"What do you know how he looks?" Parker moaned. "You ain't seen him."

"He don't *look*," Sarah Ruth said. "He's spirit. No man shall see his face . . .

"Idolatry," Sarah Ruth screamed. "Idolatry . . . I don't want no idolater in this house!" And she grabbed up the broom and began to thrash him across the shoulders with it . . . and large welts . . . formed on the face of the tattooed Christ. Then he staggered and made for the door . . .[18]

Sarah Ruth can neither understand nor appreciate the incarnation. For her, God is a spirit, and no one can see his face. The idea that God has taken on human flesh and walked among us is beyond her comprehension and her spirituality. She prefers her Deity far beyond and distant. It is even less likely that she could comprehend the idea that her husband has chosen to incarnate God in his own body. The welts she leaves across the tattooed Jesus' face mirror the beatings that the real Jesus bore in his passion. The story ends most poignantly. Still gripping the broom and filled with rage, Sarah Ruth looks out toward a pecan tree in her yard: "her eyes hardened still more. There he was—who called himself Obadiah Elihue—leaning against the tree, crying like a baby."[19]

In this, the closing line of the story, O'Connor reminds us of Parker's full name. Obadiah, "servant of the Lord," Elihue, "God is he." Hanging on a tree, beaten by one who doesn't recognize his identity, bearing the hatred and condemnation of the woman who watches him, Parker is an embodiment of the incarnation. He is the suffering servant, the crucified one, and perhaps O'Connor is hinting that he has finally stepped into his name, living up to his calling at birth to be marked by God.

We confess that this calling is ours as well. Like Father Vaillant in *Death Comes for the Archbishop* and OE Parker, we too feel marked by Jesus and, as a result we see God, the church, and our world differently. We see God as the *missio Dei*, the church as the *participati Christi*, and the world as the *imago Dei*. And we echo Father Vaillant when he says, "I confess I am covetous of that mission. I desire to be the man who restores these lost children to God. It will be the greatest happiness of my life."

⟵ Notes

1. Frost, *Exiles*, 28–49.

2. M. Scott Peck, *Further Along the Road Less Traveled: The Unending Journey Toward Spiritual Growth* (New York: Simon and Schuster, 1993), 210.

3. Charles Sheldon, *In His Steps* (1896; repr., Peabody, Mass.: Hendrickson, 2004), 9. Originally published in 1896, this book was translated into twenty-one languages by 1935. It was the basis of the global campaign to take Jesus as guide and model that became known as the WWJD (What Would Jesus Do?) movement.

4. Terry Eagleton, "Was Jesus Christ a Revolutionary?" *New Internationalist*, May 1, 2008, 24.

5. Nick Cave, *The Gospel According to Mark with an Introduction by Nick Cave* (Melbourne: Text, 1998), xi.

6. Ibid.

7. Quoted in Laura Simmons, *Creed Without Chaos: Exploring Theology in the Writings of Dorothy Sayers* (Grand Rapids, Mich.: Baker, 2005), 78.

8. Dorothy L. Sayers, *The Man Born to Be King* (London: Victor Gollancz, 1955), 21.

9. Simmons, *Creed Without Chaos*, 79.

10. See Augustine *In John* 35.5; 36.8; 40.6; Chrysostom *In John* 53.2.

11. David Jacobus Bosch, *Transforming Mission: Paradigm Shifts in Theology of Mission* (American Society of Missiology 16; Maryknoll, N.Y.: Orbis, 1991), 390.

12. Jacques Matthey, "Congress 'Mission Dei' God's Mission Today: Summary and Conclusions (Reflector's Report)," (50th Anniversary of the World Mission Conference, August 16–21, 2002), 3.1. Cited 25 September 2008. Online: http://www.wcc-coe.org/wcc/what/mission/willingen.html.

13. Bosch, *Transforming Mission*, 519.

14. Robert McAfee Brown, quoted in "The Meaning of Life," *Life*, December 1988. Cited 25 September 2008. Online: http://www.maryellenmark.com/text/magazines/life/905W-000-037.html.

15. John Eldridge, *Wild at Heart* (Nashville: Thomas Nelson, 2006), 34.

16. Willa Cather, *Death Comes for the Archbishop* (1927; repr., New York: Vintage, 1990), 206–7.

17. Flannery O'Connor, "Parker's Back," *The Complete Stories of Flannery O'Connor* (New York: Noonday, 1992), 519.

18. Ibid., 529.

19. Ibid., 530.

ReJesus and Personal ReNewal

My mission is to introduce Christianity into Christendom.
—Søren Kierkegaard

> *We have to admit that there is an immeasurable distance between all that we read in the Bible and the practice of the church and of Christians. This is why I can speak validly of perversion or subversion, for, as I shall show, practice has been the total opposite of what is required of us.*
> —Jacques Ellul

We believe it is not possible to be following the biblical Jesus and not end up being molded by the *missio Dei, participati Christi,* and *imago Dei.* When taken captive by Jesus, we cannot help but see God, the church, and the world very differently. They are fundamental elements of a Jesus-shaped people. So, taking them as our starting point, let us now look more deeply into the nature and dynamic of the lifestyle and faith that Jesus taught and exemplified. We do this not so much to outline the contours of his teaching—so many books have done a better job of that than we can possibly accomplish—but rather to try and find its spiritual centers, to touch the wild and primal energy that radiates out of Jesus. In doing so, we believe we can begin to understand why it is that his people historically have obscured the dynamic of his message in various ways. And so from the broad framework we have explored so far, let us turn our attention to an exploration of connection between Jesus, the disciple, and the community of disciples, that is, the church. We use the term "disciple" deliberately because it emphasizes the kind of relationship that is decisive for the maintenance of a living connection with Jesus. For what is a church if not a community of disciples, of people devoted to following Jesus? If the New Testament is our guide in these matters, then discipleship should be the defining quality of the Christian life. And if this is the case, then we can never move from the more primal commitment that is involved in becoming his follower in the first place.

And yet, the ethos of discipleship and the presence of the wild Messiah are not readily associated with church and Christianity of our day. Far from it, our expressions of church range generally from what we might call high church, where Jesus tends to be relegated to some place in the outer echelons of the cosmos, to the more prevalent contemporary seeker-sensitive model where the radical message of Jesus is easily trivialized into some form of spiritual accessory in a consumerist paradise. From the fundamentalist co-option of Jesus as a religious fanatic to the liberal reduction of him into a schmaltzy moralist, it is probably fair to say that we have largely lost touch with our loving, wildly passionate, dangerous, radically merciful, and always surprising Redeemer-Lord. This is the Jesus so powerfully portrayed in the Gospels. The loss of the presence and power of *this* radical Jesus must surely account for a significant part of the spiritual bankruptcy of the church in the West. And therefore the importance of reJesus for spirituality and mission cannot be underestimated.

⬅ Rebooting to Jesus

If it is not already clear, let us state it emphatically: We believe that Christology is the key to the renewal of the church in every age and in every possible situation it might find itself. The church must always return to Jesus in order to renew itself. When, for whatever reason, the church gets stuck or loses its way in the world, it needs to recover its primal identity in its founder. It is not good enough to return to the founder of whatever denomination or organization we find ourselves in, although revitalization of that kind is not without merit. For Salvationists to rediscover the fire and fight within William Booth or for Methodists to have a re-encounter with John Wesley's passion and theology is valuable. But, when there is something fundamentally wrong in the basic equation of the faith, then it is time to recover a vital and active sense of Jesus: who he is, what he has done for us, the way of life he laid down for us to follow. His passions and concerns must become ours. In other words, as stated earlier, Christology must determine missiology (our purpose and function in this world), which in turn must determine ecclesiology (the cultural forms and expressions of the church).

Putting aside the issue of how missiology must inform ecclesiology (as that is dealt with in our previous books, specifically *The Shaping of Things to Come* and *The Forgotten Ways*), we believe that Christology is the singularly most important factor in shaping our mission in the world and the forms of *ecclesia* and ministry that result from that engagement. There must be a constant return to Jesus in order to ascertain that we are in the Way. It is no good just revamping our missiology or inventing new cultural forms of *ecclesia* unless we have first and foremost related them to Christology. This has become the mis-guided task of many so-called church renewal projects currently underway. Some such projects maintain that we need to get our theology and preaching right and renewal will flow from there. Others insist on Spirit-filled worship or alternative worship or church planting or a postmodernized approach to the faith. We are skeptical. Whenever these strategies are not anchored directly in a biblical Christology, they are doomed to limited effectiveness.

So, allow us to portray it this way:

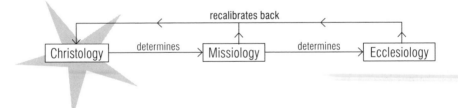

Before there is any consideration given to the particular aspects of ec-clesiology, such as leadership, evangelism, or worship, there ought to be a thoroughgoing attempt to reconnect the church with Jesus; that is, to reJesus the church as the first order of business. So much is bound up with this re-covery of a radical New Testament Christology. The church's mission as well as its experience of community can be revitalized only by a renewed encoun-ter with Jesus the Lord. And this is not something that is casual and intermit-tent. It requires a constant attention to the Lord of the church. As Wilhelm Visser T'Hooft once put it, "It belongs to the very life of the people of God that it must accept again and again to have its life renewed by a new confrontation with its Lord and his holy will."[1]

Think of it like a form of recalibration. When a machine gets jammed, the only way to kick-start it is to reset it to its original formulation. It's like a computer. When things go haywire and all else fails, we reboot it. By rebooting a computer, we restore its original operational settings, thus allowing it to function properly again. The software is back in sync with the

Resisting Evil

As a little Jesus, Dietrich Bonhoeffer refused to bend his knee to the Nazis, the empire of his time. His public resistance in 1933 to Hitler's policy to merge all Protestant churches into a pro-Nazi Protestant Reich Church put him at risk from the beginning. Bonhoeffer claimed defiantly that the church is not an organ of the state, but is subject only to Jesus and his mission. In 1939, faced with being drafted into the German army, he accepted an offer to teach at Union Seminary in New York. He returned home barely a month later, however, convinced that he would never have a voice in Germany after the war if he didn't

Dietrich Bonhoeffer

stand with his people during it. He found an opportunity to resist Hitler through his brother-in-law Hans von Dohnanyi, an officer in the military intelligence agency Abwehr and a key figure in the covert resistance movement. Von Dohnanyi arranged for Bonhoeffer to travel to the Vatican and to Switzerland, where he helped a group of Jews cross the border, as well as to Sweden, where he met with British bishop George Bell to try to secure Allied support for a planned coup against Hitler. When the money used to smuggle the Jews across the border into Switzerland was traced to Bonhoeffer, the Nazis arrested him in 1943. While he was in prison, a group of Abwehr officers, including von Dohnanyi, attempted to assassinate Hitler but failed. The Nazis tied Bonhoeffer to this plot as well, and in 1945, a month before the surrender of the Germans, he was executed by hanging. Bonhoeffer's writings have inspired millions, but his courage in resisting evil and in paying the ultimate cost for his fidelity to the gospel is his greatest and most enduring legacy.

hardware again. This is precisely the image that we wish to convey—that by rebooting the church to Jesus, it will recover itself and become fully operational again.

The Bible describes Jesus as Alpha and Omega (Rev 1:8; 21:6; 22:13). It also describes him as founder and perfecter of faith (Heb 12:2). Surely these divine titles (functions?) must say something about the ongoing role of Jesus in the life of the disciple and in the life of the Christian community. If Jesus is as he claims, the Beginning and the End, then surely this must indicate that Christology claims central place in our self-understanding. If he is founder and perfecter, then he not only sets the primary template for authentic faith but also works at helping us bring it into mature expression.

We want to address this in two primary dimensions. First, the reJesus project for individual followers of Jesus is the reJesusing of personal discipleship. Second, in the next chapter, we will explore the impact of reJesus for the renewal of the church as an organization. This chapter is individually oriented; the next chapter is communal in focus.

⟿The Capturing of Our Imaginations

Ignatius of Loyola, the founder of the Jesuits (one of the most significant Catholic missionary orders), developed a set of spiritual exercises for the initiation of new Jesuit candidates. The novel, and perhaps the most significant, aspect of the exercises was the requirement of the novitiate, as well as the established member, to activate their imaginations in order to encounter Jesus more directly. We will return to what this entailed in a later chapter, but for now it's enough to highlight why engaging Jesus through activating our imagination is an important thing to do.

Ask yourself what stimuli provoke your imagination on any given day. In other words, what stuff, coming at you from the world in which you live, most arouses or inspires you and your worldview? Television? Movies? Video games, sports, novels, business, the Internet? And yet these are not benign or valueless entertainments. They are owned or controlled by powerful forces in our society. They collectively contribute to a collective imagination that shapes us all: consumerist, materialist, individualist. In *Exiles*, Michael explored the way in which our post-Christian culture is not dissimilar to the empires into which the Old Testament exiles, Daniel, Esther, and Joseph, were repatriated. Our current empire is no more friendly to our faith than Babylon was to, say, Daniel's faith. Like all empires, our society seeks to maintain control over us in a variety of ways. These ways include

- ⟼ the threat of violence (having a powerful army helps)

- ⟼ the dominance of the economic system

- ⟼ the capturing of the imagination of the people by various means (e.g., the ubiquitous use of Caesar's image throughout the empire on coins, artifacts, and statues)

On the last point, how is the ubiquity of Caesar's image any different from the intrusive and all-pervasive nature of the tools employed by our current empire for manipulating our imaginations? It, like all pervasive systems, seeks to claim our total allegiance by dominating our imaginations. Brian Walsh and Sylvia Keesmaat deal with this issue in their commentary of Paul's letter to the Colossians. They suggest that in order to overcome the ubiquitous and dominating claims of the Roman Empire, the Colossian Christians organized their lives and their thinking around a christological center. They cultivated an alternative imagination to the dominant imagination around about them and in so doing structured their lives around Jesus.[2] As we saw in chapter 1, this reorientation around Jesus changes everything.

One of the most urgent reasons why we need to re-envision ourselves around Jesus is that our imaginations so easily become captive to the dominant forces in our culture, whether those forces are economic, political, religious, or ideological. Furthermore, as we have already observed, our perceptions of Jesus readily become domesticated through familiarity, fear of change, spiritual indolence, or whatever keeps us from engaging Jesus as living Lord. Idolatry still has its lure, and in modern democratic societies and in the globalized, market-based economic system within which we all live it seems to have become almost totally pervasive and yet more subtle at the same time. There seems to be little ideological or religious alternative to the domination of the free-market-based consumption other than the reactionary responses of Islam. The Western church seems to have almost totally capitulated to the economic ideology of our day. Says Tom Sine,

> This imagery of the good life and a better future, that pervades Western society, is born of the Enlightenment and the rise of modernity. Essentially, the storytellers of the Enlightenment took the vertical quest for God's kingdom, which had been a centerpiece of European culture, and turned it on its side. It became the horizontal pursuit of western progress, technological mastery and economic growth.

> This vision of a better future is called the Western Dream or the American Dream, and now it is the driving myth behind the new imperial global economic order. In fact, as we will see, marketers of the new global order called McWorld, and the merchants of "cool" are seeking to influence people everywhere on this planet to live into this dream. And they are having stunning success.[3]

Furthermore, Walsh and Keesmaat state, "The messages are all telling the same story. . . . economic growth is the driving force of history, consumer choice is what makes us human, and greed is normal. If we live in an empire, it is an empire of global consumerism."[4] And the empire has a plan for our lives.

Into this profoundly religious empire, made up of the idolatrous lure of money, sexuality, competing ideologies and visions, comes an alternative vision of reality in the form of Jesus. The WWJD campaign invited us to imagine how Jesus would respond to the cultural and religious issues of our day. However, this question tended to become captive to a religious pietism that limited the issue to private morality and then further trivialized into an international campaign that focused almost entirely on the sexual ethics of young adult Christians. This is unfortunate, because WWJD has in it the capacity to become a global movement that takes the claims that Jesus makes over all of life seriously indeed. We would like to relaunch the campaign but this time keeping the broader issues in mind as well. What would Jesus do in the consumptive world in which we live? How would he respond to the environmental crisis? What would Jesus do with the banal depravities of reality television? What would Jesus do with our money and resources in a world of poverty and in need of grace and mercy? As we shall see in a later chapter, the lordship of Jesus cannot be limited to personal piety and must extend to all issues common to human experience. WWJD must extend to the issues of economics, environment, and politics if we are to truly unlock the world-renewing power inherent in the question.

Our imagination is such a powerful force. Jesus pointed out, "For where your treasure is, there your heart will be also" (Matt 6:21). In other words, the things that capture our imaginations (our treasures), whether they are wealth or sex or power, drag our hearts (our actions, our priorities) along with them. This is why he insisted that we store ourselves "treasures in heaven" (Matt 6:20). If we allow Jesus to capture our imaginations, our actions and priorities will mirror his lifestyle and teaching. The church needs an alternative imagination to that of the empire in which it finds itself.

In this respect, Walter Brueggemann comments on the role of the preacher as the source of an alternative, Christ-centered imagination. If the church needs to be continually reJesused, then those who give voice to the church's public speech ought to be committed to drenching the church's collective imaginations in the gospel. Says Brueggemann,

> The event of preaching is an event of transformed imagination . . . Because finally church people are like other people; we are not changed by new rules. The

deep places in our lives—places of resistance and embrace are reached only by stories, by images, metaphors and phrases that line out the world differently apart from our fear and hurt.[5]

We've heard too many sermons about how to be better citizens. Too much preaching is concerned with the fostering of a capitulation to the mores and values of a post-Christian empire rather than a call to allow our imaginations to be overtaken by Jesus and focused on treasures in heaven.

⌐ The Conspiracy of Little Jesuses

Often the wake-up call to embrace an alternate imagination has to be made in a stark and uncompromising fashion. The 2005 film V *for Vendetta* is set in a totalitarian Britain in the not-too-distant future. The English have handed their imaginations (so to speak) over to a dictator whose empire is every bit as controlling as Caesar's. In fact, it resembles the Orwellian Britain of the novel 1984. A revolutionary in a mask, calling himself only V, embarks upon a program of civil unrest to shake people out of their stupor. In one scene, he takes over a British television studio and broadcasts an incendiary call to arms, concluding in the following manner:

> . . . the truth is, there is something terribly wrong with this country, isn't there? Cruelty and injustice, intolerance and oppression. And where once you had the freedom to object, to think and speak as you saw fit, you now have censors and systems of surveillance coercing your conformity and soliciting your submission. How did this happen? Who's to blame? Well certainly there are those more responsible than others, and they will be held accountable, but again truth be told, if you're looking for the guilty, you need only look into a mirror. I know why you did it. I know you were afraid. Who wouldn't be? War, terror, disease. There were a myriad of problems which conspired to corrupt your reason and rob you of your common sense. Fear got the best of you, and in your panic you turned to the now high chancellor, Adam Sutler. He promised you order, he promised you peace, and all he demanded in return was your silent, obedient consent. Last night I sought to end that silence. Last night I destroyed the Old Bailey, to remind this country of what it has forgotten. More than four hundred years ago a great citizen wished to embed the fifth of November forever in our memory. His hope was to remind the world that fairness, justice, and freedom are more than words, they are perspectives. So if you've seen nothing, if the crimes of this government remain unknown to you then I would suggest you allow the fifth of November to pass unmarked. But if you see what I see, if you

feel as I feel, and if you would seek as I seek, then I ask you to stand beside me one year from tonight, outside the gates of Parliament, and together we shall give them a fifth of November that shall never, ever be forgot.[6]

The film climaxes after V's death, with thousands and thousands of Britons, all wearing Guy Fawkes masks, marching on the Houses of Parliament in an unstoppable wave of resistance. V has duplicated himself in the lives of others. He has catalyzed a movement for change, for revolution. In this respect, V epitomizes what we've been talking about. He captures the imaginations of those who were previously held captive to the empire. He fashions a grand conspiracy in which hundreds of thousands of little Vs stand irresistibly against the totalitarian regime.

As mentioned earlier, Alan coined the phrase "the conspiracy of little Jesuses" to describe this same idea as portrayed in V *for Vendetta*. Jesus takes captive the imaginations of his followers and then replicates himself in them. In fact, we can sum up the task of discipleship as the lifelong project of literally becoming like him, of becoming a little Jesus. But the whole process of becoming more like him moves quickly beyond the individual to the group and from there to a movement. Even a superficial reading of the New Testament indicates that it was Jesus' strategic intention to create a movement consisting of Christlike people inhabiting every possible nook and cranny of culture and society—hence the idea of a mass conspiracy.[7]

Whether one talks about becoming a little Jesus or uses that wonderful old phrase "imitation (or following) of Christ," the essential function is clear—the modeling ourselves upon his life lies at the center of our spirituality. Says Kierkegaard,

> To be truly redeemed by Christ is, therefore, to impose on oneself the task of imitating him; As man Jesus is my model because as God he is my Redeemer; Christianity can be defined as a faith together with a corresponding way of life, *imitation of Christ*.[8]

The climactic scene in V *for Vendetta*, with countless Vs streaming out of side streets, leaping over barricades, and flowing like a torrent toward Parliament, represents the power that resides in such a conspiracy of imitation. Kierkegaard also said, "Unlike the admirer who stands simply aloof, the follower of Christ strives to be what he admires. Without this essential condition all attempts to be a Christian are fruitless."[9] This is the conspiracy of little Jesuses.

David Bosch rightly noted, "Discipleship is determined by the relation to Christ himself not by mere conformity to impersonal commands."[10] He said this when commenting on how preachers have used the Great Commission (Matt 28:18–20) to pressgang Christians into missionary service. Many well-intentioned church leaders have simplistically presented the words of Jesus, "Go therefore and make disciples of all nations," as some remote order barked by a stern sergeant-major. If Jesus said it, we should do it! But Bosch points out that missionary service that is motivated by blind obedience to an impersonal order from Jesus is built on a flimsy foundation. If our commitment to mission is only based on Jesus' "order" in Matthew 28, it makes mission an obligation for us rather than an act of love and grace. It's not unlike a woman who complains that her husband never brings her flowers. When the guilty husband rushes out and buys her a bouquet and presents it to her, she is still dissatisfied, because it wasn't that she wanted flowers in particular. What she wanted was for him to be motivated by his devotion for her so as to buy a gift. When we engage in mission only because we feel guilty that we haven't pleased Jesus and his order in the so-called Great Commission, we satisfy neither Jesus nor our own sense of calling. Rather, says Bosch, mission emerges from a deep, rich relationship with Jesus. The woman whose husband never brings her flowers doesn't want flowers. She wants him and his devotion. What Jesus is saying to his disciples in Matthew 28 is that little Jesuses will be naturally and normally about the business of making disciples, not to satisfy Jesus' demands but out of complete devotion for him. To paraphrase Bosch, the Great Commission is not a commission in the ordinary sense of the word, but rather a creative statement about the new order of things. Or as Garrett Green was noted for saying, "God is the one who conquers not by force, but by capturing the imagination of his fallen creatures."

However difficult it is to remain open to God, it is vital that this relationship must take the form of a direct and unmediated relationship with Jesus. It must involve a constantly renewed, up-to-date experience with our Lord. The loss of covenantal relationship results in a religion other than the one Jesus started. Even though it might take the forms of Christian faith, it will lack the reality of it.

That discipleship is foundational to Christianity and its mission therefore goes without saying. If we fail here, we will fail everywhere.[11] But the critical role of discipleship in the mission of the church once again highlights the role of the radical Jesus in the life of faith. And this bond cannot primarily merely involve a cerebral, objective, indirect understanding of Jesus and the Christian faith. This substitution of thinking about Jesus for existential encounter with Jesus is a constant temptation for the follower. This is partly because a living relationship with the Lord of the universe is a risky, disturbing, and demanding experience. We never get the better of him, and it is a whole lot easier, and less costly, to think than to do. It is not good enough that we just follow his teachings or a religious code developed in his wake. Discipleship requires a direct and unmediated relationship with the Lord, and the loss of this immediacy is catastrophic to the movement that claims his name.

Dallas Willard rightly bemoans the fact that for quite a while now the churches in the Western world have not made discipleship a condition of being a Christian.

> One is not required to be, or to intend to be, a disciple in order to become a Christian, and one may remain a Christian without any signs of progress toward or in discipleship. Contemporary Western churches do not require following Christ in his example, spirit, and teachings as a condition of membership— either of entering into or continuing in fellowship of a denomination or a local church. . . . So far as the visible Christian institutions of our day are concerned, discipleship clearly is optional. . . . Churches are therefore filled with "undiscipled disciples." "Most problems in contemporary churches can be explained by the fact that members have not yet decided to follow Christ."[12]

This living link between Jesus, discipleship, and authentic Christianity was highlighted by Dietrich Bonhoeffer when he says,

> Discipleship means adherence to Christ and, because Christ is the object of that adherence, it must take the form of discipleship. An abstract theology, a doctrinal system, a general religious knowledge of the subject of grace or the forgiveness of sins, render discipleship superfluous, and in fact exclude any idea of discipleship whatsoever, and are essentially inimical to the whole conception of following Christ. . . . *Christianity without the living Christ is inevitably Christianity without discipleship, and Christianity without discipleship is always Christianity without Christ.* [italics added][13]

The last sentence of this quote highlights the issue for us. At stake at the heart of discipleship is nothing less than the embodiment and transmission of the gospel. Who wants a Christianity without Christ? Well, if we are to avoid the ever-encroaching possibility of this form of spiritual deception, we had better be sure we keep our focus on disciple making as a key task. It is embodiment (our willingness to embody and live out Jesus' life and message) that creates spiritual authority. It also gives much needed credibility to our witness. And in the credibility of the message laid down through our lives lies the foundation for its authentic transmission from generation to generation and from culture to culture. Embodiment and (trans)mission therefore go together and all are bound inextricably to our relationship with Jesus.

Critic of Religiosity

Søren Kierkegaard

Like Jesus attacking Pharisaism, Søren Kierkegaard came out swinging against every phoney form of institutionalized Christianity. "An apostle proclaims the truth, an auditor is responsible for discovering counterfeits," wrote this nineteenth-century Danish philosopher and theologian. He saw it as his mission to be an auditor of Christendom, an institution he charged with sanitizing Jesus and making light of his message. Denmark's state church, he wrote, was "just about as genuine as tea made from a bit of paper which once lay in a drawer beside another bit of paper which had once been used to wrap up a few dried tea leaves from which tea had already been made three times." One of the fathers of existentialism, this remarkably complex and intelligent man underwent a profound spiritual transformation at the age of thirty-five and thereafter sought to apply some of his existentialist ideas to Christianity and thus reintroduce his nation to Jesus. Individuals, not the state, Kierkegaard argued, needed to make a "leap of faith" in order to enter into authentic Christianity. As a little Jesus, he hoped that his brutal attacks against the banality of institutional religion would anger Danish Christians enough to make them re-examine their relationship to Jesus.

The difficulty that we face in this issue of embodiment and transmission is that it is directly related to the credibility of the gospel. Our witness is a vital link in giving the claims of Jesus credibility in the eyes of non-Christian people. We are not allowed off the ethical hook by admitting that while our practice is poor, the beauty, purity, and truth of the Bible are nonetheless undiminished. The Bible, claims Jacques Ellul, insists on the unity of the two:

> We have to understand this. No recognizable revelation exists apart from the life and witness of those who bear it. The life of Christians is what gives testimony to God and to the meaning of this revelation. "See how they love one another"—this is where the approach to the Revealed God begins. "If you devour one another, you do not have the love of God in you," etc. There is no pure truth of God or Jesus Christ to which we can return, washing our hands of what we ourselves do. If Christians are not conformed in their lives to their truth, there is [effectively] no truth. This is why the accusers of the eighteenth and nineteenth centuries

were right to infer the falsity of revelation itself from the practice of the church. This makes us see that in not being what Christ demands we render all revelation false, illusory, ideological, imaginary, and non-salvific. We are thus forced to *be* Christians or to recognize the falsity of what we believe. This is undeniable proof of the need for correct practice.[14]

Whether we like it or not, we carry the burden of having to live out the truth in such a way as to establish its viability among those who are watching. Shane Claiborne, author of *The Irresistible Revolution*, once surveyed a group of people who identified themselves as "strong followers of Jesus" and asked them, "Did Jesus spend time with the poor?" Around 80 percent replied in the affirmative, leaving a disturbing 20 percent of so-called strong followers of Jesus who think Jesus didn't spend time with the poor. That this could be the case should remind us of the levels of Christian ignorance about our founder and Lord. But the more disturbing fact is that Claiborne asked the same group, "Do you spend time with the poor?" Only 2 percent replied that they did. There is for many an almost complete disconnect between our beliefs about Jesus and our actions. This disconnection lies at the nub of the problem facing the church. Søren Kierkegaard expressed it this way: "Christ is the Truth inasmuch as He is the way. He who does not follow in the way also abandons the truth. We possess Christ's truth only by imitating him, not by speculating about him."[15]

But beyond issues relating to the mission of Jesus' people, the whole matter of the leadership and ministry of the church is also directly bound to discipleship. This is no small matter, and focused effort here must yield exponential results in terms of spirituality, ministry, and mission, because Jesus is thus made manifest in the life of his people.

⟵ Face Time with Jesus

Why the church tends to so easily lose this central focus on discipleship is a bit of a historical puzzle because it forms such a strategically significant part of our task as his people in the world. Perhaps it is because it is an essentially simple act that we tend to lose focus. Modeling ourselves on a hero comes naturally to us. We do it unconsciously all the time. This task of integrating life with our message has a long history of reflection and practice, even though it has seldom, if ever, been widely accepted by the majority of believers in the Western Christendom church. One of the particularly christocentric ways of seeing this process is called conformation (Rom 8:29; 2 Cor 3:18).

The Bible understands Christian formation in a way that is largely unfamiliar to us. In the New Testament, Jesus does not disciple people by generating information, developing programs, or implementing plans. Rather, Jesus' discipleship always involves a deeply personal process of being drawn into becoming more like the image, or form, of Jesus. The great German theologian Dietrich Bonhoeffer latched onto this idea and made it central to his understanding of discipleship and ethics. He said, "It comes only as formation into his likeness, as conformation with the unique form of Him who was made man, was crucified, and rose again."[16] For him, *conformation* was the way Jesus continues to incarnate himself in the world through his people: "The way in which the form of Jesus Christ takes form in our world is the concrete, obedient, con-formation of human beings to the form of the biblical Christ, the man whose existence for others is the world's true reality."[17] But he too pointed out that this cannot be a matter of abstract theologizing or merely developing discipleship programs or the like, but rather by the way of obedience to Jesus and his commands.

The image of Jesus to which we are called to conform to is not some sort of religious nut concerned with other-worldly religious matters as if the human issues don't matter. No, if the pattern is Jesus as we encounter him in the Gospels, then it means being drawn into the pattern of true humanity because Jesus models for us what it means to be a human being in the fullest sense. In Jesus, God has given us the archetype of what it means to be truly human. Now we must become more authentically human in the way that Jesus has set out for us, using Jesus' life as a model. It was never meant to be a matter of becoming a religious person but rather the forming of Christ in every person and in the life of the community of disciples.[18]

This idea of conformation focuses attention on the direct link with Jesus and his people. The loss of this relationship and this consciousness must surely lead to the decline in the spiritual keenness of the Christian. Conversely, the rekindling of our relationship with Jesus must surely lead to a renewal of the spirit. Surely the true disciple is the person who acknowledges Christ as a present reality in his or her life. This is what trusting Jesus is all about. It requires that we draw near to Jesus, live under his lordship, trust his saving work on our behalf, and in a concentrated act of worshipful and responsive love, conform our lives to his. Participating in the life of God "does not take place through ecstasy or any religious *tour de force* (feat of strength) but through Jesus

Christ. The saints are those who penetrate into the existence of Christ, who lift themselves not by their 'bootstraps', but by Christ's humanity into Christ's divinity."[19]

In trying to convey this need for immediacy between believer and Jesus, Kierkegaard coined a rather strange term, *contemporaneousness*. Although a cumbersome term, it is a useful one because it highlights the need for unmediated closeness between Jesus and his followers. He notes that for the believer, Jesus must be a "living reality, seen through the eyes of faith, and contemporaneous with each generation. His reality must be such that it transcends both time and space."[20] In Kierkegaard's thinking, therefore, contemporaneousness is a conscious effort by the believer to reach beyond the church's entire two-thousand-year tradition and, free of inherited presuppositions, encounter Jesus, seeing him with the eyes not of the first Christians but of the first eyewitnesses (crucifiers as well as disciples), and there, "in the painful tension of that dilemma; make his own choice as to whether Jesus is the God-Man who has an absolute claim to his life or a madman who should be avoided at all costs."[21] If Kierkegaard is right, then it is impossible to avoid this rather direct appointment with Jesus if we are to be saved and to truly follow him. A Christian must be a person who has engaged, and is engaging, Jesus directly. And it is only through the lifelong imitation of Christ, not just one encounter, that genuine contemporaneousness is fully achieved.

Without laboring the point, let us reinforce our conviction that such contemporaneousness is not simply a matter of getting one's theology right (whatever *right* might mean). Biblical faith cannot be reduced to believing in a set of doctrines, and neither can discipleship be seen in these terms. Faith, as Luther (re)discovered, is more like the supreme gamble in which we stake our lives upon a conviction. It can't be reduced to belief in a set of propositions. It is a profoundly existential act in which we are fully and personally involved. Contemporaneousness cannot be attained by speculation but only by the active presence of Christ in my own existence. There is much more to being a disciple than believing and trusting Jesus at the outset; Christianity also involves a well-defined way of existence, a way of life that can be summed up in the phrase "the imitation of Christ." When we choose this way, we take it upon ourselves to be his constant companion, his follower, his contemporary. All the aspects of our discipleship (worship, ritual, prayer, mission, theologizing) are in one sense or another directed toward the achievement of contemporaneousness. Christ's whole life in all its aspects must supply the norm for the life of the following Christian and thus for the life of the whole church.[22]

↤ The Who? And the What?

So what can we use as our flashlight as we travel along this path towards Jesus? There are core truths about Jesus that provide the broad contours of the faith he set for us to journey toward. Understanding these enable us to repeatedly touch base with the elemental aspects that make Jesus and his way so special. They can provide the compass, if you will, that we can consult to see if we (individual followers and/or community of faith) are consistent with the wild and untamable Lord of the church.

Jesus' Life and Teaching	Implications for Disciple/Church	Examples of How These Could Be Lived Out
Ushers in the kingdom of God and focuses it around his own person (e.g., Mark 1:14–15; Luke 11:20)	Living under the King (see later chapter on existential monotheism, ch. 5). The kingdom of God is central and extends in and beyond the church to his entire cosmos. We are agents of the kingdom in all spheres of life common to human being. Jesus is Lord/King! We can live and work wherever we are, and we can expect the kingdom to already be there.	When we are at work, we invite Jesus to accompany us there. We look for opportunities to enact Jesus' qualities while we are working. We look for ways to mirror the work of God even through the most mundane and everyday activities.
Demands direct and active faith/trust in God (e.g., Mark 1:14–15, Matt 17:20)	Requires a radical openness to the sovereign and miraculous intervention of God in us. Faith as trust demands a distinct form of spiritual openness on our behalf. We should expect God to be involved in all aspects of our lives.	We refuse to give up when a situation seems hopeless; we have faith in God to work in the situation, somehow. We must not give in to our fears.
Mediates the grace and mercy of God (e.g., Matt 12:7)	Openness to receive as well as impart grace/mercy to others. The measure we give will be the measure we receive. We can be generous with both our resources and our time. God is merciful; we must try to find ways to be like God in daily life.	We refuse to rule out the unlikely agents of grace in our midst. Whether someone is uneducated, elderly, divorced, an ex-convict, disabled, or even just needy or annoying, we humbly accept their gifts to us as if they were from God.
Offers forgiveness of sins (e.g., Matt 9:2; Luke 7:47)	Repentance and forgiveness are a way of life (70x7). Radical openness to a holy God will require that we be constantly aware of our sinfulness and the possibility of radical evil that lurks in the human soul. Also, we must be a forgiving people (Matt 6:15).	We examine ourselves carefully for any bitterness or lack of forgiveness toward others. We place ourselves in relationships of accountability. We are open to the rebuke of the loving friend. We confess our limitations regularly.
Demonstrates the love of God for his world (e.g., John 3:16; 14:21)	Demands our primary love for God and a secondary love for others in his name. We need to know we are a loved people, and this should be expressed towards others. This love should include but extend beyond our family members to embrace even our enemies. We should be known as a people of love.	Our loves shows God's love. We show love to our family members and do so reflecting on the way it is an outpouring of the love we have received from God. We practice hospitality to the stranger. We create spaces in which others can grow and find grace.

Jesus' Life and Teaching	Implications for Disciple/Church	Examples of How These Could Be Lived Out
Heals the sick and casts out demons (e.g., Mark 1:23ff.; Luke 11:20)	Healing ministry should be part of the church's service in the world. These are signs of the kingdom's presence (John 14:12). We live in a wounded world: we should actively look for opportunities to heal people in body, psyches, and relationships.	We look for opportunities to pray for people, comfort people, reconcile with people. We must not shrink back from prayer for the sick or from engaging in spiritual warfare when necessary.
Calls all to follow and imitate him (e.g., Matt 4:19; 8:22)	He is the image of the human. Not only Savior but also God's pattern for authentic human life. This requires a following after, an imitation of Jesus . . . discipleship. It also involves a willingness to go against the flow and to stand with Jesus and his cause in the world. Even to the point of suffering and martyrdom. It will also mean we are more "attractive" to sinners and outcasts (as Jesus was).	We look for opportunities to disciple other Christians. We volunteer at a soup kitchen and sit down and talk with the clients, even if their appearance and actions make us uncomfortable.
Radicalizes the current standards of holiness (e.g., the Sermon on the Mount) (e.g., Matt 5–8)	Jesus sets a challenging ethical and moral code for the disciple/church to follow. The Sermon on the Mount is the most used discipleship text in the history of the church. This not only describes but prescribes the life of discipleship. We should make it a basic reference text and seek to live it out.	We practice hospitality, generosity, humility, and justice. We believe our faith brings not just personal salvation but a motivation for changing the world to reflect the justice and peace of God.
Introduces a distinctly non-religious (even anti-religious) way of loving and worshiping God (e.g., Matt 21; John 4:20ff)	Real countercultural forces are unleashed in the gospel. We therefore should be willing at times to go against the flow and status quo. People should be able to see that we are followers of Jesus—not that we are religious. Religious people can be off-putting to many non-Christians.	We challenge our faith community to join a secular group doing work that Jesus would approve of, even if we disagree with some of the other views the group holds.
Shows love and compassion for the poor and oppressed (e.g., Luke 4:18–19; 7:22–23)	We must serve the marginalized and downtrodden in Jesus' name. And this will mean we sometimes stand in direct opposition to systems and lifestyles that engender oppression—be they political, social, or religious systems.	We work with a group that helps HIV/AIDS victims, even though some of our Christian friends think this isn't a cause Christians should be involved with.
Befriends the outcast and misfit (e.g., Matt 9:9–12; Luke 19:10)	We should refuse to exclude people from fellowship based on cultural preferences. Also, we should be hanging around a lot more "freaks" than we ordinarily do. There is something we have to learn from the margins of society that we cannot learn from the center.	We make a point of welcoming visitors to our church who do not appear to fit in. We collect "freaks" and outcasts and look for what they can teach us about Jesus.
Follows the pattern of God's redemption (e.g., Luke 15:4–32)	We must act redemptively because God is a redeemer. We restore what has been lost or broken. Mission involves the redemption of broken people and lost culture. We don't judge, we redeem.	We aim at restoration and beauty, creativity and grace, hospitality and generosity. We live, love, play, and suffer, better than anyone else, for God is our Redeemer.

Jesus' Life and Teaching	Implications for Disciple/Church	Examples of How These Could Be Lived Out
Proclaims (as well as lives) the good news of the kingdom (e.g., Matt 5:13–16)	We should proclaim (as well as live) the good news of Jesus. In a sense we are (and must become) good news. (We *are* salt/light.) Love, forgiveness, mercy, compassion, righteous anger . . . these are the marks of a disciple.	We socialize with unbelievers. We pray with them. We model an alternate reality by our alternate lifestyle. We are always ready to give an answer for the hope within us. We acknowledge the ministry of the gifted evangelists among us.
Presents an existential call to the whole person (e.g., Matt 22:37–40)	We must respond with all that we are, not just believe with our heads or our bodies. The love of God engages heart, head, mind, will, body, etc. We cannot compartmentalize our lives in ways that divide our total devotion to God.	We see that pleasures are from God. But we direct them towards God, acknowledging that God gave them to us in the first place. We engage intellectually, emotionally, and bodily in the life God has given us.
Offers new beginnings (e.g., John 3:1–7; Luke 7:38–50)	We must be born again. We are the people of the new start! We must offer new starts to others. Give people a go. Learn to actively forgive.	We remember that we have received forgiveness and that others need it as well. We tell others of Jesus' gift of a new start and a life with God.
Hates hypocrisy (e.g., Matt 23:28ff.; Luke 12:1)	In Jesus' teaching, self-righteousness is abhorred! Mentioned far more than sexual sin, this is unacceptable sin of the spirit for disciples of Jesus. We have been forgiven much; we must be willing to offer the same grace to others.	We listen humbly when others point out our faults. We remember not to put sexual sins higher on the scale of sin than the more "spiritual" sins of hypocrisy and pride, since Jesus said more about these than about sexual sin.
Is coming again (e.g., Luke 11; Matt 25:1–13)	An adoring and expectant longing for his presence and return (like a betrothed virgin awaiting the bridegroom). He completes us. He also comes in judgment on unrighteousness. It's going to be a big day!	We hold on to a sense of Jesus' return and our need to live urgently. Seize the day! "Live as if Jesus died yesterday, was raised today, and is coming tomorrow" (Luther).
Lays down life for friends (e.g., John 15:13)	Calls us to self-sacrificial lifestyle. We are called to be servants to a lost and broken world (Matt 23:11–12).	We decide to give up a luxury—perhaps cable TV, dinners out, or cell phone games—and give the money to a good cause.
Brings salvation (e.g., Luke 1:76–77; 19:9)	We need to be saved. This is not only a decision, it is a lifelong process (Phil 2:12). Also, we are the messengers of salvation. Salvation in the Hebrew mind has connotations of healing and wholeness. We need to apply salvation holistically.	We hold on to the idea of salvation as a process in which we are involved on a daily basis.

We don't believe this list is exhaustive, nor do we think that it is even an adequate summary of the faith that has captured the hearts and imaginations of hundreds of millions over two thousand years of history. In fact, we suggest that readers might wish to compile a list of the central ideas and implications of Jesus and his teaching for themselves. It's a great exercise to remind the disciple of the essentials of the faith.

⟵ Following Missional Jesus

Scot McKnight, biblical scholar and blogger, has done something similar with his blog series called "Missional Jesus." He draws no conclusions as to how we ought to live as followers, but we believe that it should be reasonably clear how Jesus acted and affected those around him—readers can draw their own conclusions. Here is our summary/excerpting of the series.[23]

Bible Text Examined	Subject of Blog Entry
Luke 4:16–30	• Missional Jesus publicly announces the centrality of himself to the mission of God (4:21). • Missional Jesus sees his own mission in Isaiah 61:1–2, that means his mission involves justice for the poor, prisoners, the blind, and the oppressed. • The mission of Jesus is a Jubilee mission (4:19). • The mission of Jesus creates disturbances and rejection (4:24). • Homies reject Jesus (4:24–29). • The mission of Jesus will extend beyond the normal boundaries.
Luke 5:1–11	• Missional Jesus is a preacher of the word (5:1–3). • Encountering the missional Jesus brings bewilderment, wonder, and awe—leading to repentance (5:5, 8, 9–10). • Missional Jesus shares his mission with those who are attached to him (5:10). • Those who participate in the mission of Jesus are called to enlist others in the mission of Jesus (5:11).
Luke 9:57–62	• Missional Jesus knows the cost to the body (9:58). • Missional Jesus knows the cost to the family life when it comes to sacred customs (9:59–60). • Missional Jesus knows the cost to the family life when it comes to simple social courtesies (9:61–62). • Missional Jesus wants all from his followers, he wants them to make that decision now, and he demands all because he knows the kingdom of God is worth it.
Matthew 4:23–25	• Overall, missional Jesus did what was good for others. • Missional Jesus taught in typical centers of religious education. • Missional Jesus preached—which means declared good news—about the kingdom of God. What is the kingdom of God? Kingdom for Jesus is the "society in which God's will is established and transforms all of life." • Missional Jesus healed. • Missional Jesus was attractive.
Matthew 7:12	• Missional Jesus accepts anyone who comes to him for healing. • Missional Jesus breaks down boundaries between Gentiles and Jews. • Missional Jesus heals Gentiles too. • Missional Jesus believes that what mattered was faith in God (through Jesus) and not ethnic heritage and religious association. • Missional Jesus lauds the perception of faith in him as faith in the One who is sent by God with authority.

Bible Text Examined	Subject of Blog Entry
Mark 12:29–31	• Missional Jesus confronts the evil at home in persons ravaged by evil spirits. • The evil world recognizes missional Jesus as a threat of power. • Missional Jesus' power is intimidating and awe-inspiring, but it doesn't mean everyone who perceives turns into a follower of Jesus. • Missional Jesus summons those released from evil to witness to the mercy he [the Lord] has shown them. • Missional Jesus knows his mission is a spiritual battle.
Matthew 9:32–34	• Missional Jesus attracts those who are possessed by evil—the way flames attract moths. • Missional Jesus, therefore, attracts folks who know that Jesus can heal them. • Missional Jesus can flat-out cure folks. • Missional Jesus is opposed by the religious authorities: to the degree that they call him demon-possessed.
Matthew 9:35–10:4	• Missional Jesus participates in the mission of God. • Missional Jesus therefore prays to God for "extenders" of his mission-working kingdom of God. • Missional Jesus prays because he is moved by oppression and the need for mercy on so many. • Missional Jesus specifically identifies 12 workers for the kingdom and appoints them as his personal representatives in the kingdom work. • Missional Jesus appoints his "extenders" to do what he has been doing in Matthew. They are therefore extenders of Jesus and not doers of their own mission. Missional work is Jesus work. • Not all of Jesus' "extenders" follow Jesus faithfully.
Matthew 10:5–8	• Missional Jesus has a targeted audience. They are Jews. • Missioners of the missional Jesus have one message: God's kingdom. • Missioners do what Jesus did and extend what Jesus did and say what Jesus said. They are to "be" Jesus in a new place in order to extend Jesus and his kingdom into new places.

What we can say is that without qualification, the Gospels present us with the most compelling portrait of a person who was so wonderfully human, and yet one who lifted us up beyond the merely human and has shown us the life of God (John 14:9). He is the God whom we love and who is worthy of adoration. We will not let go! And we refuse to subvert this life in the petty concerns of church polity or middle-class mediocrity. We will strive to do anything in our strength to assure that in his church, he is named as Lord.

Another voice singing from this same song-sheet is Irish songwriter Sinéad O'Connor, who in 2007 released her album *Theology*, an anthology of reflections on various Old Testament passages that cry out in anguish for a faith not stained by the church that bears God's name. Raised Catholic, the brunt of her attacks has invariably been borne by the church of her childhood, but the sting in her beautiful songs can be felt by any church or denomination that shuts Jesus out of its religious system. In her searing lament, "Out of the Depths," she captures the psalmist's brokenhearted cry for mercy. It begins with a paraphrase of Psalm 130:1:[24]

> Out of the depths I cry to you
> O Lord.

In her song she imagines this lament being sung for a God who is locked out of his own church. The song closes with the lines:

> And it's sad but true how the old saying goes
> If God lived on earth people would break his windows

What a line! To truly understand God we must see him as the humbled one, the attacked one. Jesus' windows were all broken by the time he ascended the gentle slope of Golgotha. Sinéad ends the song by breathlessly repeating several times the Old Testament line (Ps 130:6a):

> I long for you as watchmen long for the end of night.

This is our longing, too. Renewal will begin with each of us. But like the conspiracy of the little Jesuses, it will have consequences for the renewal of the church as a whole. And to that subject we now turn our attention.

⟵ Notes

1. Wilhelm Visser T'Hooft, *The Renewal of the Church* (London: SCM, 1956), 1.
2. Brian J. Walsh and Sylvia C. Keesmaat, *Colossians Remixed* (Downers Grove, Ill.: InterVarsity, 2004), ch. 2–3.
3. Tom Sine, *The New Conspirators* (Downers Grove, Ill.: InterVarsity, forthcoming).
4. Walsh and Keesmaat, *Colossians Remixed*, 85.
5. Walter Brueggemann, *Finally Comes the Poet* (Minneapolis: Augsburg Fortress, 1989), 23.
6. *V for Vendetta*, directed by James McTeigue (Burbank, Calif., Warner Bros., 2005).
7. Hirsch, *Forgotten Ways*, 113.
8. Louis K. Dupré, *Kierkegaard as Theologian: The Dialectic of Christian Existence* (London: Sheed & Ward, 1964), 171.
9. Ronald Grimsely, *Kierkegaard: A Biographical Introduction* (London: Studio Vista, 1973), 103.
10. Bosch, *Transforming Mission*, 67.
11. Hirsch, *Forgotten Ways*, 102.

12. Dallas Willard, *The Spirit of the Disciplines*, quoted in R. J. Foster and J. B. Smith, *Devotional Classics*, rev. ed. (San Francisco: HarperOne, 2005), 14.

13. Dietrich Bonhoeffer, quoted in John A. Phillips, *The Form of Christ in the World: A Study of Bonhoeffer's Christology* (London: Collins, 1967), 100.

14. Ellul, *Subversion of Christianity*, 6–7.

15. Søren Kierkegaard, *Training in Christianity*, quoted in Dupré, *Kierkegaard as Theologian*, 172.

16. J. A. Woelfel, *Bonhoeffer's Theology: Classical and Revolutionary* (Nashville: Abingdon, 1970), 254.

17. Ibid.

18. Ibid., 255, 256.

19. Romano Guardini, *The Lord* (London: Longmans, 1954), 447.

20. Vernard Eller, *Kierkegaard and Radical Discipleship: A New Perspective* (Princeton: Princeton University Press, 1968). Cited 25 September 2008. Online: http://www.hccentral.com/eller2/part12a.html.

21. Ibid., e-text.

22. Søren Kierkegaard, journals, November 26, 1834, quoted in David J. Gouwens, *Kierkegaard as Religious Thinker* (Cambridge: Cambridge University Press, 1996), 173.

23. Scot McKnight's "Missional Jesus" series can be found online at http://www.jesuscreed.org/?cat=39.

24. Sinéad O'Connor, "Out of the Depths," *Theology* (Koch Records, 2007).

Chapter Three

ReJesus for the Church and the Organization

*Christ's whole life in all its aspects must supply the
norm for the life of the following Christian and thus for
the life of the whole Church.*
—Søren Kierkegaard

*All religious institutional embeddedness—whether
in the form of temple worship, unjust social systems,
or repressive religious practices—is challenged
by the revelation of God in the life, death, and
resurrection of Jesus.*
—Gail O'Day

In Revelation 3:20, we hear these famous words of Jesus: "Listen! I am standing at the door, knocking; if you hear my voice and open the door, I will come in to you and eat with you, and you with me." We generally interpret this to say that Jesus is standing at the door of our hearts and asking us to allow him to come in. Even though we can appreciate the sentiment, the verse itself has nothing to do with personal evangelism. The specific church in question in Revelation 3 is that in Laodicea, the famously lukewarm church that Jesus wanted to vomit out of his mouth. The image here is of Jesus standing outside of the church asking to come in. The question that should spring to our minds is, "What is he doing on the outside of the church when he is meant to be the Lord of that very church?" But of course, John's revelation of the seven messages to the seven churches is given to us as a warning that we not make the same errors. Jesus is outside the door of the church in Laodicea! How is this also true for many communities and organizations that claim the name Christian? The question we ask in introducing this chapter must be, is Jesus similarly outside the door of your church? Have we shut him out of the fellowship of the insiders? And what has been the result?

⌒ReJesusing Our Organizations

As is now clear, our basic assumption is that Jesus provides the primary template for us as individual followers but also for the church as the community that is in Christ and that walks in his way. As stated earlier, we believe that the church must constantly return to Jesus to find itself again, to recalibrate, to test whether we are indeed in the faith. The inference is that by and large the church as we currently experience it in the West has to varying degrees lost touch with the wild and dangerous message that it carries and is duty bound to live out and to pass on. As Jesus' disciples we are called to a Christlike life, and no matter how we configure it, that must surely mean that somehow our lives and our communities must be in significant congruence with the life, teachings, and mission of Jesus. The degree that we are living the life laid out by our Master is directly proportional to the degree that we can call ourselves authentic disciples.

This might well sound like idealism to some more pragmatically inclined readers, and perhaps rightly. They may well point out the fact that as things now stand, we have built and established a massive global religion comprising thousands of organizations with massive capital and resources. And there is no denying that such organizations do manage to help many people and bring many to faith. Therefore, they might consider it an indulgence on our part to be prattling on about the radical life of Jesus when, whether we like it or not, we are now obligated to maintain those religious organizations with their associated programs, paid professionals, ideologies, capital, buildings, and so on. Theirs is a call to pragmatism over radicalism, although, we suspect, in more honest moments many of them would probably admit that much that we do seems to have only an indirect correlation to the uncluttered, nonreligious, life-oriented faith so compellingly portrayed in the Gospels. These objectors might, in spite of their deepest spiritual intuitions, simply say that we have no choice but to continue to operate the services and maintain the system or else the whole edifice might crumble.

And others still might add the fact that along with the institution of the church we have long and complex histories that have shaped us, carried us, and landed us where we are today. They would suggest that we are indeed inheritors of a grand religious tradition with rich rituals that has evolved from the early Christian movement even though it is not really the same phenomenon now. For them, the church as we have it is their reality, and they can't, indeed they won't, go back to some simple, somewhat naïve, aesthetically bankrupt, primitive Jesus-like faith of biblical Christianity. Such people will no doubt believe that for good or ill, Christianity now exists, embedded, in its rituals, dogmas, priesthoods, cathedrals, and other religious accoutrements and that the idealism of a reJesus project has no place in the sensible Christian religion we now have.

And we must admit that there is substance to both these responses—the pragmatic and the traditionalist. The institution of the church (traditional and contemporary) is not without God, beauty, or blessing. And we recognize that deeply spiritual people have tirelessly worked for their advancement. We don't wish to suggest that it is worthless (and please forgive us if we have given this impression), but we cannot escape the question, "Is this really what Jesus intended for his movement?" And isn't all this paraphernalia the very thing that partly obscures our access to the vital faith that we all seek and long for? Does advancing in the kingdom of God boil down to this? Running programs and services and/or guiding the laity through liturgical complexities in order to help people get to the God they are all meant to access directly through Jesus anyhow? Was this what Jesus had in mind when he established the church (Matt 16:18–19)?[1] And, whatever happened to the doctrine of the priesthood of all believers that many within the Protestant movements are meant to adhere to (1 Pet 2:9)?

We are not insensitive to the fact that a great many people feel connected to Jesus via the stained-glass imagination of grand ecclesiastical traditions. Nor do we dispute that contemporary-style seeker churches have given many people new hope and led them into a real experience of Christian faith. It would be ignorant of us to do so. God is everywhere, and his grace is manifest wherever he so chooses.

However, whatever case can be made for the status quo, none of us can, or should, avoid the spiritual test of evaluating the validity of our preferred expression of church by cues offered by Jesus the Messiah. Unless we can validate who we are and what we do by lining ourselves up with the measure that Jesus laid down in his life and work, then what in God's name are we doing? And how can we legitimately call ourselves Christ-ian, unless what we are doing is built squarely on the rock of Jesus and takes its direct agenda (and direct cues for its organizations and lifestyle) from him? His *modus operandi*, his teaching, his critique of religion, his commitment to the way of the kingdom, must become our primary source of guidance. We believe that in order to find renewal (organizational, communal, and personal) we need to rediscover Jesus

Evangelistic Activism

Alan Walker

Alan Walker was an Australian evangelist and theologian born in 1911 who devoted his life to both social activism and evangelism. In the 1950s Alan Walker launched a three-year-long evangelistic tour across Australia and New Zealand, in which he preached to more than half the total populations of each country. Evangelistic rallies like this were relatively common in Australia at the time; by the early twentieth-century fundamentalist preachers from the United States had begun regular visits to the country to conduct similar evangelism circuits. But the scale of Walker's itinerary was unique in that he heralded the integration of evangelism and social activism in a day when the Protestant church generally saw the two realms as incompatible. He also had the moral courage to be an outspoken critic of the racist "White Australia" policy as early as 1938, when the church had been largely silent on the issue. As a pacifist during World War II, and the Vietnam War, he attracted the ire of the media but remained true to his convictions. After his last evangelical tour in 1958, he took over the leadership of the Methodist Central Mission in Sydney, Australia and developed it into one of the country's largest social justice agencies. He was expelled twice from South Africa for his anti-apartheid stance and was knighted by the Queen of England, befriended by Martin Luther King Jr., and dubbed "the conscience of the nation" by the Governor-General of Australia. Alan Walker embodies Jesus because his social activism was never at the expense of his evangelistic passion; "Let it never be forgotten that it is Christ we offer."

afresh even though this be a dangerous course of action because it calls into question so much of what we might build our various religious houses on. At the beginning of this new century, we have never needed so desperately to re-discover the original genius of the Christian experience and to allow it to strip away all the unnecessary and cumbersome paraphernalia of Christendom.

It has surprised us that in recent years even our secular culture has been demanding this project of reJesusing the church. A number of filmmakers (secular prophets of our time?) have recently depicted Christlike characters in conflict with the institutionalized church. Those church leaders who have dis-missed these films as savage attacks on Christ have missed the point. Films such as *Jesus of Montreal*, *Chocolat*, and *As It Is in Heaven* are not attacks on Jesus. They are scathing critiques of institutional Christianity, but they all portray their messianic-like protagonists with great sympathy, even reverence.

The most allegorical of them, the Canadian film *Jesus of Montreal*, depicts an out-of-work actor, Daniel, who is commissioned to breathe new life into a church passion play but who enrages the religious authorities when he stages it in an all-too-real manner. As he researches and rehearses the story of Jesus (tellingly, under the gaze of a stone statue of Christ outside the church), Daniel's life begins to mirror that of Christ's. Like Jesus, he gathers around him a troupe of misfits and outcasts—a man who dubs porno films, an overlooked middle-aged actress, a model often reduced to exposing her breasts for casting agents. Like Jesus, Daniel molds this band into a proud, functional community of grace and forgiveness. Like Jesus, Daniel appeals to the common people. His play is soon the talk of Montreal, with hundreds of non-churchgoers lining up for tickets. And inevitably, like Jesus, he finds himself in serious conflict with religious leaders, who are so outraged by his earthy, passionate portrayal of Christ they decide to shut the play down, resulting in Daniel's tragic death.

Jesus of Montreal is more than a drama about an actor who becomes consumed by his role. It is an allegory in which Daniel is essentially a Christ figure right from the opening John-the-Baptist parallel scene. And while it offers us an agnostic retelling of Jesus' life, we wouldn't expect a secular filmmaker to do anything else. But if we're wise, we'll listen to the film's basic premise: if Jesus really did turn up in Montreal, the church would be his greatest enemy!

Likewise, in two other films, Christ figures turn up in small communities, offering hope to the marginalized but ending up in conflict with the church establishment. In *Chocolat*, a woman called Vianne transforms a dour French village with love and grace (and, of course, chocolate) and is nearly run out of town by the mayor, who is the overbearing power behind the meek priest. In *As It Is in Heaven*, an internationally famous symphony conductor retires to the small Swedish town of his childhood and is inveigled into directing the local Lutheran church choir. His methods are so radical that he transforms the rag-tag amateur singers into a world-standard choir, but in so doing he finds that the Lutheran minister has become his sworn enemy. Like Daniel, he too dies tragically but leaves behind a group of men and women who will never be the same.

We don't suggest that we should take our cue from filmmakers, but these movies have intuited something important and are popular precisely because they hit a nerve in their audiences. Even though they might prefer to depict decidedly nondivine Christ figures, they do speak to an audience that believes the real Christ was more about transforming a small band of followers than running a wealthy religious institution. These films, and many more besides, insist that a faithful, determined, loving, honest community of friends, inspired by an extraordinary visionary, can change its worlds. Daniel's acting troupe resolve to carry on his work by establishing an avant-garde actors' studio. Vianne's friends from the chocolate shop initiate a revolution that eventually sees the dismal village change into a vibrant colorful community. And in *As It Is in Heaven*, the conductor, also called Daniel, dies of a heart attack listening to his choir win a prestigious choral contest in Austria, knowing they have achieved a sense of harmony rarely accomplished by even the best choirs.

The message these films seem to be making was also expressed by anthropologist Margaret Mead, when she wrote, "Never doubt that a small group of thoughtful, committed citizens can change the world. Indeed, it is the only thing that ever has."[2] How different is this from the revolution forged by Jesus? We do well to remember Roland Allen's profound observation about missional movements and how they center on Jesus:

> The spontaneous expansion of the Church reduced to its element is a very simple thing. It asks for no elaborate organization, no large finances, no great numbers of paid missionaries. In its beginning it may be the work of one man and that of a man neither learned in the things of this world, nor rich in the wealth of this world. What is necessary is faith. What is needed is the kind of faith which uniting a man to Christ, sets him on fire.[3]

We feel that at this critical juncture of history, when the church is forced to find itself again by the sheer circumstance of the adaptive challenge of the twenty-first century, we must return to being that simple, uncluttered, passionate community of Christ, filled with the love of God that so imbued our spiritual ancestors. We must reignite our passion directly from Jesus' flame. This process of going back to our generative center will mean a process of rediscovering Jesus afresh. We need to reJesus our organizations.

Christianity Minus Christ Equals Religion

In order to get to the nub of the problem, let's reverse the way of looking at the process of reJesus: let us think about what happens when you take Jesus out of the experience of Christianity. To see this consider the following equation:

Christianity − Christ = Religion

It makes sense, doesn't it? Some statements have an immediate ring of truth about them, and for many Christians this is one of them. Of course, Christianity without the lifeblood, the vision, the love of the real Jesus is a soulless religious institution. If you have not already noticed, we tend to use the word "religion" in rather negative sense—as a set of inherited rituals, rules, and structures devoid of a vital spirituality. Mostly religion in this sense tends to be quite oppressive and controlling. And this is how we mean it here. The removal of Jesus from the faith does result in the rise of religious consciousness and institutional expression. A study in European church history will more than adequately prove this point. The Inquisition was not a freak of history but rather was the logical result of a highly coercive and controlling religion that had lost sight of its reason for existence—had lost contact with its founder. But how does this happen? How does a movement as vital as that of early Christianity find itself having drifted so far from its foundation? This is not so mysterious a matter. In fact, it can be readily explained by the sociology of religion. Sociologists recognize that the fading of the initial founding impulse of a movement is not unique to Christianity but is true of all religious expressions. Sociologists call this the *routinization of charisma* and say it accounts for the decline of religious organizations and people movements. What happens in the beginning of a movement is that the people encounter the divine in a profound and revelatory way, but with successive generations this encounter tends to fade like a photocopy of a photocopy of a photocopy. What begins as a revolutionary, life-transforming, confrontation with Jesus eventually subsides into a codified religion and is subsequently incorporated into normal social life.

And herein lies an irresolvable dilemma for all people of faith: Although genuine faith is born out of direct encounters with God, it cannot survive and prosper without some form of stability and order. Viewed positively, rituals, creeds, and organizations can help people structure their relationship with God. In fact, we believe this is what they initially were designed for. But unless the worshipper is very wary, the glory of the God encounter will slowly fade and the ritual, creeds, and rules intended to preserve the encounter will take its place. The crisis dawns when the outward forms of worship no longer match the inward experience and spiritual condition of the participants. At that point, decline becomes inevitable, authentic Christianity is subverted, and constant renewals become necessary . . . hence the need to reJesus.

It is, as O'Dea says, a dilemma born of the tragedy inherent in the human condition in a fallen world. But for the disciple, the simple truth must remain; one cannot bolt down, control, or even mediate the essential God encounter in rituals, priesthoods, and theological formulas. We all need to constantly engage the God who unnerves, destabilizes, and yet enthralls us. The same is true for our defining relationship with Jesus. It is like the story of the Israelites in the wilderness. They tried to store up the manna from heaven for another day. Religion can give into the same temptation to try to store up and rely on the souvenirs of a past spiritual experience. For how many years did the church rely on the system of holy Christian relics—a bone from Peter's finger, a wooden shard from the cross of Christ, cathedrals and sacred buildings, inherited rituals, even creedal formulas, more than it relied on a fresh, daily encounter with Jesus? We, like Israel, are called to be willing to collect the fresh manna every day—and we are to do this without becoming spiritual thrill seekers but rather lifelong worshipers. To do otherwise is to "outsource your encounter with Jesus" to a religious system of souvenirs, ritual, and religious paraphernalia. Said Maurice Friedman:

> Theophany *happens* to man, and he has his part in it as God has His. [Religious] forms and ideas result from it; but what is truly revealed in it is *not* a form or an idea but God. [Genuine] religious reality means this; it is the undiminished relation to God Himself. Man does not possess God; he meets Him.[4]

The more one replaces a fresh daily encounter with Jesus with religious forms, over time he is removed from his central place in the life of the church. The result of this removal (by whatever means) is the onset of dead religion in the place of a living faith.[5] And to be honest, much of what has gone under the name Christendom can readily be called religion and not Christianity as defined by the Bible. Centuries ago, Blaise Pascal uttered these incisive words about the spiritual condition of the Christianity of his day: "Christendom is a union of people who, by means of the sacraments, excuse themselves from their duty to love God."[6] And while religious people tend to be sincere, they do use religion to qualify the God experience–to soften it and control it. One of the functions of religion, sociologically speaking, includes that of avoiding God. All attempts to reduce the faith to intellectualism, or to condition our understanding of God, or to domesticate Jesus, or to diminish the call to lifelong discipleship will result in the loss of the God experience and the encroachment of some form of religion. Anglican missiologist John V. Taylor says, "We need not go all the way with Karl Barth in defining all religion as unbelief. But . . . it is plain that man uses religion as a way of escaping from God. This is true of Christianity as of any other religious system."[7] And it was yet another Anglican who rightly said, "Jesus was inaugurating a way of life which had no further need of the Temple."[8] Any attempt then to reconstruct a temple theology of church goes clean contrary to the work of Jesus. He is the new temple.

Martin Buber, the great articulator of dialogical Hebraic spirituality, says that what were originally the true forms of the God encounter soon deteriorate and then become obstacles or substitutes for God. We do very well to heed the warning he gives:

> The ur-danger of man is "religion" and mystic ecstasy. It may be that the forms by which man originally hallowed the world for God have become independent . . . then they eventually cease to embody the consecration of the lived, everyday life, and become instead the means of its separation from God. Life in the world and religious service then begin to run on unapproachably parallel lines. But the "god of this divine service" is no longer God, it is the mask, the real partner in the communion is no longer there, the worshipper gesticulates into the empty air. Or, it may be that the state of soul underlying the divine service that becomes independent, the devotion, the reaching-out, the absorption-in, the rapture; which was meant to be and intended for a verification, flowing from the fullness of life, becomes instead detached from life. Now the soul only wants to deal with God; it is as if she [the soul] desired to exercise her love for Him and for Him alone, and not on His world. Now, the soul thinks, the world has disappeared, and only she alone, the soul is left. What she now calls "God" is only a figment in herself, the dialogue which she thinks she is carrying on is only a monologue with divided roles, for the real partner in the communion is no longer there.[9]

As harsh as this might seem, the Hebrew Bible sustains a constant critique of its own religious forms. Psalm 50 is a classic example of a prophetic railing against the formulization of faith. The prophets were the guardians of the covenantal relationship between God and his people. They were obsessed with the call to faithfulness to God. And they insisted that true faithfulness toward God could not be fulfilled through religious ritual, but only with a heart given over to him. This basic challenge is repeated throughout the prophetic wrings. For instance, Isaiah cries, "The Lord said: Because these people draw near with their mouth and honor me with their lips, while their hearts are far from me, and their worship of me is a human commandment learned by rote . . ." (Isa 29:13, cf. Isa 58; Jer 7:3–16; Amos 5:21). It's not about sacrifice in itself that the prophet rails against; it is the loss of covenantal worship. It is the intent one brings to religious forms that gives them their true meaning.

⟿Christianity as Antireligion

As we are thinking about the dangers of formulaic religion, it might be useful to take a look at the Pharisees. Most readers of the New Testament would agree that the Pharisees are often portrayed as the bad guys and not as a group of people we would want to join. Let's take a closer look at the Pharisees. What do we know about them?

Well, from the Bible and from historical research, we can say that

- ⟿ They were very sincere in their belief system.

- ⟿ They were an extremely zealous and passionate bunch—the commitment of a suicide bomber would probably be similar to the zeal of a good Pharisee.

- ⟿ They were meticulous tithers and gave beyond what was required of them (mint, rue, and cumin were not listed in the things needed to be tithed).

- ⟿ They upheld a strong moral code—they were very decent people.

- ⟿ They believed in the authority of the full Hebrew Scriptures. And in this they opposed the Sadducees, the theological liberals of their day, who limited the canon to the first five books and then began diminishing their authority over matters of life and faith.

- ⟿ They believed in miracles. They believed that God can and did break into the course of human affairs in the form of miraculous intervention. Against the theological liberalism of their day, they fiercely defended the doctrine of the resurrection (the primary miracle), which the Sadducees denied.

- ⟿ They were the keepers of the tradition, and therefore the custodians of the identity of Israel. It is unlikely Israel would have survived the stormy intertestamental period without their presence and contribution.

- ⟿ They were what we would call missional. Imbued with messianic causes, they went over land and sea to make just one convert.

- ⟿ They prayed arduously and often with set prayers prescribed for all possible situations in life.

⟵ They were strongly messianic. They longed for Israel's (and the world's) redemption.

We would be wrong to characterize Pharisees as mean-spirited people with nothing but evil on their minds. Generally they were sincere and well-intentioned in all they did. As degenerate and in need of renewal as the Judaism of Jesus' time was, they were nonetheless exemplary religious people as far as religions go.

We might want to ask ourselves the question, "Which brand of contemporary Christianity most closely adopts this form of spirituality?" To which we must surely answer, "It is the Bible-believing Christians . . . the evangelicals!" And the most frightening aspect of this realization, as just noted, is that these were the people who were most responsible for putting Jesus on the cross. So herein lies the rub. They are us, or at least what we can become if we are not attentive to the dynamics involved in the slow erosion of faithfulness into religion. They are living mirrors of what can happen to all well-meaning and sincere people when they lose focus on the central issues of faith—the "weightier matters of the law" (Matt 23:23). The horror of this realization is complete when we remember that these fine, upright, devoted religious people—people not unlike us—were hell-bent on murdering Jesus.

But let's press this exercise even further. Remember that, theologically speaking, Jesus was a true Pharisee. He affirmed all the things on that list regarding the authority of the Bible, the reality of miracles, the resurrection, the need for an ardent holiness, and so on. The world of difference exists in how we inhabit the theology we adhere to—how we believe it. Divorced from love, humility, and mercy, it readily becomes a dead and/or oppressive religion. And here again Jesus is the key. Without the active love for, and presence of, the radical Jesus, Christianity easily degenerates into an oppressive religion. Make no mistake, the Christendom project is full of atrocities perpetrated in the name of religion; the Inquisition and the Crusades stand out, but they were not isolated incidents. One can even argue that it is partly from the snares of religion that Jesus came to save us. We do well to remember the judgment that came upon the legalistic moralism that the Judaism at the time of Jesus had degenerated into. The parables of judgment have ongoing validity to all religious people, not just the scribes and the Pharisees.

While teaching at a seminary in the American Bible Belt, Alan once posed the question, "What would we do with Jesus if he turned up at our churches?" One brave soul answered with heart-stopping honesty, "We would probably kill him!" And we all somehow knew that his answer was disturb-ingly true. But the disquieting question remains: what *would* your local church do if Jesus, the real, undiminished reforming revolutionary that we see por-trayed in the Scriptures, came into the community? For most of our churches, we expect that sparks would fly! Why? Because Jesus and religion just don't mix. Jacques Ellul is absolutely right when he says that

> For the Romans nascent Christianity was not at all a new religion. It was 'antireligion.' . . . What the first Christian generations were putting on trial was not just the imperial religion, as is often said, but every religion in the known world.[10]

> Christianity claims not to be a religion that is superior to others, but to be an antireligion that refutes all the religions that attempt to link us with a divine universe. No doubt Christianity constantly becomes a religion . . . [however] the Christian religion itself is constantly called into question by the absolute that is revealed in Jesus Christ.[11]

In Jesus we have the undoing of all that we call religion. In the place of a mediating system with its temples, rituals, creeds, and priestly cultus, he opens up the God experience to all and shatters the oppressive religious sys-tem of the day (Matt 21:28–46; Luke 19:10–26; 23:45). That the advent of Jesus signaled the demise of the temple system is clear. Says N. T. Wright, "Jesus was inaugurating a way of life which had no further need of the Temple."[12] Even a cursory reading of Mark reveals that immediately after his Spirit baptism and ordeal in the desert, Jesus immediately begins confronting the forces that op-press human life—the demonic forces and the religious system. His attack on religion is relentless and cuts deep. In the ministry of Jesus, the kingdom of God breaks out among those whom the religious system had marginalized—the poor, the oppressed, the prostitutes—and the religious people find them-selves under the judgment of God (e.g., Matt 23:13–39). And in Jesus' answer to the Samaritan woman we see Jesus delegitimizing all attempts to localize and thus mediate and control God through the operation of sacred spaces (John 4:20–24).[13] Furthermore, Jesus' parables of judgment all call into question any attempt to control God and people and are therefore undeviating condemna-tions of religion in all its forms. Taken as a whole, it is difficult to see Jesus fitting into any religious system. In him is the undoing of all religion.

And because of this, the religious people hated Jesus and constantly plotted to kill him . . . and eventually did, in cahoots with the politicians and the mob. And we would suggest that all religious people will likewise hate Jesus and seek to remove him from the equation because what he does is effectively invalidate the system that they have so deeply invested in. To reJesus the church, we must first look in the mirror and ask ourselves whether the strange and wonderful God-Man has invaded our life with purpose and freshness. If Christianity minus Christ equals religion, then Christianity plus Christ is the antidote to religion.

The Founder and the Found

Part of the basis to this claim comes from an understanding of the defining role that Jesus plays for the movement that sprang from his life and work. In all people-movements, including religious movements, there is a defining relationship between the originator and the subsequent movement that forms from the work and teachings of that person. In some rare cases, a movement might well evolve from the original template set by its founder, taking on a broader vision or a new philosophical base while still remaining essentially true to its original self (e.g., the women's movement as it has evolved from the original suffragettes to modern-day feminism). But we would suggest that this ought not to be the case for the church. The living link between the founder and the found is critical for the health of Christianity in particular, as we have already tried to articulate.

Max Weber, the famous sociologist, was one of the first to broker these insights when he described the role of the "charismatic leader" in the founding of a movement. The charismatic leader in his view is distinguished from other types of leaders by his or her capacity to inspire loyalty toward himself or herself. And the source of this authority exists apart from any status gained from membership in an established institution. He also noted that movements, particularly religious movements that survive beyond the first generation, are started by such an extraordinarily gifted (charismatic) person who in a crisis situation puts forward a radically alternative vision of the world and thus initiates an ensuing mission to change the world in order to fulfill that vision. This annunciation of a radical vision and mission subsequently attracts a set of followers who collectively experience various successes and encounters that further validate the charismatic's mission. And so we find that eventually a team of devoted followers emerges to further advance the radical message of the founder.[14]

The point we make in referring to Weber here is that he rightly understood the critical factors that made for significant people movements and transformational organizations. For one, he clearly understood the role of

Radical Hospitality

Jean Vanier

By his mid-thirties, Jean Vanier, a native of Geneva, Switzerland, had also lived in England, France, and Canada; served in the British Navy and the Royal Canadian Navy; completed his doctorate in philosophy; and become a dynamic young professor at the University of Toronto. But it wasn't until 1964, when Vanier was thirty-six, that Vanier discovered what would become his true life's work. After witnessing the desperate situations of thousands of intellectually disabled people in mental institutions, he bought an old house in Trosly-Breuil, France, invited two men from such institutions to live with him, and established a community with them. Naming the home L'Arche, which means "the ark" in French, Vanier and the two men opened their home to others, gradually building a mutual community in which people with mental disabilities and people without maintained a genuine community. Since then, 130 other community homes have been formed in places all over the world. Although he has become internationally regarded, Vanier still makes his home in the original community of Trosly-Breuil. Jean Vanier is a little Jesus because he embodies the Christlike motivation to live among, befriend, and serve those who are otherwise treated as social outcasts in our world.

the founder as decisive, not only for the initiation of the religious movement but also in defining the ongoing life of the organization that outlives him or her. He also noted that in order to survive the loss of the founder, the movement has to somehow build the charisma of the founder into the life of the organization.[15] He said, "The genuine charismatic situation quickly gives rise to incipient institutions, which emerge from the cooling off of extraordinary states or devotion and fever."[16] In fact, it was Weber who coined the phrase we have already introduced: the routinization of charisma.

Thomas O'Dea refers to these catalyzing encounters that kick-start movements and then fade with the passing of time. He points out how consecutive generations tend to construct religious systems to take the place of the original encounter. He says, "Worship is the fundamental religious response [to such encounters] but in order to survive its charismatic moment worship must become stabilized in established forms and procedures."[17] In fact, he argues that this is an unavoidable paradox for religious movements.[18] The ultimate and the sacred cannot be expressed in institutional structures without those structures taking on a life of their own and corrupting what they are meant to represent. Yet without some form of institutionalization, religious experiences of themselves will not sustain a religious movement.

And herein lies an irresolvable dilemma for religious organizations: although religious movements are born out of firsthand religious experiences, they cannot survive and prosper without some form of stability and order. The *charism* (the originating grace or gift) has to be diffused, ritualized, and mediated by the organization so that the initial gift of the founder can be made accessible through the organization itself. While O'Dea saw this process of institutionalization as inevitable and even necessary, he also saw that it was paradoxically the process that would dilute or possibly even obliterate the initial message and ethos of the founder. Yet this routinization of charisma has a tendency to snuff out the life it was meant to protect and enhance. The crisis inevitably dawns when the outward forms of worship no longer match the inward experience and spiritual condition of the participants. Decline becomes inevitable. Authentic Christianity is subverted and constant renewals become necessary . . . hence the need to reJesus.

Weber maintained that the process of institutionalization and renewal involved a constant return to the charismatic center in order to relegitimize, or in our language, refound, the subsequent movement. To remain true, all religious organizations require a form of renewal that requires a return to the original ethos and the power of the founder. And whether one applies this to a denomination or to Christianity as a whole, one can call this rediscovery of one's original message radical traditionalism because it involves going back to the organization's deepest tradition and reinterpreting it for a new context.

In fact, there is a certain way of thinking and acting within an organization that can be traced back to its founder. This is called the organization's foundational culture, and it is formed through three sources:

- ⟵ The beliefs, values, and assumptions of its founders

- ⟵ The validation of these beliefs through the learning experiences of the group

- ⟵ The enhancement of these beliefs by the new beliefs, values, and assumptions brought by new group members.

But we can say categorically that the impact of the founder is the most important factor in determining the resultant culture of an organization or religion.[19] In relation to the church we can call this process refounding the church, or simply reJesus.

In the formation of Christianity we can clearly see all these forces at work. In the New Testament (even the word "new" implies a departure from, or at least a radical reinterpretation of, the "old") Jesus redefines the way people had previously understood and experienced the kingdom of God. As the true prophet of God, he totally radicalizes the kingdom by negating and bypassing the religious institution that has inadvertently begun to block its operations and activity (Matt 23:13ff.), and in so doing he opens up direct access for the people, for all who would draw near (e.g., Matt 11:28–30; 21:43; John 4:20–24). In doing these things, Jesus explicitly becomes the founder and initiator of a new covenant with the people of God. He initiated a way of engaging the God of Israel that later came to be called Christianity, the religion that takes its cue from him. We also know from the Gospels that Jesus spent significant and strategic time devoted to initiating his followers into the ways of the kingdom and to discipling and teaching them to recognize the dynamics of what it meant to be one of his followers. The basics of what it means to be a disciple are thus built into the system at its inception.

It was Peter Berger who alerted us to the fact that reality is in fact socially constructed. The social process is exactly how leaders get their ideas implemented. Their ideas are taught to the group, even imposed at times in the form of commands, as we can see in some aspects of Jesus' teaching. But they are generally passed on to the followers through a combination of socialization, through the charismatic power of the founder, and by acting, by doing, by living out confidence in the message.

They knew they were bound to his teaching and template. Any apostolic development of the teachings of Jesus are authentic only insofar that they refer directly to the person, and extend the work of, Jesus. They are all bound to the revelation of God given in and through Jesus. They have no authority to speculate beyond that. They can, however, interpret Jesus and his teachings and reapply them in fresh cultural ways. As such the whole movement grows and evolves, but the nascent ethos of the founder is maintained. This is exactly what Paul does. The most cogent example of apostolic imagination and practice was given to us by Paul who spent his best energies in establishing new ground for the gospel and in working out the redemptive significance of the Messiah, in terms of both his person (e.g., Ephesians and Colossians) and his work (e.g., Romans and Galatians). But he too is self-consciously bound by the revelation given in and through Jesus (Gal 1:8; Col 1:15–20; 1 Cor 3:11; 9:16–23). In a real sense his work always harks back to the Christ event to be true and authentic.

Early on, the original church had cause to recalibrate to Jesus. The original believers were largely Jews, and The Way was considered a sect under the broader umbrella of Judaism. As such, many of their expectations were colored by their Jewish nationalism. For instance, expectations of a restored Jewish kingdom were not met within a generation. In fact, rather than being liberated from foreign control, Jerusalem and the temple were brutally destroyed by the Romans, and Jews were scattered throughout the empire. The Jewish believers had cause to seriously rethink the bases of the faith. Their assumptions had to be radically reconsidered. Note the way that within a generation the Christian movement was already forced back to its founder to rediscover its original charism. Was it a Jewish renewal movement or something more? The Christian movement would have ample reason to do this again and again throughout history. It is what renewal of the faith, ministry, and mission of the church is all about.

And remember, we are talking here about both the founder and the found. Whatever sociological process we might use to understand the role of the founder of a movement, in order to be valid, his or her followers must somehow strive to embody the life, ideals, and reality of that founder. Likewise for the Christian movement, the founder must be able to be seen in the lives of the found. This is the process of embodiment, which is so essential to movements.[20] This is what it means for the church to have Jesus in its midst. This must surely partly be what it means to live "in Christ" and he in us. Observers should be able to encounter Jesus in and through the life and community of his followers. People observing us ought to be able to discern the elements of Jesus' way in our ways. If they cannot find authentic signals of the historical Jesus through the life of his people, then as far as we are concerned they have the full right to question our legitimacy.

Tony Campolo tells the story of a drunk who was miraculously converted at a Bowery mission in New York. Like all Campolo stories, it has a jokey punch line that betrays a far more serious and convicting point.

The drunk, Joe, was known throughout the Bowery as the worst kind of wino, a hopeless derelict of a man, living on borrowed time. But following his conversion, everything changed. Joe became the most caring person that anyone associated with the mission had ever known. He spent his days and nights hanging out at the hall, not balking at even the lowliest job. He mopped up vomit and urine and cleaned up drunks whatever their condition. He considered nothing too demeaning for him.

One evening, when the director of the mission was delivering his evening evangelistic message to the usual crowd of still and sullen men, their heads hung in penitence and exhaustion, there was one man who looked up, came down the aisle to the altar, and knelt to pray, crying out for God to help him to change. The repentant drunk kept shouting, "Oh God, make me like Joe! Make me like Joe! Make me like Joe!" The director of the mission leaned over and said to the man, "Son, I think it would be better if you prayed, 'Make me like Jesus!'" The man looked up at the director with a quizzical expression on his face and asked, "Is he like Joe?"[21]

The New Testament writers likewise call people to emulate their example, knowing that they had committed their lives to Jesus and that he indeed "lived in them." It takes either self-delusion, a lot of chutzpah, or a real commitment to the embodiment of Jesus' message to be able to say "follow me as I follow Christ." But Paul was never coy about calling people to follow his example. This might seem like arrogance to us, but, like the ex-drunk in Campolo's story, he was so given over to the example of Christ that he had become a living embodiment of Jesus. It was Jesus he was pointing to, but it is Jesus through the medium of his own life. He understood Jesus lived in him and he in Christ. It is out of this conviction that he could say,

> Be imitators of me, as I am of Christ. (1 Cor 11:1)

> Join in imitating me, and observe those who live according to the example you have in us. (Phil 3:17)

> For you yourselves know how you ought to imitate us; we were not idle when we were with you . . . (2 Thess 3:7)

Note how in Philippians 3:17 he also directs his readers to observe others whose lives mirror that of Jesus. In effect, the found are to replicate the founder to outsiders and to each other.

But to push the point a little further, consider the difference between Christianity and Islam. In both cases, the founder sets the primary pattern for others to follow—they provide the authenticating human image of the spiritual person for their followers to emulate. There is in all religions some real expectation of continuity between the founder and the follower. So, when we see a person or organization claiming to be Christian but acting in a gratu-itously violent and unloving way, we can say that that person or organization is clearly out of sync with the way of Jesus. We can say with some confidence that one cannot follow Jesus and at the same time act in ways deeply incon-sistent with his teachings. That is why violent fundamentalisms are aberra-tions of Christianity as defined by Jesus. They distort the reality of love and forgiveness that are embodied in the Messiah.

But in the case of Islam, the founder set an entirely different model from that of Jesus. The Koran depicts Muhammed as a passionately spiritual man who called people into the worship of *Allah*. And there are some great spiritual insights in the Koran. However, the same Koran depicts Muhammad as a man with a rigid morality, an assertive sexuality, a bad temper, and dis-tinctly warlike tendencies. So following the logic, we can say that when Islam acts similarly it is not entirely inconsistent with its founder at this point.

However, when Christianity is warlike and voracious, it betrays Jesus in a significant way. This is why racism, the Crusades, the Inquisition, or the Christian endorsement of unbridled capitalism of our day are such apostate distortions of the faith—apostate because they run contrary to the faith ex-pression, the initial pattern, that Jesus set for us to follow. The founder's influ-ence must imbue the movement because we get our sense of place and our ongoing identity from him.

The following chart will give the reader a feel of what we are saying here: we ought to get a feel of what a religion stands for by examining the lives and teachings of the founders (or key figures).[22]

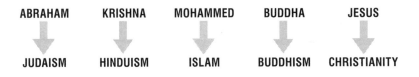

⟵Discerning the Inner Voice of the Organization

But beyond the role of the founder in the ongoing renewal of the church, we must briefly return to the idea of radical traditionalism. Another useful way of conceiving the renewal of organizations is to talk in terms of reform-ing, or even better, refounding the organization. Movement expert Steve Ad-dison calls this discerning the inner voice of the organization.[23]

Drawing on the insights of organizational theorist Robert Quinn,[24] Addison says that rather than us finding a purpose, a purpose finds us. Quinn argues that every organization has an inner voice that constitutes its moral core. Following this cue, then, we can say that in various forms of organizational renewal, the goal is not so much to impose a purpose on its members but to help them rediscover it, to train them to listen for the inner voice of the organization. Still, we can be sure that any attempt to realign the organization with its inner voice will threaten the existing culture, whose central impulse is self-preservation. Nonetheless, as Quinn says, this "articulation of the inner voice of an organization is often the first step toward revitalizing a company and uncovering a vision filled with resonance."[25]

Similarly, in his study of religious orders, Lawrence Cada refers to the "founding charism" of an order to describe its unique vision of the world transformed by the gospel.[26] The use of the term *charism* (grace) implies that the purpose of an organization is a gift that lies at the heart of the organization—a divine bequest, unique to that particular organization. And the recovery of that gift means a "return to the sources."[27] Organizational renewal is about the discovery of an organization's true identity and mission. The authority to bring transformation to the church does not rest in the person of the leader or group but in God's calling. If this is so, then the key to the revitalization of religious organizations is to reappropriate, or recover, their founding charism.

But as mentioned earlier, this must not be the blind return to traditionalism but an innovative insight into how the founding charism is to be expressed in the contemporary world. This involves a rediscovery of the founder's vision matched with spectacular innovations that are as yet unheard of.[28] Addison suggests then that revitalization requires an innovative return to tradition.

While many people use the term "radical" to mean a departure from the traditional, it refers to a return to the root cause of a thing. Webster defines "radical" as "of or pertaining to the root or origin; reaching to the center, to the foundation, to the ultimate sources, to the principles, or the like; original; fundamental; thorough-going; unsparing; extreme; as in, 'radical evils': 'radical reform'; 'a radical party.'"

We have been called radicals in our time, but using this definition, aren't we all meant to be radicals in some form or another? We are hardly calling the church into new, uncharted territory. Rather, we advocate a return to our most fundamental cause. If that's radical, then we are radicals indeed!

Central to the organizational renewal process is the rediscovery of the organization's identity and at the same time the innovative interpretation of that identity in a changed world. Thus, there is both a continuity and discontinuity in the revitalization process, involving both a conservative dimension as well as a radical one. Addison illustrates by referring to Volkswagen's innovative reinterpretation of the Beetle to illustrate this process. This iconic motorcar ceased production in the late 1970s before being resurrected for the new millennium. The new Beetle that emerged definitely has continuity with the original one but was in some sense radically new. It was a great success and a powerful illustration of radical traditionalism involved in refounding organizations.

But we can also learn from educational psychology in this matter. Jean Piaget, the great educational psychologist, conducted much of his early research on the streets of Geneva, interviewing children and observing how they played structured games together. He noted that very small children unquestioningly played games according to the inherited rules. They slavishly obeyed the traditional rules of, say marbles, because their older siblings or their parents had taught them how to play that way. Piaget then noted that at a certain stage in the development of the child he or she wanted to throw these rules away. A rule-less game of marbles on the streets of Geneva last century was exactly as you'd expect it to be—chaos! Later in childhood, these same children, fed up with chaotic games that were always won by bullies or the most crafty, rediscovered the original rules of the game. Piaget noted how much more powerfully these rules worked in the lives of the older children. They were the same rules they were taught as tiny children. But the difference now was that they had discovered these rules as an antidote to disorder. They felt these rules were *their* rules. In a sense, this process of childhood development mirrors what we've been discussing.

What we are advocating is a radical traditionalism. The church needs to follow the same path as the children did with their games of marbles. ReJesus, the refounding of the church, means departing from a blind, slavish allegiance to religious rules inherited from our parents and forebears. It means walking into the turmoil of chaos and daring to trust that the at the end of the path will be not bedlam but a rediscovery of the way of Jesus, a rediscovery of the original rules that we can own ourselves with greater conviction and authenticity. Jesus, as our founder, is our guide on this path. His words and his example are the constants as we leave our old traditions and look to bring the church and the gospel into new contexts of traditional radicalism.

⟵Notes

1. "And I tell you, you are Peter, and on this rock I will build my church, and the gates of Hades will not overcome it. I will give you the keys of the kingdom of heaven, and whatever you bind on earth will be bound in heaven, and whatever you loose on earth will be loosed in heaven."

2. This quote has appeared everywhere from fridge magnets to school blackboards. We found it online at http://www.quotationspage.com/quote/33522.html.

3. Roland Allen, The Compulsion of the Spirit (ed. David Paton and Charles H. Long; Grand Rapids, Mich.: Eerdmans, 1983), 47–48.

4. Maurice S. Friedman, Martin Buber: The Life of Dialogue (Chicago: University of Chicago Press, 1955; repr. New York: Harper's N.Y., 1960), 32. Cited 25 September 2008. Online: http://www.religion-online.org/showchapter.asp?title=459&C=377.

5. The word "religion" can be used in either a positive or a negative sense. We almost use it always in the negative.

6. From Abraham Heschel, A Passion for Truth (New York: Farrar, Straus and Giroux, 1973), 169–70.

7. John V. Taylor, The Go-between God: The Holy Spirit and the Christian Mission (London: SCM, 1972), 190.

8. N. T. Wright, quoted in Bruxy Cavey, The End of Religion: An Introduction to the Subversive Spirituality of Jesus (Ottawa: Agora, 2005), 62.

9. Martin Buber, Mamre (Melbourne: Melbourne University Press, 1946), 103–4.

10. Ellul, Subversion of Christianity, 55.

11. Ibid., 141.

12. Quoted in Cavey, End of Religion, 62.

13. He says to her, "Woman, believe me, the hour is coming when you will worship the Father neither on this mountain nor in Jerusalem. . . . But the hour is coming, and is now here, when the true worshipers will worship the Father in spirit and truth, for the Father seeks such as these to worship him. God is spirit, and those who worship him must worship in spirit and in truth."

14. Weber's ideas are widely discussed and freely available. See, for instance, H. H. Gerth and C. W. Mills, From Max Weber: Essays in Sociology (New York: Oxford University Press, 1958), 262ff.

15. See the work of Ichak Adizes, Corporate Life Cycles (Englewood Cliffs, N.J.: Prentice Hall, 1988).

16. Quoted in H. B. Jones, "Magic, Meaning, and Leadership: Weber's Model and the Empirical Literature," Human Relations 54/6 (2001): 753.

17. Thomas F. O'Dea, "Five Dilemmas of the Institutionalization of Religion," Journal for the Scientific Study of Religion 1/1 (October 1961): 34.

18. Ibid., 32.

19. Edgar H. Schein, *Organizational Culture and Leadership* (San Francisco: Jossey-Bass, 1990), 209–10.

20. Hirsch, *Forgotten Ways*, 114–16.

21. Michael heard Tony Campolo tell this story in a presentation many years ago.

22. Adopted from online podcast notes by Canadian writer and speaker, Bruxy Cavey, available at http://www.themeetinghouse.ca/podcast/TMH.rss.

23. From Addison's exceptional but unpublished work on Christian movements. Material used with permission. See also his blog on movements called *World Changers* at http://www.steveaddison.net/.

24. Robert E. Quinn, *Change the World* (San Francisco: Jossey-Bass, 2000), 61.

25. Ibid., 138.

26. Lawrence Cada et al., *Shaping the Coming Age of Religious Life* (New York: Seabury, 1979), 92.

27. Raymond Hostie, *The Life and Death of Religious Orders* (Washington, D.C.: Center for Applied Research in the Apostolate, 1983), 277.

28. Ibid., 278.

Chapter Four

I've Got a Picture of Jesus

It's been said often enough, but it bears repeating:
without the real human Jesus of Nazareth, we are
at the mercy of anybody who tells us that "Christ"
is this, or that.
—N. T. Wright

Our passion for Jesus is the only passion
that will not destroy us.
—Larry Crabb

To embrace the radical traditionalism we have been discussing requires a rediscovery of our foundation—the person, Jesus. It will require us to let go of our much-loved but inaccurate assumptions about him and be prepared to venture back to the Gospels to see him in all his strange radicalness. We don't for one minute assume that this will be easy for many Christians. The benign images of gentle Jesus, meek and mild, have comforted and encouraged many believers. But we ask you to reacquaint yourself with the biblical record and to be brave enough to encounter the disquieting, unsettling, perplexing, unfamiliar Jesus found there.

It has been said that God made us in his image, and we returned the favor (was it Voltaire?). This innate tendency to co-opt God to our own egos and agendas is deeply embedded in the human condition. An illustration: Some time ago Michael was speaking at a conference and was teamed with a worship leader for each of his sessions. Michael was calling the participants to the reJesus project with all its implied radicalism. The worship leader, though, was on an entirely different page. He spoke about Jesus as a cuddly, fatherly type, as all-gentle, all-kind, all-forgiving. He led the audience through a visualization experience in which they were to imagine themselves returning home to Jesus, feeling his strong, warm embrace around them. They were invited to cuddle him, secure in his love and knowing he adored them like his gorgeous little boys or girls. You can imagine the disconnect when Michael stood up after this and spoke about the wild, radical, mysterious, revolutionary Messiah from Nazareth!

In fact, the shift required by the participants to get from the warm, sentimental Jesus of the worship leader to the wild, revolutionary Jesus of the keynote speaker was so great that Michael and the worship leader met for breakfast the next day to try to integrate their approaches as best they could. During this conversation, the worship leader spoke about growing up in a cold and austere German family, with a distant, unpleasant father. All his life he had tried to fulfill his father's high standards, only to fall short time and again. It was through discovering the unconditional love of Jesus that he finally felt free from the scathing and debilitating self-criticism that he had inherited from his childhood. This experience had been so formative that it had shaped his whole view of Jesus. His Jesus had become an end-lessly loving daddy-figure, a sentimental parent who was proud of his son and who cheered him on and was thrilled with his every achievement no mat-ter how small. Can you see how our understanding of Jesus can be so easily shaped by our own psychospiritual needs? Show me your Jesus, and I'll tell you who *you* are.

So, was the worship leader wrong? Doesn't Jesus love us uncondition-ally? Of course he does, but we need to know what it means for Jesus to love us lest we romanticize it and thus distort the type of love that Jesus has for us. Is it soft and sentimental? Doesn't Jesus' understanding of love involve action and sacrifice more than just feelings? And besides, is that really all there is to Jesus? If hugs and kisses were the sum total of Jesus' character, why would anyone have wanted him dead? No one wants to kill a big ball of daddy love, do they? Jesus' character must at the least be viewed through the knowledge that his whole public ministry was marked by a resolute march toward the cross. Death becomes him! He embraces it early in his ministry and barely flinches from it all the way to Golgotha. We don't mean to sound insensitive to the terrible craving for acceptance that many people are left with because of poor parenting. Jesus unquestionably meets that deep need. But if we limit Jesus to the meeting of our psychological needs, we end up following only part of Jesus. That's how we get this daddy-hunger Jesus.

Earlier we talked about the distorted view of Jesus promulgated by the Ku Klux Klan. Since their deepest need is to justify their fear and loathing of blacks and Jews, they construct racist Jesus. Similarly, many churches have constructed Jesuses who meet their needs. There is a schmaltzy Jesus, or a middle-class Jesus, or a meek and mild Jesus who speaks in platitudes that don't upset their closely controlled lives. And then there is that annual cultural distortion, baby-in-a-manger Jesus, a harmless little child that everyone can "oohh" and "ahhh" over without having to take seriously. And so it goes. Our concern here is not to suggest that Jesus doesn't address our deep longings and needs but rather to affirm that he can never be limited to meeting those deep longings. Sometimes he challenges those needs. Many of us are familiar with the scene in C. S. Lewis's *The Lion, the Witch, and the Wardrobe*, when Lucy is about to meet Aslan the lion, the allegorical Christ figure in the books. She asks Mr. Beaver, "Is he safe?" "'Safe?' said Mr. Beaver . . . 'Who said anything about safe? 'Course he isn't safe, but he's good. He's the King, I tell you.'"[1] Following Jesus is never safe when it comes to our culturally adopted lifestyles, but it is always good.

To be sure, there are times when the word we hear from Jesus is, "I have desired to gather your children together as a hen gathers her brood under her wings." But at other times it might just as well be, "Do you not perceive or understand? Are your hearts hardened? Do you have eyes, and fail to see? Do you have ears, and fail to hear?" Both these statements appear on the lips of Jesus. The first one, from Luke 13:34, refers to his love for the people of Israel, and the second, from Mark 8:17, is directed in frustration toward his disciples. Our point is that Jesus was more than willing to express his disappointment and annoyance at his friends as well as his love and compassion. We need to remember that even though he deeply loved his disciples (John 17, for instance), he also continued to surprise, amaze, frighten, disturb, and challenge them. To limit Jesus to a spiritual tap that can be turned on and off according to our need for affirmation is a terrible mistake. It leads to us remaking Jesus in our image, rather than us being molded to his likeness.

In *Talladega Nights*, Will Ferrell, in typical over-the-top style, plays the fictional Nascar champion, Ricky Bobby. In a mostly inane film, filled with ridiculous set pieces, one scene surprises us. Ricky Bobby sits down to dinner with his wife, Carly; his two sons, Walker and Texas Ranger; his father-in-law, Chip; and his racing partner, Cal, and says grace. Addressing his prayer to "dear Lord baby Jesus," Ricky begins with thanks for the bountiful harvest of Dominoes, KFC, and Taco Bell set before him, as well as for his family and his best friend, Cal. He then asks Jesus to use his "baby Jesus powers" to heal Chip's bad leg, at which point his wife, Carly, interjects:

Carly: You know Jesus did grow up. You don't always have to call him "baby."

Ricky: I like the Christmas Jesus best and I'm sayin' grace. When you say grace you can say it to grown-up Jesus, teenage Jesus, bearded Jesus, or whoever you want . . . [continues praying] Dear tiny Jesus, with your golden fleece diapers, with your tiny little fat balled-up fist . . .

Chip [yelling]: He was a man! He had a beard.

Ricky: Look, I like the baby Jesus version the best. Do you hear me?

Inspired by this discussion about Jesus, Ricky's friend Cal decides to throw in his favorite image as well:

Cal: I like to picture Jesus in a tuxedo T-shirt, cos it says, like, I wanna be formal, but I'm here to party too. I like to party, so I like my Jesus to party.

Walker: I like to picture Jesus as a ninja fighting off evil samurai.

Cal: I like to picture Jesus with, like, giant eagle's wings, and singin' lead vocals for Lynard Skynard with, like, an angel band, and I'm in the front row, and I'm hammered drunk.

After Carly puts an end to the theological discussion by asking Ricky to finish saying grace, he continues praying: "Dear eight-pound, six-ounce infant Jesus; don't even know a word yet, just a little infant so cuddly, still omnipotent, we just thank you . . ."[2]

The bulk of Ricky's prayer is an expression of gratitude for his hot wife, his success on the track, and the millions of dollars he's made in endorsements (he even fulfills his contractual obligation to mention his sponsor Powerade). The whole scene is a farcical reminder of the temptation felt by those who don't read the Gospels to fashion Jesus in their own image.

To paraphrase Anne Lamott, you know you've remade Jesus in your own image when he hates all the same people you hate! We have all tried to shoehorn Jesus into our own agendas, making him hate those we hate, whether it's gays, Muslims, liberals, Catholics, fundamentalists, or postmoderns. But not even his own community could compel Jesus in that way. In Luke 4, Jesus commences his public ministry in his hometown with a reading from the scroll of the prophet Isaiah. The first half of his sermon that day is often repeated in churches today; having read of the day of the Lord, he impetuously announced, "Today this scripture has been fulfilled in your hearing" (Luke 4:21). The second half of his message, however, is rarely celebrated today. But it is every bit as radical as his announcement that he is the fulfillment of the prophecy made in Isaiah 61. It is so radical, in fact, that his audience was prepared to murder him. What does he say?

He plucks from the pages of 1 and 2 Kings two stories that have appeared in so many children's Sunday school curricula that their potency has been leached from the narrative. And yet they are both subversive and radical stories. In the first, he alludes to Elijah's retreat to the home of the widow at Zarephath in Sidon (1 Kgs 17:8–24). Of all the widows in Israel to whom God might have sent Elijah, he chose to provide him with sanctuary in the home of a Sidonite, says Jesus. But furthermore, as if to press his case even harder, Jesus jumps to 2 Kings 5 and the healing of the leprous Aramean warlord, Naaman. Of all the lepers in Israel, God chose to heal the leader of one of their enemy's armed forces. What do the widow at Zarephath and General Naaman of Syria have in common? They were both outsiders, enemies, despised by Israel. And yet it is to both of them that the grace of God is revealed. Indeed, in the widow's case, it is through her that God's grace is revealed. Jesus picks two characters he knows his Sabbath-day audience in Nazareth would have hated, and he dares his audience to admit that God loved them as much as anyone in Israel. He will not be co-opted, even by Israel, to a cause fueled by hatred and racism.

Later, the religious leaders of Israel send an emissary to try to trick Jesus into making politically inflammatory statements against Rome. We know how cleverly Jesus repels their trick with his statement, "Give therefore to the emperor the things that are the emperor's, and to God the things that are God's" (Matt 22:21), but it's the emissary's opening line that caught our eye: "We know you are sincere, and teach the way of God in accordance with the truth, and show deference to no one; for you do not regard people with partiality" (Matt 22:16).

No doubt, these are falsely flattering words. But we can't help but notice the irony of Jesus' enemies correctly identifying the fact that he cannot be swayed by the agendas of others, no matter who they are. So, why do we constantly persist in trying to co-opt him for our purposes?

Having said that, we are not foolish enough to suggest that knowing Jesus is a purely objective task. Of course, we all bring our own needs, hopes, and longings to our quest to understand Jesus. The poet Robert Frost once wrote, "Heaven gives its glimpses only to those not in a position to look too close." Here we have a deeply insightful understanding of Christian revelation. Those of us taken by Jesus have, in faith, glimpsed him. However, when we try to describe the content of that glimpse, the vision and the viewer inevitably become one. Though the glimpse is real, we are not in a position to sort out where it ends and we begin. We have the Gospels to provide us with the parameters outside of which we mustn't stray lest our glimpse of Jesus be more about us than about Jesus. And of course, we have the Holy Spirit.

The apostle Paul was bold enough to claim that if we are in the Spirit of God, "we have the mind of Christ" (1 Cor 2:16). If this is true, then any supposed necessity of separating ourselves in our subjectivity from the objective reality of Jesus Christ is questionable. So-called pure objectivity is a fallacious quest. We are always subjectively (personally) involved in the knowledge of God because God cannot be known in pure objectivity. In fact, objective detachment from the object of faith, which is Jesus Christ, is not consistent with a biblical way of knowing (see ch. 5). It is also out of our subjectivity that we can discover who the real Jesus is, for his mind is present in the world. But it is present only in his followers, as a gift of the Spirit. Bringing both to bear—our objectivity and our subjectivity—is more likely to yield a clearer glimpse of Jesus than either one alone.

⟿ Vandalizing Our Portraits of Jesus

One of the best ways to expose our co-option of Jesus to our own personal, religious, and cultural agendas is to interpret the many images of him that we entertain. The artistic talent of the Spanish painter Bartolome Murillo first emerged when, as a boy, he vandalized his parents' much-loved icon. Murillo converted the holy and other-worldly image of Jesus the shepherd boy into the depiction of a playful, rough-and-ready Spanish child. With the intuition of a child, young Murillo couldn't bear the almost frightening image of the pristine holy boy that hung in his childhood home. He had to rescue Jesus from the gilt frame and put him back on the dusty streets of Seville. We respond to this story strongly.

The thought of the young Murillo vandalizing his family's icon stays with us and informs a good deal of what we do. We see ourselves as iconoclasts, as holy vandals, defacing the church's cherished but unhelpful images of Jesus. Some of these images are relatively benign, like the daddy-love Jesus of the worship leader just mentioned. Others are sinister, like the KKK's Aryan Christ. But they are both inaccurate. And it's their inaccuracy that leads many people off in an unhelpful trajectory. Allow us to apply our vandals' spray cans to some of the classic glimpses of Jesus.

The Bearded-Lady Jesus

In the early 1850s, William Holman Hunt, one of the founders of the avant-garde Pre-Raphaelite movement, painted an immeasurably popular picture, *The Light of the World*. In this image, Jesus is standing outside a closed, heavy, wooden door, under a stone archway. He gently raps on the door with the back of his open hand. In his other hand he holds a jewel-encrusted lantern. The scene is dark, and behind him can be seen wild woods with twisted branches silhouetted against the setting sun. It seems that Jesus has braved an inhospitable terrain to make it to this ivy-covered door. Hunt said, "I painted the picture with what I thought, unworthy though I was, to be by Divine command, and not simply as a good subject."[3] The picture is certainly reminiscent

Jesus. *The Light of the World*, William Holman Hunt. Oil on canvas over panel.

of the text we mentioned earlier: "I am standing at the door, knocking; if you hear my voice and open the door, I will come in to you and eat with you, and you with me" (Rev 3:20).

It's hard to quantify the popularity of this image. At the turn of the twentieth century, it toured Canada, Australia, New Zealand, and South Africa and was seen by thousands. In our homeland of Australia more than five hundred thousand people saw it in Sydney and Melbourne in a time when the combined populations of those cities was fewer than a million people. Across the United Kingdom, postcard-sized copies were made, and people couldn't get enough of them. They carried the image like a keepsake or a relic. Servicemen were given copies to keep in their uniforms, a physical reminder of the closeness of Jesus to them in their time of battle. The Salvation Army composer, Sir Dean Goffin, was inspired by the painting to compose his most famous piece, also entitled *The Light of the World*. Hunt's original is now in a side room off the large chapel at Keble College, Oxford, and he painted a large copy toward the end of his life, which is now in London's St. Paul's Cathedral.

A closer examination of Hunt's Jesus reveals some interesting observations. For example, the wooden door has no exterior handle. It can obviously only be opened from the inside, adding weight to its portrayal of the passage from Revelation 3. Furthermore, Jesus is somewhat feminized. He is wearing a silk ball gown (we're not sure what else you'd call it) and a royal red robe or cape. He has a golden crown on his head, flattening his glorious blond, shoulder-length hair. His beard is blond, too, and his serene gaze makes him look more like a mythic English king than a Middle Eastern radical. In his genuine attempt to portray Jesus' kingly grandeur, Hunt has cast him as King Arthur or Richard the Lionheart perhaps, a wise, unruffled, beautiful English monarch. A classic co-option.

William Holman Hunt was to influence the popular perception of Jesus more than just about anyone else in Western cultural history, even, dare we say it, the Gospel writers. His rendering of the door-knocking Jesus as a blond, bearded royal was seared into the public consciousness of Britons and carried throughout the British Empire as far away as South Africa, Australia, and New Zealand, until today. Hunt's rendering heavily influenced the most common image of Jesus you can find—Warner Sallman's painting, *Head of Christ*. We don't have permission to include it in our book, but it is easy to find on the Internet. (We suggest you Google the artist and painting title to see if you recognize this.)

We call it the bearded-lady Jesus. Flowing blond locks swept back from the face, high cheekbones, groomed eyebrows, full lips, with heavenward gazing, gentle eyes—he's beautiful. But is this a valid biblical representation of Jesus? Or is this a mere fantasy object for an overly sentimental, cultural Christianity? This is the inoffensive Messiah, clean and tidy, pleasing to the eye. This is no disturber of our souls. This image of Jesus reflects a spirituality that is anchored in an adoration of the wonderful Christ, the unattainable Jesus.

A few years back, when Michael was teaching a seminar to Salvation Army officers in New Zealand, he noticed that most of the members of the audience were wearing black T-shirts with the revolutionary slogan, "I'll fight," emblazoned in red across the back. This was an allusion to a famous sermon by the Salvation Army founder, William Booth, who claimed that while there was poverty, alcoholism, and suffering on the streets of London, he'd fight it with all his might. It's a dramatic and motivational slogan. But hanging on the wall in the seminar room, dominating the whole space, was the picture of Jesus shown above. Michael pointed this out and asked whether the Jesus depicted in that painting would ever fight against anything, let alone get down into the filthy alleys and laneways of nineteenth-century London to serve the poor. One officer present admitted that the bearded-lady Jesus probably informed their Christology far more than the example of William Booth, a holy warrior if ever there was one.

The bearded lady in these paintings exudes an abstracted serenity, gentleness, and peace. And yet the Jesus we meet in the Gospels is at times frustrated, disappointed, annoyed and, worse still, angered. He is full of holy pathos. He exasperated his rivals, unsettled his friends, and drove his enemies mad. Says Alison Morgan, "Jesus was a difficult and uncooperative revolutionary who so threatened the established order of the day that there seemed to be no option but to have him executed."[4]

Spooky Jesus

Another series of images of Jesus that affects the imaginations of many can go under the heading of what we call spooky Jesus. They are similar to the bearded-lady Jesus in that they present a somewhat feminized picture of Christ, but they go further by adding a variety of highly symbolic, ethereal elements to the picture. These immensely popular portrayals of Jesus present him as an otherworldly being, swathed in swirling haloes and unearthly auras (probably to ensure that the viewer would not miss the fact of his divinity). This Jesus seems almost heretical. Why? Because these images seem to portray Christ's divinity at the expense of his humanity. It's as if his God nature can be barely contained by his ill-fitting human shell. It is almost as if he is one of those aliens who take on a human disguise in the movie *Men in Black*. Every now and again the alien breaks through the skin to reveal the otherworldly creature who has co-opted a human vehicle, a disposable pod, for his purposes.

Jesus. *Sacred Heart,* Pompeo Batoni.
Oil on canvas.

The early church worked hard to ensure that while it affirmed Jesus' divinity, it did not lose sight of his complete and total humanity. And it was right to reject any notions that diminished his humanity. Portrayals like spooky Jesus can rightly be labeled docetic (the heresy that claims that Jesus only seemed to be a human but was not) and should be rejected as such. When we look at the Jesus of the Gospels, we find that in fact this was exactly what Jesus was not. The incarnation emphasizes the fact that Jesus' humanity so contained the divinity of Jesus that his family, his neighbors, his friends, and even his disciples did not fully realize that God was present in the human person that they encountered in Jesus—so hidden was his divinity in his humanity. Glowing halos, exposed hearts, and dramatic posturing—all regularly included in these depictions—take us away from the Gospels rather than toward the real Jesus.

If the William Holman Hunt Jesus is a benign, insipid, emasculated man, then spooky Jesus is an otherworldly and distant being. One raps respectfully at the door to your heart, while the other waits serenely for you to approach him. The Hunt Jesus cares, while the Romanesque Jesus knows! If we asked you to show us your Jesus and you said he looked like spooky Jesus, we'd guess you feel most comfortable with the intangible, wise, ethereal, otherworldly, composed aspects of Jesus.

And yet the Jesus we meet in the Gospels is at times frustrated, angry, and disappointed. He is not always serene, his emotions held masterfully in check. Nowhere is this more movingly portrayed than on the night of his betrayal and arrest. After celebrating Passover, the grand Hebrew story of exile and restoration, Jesus and his friends take a late-night stroll in the garden called Gethsemane. There, as he prepares himself for the sacrifice he is about to make, Jesus asks, even begs, his Father three times for some alternative course. Far from the unflinching automaton he can sometimes be portrayed as, Jesus is filled with anxiety and uncertainty. Having asked his dearest friends to wait with him and pray during this his darkest hour, he expresses such sadness and loneliness when they fall asleep: "Could you not watch with me and pray for just one hour?" More than sadness, we can sense his frustration and annoyance at their abandoning him for sleep.

Scott Peck once noted that one of the chief reasons for his trusting the Gospels was their all-too-real description of Jesus. In his agnostic days, before reading them, he had assumed that the Gospels were simply works of hagiography, exaggerated accounts of this mythic holy man, invented by those of his followers committed to creating a cult of personality around him. However, when Peck first read the texts themselves, he was astonished to discover that the Jesus in their pages was nothing like the Romanesque icons he had seen before. He was richer, more textured, more authentically human than any invented folk hero could possibly be. In fact, Peck went on to conclude that the Gospels must be true. If they were inventions by Jesus' followers, those followers would have invented a better messiah than the one found in the Gospels. By that he meant that they would have invented a flawless messiah, one who never showed fear, sadness, or anger. That he isn't a "perfect" Jesus was proof enough that the Gospel writers were faithful reporters, not cunning inventors.

Ordinary Galilean Jesus

N. T. Wright was noted for having said that after the novelist and amateur New Testament scholar A. N. Wilson had finished with Jesus, all we were left with was "a moderately pale Galilean."[5] In fact, Wilson epitomizes that approach to Christology that seeks to strip away all the historical dogma only to find a simple Galilean holy man who had no idea he was launching a major new faith movement by his folksy parables and general good nature. In his surprisingly popular book, *Jesus: A Life*, Wilson concludes rather dramatically that if Jesus "had foreseen the whole of Christian history, his despair would have been even greater than it was when he cried out, 'My God, why hast thou forsaken me?'"[6]

According to Wilson, Jesus didn't think he was the messiah, far less the second person of the Trinity. He was born in an ordinary fashion in Nazareth, not Bethlehem. He taught an inner morality, and his kingdom was more a kind of indestructible inner kingdom than any external reality. He tried to raise the status of women, and he opposed extreme Jewish nationalism. However, when some people tried to foist certain messianic pretensions upon him, he was arrested by the Romans and summarily executed. He stayed dead and was buried in Galilee. Ultimately, he failed. His message was not taken up. When his brother James set about rehabilitating his damaged reputation by reassuring his followers that all had happened according to the Scripture, some people mistook him for his dead brother and a rumor began circulating that Jesus had been resurrected. But the resurrected Jesus was no more than James, who bore a striking family resemblance to his now-deceased brother the *hasid*, or holy man.

For Wilson, Paul is the great inventor of Christianity. Paul took the sayings of Jesus and the passion of the earliest Christians and constructed the complex theology of the New Testament, moving it far away from the simple teaching of Jesus. And the rest is history!

Wilson's speculation gives us a Jesus who is an ordinary itinerant storyteller and religious guru. He probably married (some writers believe he married Mary Magdalene and fathered children or a child with her). Jesus is damned with faint praise. He was a "great teacher," "a good man," "a holy man." What this means is he was an ordinary man, and the only way to explain the incredible movement of Jesus followers that combusted soon after his death is to give the credit to someone else. That someone is the villain of the piece, the dastardly Apostle Paul. He took Jesus' uncomplicated folk Judaism and perverted it into the complex system known today as Christianity.

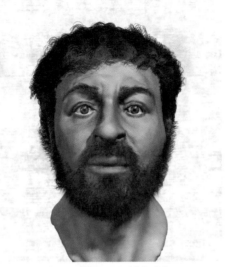

Jesus. Computer Model.
From the BBC's *Son of God.*

The picture above was created for a BBC special on Jesus in 2001. Forensic scientists took a skull from first-century Palestine and, using the reconstructive techniques currently employed by police investigators when trying to determine the identity of an unidentified skull, constructed this face. They added facial hair in keeping with what historians know of the fashion of the time and colored its skin to reflect Middle Eastern men today. The BBC wasn't claiming that this is the face of Jesus. Rather, they pointed out that this is what a typical Jewish man in Palestine looked like two thousand years ago. The heavy brow, swarthy complexion, and thick features are a world away from the bearded lady or the Romanesque Jesus. According to Wilson, this is the Galilean we mistook for the savior of the world.

Suffice to say, this is an image of Jesus that's not too popular in churches. Try this: conduct an exercise with church folk or even seminarians. Display a number of images of Jesus, including the ones we've looked at here, and ask them to rank the images from favorite to least favorite. It has been our experience that in almost every case, the BBC Jesus ranks last. Church folk seem to prefer their Jesus to look more impressive than this guy. However, we strongly suspect that outside the church, more and more people are being taken by the ordinary Galilean of Wilson. For instance, Robert Funk from the Jesus Seminar paints Jesus as a radical, gadfly, and social deviant who serves up some alternate construction of reality through his esoteric parables. Funk's colleague, John Dominic Crossan, offers a Jesus who was setting up an egalitarian community in Galilee by free healing and meals open to all comers. For them, Jesus is more easily dealt with as a great poet or a teacher of love. Of course this only begs the question, how does the poet-cum-social-worker Jesus heal the sick? The silence is deafening.

Such attempts to domesticate and secularize Jesus are flawed from the start. When rock star Bono was challenged that Jesus could be ranked among the world's great thinkers, but that to consider him the son of God was far-fetched, he had a great response:

> No, it's not farfetched to me. Look, the secular response to the Christ story always goes like this: he was a great prophet, obviously a very interesting guy, had a lot to say along the lines of other great prophets, be they Elijah, Muhammad, Buddha or Confucius. But actually Christ doesn't allow you that. He doesn't let you off that hook. Christ says: No. *I'm not saying I'm a teacher, don't call me teacher. I'm not saying I'm a prophet. I'm saying: "I'm the Messiah." I'm saying: "I am God incarnate."* And people say: No, *no, please, just be a prophet. A prophet, we can take. You're a bit eccentric. We've had John the Baptist eating locusts and wild honey, we can handle that. But don't mention the "M" word! Because, you know, we're gonna have to crucify you.* And he goes: No, no. *I know you're expecting me to come back with an army, and set you free from these creeps, but actually I am the Messiah.* At this point, everyone starts staring at their shoes, and says: Oh, *my God, he's gonna keep saying this.* So what you're left with is: either Christ was who He said He was—the Messiah—or a complete nutcase. I mean, we're talking nutcase on the level of Charles Manson. This man was like some of the people we've been talking about earlier. This man was strapping himself to a bomb, and had "King of the Jews" on his head, and, as they were putting him up on the Cross, was going: OK, *martyrdom, here we go. Bring on the pain! I can take it.* I'm not joking here. The idea that the entire course of civilization for over half of the globe could have its fate changed and turned upside-down by a nutcase, for me, *that's* farfetched . . .[7]

And he's right! The secular Jesus doesn't make any sense when you read the Gospels and hear his personal claims of messiahship. For him to pull it off, Wilson has to turn Paul into the architect of the faith, scripting the false claims and putting them in the mouth of the unsuspecting Galilean. Theologian Barbara Thiering and Episcopalian bishop John Spong each developed a whole approach to biblical hermeneutics that required a sophisticated understanding of the encoding of *midrash*, explaining away Jesus' more embarrassing claims to be the Son of God. Dan Brown, author of *The Da Vinci Code*, blames the Emperor Constantine and his cadre of fake gospel writers. But if we take the Gospels' claims about Jesus seriously, we are left with exactly the dilemma Bono outlines—either Jesus is the Christ or he just thought he was the Christ.

We confess we do like Bono, but to give credit where it's due, it was C. S. Lewis who first posed this formulation for dismissing those who prefer the "good teacher" Jesus:

> I am here trying to prevent anyone from saying the really foolish thing that people often say about Him: "I'm ready to accept Jesus as a great moral teacher, but I don't accept his claim to be God." That is the one thing we must not say. A man who was merely a man and said the sort of things Jesus said would not be a great moral teacher. He would either be a lunatic—on the level with the man who says he is a poached egg—or else he would be the Devil of Hell. You must make your own choice. Either this man was, and is, the Son of God; or else a madman or something worse. . . . But let us not come up with any patronizing nonsense about his being a great human teacher. He has not left that open to us. He did not intend to.[8]

This is the "liar, lunatic, or Lord" approach and it makes a good argument: you cannot dismiss Jesus as a good teacher or an ordinary Galilean holy man. Neither can you be satisfied with the serene, bearded-lady Jesus or the more alien-like spooky Jesus. The Gospels don't allow you that.

Revolutionary Jesus

As we have noted already, the Gospel story makes clear that those who understood Jesus and his message the best were those who most wanted him dead. He was considered a threat and a danger to the religious system of Judaism but presumably also to the impressionable masses. It's hard to imagine the bearded-lady Jesus, spooky Jesus, or ordinary Galilean Jesus threatening anybody. But Jesus' contemporaries saw him as a usurper of institutional religion, a blasphemer, a heretic, a drunkard, a glutton, and a false teacher. He was an unschooled rabbi from the God-forsaken north who had run amok and begun to stir up trouble among the equally uneducated populace. In his enemies' minds he was an extremist, a radical, a revolutionary.

There have been a few attempts over the years to react against the insipid depictions of Jesus. In the 1960s, the radical Italian filmmaker Pier Paolo Pasolini, a homosexual, a communist, and an atheist to boot, made a remarkable film based on Matthew's Gospel. His Jesus is a sinister-looking man, nearly always shrouded in a dark hood, presenting his parables not as heart-warming stories but as revolutionary tracts. He is stern, brusque, and demanding, insisting that he's come not to bring peace but a sword. Pasolini presents him as a subversive, covertly moving from place to place near the Sea of Galilee, sometimes attracting a multitude, sometimes being driven away. Interestingly, Pasolini's script for the film, entitled *The Gospel According to Saint Matthew*, is taken directly from Matthew's gospel and includes a clear depiction of the resurrection. Given that Pasolini was considered an unsavory character and that his Jesus is played as an unsettling radical, this film doesn't get much play in most church circles.[9] And yet Pasolini presents a conservative portrayal of Jesus, more in keeping with the Gospels than that of the pious William Holman Hunt.

Jesus. Film still from *Il Vangelo secondo Matteo (The Gospel According to Saint Matthew)*, directed by Pier Paolo Pasolini.

Then, in 1999, at the end of the Church of England's so-called decade of evangelism, the following advertisement appeared across the United Kingdom. It portrayed Jesus as a kind of Che Guevara character on a revolutionary red banner with the slogan, "Meek. Mild. As If." We thought it was cool, but on the original posters the bottom line read, "Discover the real Jesus. Church. April 4." We suspect that those who dared to go with the idea that Jesus was a revolutionary were less likely to believe they could find him in an Anglican church on a Sunday in England on April 4, or any other day for that matter. The usual image of the local parson hardly correlates with the Che-Jesus image below.

In the correct sense of the terms, Jesus was probably more a reformer than a revolutionary. He wasn't committed to overturning the whole religious system of which he was part. Indeed, as he points out, "Do not think that I have come to abolish the law or the prophets; I have come not to abolish but to fulfill" (Matt 5:17). His work was to transform Israel, and beyond

Jesus. Church of England poster, 1999.

that the world, not by rejecting or abolishing Israel's faith but by embodying it and calling Israel back to its true belief. Such radical reformation would have considerable impact on the structures of the religious institutions of Israel, and those beholden to such structures saw this a mile off. In this respect, Jesus is calling Israel to what we referred to earlier as radical foundationalism.

Is it any wonder that those equally beholden to the structures of the religious institutions of Christendom are just as concerned about the revolutionary Jesus being set loose in their churches! Our hope is that church leaders would recognize that Jesus doesn't want to destroy what they've got now—he just wants to reshape it radically.

Fully Human Fully Divine Jesus

One ancient icon seems to us to be more balanced. It was found in the monastery of St. Catherine in the Sinai desert. While still sporting a dramatic halo, the St. Catherine's icon depicts Jesus as tranquil and unruffled. To be sure, he has the face of a Roman scholar rather than a Palestinian rabbi, but the artist has none of the spookiness seen in other pictures of Jesus. He has painted him as an all-wise teacher. His face is not symmetrical like that in many spooky Jesus icons. It is more flawed, less lovely than the others. Such religious portraiture was rare though. The Romanesque depiction of Jesus' face characteristically portrayed him with a mask-like visage and a radically expressionistic, transfixing gaze. This, along with the halo, was supposed to convey a sense of the transcendent or the holy. Early Christian artists were conscious that Jesus was both fully human and fully divine, but when depicting him in icons, paintings, murals, and stained glass, they erred on the side of the divine, assuming that a divine human wouldn't look quite like a, well, human human.

Jesus. *Christ Pantocrator.* Icon at
St. Catherine's Monastery, Sinai.
Encaustic on panel.

↜The Jesus of the Age

Having attempted to debunk the many inadequate and even false images of Jesus that distort our true appreciation of him, we acknowledge that every age brings with it a new perspective on the multifaceted Jesus who has so captured the minds and hearts of millions throughout history. As selective as these images must be when viewed against his wholeness, nonetheless there is merit in surveying the effect that these images have had on forming the culture and societies of their day. Jaroslav Pelikan has done precisely that in his fine work *Jesus Through the Centuries*. In this book he reveals how each image of Jesus created by each successive era is a key to understanding the temper and values of that age—its strengths and its deficiencies. His table of contents provides us with a list of some of the successive images that have informed history over two millennia:[10]

- ↜ *The Rabbi*: informs the early New Testament period, particularly that of Jewish Christianity.

- ↜ *The Turning Point of History*: encapsulates the increasing significance of Jesus for the first and second centuries.

- ↜ *The Light of the Gentiles*: highlights the pagan anticipations of Christ as prefigured in Socrates and Virgil and the other poet-philosophers of the pre-Christian period.

- ↜ *The King of Kings*: highlights the lordship of Jesus over against the lordship of Caesar culminating in the Constantinian contract and the rise of the Christian Empire.

- ↜ *The Cosmic Christ*: focuses on Christ as Logos, mind, and reason informing the rising Christianized Platonism of the third and fourth centuries.

- ↜ *The Son of Man*: informs the Augustinian Christian psychology and anthropology of the fifth century.

- ↜ *The True Image*: Christ as the inspiration for true art and architecture in the Byzantine period.

- ↜ *The Christ Crucified*: in the Middle Ages, the cross becomes the most significant image in art and literature, emphasizing the saving work of Jesus (tenth and eleventh centuries).

- ↩ *The Monk Who Rules the World*: the triumph of the Benedictine vision of the world represents the triumph of monasticism.

- ↩ *The Bridegroom of the Soul*: the rise of Christian mysticism interprets the Song of Songs as an allegory of the love of Christ and the believer.

- ↩ *The Divine and Human Model*: Francis of Assisi helps restore the full humanity of Jesus and leads to the transformation of the institutional church of the thirteenth and fourteenth centuries.

- ↩ *The Universal Man*: the image of the Renaissance period with its rediscovery of Christian humanism.

- ↩ *The Mirror of the Eternal*: Christ as mirror of the true, the beautiful, and the good that features in the Reformation period.

- ↩ *The Prince of Peace*: the Crusades and the wars of religion also cause a resurgence of Christian pacifism, especially mirrored in Anabaptist circles.

- ↩ *The Teacher of Common Sense*: the quest for the historical Jesus in scholarship and philosophy of the Enlightenment period.

- ↩ *The Poet of the Spirit*: idealism and romantic philosophy of the nineteenth century arises in protest against orthodox rigidity and rationalist banality.

- ↩ *The Liberator*: applies to both nineteenth and twentieth centuries. From Marx to Tolstoy, to Gandhi and Martin Luther King Jr., Jesus' prophetic opposition to economic and political oppression and injustice is highlighted.

- ↩ *The Man Who Belongs to the World*: the unprecedented spread in the twentieth century of the message of Jesus means that massive populations in the Third World come into the fold. Jesus becomes a truly world figure engaging the other religions in a more significant way.

Although we think that it is just about impossible to sum up an era in one image and Pelikan's choices might seem arbitrary, nonetheless as a historian, his approach highlights the ongoing role of Jesus in shaping the culture and history of the West. But mostly it is helpful in understanding the images of Jesus that seem to capture the spirit of an age. What is most helpful perhaps is seeing that Jesus is all of the above. He is Rabbi, King of kings, Cosmic Christ, Light of the Nations, and so on. And herein lies the problem: to limit him to one image is to limit the magnificence of the person that we meet in Jesus.

⟵ What Kind of Man Is This?

Some time ago, Michael had the opportunity to conduct a regular worship gathering with a group of people who felt uncomfortable in traditional churches. They were an interesting collective of artists, writers, and cultural creatives, some of whom had church backgrounds but had rejected it all and others who had never set foot in a church building. They met for a whole summer in a cramped art gallery above a café. The gallery owners were intrigued by Jesus and had gathered a motley crew of unlikely people together to worship him. Some were unemployed. Some were working only occasionally as artists. Others were suffering with mental illness. Michael and his wife, Carolyn, would lead them through a short, simple liturgy of prayers and music, using uncomplicated symbols like stones, broken pottery, candles, and, of course, bread and wine.

One of the features of the gathering was a brief study of John's Gospel followed by a discussion about the text. John's Gospel launches right in with John the Baptist's ministry and his identification of Jesus as the Lamb of God, followed quickly by the turning of water into wine at Cana and the cleansing of the temple and Jesus' late-night conversation with Nicodemus about being born again.

What was interesting was how this group approached the text. They immediately saw things that most churched groups don't see. They saw Jesus siding with the oppressed and the marginalized. They read the scenes at the Jordan River as John and Jesus leading the forgotten, the poor, and the downtrodden out of the desert through the refreshing waters toward hope and strength. They saw Jesus' transformation of ceremonial waters into wedding wine as his subversive act of taking those religious symbols designed to separate the holy from the unholy and converting them into something delicious for all to enjoy. They identified his fury in the temple as his shattering of the institutional system that denied access and equity to the poor penitents who were forced to change their money and purchase birds for religious sacrifices. They overheard Jesus telling Nicodemus about how the transformation he was initiating began with a transformation of the heart, the inner things over which all people have control, not the outer world, which only the rich or powerful have the capacity to change.

In effect, they read the Gospel as being largely about exile and restoration (not that they would have expressed it in these terms). They read it this way because they felt like exiles from institutional religion. To these exiles who felt too dirty to attend church, the Jordan River scenes were a reminder that Jesus is calling everyone, not just the clean, to his side. To these exiles who had been told that they needed to be washed before they could approach God, the wedding at Cana convinced them that in Jesus' kingdom they were welcomed guests and that there was plenty of wine for all. Likewise, to them the cleansing of the temple presented a Jesus who would stop at nothing to demolish every religious hoop put in the way of repentant people accessing God.

In *They Like Jesus but Not the Church*, Dan Kimball reports on similar experiences he has had with unchurched people. The title of the book pretty much sums up his main point and summarizes the words of a number of young adults who are drawn to the Jesus of the Gospels but who cannot find a place in the church.[11] This has been our experience as well. That group of desperate Jesus seekers who gathered in that gallery that summer are not dissimilar to the first-century Jews to whom the Gospels were first written. They feel exiled from institutional Christianity. But they are desperate for restoration. What kind of Jesus will restore them? The pristine, pure, serene, bearded lady? He only makes them feel more guilty about their inadequacies. Spooky Jesus? He intrigues them, but ultimately he belongs in the church world of stained glass and flying buttresses, the very world they feel is off limits to them. The ordinary Galilean teacher? At least he's safe. He teaches compassion and kindness, and many exiles would prefer him to the other options, but ultimately he leads them nowhere. He might appeal to their experience of exile, but he promises no restoration.

⟵ Setting Free the Wild Man

One of the stories told about Jesus goes like this: It was said that people didn't venture down to the cliffs on the eastern side of Lake Galilee after dark. In fact, even in broad daylight, unless one had a good reason to be on the steep and desolate banks on the water's edge it was best to stay away. The wild man lived there. An insane, naked man scurried about on all fours out there. More like an animal than a man, he ate what he could scavenge from the pigs that grazed nearby and slept in the cave-tombs among the bones of the dead. His bloodcurdling shrieks could be heard day and night.

He was the stuff of local legend and lore. Parents threatened bad children with setting the wild man on to them. He has the strength of ten men, they warned; no one can hold him down. Half starved and insane, the wild man's hairy body was covered with scabs and sores. He was the object of both mirth and genuine fear among the residents of the Greek-speaking town of Gadara, and they thought that the sooner he died from starvation or infection, the better.

Jews who lived beyond this region had given them all in Gadara up for dead. This, the eastern shore of Lake Galilee, was almost entirely populated with Gentiles. It had been colonized by Greek speakers, who had built as many as ten cities there. Pious Jews had long since left the area to avoid contamination, and those who remained knew they were in pagan territory. Little wonder, some said, that it was overrun by maniacs and lunatics.

When Jesus stepped out of his boat onto the beach near Gadara, he must have suspected what he was in for. Strange it must have seemed to many Jews that he, such a renowned prophet, would even bother with Gadara. Leave them to their own devices, they would have sniffed. They are not ours, or God's, concern.

It's no mistake that Jesus disembarks at the desolate stretch of shoreline under the steep cliffs near the town. In every likelihood he has spotted the wild man from his boat as it approached land. His pathetic wailing and scampering about on the cliffs would have made him conspicuous, to say the least. Where other boatmen would have put to shore far from this madman, Jesus makes a beeline toward him. And no sooner do his feet touch the soil than the wild man rushes him. This might have scared off many an unwary traveler, but Jesus, something of a wild man himself, is unmoved.

"What do you want with me, Jesus, Son of the Most High God? Swear to God that you won't torture me," he shrieks. Such a knowing request betrays his condition. He is a demoniac, meaning that his personality is under the mastery of an evil power or powers. The effect is the destruction of human character. He has been brought to isolation from society, stripped of his moral integrity, and reduced to a state of utter physical degradation.

This man, despised and rejected by men, has not just stumbled fortuitously upon Jesus but has been sought out by him. The demons declare themselves to be in great number. "I am called Legion," cries the pathetic man, overwhelmed by evil forces who have the audacity to beg Jesus to cast them not into hell but into a nearby herd of swine. And remarkably, Jesus, having negoti-ated with demons, agrees to their request and sends them skittling into the pigs, who end up plunging over the cliffs into the lake and drowning.

What kind of Messiah accedes to the wishes of demons? What kind of Messiah destroys the income of a local swineherd? It would be like blowing up a grocer's corner store! These poor farmers don't deserve to watch their bloated, drowned pigs floating in Lake Galilee, do they? Shouldn't the Mes-siah be on the side of the poor? The demons get more courtesy from Jesus than do the swineherds. What kind of prophet is this?

This is the kind of prophet who finds clothes for the wild man, who dresses him and feeds him and treats him with the dignity and respect, the attention and love every human being deserves. When they come running to see what's happened, the locals find dead pigs, destitute farmers, and the un-tamed, naked wild man now clothed and in his right mind. The bizarre scene scares the daylights out of these pagan people. Strong magic has come to their shores, and they beg the strange magician to leave the area quickly.

As Jesus climbs into his boat, the wild man takes his arm. "Let me come with you. There's nothing for me here. I will serve you all my days."

Yet while the demons' request was granted, the wild man's is denied. Forced to remain in the Gadarenes, he goes on to be confirmed as part of local lore forever as the wild man who was rehabilitated by the even wilder Messiah from Nazareth.

Is it any wonder than Jesus is at home among the wild things? He inau-gurated his public ministry by fasting for forty days in the wilderness where the wild beasts roam. He is untamed and unfettered, and his ministry is in-dicative of this. It runs amok wherever he goes. Indeed Jesus conducts his ministry as a kind of fugitive. As we've seen, after his inaugural sermon in Luke 4, he is manhandled toward a cliff in an attempted assassination. He evades the baying mob, but his public ministry is then conducted in a ren-egade fashion. Then in Mark 3, when Jesus returns to his old hometown, the neighbors are repulsed by his teaching, declaring him to be insane ("He has gone out of his mind"). Even his family are so outraged by his behavior that they attempt to restrain him for his own good. They are embarrassed by his wild ideas. In John 7, his brothers rebuke him because they see him as skulk-ing around in Galilee: "No one who wants to become a public figure acts in secret. Since you are doing these things, show yourself to the world" (Luke 7:4). Later in that same chapter (v. 32), when the Pharisees send out temple police to arrest him, he evades capture and continues on the run.

Somehow we ignore these indications that Jesus' public ministry was operating "under the radar" with a band of impressionable young men by his side. One of his inner circle was Simon the Zealot. The Zealots were an underground anti-imperialist movement dedicated to driving the Romans out of Israel. They wanted political freedom but also they wanted a purified, traditionalist theocratic Jewish state free from the interference of pagan Rome. As well as the militant Simon, Jesus also attracted James and John. Some New Testament scholars think that their nickname, "the sons of thunder," may link them to the insurrectionists as well. Furthermore, some of Jesus' first followers had been disciples of the ascetic and ferociously anti-social John the Baptist. Having attracted these disaffected radicals to his side, Jesus was seen as a danger to society.

And why wouldn't he be? Even his friends were somewhat frightened by him. When Jesus asks them what people are saying about him, they reply that some think he is a resurrected John the Baptist, or even Elijah (Luke 9:18f). They're not saying they think he is a real softy, a big, gorgeous guru of love and goodwill. They think he's a resurrected wild man, for that's surely what both John and Elijah were when alive. Indeed these rumors had reached even King Herod, who had had John executed (Luke 9:7). John the Baptist back from the dead! That would be a frightening sight.

Our point is that to reJesus the church, we need to go back to the daring, radical, strange, wonderful, inexplicable, unstoppable, marvelous, unsettling, disturbing, caring, powerful God-Man. The communities around us are crying out for him. They are turning up in droves to hear the Dalai Lama speak. They are buying mountains of books on popular theology. They are traipsing over sacred sites across the globe. They are searching for the promised one, the one who offers them restoration and peace. The church needs to find itself in league with this Jesus, staring at him in amazement and saying, as Peter did, with a trembling voice, "What kind of man is this?" Even the wind and waves obey him. Even the wild demons obey him. Even the Pharisees quake at the thought of what he might unleash if left to his own devices.

⟵ Notes

1. C. S. Lewis, *The Lion, the Witch, and the Wardrobe* (New York: Macmillan, 1981), 74.

2. *Talladega Nights: The Ballad of Ricky Bobby*, directed by Adam McKay (Culver City, Calif., Sony Pictures, 2006).

3. C. Forbes, "Images of Christ in Nineteenth-Century British Paintings in the Forbes Magazine Collection," *Magazine Antiques*, December 2001, 12.

4. Alison Morgan, *The Wild Gospel* (Oxford: Monarch, 2007), 36.

5. N. T. Wright, *Who Was Jesus?* (London: SPCK, 1992), 37ff.

6. A. N. Wilson, *Jesus* (London: Sinclair-Stevenson, 1992), quoted in Wright, *Who Was Jesus?* 38.

7. "Bono: Grace over Karma," excerpt from *Bono: In Conversation with Mischka Assayas* (New York: Riverhead, 2005), ChristianityToday.com, August 8, 2005. Cited 1 August 2008. Online: http://www.christianitytoday.com/music/interviews/2005/bono-0805.html.

8. C. S. Lewis, *Mere Christianity* (New York: Macmillan, 1952), 55–56.

9. Interestingly, this film was included in the 1995 Vatican list of films "suitable for viewing by the faithful."

10. Jaroslav Pelikan, *Jesus Through the Centuries* (New Haven, Conn.: Yale University Press, 1999), vii–ix.

11. Dan Kimball, *They Like Jesus but Not the Church* (Grand Rapids, Mich.: Zondervan, 2007).

Chapter Five

The Shema Schema
(One God, One Love)

Monotheism is a outcome of the exclusive claim of
Yahweh, rather than a conceptual hypothesis resulting
from human effort to gain a unitary view of his world.
—Paul Minear

R. Joshua ben Korba said: Why does the section
"Hear, O Israel" (Deut 6:4–9) precede the section
"And it shall come to pass if ye shall hearken
diligently to my commandments"? So that a man
may first take upon himself the yoke of the kingdom
of Heaven and afterward take upon him the
yoke of the commandments.
—The Talmud

All this talk about Jesus, discipleship, and the church raises a whole set of
questions relating to a broader understanding of God. Where is the place
of God in a discussion on Christology and the missional church? We mean to
turn our attention to this very question, and in doing so we hope to frame the
discussion within the most fundamental revelation of God in the Bible, namely,
that he is One and that he claims us and that this claim excludes all other
claims for ultimate loyalty. In effect, we are going to look at biblical (existential)
monotheism and its implications for a missional worldview, as well as some of
the practical outworkings of it for life and faith. Monotheism, interpreted from
within the biblical worldview, is the belief that the one God, Lord and Creator
of all, has rightful claim to sovereignty over all that he has created. Viewed in
this way, Jesus' teachings of the kingdom of God are one way of expressing the
claim of the one God over all creation.

The reader might well be tempted to dismiss this chapter as being overly theological and therefore choose to skip it to get to the more practical stuff. We believe this would be a serious mistake, not because the practical isn't important but because so much of the practical stuff is bound up directly with our understanding of God. This goes to the issue of worldview—if we go wrong on monotheism, our most elemental view of God, the whole enterprise is threatened. We ought to be mindful once again of William Temple's warnings about the nature of theological error when he noted that if our conception of God is radically false, then the more devout we are the worse it will be for us. We believe that the fundamental correction for the church at the dawn of the twenty-first century must be a christological one that will in turn revolutionize our missiology as well as our ecclesiology. But we must be patient, and we need to be as accurate as we can, because when one is journeying to the moon, one degree off at launch and we will miss it by thousands of miles. If this is not already obvious, this theological corrective must take place in the realm of Christology. But to understand Christology properly, we need to probe the most basic assumption in the biblical revelation of God, namely, the assumption that God is One and that he redeems and claims us in and through Jesus the Messiah.

⟿ One God

The representative text on this topic is what Jewish people call the *Shema*. "Hear, O Israel: The Lord our God, the Lord is one; and you shall love the Lord your God with all your heart, and with all your soul, and with all your mind, and with all your strength." As a righteous Jew, Jesus himself affirms that there are no greater commandments than these (Mark 12:31).

The word *shema* is the first word in the text of Deuteronomy 6:4–9, and it means "hear" or " pay attention." This call to attention highlights what follows. And what follows is more than simply a statement about God and God's relationship to the people of God (and it is that). It also contains within it the fundamentals of the worldview of the Bible because it ties together a distinct way of ethical living with a distinct understanding of God. The *Shema* also assumes the whole idea of a covenant relationship between the players—a deeply personal and well-defined connection between God and the people Israel. Observant Jews of all varieties confess the *Shema* three times a day, thus highlighting its nature as a prototypal summary of biblical faith. This text is of essential importance because it contains the guiding idea of God that is basic to Jewish faith, is assumed by all the writers of the New Testament, and is adopted into the faith of Islam.

This concept of the oneness of God represents a striking contrast to that of the religious thought of the cultures that surrounded Israel where the multiplicity of gods in turn led to great upheaval and tension in human life. For polytheists, though a person might carry out his religious duties with care, he or she could not be guaranteed any security, for if there was strife among the gods, this would radically affect human life. Though a given god might promise much to the individual person, a more powerful god might still bring disaster. The resulting tension often led to a deep pessimism in religious life and thought. This is not as theoretical as it sounds at first. The average modern polytheists-next-door also lack an integrating center of life. They live under the rules of economics, nationalism, sex, family, and whatever other idols they set up. And make no mistake; these are idols that can dominate a person's life and consciousness. History is clear about that. People will kill for these if necessary. These idols compete with one another and demand loyalty and obeisance, but they can never deliver ultimate meaning to life. Because life is fragmented, distributed among the many, it therefore allows no unified vision of reality to emerge. In radical contrast to the belief in many gods, Yahweh is the one and only God who redeems his people and subsequently requires that they love him as he had already loved them.[1] And the nature of this God and the form this love of God should take is made known to us in Scripture, nature, and history. He is good, holy, just, and compassionate, and he requires us to be the same. To be in relationship with him therefore brings meaning, focus, moral vision, and an ultimate reality to human life.

This revelation of God as One speaks not only of the uniqueness of God (over against the many) but also the unity within God and therefore the world God has created. The God of the universe *is* the God of history. We assert that this understanding of God lies at the root of the whole biblical worldview. It clearly motivates and inspires the faith of the New Testament. Monotheistic statements permeate the New Testament, whether they are statements of faith in the one God (1 Cor 8:4–6; Eph 4:6; 1 Tim 2:5; Rom 3:30; Jas 2:19), the only God (Rom 16:27; 1 Tim 1:17; 6:15; Jude 25; John 17:3), or the God from whom all things derive (Rom 11:36; Heb 2:10; 1 Cor 8:6; Rev 4:11). These affirmations demonstrate a complete continuity with the Old Testament and its fundamental proclamation of existential (Deut 5:7) and theoretical

(Deut 4:35) monotheism.[2] And as such it forms the most basic assumption from which apostle, prophet, priest, and king operate.

But this concern with monotheism is especially present in the teachings of Jesus where he places strong emphasis on the affirmation of one God.

Release to the Captives

William Wilberforce

William Wilberforce is accredited with leading the campaign for the abolition of slavery in the British Empire in the early nineteenth century. A descendant of a wealthy family, a member of the British House of Commons, and a man with a weak constitution, Wilberforce perhaps seems an unlikely little Jesus. But his conversion to evangelical faith in 1784 led to his joining the Clapham Sect, a group of evangelical and abolitionist members of the Anglican Church. It was in this group that Wilberforce's interest in social reform was piqued. In 1789 he made his first speech against the slave trade, which launched him on what would become a monumental political battle to end slavery, a struggle dogged by many failures and setbacks. It wasn't until 1807 that the Abolition of the Slave Trade bill was finally passed through both British Houses of Parliament. Though celebrated as a milestone in the abolitionist cause, outlawing the slave trade didn't actually end slavery itself, and many slave traders continued to flout the new laws. Wilberforce helped launch a new phase of the campaign and sought to end human slavery for good. Exhausted by the campaign and the parlous state of his health, Wilberforce retired in 1825. In 1833 he received news of the impending passing of the Slavery Abolition Act. "Thank God that I should have lived to witness a day in which England is willing to give twenty million pounds for the abolition of slavery," he is quoted as saying. He died two days later. As a little Jesus, Wilberforce is commended for his unstinting effort to abolish slavery and promote equality among races in a turbulent time.

In Mark 12:28–34, Jesus responds to a question about the greatest commandment by directly quoting the *Shema* (Deut 6:4–5), thus affirming the primacy of monotheistic faith. Yet the fullness of this quotation, with its emphasis on total devotion to God, and the addition of a "second like it," the loving of one's neighbors as oneself, draws out the ethical consequence of faith that is so distinctly in *Shema* faith.

In Mark 10:18–19 this same idea is stressed, for the affirmation of God's unique goodness ("No one is good but God alone") is immediately followed by a list of ethical imperatives that derive from the uniquely good God. The monotheistic confession was thus taken seriously by Jesus, not because there was a pervasive rational challenge to it but because its ethical implications were so serious. Dedication to the one God, according to Jesus, must be demonstrated by living out God's ethical demands.[3] Scot McKnight's *Jesus Creed: Loving God, Loving Others* explores how the foundational monotheism in the *Shema* informs Jesus' teachings and the New Testament.[4]

This connection between belief in the one God and the way of life in the believer has been given the rather unappealing label *ethical monotheism*. We prefer, for reasons that will become obvious, to call it existential monotheism. And what it means is that inherent in the whole notion of monotheism, genuine relationship with the biblical God must result in a lifestyle consistent with the nature of the covenant God.[5] So the *Shema* is not so much a statement about the unity and oneness of God as it is a statement about the relationship that God has to Israel and the church.

So we can see that linked with ethical monotheism is the whole spirituality of the people born of this revelation. Therefore discipleship, worship, and mission must take a direct cue from the claim of the one Lord over our lives. This has far-reaching consequences for us, because, as we shall see, it also implies the obliteration of all the life-cramping dualisms (e.g., sacred and secular, the body and the spirit) that have plagued Christian thinking in the Western tradition. This can be represented something like this.

The diagram shows our view of God at the top, and our response at the bottom. Our response is the way we act based on our view of God. The above illustrates the unifying and all-compassing nature of the claim that

God makes over the lives of his chosen people. Everything is caught up into the redemptive lordship of the One. We use the term "existential" here because for us it best describes the dynamics of biblical monotheism, not so much as a philosophy or doctrine but as the impact that an encounter with the one God has on the whole lives of those who truly encounter him.[6]

⬸ One Love

Monotheism, as the biblical players experienced it, is not so much an attempt to probe the inner nature of eternal Being but rather a response to an encounter with the living God. There is a clear, direct, and indissoluble link between God and the lifestyles that ought to emerge from an encounter with God. But biblical faith in God moves us beyond mere ethics and intellectual knowledge of God to something far more impacting and all-embracing.[7] The whole of life is caught up, focused, and directed in the God encounter. To attempt to avoid this far-reaching claim that God makes on our lives is to miss a truly godly experience. To try and explain the situation created by God's visit, we can do no other than exclaim, "the Lord our God, he is the one Lord." This is a profoundly existential confession, an act in which our whole being, our very lives, are drawn together and concentrated.

There is a gulf of difference between the existential view of monotheism and the philosophical one. The philosopher poses the question of the nature of God in a form quite alien to the outlook of the biblical writers. The philosopher makes the problem one of intellect rather than of action; he or she views the problem speculatively to gain objective understanding of a concept of God rather than existentially in terms of personal involvement with God.[8] To us who claim the name of Jesus, only one power is sovereign—the God we encounter in our Lord Jesus Christ. And we are called to respond with our lives. As Paul Minear writes:

> The sole sovereignty of God is realized only by stern struggle with other gods, with all the forces that oppose his will. This is to say that, to the biblical writers, monotheism begins not as a stage of metaphysical speculation, not as a final step in the development out of polytheism, not as the merging of all gods into one (as in Hinduism), but when one God becomes the decisive reality for a particular man and thereby calls for the dethronement of all his other gods.

> This helps to explain why early Christians found in the total obedience of Jesus a supreme and final manifestation of God, a manifestation of which by its very

nature transcended history, judged history, and redeemed history. It points to the reason why, in dying to the world, they experienced true knowledge of God and true power from God. And this message of the oneness of God intensified their struggle against false gods. To them, the conflict with heathen gods had entered its final stage. Everywhere their testimony is ambivalent: there are no such gods for us, yet there are many daemonic powers that are attacking us most viciously. Their ambivalence in the struggle between God and upstart deities will disappear only when all others have been subdued by Christ and brought within the sovereignty of God.

Christian belief does not consist in saying "there is one God." The devil knows that! Christians respond to their God by faith in his deeds, by trusting in his power, hoping in his promise and passionately abandoning themselves to do his will. Only within the context of such a passionate vocation does the knowledge of the one Lord live. And this knowledge necessitates rather than eliminates the struggle with the devil and all his works. To paraphrase Kierkegaard, only in unconditional obedience, spurred by infinite passion, infinite resignation, infinite enthusiasm, is such "monotheism" wholly manifested in human existence, as for example, in Jesus.[9]

Seek First the Kingdom

Beyond the defining encounter with the One who claims us, the existential approach gets us much closer to what the Bible teaches about discipleship and genuine belief in God. And all these aspects come into clearer focus in Jesus' teaching on the kingdom of God. Viewed from the angle of existential monotheism, the kingdom of God can be viewed as "the business, or working, end" of the claim of the One God over all of life.[10]

The New Testament writers' use of the phrase "the kingdom of God" is another way of saying that God is One, and that he is indeed King, and that he claims all and rules over all. We miss it because we don't understand monotheism the way the first-century Jews did. While there might be a difference of opinion over Jesus' use of this phrase, most scholars would agree that the kingdom of God refers to the active reign of God everywhere and over everyone. It is the activity of God in all spheres of life, especially in the church, but also well beyond it. We like the way Eugene Peterson puts it:

The "political" metaphor, "Kingdom," insists on a gospel that includes everything and everyone under the rule of God. God is no religious glow to warm a dark night. Christ is no esoteric truth with which to form a Gnostic elite. The

Christian faith is an out-in-the-open, strenuous, legislating, conquering total-
ity. God is sovereign: nothing and no one is exempt from his rule.[11]

It is easy to see how the concepts of monotheism and the kingdom of
God are related. The way the earliest Christians expressed this was by restat-
ing Israel's ancient belief in the kingdom of Yahweh and by attaching the
active function of kingship/lordship to Jesus. Seen in this light, the church's
elemental confession that "Jesus is Lord" captures all the meaning and significance of the biblical teaching on the kingdom of God. Reconfiguring our
previous diagram, we can frame it as follows.

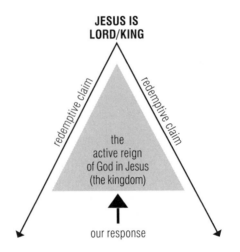

Our view of God is that Jesus is Lord, and the kingdom of God is the arena
in which we respond to God's sovereign rule over this world. All is included
(and nothing is excluded) in this claim. Once again the all-encompassing
nature of existential monotheism comes to the fore.

You Shall Be Holy Because I Am Holy

Because the claim of God penetrates so deeply into the human heart
and into every aspect of life, it must by its nature provoke a deeply personal
response in return. The *Shema* binds the believer to a love of God that demands nothing less than heart, soul, and strength as the appropriate response to the initiating love of God. We cannot encounter God and walk away
unchanged and unmotivated. We cannot confess with our lips and not follow with our lives. The call to an appropriate holiness is implied in all true

knowledge of God ("be holy, for I am holy," Lev 11:44). In other words, a true encounter with the one God generates a life-embracing, all-encompassing ethic. Anything less and it is not a biblical view of God.

For instance, Mark Sayers, comrade and commentator on culture and the gospel, suggests that while the vast majority of people in Western contexts say they believe in some form of god,[12] the god they believe in is so distant and their idea of him/her/it is so vague that it fails to generate any transforming impact. Sayers calls this the "break-glass-in-case-of-emergency-god," the being we invoke when we get into trouble or experience some form national disaster. But this god of the popular mind is so remote that it fails to have any practical impact on daily life whatsoever. In other words, popular ideas of god, whether they are new religious movements or vague notions of a higher power, almost universally fail to engender a way of life as response . . . an ethic, an ethos, a Way.

But this view of God as distant leads to a lack of engagement with God (indicated by the broken lines leading to and from the idea of God in the diagram). This creates a vacuum in the life of an individual, and so other things rush in to fill the vacuum. In our day, consumerism is the chief idol: the provider of meaning, identity, community, and purpose. In other words, the spiritual quest for happiness (the good life) is mainly pursued through the blessings of consumption. Sayers thus rightly notes that consumerism provides us with a definite form of spirituality.[13] But this combines with the other factor that kicks in as a result of the practical irrelevance of the deity, namely, the deification of the self. With the loss of the holy Other that is God, the self becomes the sole source of authority and thus the only real basis of ethics, guidance, and choices. When this happens, we end up in a vacuous prison of pleasure where the self is trapped in radical bondage to the not-so-tender mercies of the marketers. The god of mammon rears its ugly head again. To illustrate, consider the diagram on the following page.

And Christians are not exempt from this trivialization of God and the resultant deification of the self. In fact, an independent observer could be forgiven for believing that Western Christianity is consumerist to the core. But surely any diminishing of the claims of the one true God, and any deification of the self, is nothing more than another form of religious idolatry. Recall chapter 4, where we discussed the various images that Christians entertain of Jesus. Now apply these images (e.g., bearded-lady Jesus, spooky Jesus, or the iddy-baby Jesus of *Talladega Nights*) to the top of the diagram above. It is not hard to see the impact that this will have on life. For instance, there is

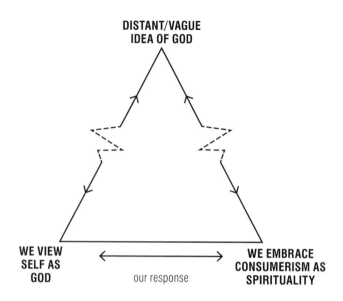

DISTANT/VAGUE IDEA OF GOD

WE VIEW SELF AS GOD ← our response → **WE EMBRACE CONSUMERISM AS SPIRITUALITY**

an iconic image of Jesus that came from the film *Dogma*. It is called "buddy Jesus." Buddy Jesus is a view of Jesus that minimizes him to being my pal, mate, a friend who covers my back. There is no reverence here, only bland familiarity. But if our primary image of Jesus is that he is my homeboy, my buddy, then we shouldn't be surprised that the religion that develops around this is a false and profoundly consumerist one.

So what does true spirituality as response look like? How do we love the Lord with heart, soul, mind, and strength, and pass that spirituality on meaningfully to later generations, as the *Shema* suggests (Deut 6:5–9; Matt 22:37–40)? Allow us to suggest a couple of broad ways.

Spirituality Beyond the Sacred and Secular

One of the outcomes of a truly monotheistic view of the world is the annihilation of the dualistic category of sacred and secular. If one God is the source of reality and the reference point for life, how can life be fragmented? When we truly claim Jesus as Lord, how can we claim that some areas of life are non-God areas . . . secular? But this is a tempting thing because integrating life under the one Lord is an arduous task. But integrate we must if we believe as true monotheists. Paul Minear suggests that the biblical writers constantly fight

against a false separation of sacred from secular, against any reduction in the territory under divine rule. It has often been observed that in neither Testament can ethics and religion be separated. One finds an ethical religion and a religious ethic precisely because every aspect of life is seen from a single centre, and every aspect is therefore potentially religious and no aspect is *per se* religious.[14]

Glocal (combining global with local) apostle Bob Roberts refers to the domains of our lives and asserts that the kingdom extends to all the domains (religion, science, politics, art, business, education, agriculture, security, family).[15] He sees that mission must entail an engagement in each and every domain and should not be limited to church and merely religious issues, as that would be to limit the activity of the kingdom to that of the church. And yet we know that the kingdom of God is God's activity in and throughout the whole cosmos, including the human and all the domains of human society. Clearly there can be no false sacred-secular divide here. One of the tasks of the church, says Roberts, is to learn how to engage in all of life in order to transform the world.

> We've segmented |our understanding of| how God works. And we've done so to our own detriment. Only when we see the bigger picture of how the pieces fit together can there be any flow or continuity. I call this way of learning, *domain jumping* |and it is| the means to bring together what was previously considered separate . . . instead of learning and mastering only one domain or specialty for a lifetime, we allow one domain to naturally lead to learning in the next related domain. We're curious. We want to know how it all relates; instead of camping out on only one |the religious| domain.[16]

Glocalnet, Robert's training organization, uses what it calls a domain map to help teach church planters to know how to engage society on a practical level. The key is to help people see that their job or vocation puts them in a domain and that is, at the same time, their chief ministry. This breakthrough in terms of our understanding of God's rule in the world and our role in it only highlights how we have failed to fully comprehend the all-encompassing nature of monotheism, whereas Judaism has understood this all along.

When we associate this idea to the christological redefinition of monotheism (as we must), then our task in the world is to be Jesus' agents in every sphere or domain of society. The lordship of Jesus extends to our sexuality, our political life, our economic existence, our family, our play, and everything in between. There must be no limitation to the claim that Jesus makes over all of life. When we get this right, Jesus' lordship takes on a missional edge. "Jesus is Lord" is more like a rallying war cry than a mere theological statement.

Oneness to the One

Judaism has well understood the nature and implications of existential monotheism, and the heart of Jewish spirituality is directly tied to the *Shema*. Jewish people know that if God is one and that all of life comes under that claim of the one God, then the only true response is that we give all of life to God as our true act of worship. They call this task *yichud*, or unification, and it involves taking all of the disparate elements in one's life and offering them up to God. No sphere or domain or aspect of human existence is to be kept out of this equation; politics, economics, family life, religious life, all are directed toward the One. In this offering, all idolatries are renounced, no domain is seen as autonomous, all motivations are to be redeemed and directed toward God, and in so doing the worshipper unifies his or her own existence. This is true holiness (Rom 12:1–3).

Seen in this light we can say that the heart of a genuinely biblical spirituality is found in response to the holy claim of Oneness. For us, as for the Israelite, worship, discipleship, and mission are rolled into the one act of unification as response to the one God, but for us it is focused in Jesus Christ. In yet another reworking of our basic diagram, we can illustrate this as follows.

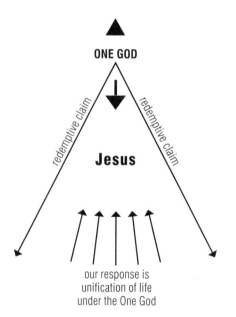

In this diagram, we see the affirmation of God and the redemptive claim of God, mediated through Jesus Christ. Our response to that claim is that we unify our lives and offer all their disparate elements toward God in and through Jesus. Here we have the spiritual meaning of worship, discipleship, and mission.

Therefore, worship as the Bible characterizes it cannot be limited to singing praise and worship songs to God. Although it includes this, it is far more all-encompassing than that. Worship is nothing less than *offering our whole lives back to God through Jesus*. It is taking all the elements that make up human life (family, friendships, money, work, nation, etc.) and presenting them back to the One who gives them their ultimate meaning in the first place. But what is discipleship if it is not the same type of action? Surely, discipleship is taking all that is me (body and soul) and over a lifetime, directing it to God through Jesus. But the discerning reader would immediately notice that this sounds like a good definition of mission as well, because mission, insofar that it involves us, entails the redemption of a lost world and bringing it back to God. This is what constitutes the biblical idea of holiness—the redemption of the everyday and of everything; oneness in response to the One.

> He who divides his life between God and the world, giving the world what belongs to it in order to save for God what belongs to Him, refuses to give God the service commanded by him, that service which consists in giving the one direction to all the energy, the sanctification of the everyday in the world and in the soul.[17]

And for us, the people of the New Covenant, it is Jesus who provides us with the model of perfect worship and true holiness. Jesus is the center point where God's claim and human response correlate. He is the perfect human being, the true Israel, who has offered up perfect worship and in his redeeming death brought God's salvation in the world. In a real sense, we are his act of worship, his offering to God. And we his people are drawn into the very life and love of God through him. And our love of God is offered through him. This is what makes us Christ-ians—one's belonging to Jesus the Messiah. And it is precisely here that Christology comes to the fore yet again. It focuses our allegiance to God in and through Jesus the Messiah. We are bound to him.

Idolatrous Views of Jesus

Clearly this calls forth a response involving the whole person—what the Bible describes as an offering of the heart. Monotheistic faith has to do with the surrender of the heart. To ask and answer the question, "What is the treasure of my heart to which I owe allegiance?" For Luther, even the word

"God," understood rightly, demands ultimate allegiance. This is what the first commandment is all about. There are strong impulses to false worship inherent in the human condition. The claim of the one true God is set against the competing claims of the many false gods. In the following diagram we see an idolatrous view of god overshadowing the true monotheism. Our response is to go off in many directions, none of them leading back to God.

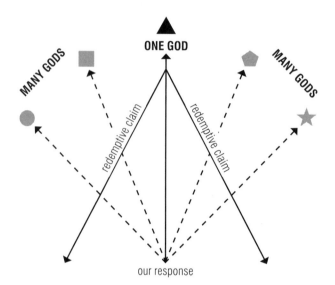

Only the true God can give unity, wholeness, and security to a human being. Therefore, the human heart, to be true to its original purpose, should have only one God. But we resist the all-encompassing claim and seek to find refuge in false gods. The question we all face is whether we will surrender our heart to the God of Israel and Jesus Christ or to an idol. In the language of Paul Tillich's existential theology, monotheism is about our ultimate concern. God, the one and only God, can be the object of our ultimate concern, since only the one God is ultimate. Without a living monotheistic faith, a person's life will inevitably be fragmentary. To paraphrase Yeats, things fall apart, the center does not hold.

Idolatry is insidious; it plays upon our deepest insecurities, appeals to our fearfulness, and therefore nourishes our fallen instinct to flee from the holy One whose love will redeem, purge, and cleanse the soul. For the person of faith, idolatry is a constant temptation, an encroachment on the true understanding of God. We can never control or manipulate the Lord. A relationship with him, while bringing utter completion to the human, paradoxically also creates a secret constant unrest in the life of the disciple. It raises a thousand questions about how we live, what we value, how we spend our money, what we do with our sexuality. The presence of God creates a constant tension in our lives, because a sort of holy terror is awakened by a contact with the Divine.

> [Our encounter with God] plunges us into an intensely dramatic participation in history. Every situation is pregnant with ultimate possibility; every moment is made explosive by the presence of infinite power. When God . . . appears, the reverberations in human existence cannot be silenced. He is not a problem to be solved; he creates problems through his nearness, his threats, his insistent demands, his irresistible intention. It is not so much that we raise questions about him, than that he raises questions of us.[18]

To encounter Jesus is to be changed by him and to embark on a lifelong journey to become like him. But to become a little Jesus is no small task. It requires real moral and spiritual effort, and few do it well. We can acknowledge without too much shame that the attempt to escape the claims of Jesus are common to all of us, no matter our situation. Hear Paul Tillich:

> Man wishes to flee from God. . . . Men of all kinds, prophets and reformers, saints and atheists . . . have had the same experience. . . . A man who has never tried to escape God never has experienced God, namely, that God who is *really* God. . . . A god from whom one can successfully flee is proved by that very success to be an idol. God is inescapable. He is God because he is inescapable . . .[19]

One of these fugitive ways is the path of idolatry. We have seen how our image of God clarifies or distorts our basic conception of God and substitutes a false experience for the true, transforming God encounter. Idolatry also invites us to give our allegiance to that which is not God, thereby fragmenting us spiritually by inviting us to give our loyalty to multiple gods. All that can be said about idolatry in relation to God can be said in relation to Jesus because Jesus is our Lord and the focal point of Christian faith.

Everyone has a god, in the sense that everyone puts something first in one's life: money, power, prestige, self, career, love and so forth. There must be something in your life that operates as your source of meaning and strength, something that you regard, at least implicitly, as the supreme power in your life. If you think your priority in life is to be a transcendent person, you will have a God with a capital letter. If you think of your highest value as a cause, an ideal, or an ideology, you will have a god with a small letter. Either way you will have something that is divine for you.

To believe that Jesus is divine is to choose to make him, and what he stands for, your God. To deny this is to make someone else your god and to relegate Jesus and what he stands for to second place in your scale of values.[20] Our way to God is through the redeeming love of Jesus Christ. Therefore, any false idea of Jesus will destroy the fabric of a New Testament faith. False ideas devastate the way of Jesus from the inside. At the least, idolatry fosters an immature following of Jesus. That is why false images of Jesus are so insidious, and this is the reason why we must strive to constantly reJesus our lives and the church.

Fifty Ways to Leave Your Lover

Human beings, including Jesus' disciples, have become artful in developing ways in which to escape from the all-encompassing claims of God in Jesus. Any discussion about true encounters with God must therefore include ways in which we try and avoid him, to qualify the God relationship, to ameliorate the tension he creates in our lives. We have found the analysis of Paul Minear in *Eyes of Faith* extremely useful, and so we use his material as a basis for this section.[21] Note how the all-encompassing nature of existential monotheism comes to the fore here.

Idolatry

Idolatry is making our own gods according to our own image and likeness. One of the basic urges of idolatry is the human desire to initiate one's own relationship to God and thereby control God. "Man worships idols precisely because of his ability to see them, to know them, to have power over them. But he can never observe God in the same way in which he can reflect on the beauty and power of his idol."[22] In becoming idolaters, we try to diminish the power and presence of God in our lives and minimize his impact on us. It's an ancient dodge.

Vacating the Arena

Vacating the arena is attempting to leave the arena of engagement and become a spectator, thereby trying to reverse the roles. God becomes the actor, and we become the critical observer. We try to become "investigators of God's claims."[23] But this attempt to escape is futile because God cannot and will not simply be observed by us. He can be truly known only by existential involvement. Key knowledge is denied to the detached observer in precisely those questions that are the most decisive in determining his destiny. Besides, people cannot forgive themselves of their own sins or even keep death away. God cannot be dodged by these means. "Existential concern expels speculative detachment."[24]

Trying to Hide

In reality there is nowhere to hide. When God invades our lives, he forces us out of our corners and into the arena. And we cannot hide from God anyway, for as the psalmist writes, "Where can I flee from your presence?" (Ps 139:7). We carry the issues deep within us. No human can fully evade the issue of God.

Religiosity

As we have seen in chapters 2 and 3, we try to escape God by attempting to "preserve mementos of God's former visits in ritual and law, to idolize these, to substitute legal observance and cultic sacrifice for 'knowledge of God' . . . The religious person is also inclined to speak of God in the third person, albeit with apparent reverence, and thus to remove himself from the magnetic field of divine compulsions. Man can forget God in the very act of speaking of him."[25] Religiosity is one of the biggest cop-outs known to the human. It objectifies God and thus seeks to control him.

Building Compartments

By building compartments the dodger consents to God's authority in the area where that seems desirable but at the same time tries to maintain his autonomy in other areas. "But God does not respect these man-made fences. Man's total existence is known by him. When he speaks, he claims total sovereignty."[26]

False Dualisms

False dualisms occur when we try to erect walls between the sacred and the secular and confining God to the sacred realm. But there is no such concept of religion in the Scriptures, "for there is no experience which as such can be defined as religious, and no experience which lies outside of the divine radius. [But] God does not call man to endorse a religion, but to view all life religiously, i.e., in its relation to God."[27]

Trying to Draw a Line Between Flesh and Spirit

As we've pointed out, the biblical God is the Creator of both body and spirit. In every personal encounter, he forces us to participate as a unit. He does not draw the false line between flesh and spirit and deal with one in isolation. We are to offer our bodies as living sacrifices.

Trying to Draw False Distinctions Between Private and Public Life

We try to distinguish between events of significance to the individual and those having social impact. But in a real way, "every event is social because it takes place within the web of personal relations and involves, in however small a compass, issues of ultimate concern."[28]

In tackling these attempts to hide, the biblical writers "fight against any false separation of sacred from the secular, against any reduction in the territory under divine rule."[29] And as disciples, we are called not to escape from God but to fully engage him, to become like him. We are the people of the way of Jesus, and as Glen Stassen and David Gushee point out, when this way "is thinned down, marginalized or avoided, then churches and Christians lose their antibodies against infection by secular ideologies that manipulate Christians into serving some other lord. We fear precisely that kind of idolatry now."[30]

⟵ The Christ-Like God

Any chapter exploring monotheism must look at how Jesus changes, or rather develops, our understanding of God. We must ensure that the link between the one God of the Scriptures and Jesus the Messiah is properly understood, because this will have massive implications for the basic thrust of reJesus.

It is clear from the New Testament that Jesus fundamentally alters the way we understand everything about God and faith. He "affects every aspect of Christian doctrine and gives distinction to its understanding of God, humanity, sin, salvation and the eschaton (the end times)."[31] To make this claim, Dennis Kinlaw focuses mainly on those texts in which Jesus reveals the nature of his eternal and intimate relationship to God. He particularly focuses on the implications of Father-Son relationship in the Gospel of John. Chapters 1, 5, 9, 10, 14, and 17 are saturated with texts about Jesus' insider status and knowledge of the Godhead. In these passages, Jesus claims to be the same as God, and he fully claims the attributes and functions of God. Then, in Mark 10:17–22, the confession of "God alone" is coupled with Jesus' command to "follow me," suggesting that faith in one God and following Jesus are one and the same thing (see Mark 2:7–12). In Matthew 23:9–10, the uniqueness of God, the "one Father," is paralleled by the uniqueness of Jesus, the "one master" who stands in contrast to the multiplicity of earthly masters. This point is also emphasized in 1 Timothy 2:5–6, where the contrast is between one God/one Mediator and the multiplicity of gods and mediators suggested by the Gnostic theology that Paul was combating. When we add this with the comprehensive high Christology of Colossians and Revelation, we can see how the person and work of Jesus qualify the oneness of God and yet never violate the essential monotheistic revelation of the Bible. N. T. Wright says,

> All the signs are that the earliest Christians came to the startling conclusion that they were under obligation, without ceasing to be Jewish monotheists, to worship Jesus . . . For Paul, "there is one God (the Father, from whom are all things and we to him), and one Lord, Jesus Christ (through whom are all things and we through him)" (1 Cor 8:6). This stunning adaptation of the Shema . . . emphasizing creation and redemption as equally originating in the Father and equally implemented through Jesus, encapsulates, at the earliest stages of Christianity . . . everything that later generations and centuries would struggle to say about Jesus. From here on, we must say that if Trinitarian theology had not existed, it would be necessary to invent it.[32]

And as startling as this sounds, we can say with confidence that the thinking about God in the early church did not begin with reflecting on God; it focused first on Jesus. Jesus reveals himself not only as the door into salvation (John 10:7) but also the entry point into the knowledge of the one true God. Again, Kinlaw makes this clear: "Logically this means we should begin our theological studies with Jesus, who, as John said, 'has made him [God] known' (John 1:18)."[33] This makes Jesus Revealer and Mediator at the same time (John 14:6).

Albert Nolan, another key New Testament scholar, says it this way, and we quote him at length because of the sheer relevance for our understanding of God:

> I have chosen this [the Christ-like God] approach because it enables us . . . to avoid the perennial mistake of superimposing upon the life and personality of Jesus our preconceived ideas of what God is supposed to be like . . .
>
> By his words and praxis, Jesus himself changed the content of the word "God." If we do not allow him to change our image of God, we will not be able to say that he is our Lord and our God. To choose him as our God is to make him the source of our information about divinity and to refuse to superimpose upon him our own ideas of divinity.
>
> This is the meaning of the traditional assertion that Jesus is the Word of God. Jesus reveals God to us, God does not reveal Jesus to us. God is not the Word of Jesus, that is to say, our ideas about God cannot throw any light upon the life of Jesus. To argue from God to Jesus instead of arguing from Jesus to God is to put the cart before the horse. This, of course, is what many Christians have tried to do. It has generally led them into a series of meaningless speculations which only cloud the issue and which prevent Jesus from revealing God to us.
>
> We cannot deduce anything about Jesus from what we think we know about God; we must deduce everything about God from what we do know about Jesus. Thus, when we say that Jesus is divine, we do not wish to add anything to what we have been able to discover about him so far, nor do we wish to change anything that we have said about him. To say now suddenly that Jesus is divine does not change our understanding of Jesus; it changes our understanding of divinity. We are not only turning away from the gods of money, power, prestige or self; we are turning away from all the old images of a personal God in order to find our God in Jesus and what he stood for.
>
> This is not to say that we must abolish the Old Testament and reject the God of Abraham, Isaac and Jacob. It means that if we accept Jesus as divine, we must reinterpret the Old Testament from Jesus' point of view and try to understand the God of Abraham, Isaac and Jacob in the way in which Jesus did . . . We have seen what Jesus was like. If we now wish to treat him as our God, we would have to conclude that our God does not want to be served by us, but wants to serve us; . . . If this is a true picture of God, then God is more truly human, more thoroughly humane, than any human being. God is, what Schillebeeckx has called, a Deus humanissimus, a supremely human God.[34]

Luther was a theologian who truly understood this christological re-framing of God and the implications for the Christian faith. And we ought to be thoroughly thankful because in rediscovering it, he once again unleashed the power of the gospel in the Western world. Commenting on the critics of one of his most important books (*The Bondage of the Will*), Luther writes, "I have written that . . . one must look at the revealed God (Jesus) when we sing in the hymn, 'Jesus Christ is the lord of hosts and there is no other God.' But they [his theological opponents] will pass over all of these places and take only those passages in my writing that deal with the hidden God."[35] A little earlier in the book he writes, "If you have Him [Christ] then you also have the hidden God together with Him who has been revealed."[36]

We admit that this sounds a little convoluted at first, but Luther is here countering the medieval theologians' tendency to focus on ontology (the being of God, the hidden God) instead of Christology (the revealed God). Speculation about the mystery of God's inner being was so wrapped up in speculative religious philosophy that the minds of average believers were frazzled and access to the love of God through the gospel was thereby restricted. This rightly infuriated Luther. He insisted that if we want to truly see God, we need only look at Jesus, for in Jesus we have received the fullness of God, and we need look no further. Says Luther, "The only God we see is the God clothed in the promises of the Gospel."[37] Or as Jesus says, "Whoever has seen me has seen the Father. How can you say, 'Show us the Father'?" (John 14:9).

The implications of this intratrinitarian shift within the revelation of God are paradigmatic. Executive lordship is now conferred directly on Jesus, and with this shift comes a realignment of the believer's focus and loyalties. So important is this shift that the Christian faith pivots on this precise point—it is Jesus who sets Christianity apart from the other two monotheistic faiths, Judaism and Islam. Our understanding of God is now always filtered through the prism of Jesus Christ. We cannot understand God if we don't engage him through Jesus. He is the way, the truth, and the life (John 14:6).

This redefinition of biblical monotheism around the role of Jesus can be called Christocentric monotheism, because it realigns our loyalties to God around the person and work of Jesus Christ. Jesus thus becomes the pivotal point in our relation to God, and it is to him that we must give our allegiance and loyalty. Jesus is Lord! And this lordship is expressed in exactly the same way that it is in the Old Testament. It is the covenant claim of God over our lives, the unshakable center of the Christian creed and confession.[38]

Alan's grandfather used to say this ditty,

Roses are red
Violets are blueish
If it wasn't for Jesus
We'd all be Jewish

Now, it's not really true, but it does highlight the role that Jesus plays in redefining the people of God. Jesus changes everything, and this is critical to understand if we are going to recalibrate the church around the person of Jesus as we must at this point of time. Wright makes this call to reJesus our understanding of God,

Unstinting Compasssion

Mother Teresa

Few people have embodied the role of a little Jesus quite as sublimely as Agnes Gonxha Bojaxhiu, better known as Mother Teresa. When she was eighteen she joined the Sisters of Loreto in Dublin, Ireland, and, shortly after taking her vows as a nun, found herself teaching high school in Calcutta, India (known today as Kolkata). In 1948, after several years of witnessing widespread suffering and poverty in Calcutta, she received permission to leave her teaching position and work among the poor population. She opened a school for slum children, relying on volunteer and financial support. Two years later Mother Teresa was granted permission to start her own order, aiming to care for "the hungry, the naked, the homeless, the crippled, the blind, the lepers, all those people who feel unwanted, unloved, uncared for throughout society, people that have become a burden to the society and are shunned by everyone." Originally named the *Diocesan Congregation of the Calcutta Diocese* by the Vatican, the order began with only thirteen members in Calcutta. Today it is known as the Missionaries of Charity and consists of more than 4,000 nuns who care for underprivileged, disadvantaged, and disabled persons through orphanages, AIDS hospices, and charity centers all over the world. Another focus of Mother Teresa's lifetime ministry was to provide people with the opportunity to die with dignity. Calcutta's Home for the Dying, a free hospice for the poor, provides residents with medical attention and allows "people who lived like animals to die like angels—loved and wanted." Mother Teresa herself passed away on September 5, 1997. Her way of loving those with no capacity to repay her for her kindness more than qualifies Mother Teresa as a little Jesus.

My proposal is not that we know what the word "god" means, and manage somehow to fit Jesus into that. Instead, I suggest, that we think historically about a young Jew, possessed of a desperately risky, indeed apparently crazy, vocation, riding into Jerusalem in tears, denouncing the Temple, and dying on a Roman cross—and we somehow allow our meaning for the word "god" to be recentered around that point.[39]

Among other things, this will mean that the confession "Yahweh is Lord" will transform into the primary New Testament confession of "Jesus is Lord," bearing within it the full implications and the weight of monotheistic understanding of God. And what this means in turn is that our loyalty to God must now be mediated via the person of Jesus. Paul insists that the actual function of lordship, normally associated with the Father, is now passed on to Jesus.[40] God actually saves as well as claims us in Jesus, and this claim demands the response of our very lives. Everything we are and all that we have is included in this claim. This was a realization that could not be avoided by the Confessing Church (led by Karl Barth and Dietrich Bonhoeffer) in Nazi Germany when they developed the Barmen Declaration to counter the heretical claims of the so-called Nazi Christians. They confessed

> Just as Jesus Christ is the pledge of the forgiveness of sins, just so—and with the same earnestness—is he also God's mighty claim on our whole life; in him we encounter a joyous liberation from the godless claims of this world to free and thankful service to his creatures. We repudiate the false teaching that there are areas of our life in which we do not belong to Jesus Christ but another lord, areas in which we do not need justification and sanctification through him.[41]

Here lies the interface between the disciple and God. It is through the redeeming lordship of Jesus. And when we talk of lordship, we are talking about God's redemptive claim on our lives and our existential response to this claim. And here is where it begins to impact us in a practical way. Perhaps we can illustrate it by going back to our basic diagram (see next page). Our view of God is as the one true God. Our response is an existential one, through the redemptive work of Jesus.

As in the *Shema*, we can see all the elements of monotheism are present. The link between the one God (monotheism) and lifestyle (ethics) are fully maintained. The difference between the Old Testament and the New Testament understandings of God is found in the person and work of the Messiah, hence Christocentric monotheism.

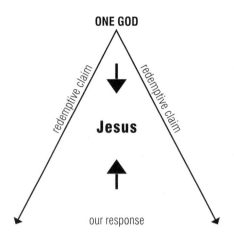

A Quick Word on the Trinity

By now, any theologically sensitive reader would have asked the question, "Does all this focus on Jesus destroy the trinitarian fabric out of which comes a genuinely Christian understanding of God and the world?" The last thing we wish to do is challenge the fundamental revelation of God as triune Being. We affirm this with all orthodox Christians everywhere. Even though the later formulations are complex, overly ontological in perspective, and missionally clumsy, they are nonetheless correct in what they affirm. Rather, what we want to do here is reinstate a more primitive form of trinitarian understanding, one much closer to the trinitarianism of the New Testament than the denser philosophical formulations of the later church. This has massive implications for any church recalibrating itself along the lines suggested in this book. Renewal involves going back to basics, recovering our elemental message, and jettisoning the unnecessary in order to focus on the essential. Missiologically speaking, it is also essential that we travel lighter than we have in Christendom past. We believe we need to be as theologically unencumbered as possible so that we may more approximate the way the early Christians understood their relation to God. This has significant implication for missional movements and the rapid transfer of ideas, as Alan has demonstrated in *The Forgotten Ways*.[42]

And as for a christological center and starting point, we would argue that any understanding of the Trinity must of necessity start with Jesus because it is he who introduces us into the Trinity in the first place. Any approach to the Trinity must go through Christology and should stress the Christ-likeness of God, thus enabling us to move from the relatively known to the relatively unknown. Furthermore, to really appreciate the trinitarian revelation, we need to frame whatever understanding we glean from Jesus in the light of the Israel story that precedes the Messiah. As we noted from Wright's scholarship, without the Israel story we cannot understand Jesus properly, and once again, everything goes awry. Or to say it another way, to understand the New Testament, we must know the story that gives it meaning.[43] And so we are back to the *Shema*, the fundamental confession of Israel then and now. Any true understanding of the Trinity arises out of an understanding of the nature of biblical monotheism. Otherwise what we end up with is tritheism, which certainly is not what the Bible teaches.

In returning to the essentials in this way, we are hoping to recover the powerful dynamic, the ethos, and the faith structure of existential monotheism. This kind of monotheism tended to recede as the dogmatic and metaphysical interests of the Greek and Latin theologians became dominant and replaced the existential demands of the faith (othopraxy) with the need for orthodoxy.[44]

To Sum Up

Any examination of our own lives and communities will no doubt reveal that we are all somehow torn between the great escape, as described above, and the trembling desire to be more like Jesus, to know God more fully, and to be truly known by him in return. Ever since the fall we have been fluctuating between the desire to hide from God in the garden and to reveal ourselves to him. In Jesus, God has come to us. We know from him that God is *for* us and that it is the nature of his love that he desires to have us fully to himself. The incarnation reveals to us a God who utterly understands our condition and yet one who is able, through his sacrificial suffering on our behalf, to raise us to be the kind of people God wanted in the first place. But we must not avoid the radical place Jesus has in this schema of redemption. In Jesus, we are not only redeemed, we are claimed, and this claim, true to the existential monotheism that gives it meaning, is exclusive. We can but echo the words of Paul and make them into our confession,

> For us there is one God, the Father, from whom are all things and for whom we exist, and one Lord, Jesus Christ, through whom are all things and through whom we exist. (1 Cor 8:6)

⟿ Notes

1. "Note in particular the example of the flood account in the Gilgamesh Epic, where the flood seems to be a result of Enlil's whim. It was only through the goodness of Enki that Utnapishtim was warned and escaped from the deluge." D. L. Christensen, *Deuteronomy* 1–11 (Word Biblical Commentary 6A; Dallas: Word, 1998; electronic ed., Logos Library System).

2. D. N. Freedman, "God in the New Testament," *Anchor Bible Dictionary* (New York: Doubleday, 1996; electronic ed.).

3. Ibid., electronic edition. Interestingly, the structure of Paul's letters indicates the same commitment to the unbreakable link between understanding of God with lifestyle. New Testament scholars talk about the indicative and the imperative structure of the Pauline letters. The first half deals with teaching about God, salvation, and other theological issues. The second half invariably talks about ethical issues.

4. Scot McKnight, *Jesus Creed: Loving God, Loving Others* (Brewster, Mass.: Paraclete, 2004).

5. "Today's church must not forget that the earliest theology in the New Testament is relational or existential rather than propositional or creedal." Marvin Wilson, *Our Father Abraham: Jewish Roots of the Christian Faith* (Grand Rapids, Mich.: Eerdmans, 1989), 138.

6. We are hardly alone in this. See Martin Buber, Søren Kierkegaard, Karl Barth, Helmut Theilicke, Paul Minear, Emil Brunner, John McQuarrie, et al.

7. "[M]onotheism is an outcome of the exclusive claim of Yahweh, rather than a conceptual hypothesis resulting from human effort to gain a unitary view of his world." Paul Minear, *Eyes of Faith: A Study in the Biblical Point of View* (Philadelphia: Westminster, 1946), 24.

8. To the philosopher, monotheism can be defined as "the doctrine of, or belief in, the existence of but one God." And following such a definition, one is either a monotheist or not. And whether one is or not can be determined by objective standards. People may hold to a doctrine of the existence of one God without ever involving the character of his or her personal relationship to that God. But this is not a biblical (existential) understanding of monotheism. In a strange sense, a biblical monotheism cannot even be defined, and no biblical writer attempts such a definition. At the most there is a witness to an encounter, a description of God's visit, to which a specific person (or community) responds in faith that for him (or her, or them) there is only one Lord. The effect on the person or community will be the confession that God alone is our Creator and Redeemer, that God and God alone has the right to determine our duty and demand our loyalty, that our destiny lies in God's hands alone. Others may have gods, but in reality they are idols.

9. Minear, *Eyes of Faith*, 25–26.

10. Hirsch, *Forgotten Ways*, 93.

11. Eugene H. Peterson, *Reversed Thunder* (San Francisco: Harper & Row, 1988), 117–18.

12. Notes from many discussions had with Mark Sayers during 2006—Alan.

13. See also Hirsch, *Forgotten Ways*, "'Little Jesus' in Disneyland," 106ff., and Frost, *Exiles*, 225–27, for a more thorough analysis of consumerism in relation to discipleship.

14. Minear, *Eyes of Faith*, 21.

15. See especially Bob Roberts Jr., *Glocalization: How Followers of Jesus Engage a Flat World* (Grand Rapids, Mich.: Zondervan, 2007), 40ff. This is an idea akin to Abraham Kuyper's idea of sphere sovereignty. See also Bob Roberts Jr., *Transformation: How Glocal Churches Transform Lives and the World* (Grand Rapids, Mich.: Zondervan, 2006).

16. Roberts, *Transformation*, 37–40.

17. Buber, *Mamre*, 107–8.

18. Minear, *Eyes of Faith*, 16.

19. Paul Tillich, quoted in Minear, *Eyes of Faith*, 17.

20. Albert Nolan, *Jesus Before Christianity* (Maryknoll, N.Y.: Orbis, 1978), 166.

21. Minear, *Eyes of Faith*, 17–22.

22. Ibid., 17.

23. Ibid.

24. Ibid., 19.

25. Ibid.

26. Ibid., 20.

27. Ibid., 20–21.

28. Ibid., 22.

29. Ibid.

30. Glen H. Stassen and David P. Gushee, *Kingdom Ethics: Following Jesus in Contemporary Context* (Downers Grove, Ill.: InterVarsity, 2003), 11.

31. Dennis F. Kinlaw, *Let's Start with Jesus: A New Way of Doing Theology* (Grand Rapids, Mich.: Zondervan, 2005), 20.

32. N. T. Wright, *The Challenge of Jesus* (London: SPCK, 2000), 78, 79.

33. Kinlaw, *Let's Start with Jesus*, 27.

34. Nolan, *Jesus Before Christianity*, 165–67.

35. Martin Luther, *The Bondage of the Will*, in *Luther's Works* (ed. Jaroslav Pelikan et al.; St. Louis: Concordia, 1955–), vol. 5, 50. However, he does admit that there is a sense in which God does hide himself; for instance, in human form (the incarnation), in suffering, in a naked man on a cross, in persecution. But he does this in order to humble the pride of human reason so that he may not be found by cleverness but by faith.

36. Ibid.

37. Ibid., 48.

38. Hirsch, *Forgotten Ways*, 93.

39. Wright, *The Challenge of Jesus*, 92.

40. "[H]e [God] raised him from the dead and seated him at his right hand in the heavenly realms, far above all rule and authority, power and dominion, and every title that can be given, not only in the present age but also in the one to come. And God placed all things under his feet and appointed him to be head over everything for the church, which is his body, the fullness of him who fills everything in every way" (Eph 1:20–23 NIV). In 1 Corinthians 15:25–28 (NIV), Paul says, "For he [Jesus] must reign until he has put all his enemies under his feet. . . . When he has done this, then the Son himself will be made subject to him who put everything under him, so that God may be all in all." Cf. Hirsch, *Forgotten Ways*, 93.

41. "The Barmen Declaration of 1934," quoted from Woelfel, *Bonhoeffer's Theology*, 242.

42. See Hirsch, *Forgotten Ways*, ch. 3, for reasons why we need to distill and simplify our message in the West.

43. Jonathan Wilson, *God So Loved the World* (Grand Rapids, Mich.: Baker, 2001), 13.

44. Harnack's famous pronouncement maintained that dogma, in its conception and development, is a work of the Greek spirit on the soil of the gospel. Although Harnack seems to have thought of this work of the Greek spirit as to some extent a deterioration, he acknowledged its necessity: "Christianity without dogma, that is, without a clear expression of its content, is inconceivable." See John Macquarrie, *Existentialism* (Philadelphia: Westminster, 1972), 28–29.

Chapter Six

Three . . . Two . . . One . . . Engage

*As civilization advances, the sense of
wonder almost necessarily declines. Such
decline is an alarming symptom of our
state of mind. Mankind will not perish for
want of information, but only for want of
appreciation. The beginning of our happiness
lies in the understanding that life without
wonder is not worth living. What we lack is
not a will to believe, but a will to wonder.*
—Abraham Heschel

*We live or die consumed by fire or fire
Our hope lies in the choice of pyre
. . . to be redeemed from fire by fire*
—T. S. Eliot

Having been claimed by the God who reveals himself in Jesus, we need to seriously consider something of the dynamic of engagement between Jesus and his people. How can we know him in the fullness of human knowledge (Eph 1:17–23)? What role does revelation play in guiding us to a true experience and life-transforming encounter with the One who saves? How do we engage the Christ of the Bible more directly? Our journey here must take us into a reconsideration of ways of apprehension and knowing, the relation between subjective and objective knowledge, direct and indirect approaches to Jesus. Most of all, we want to open up new, and yet strangely ancient, pathways into an up-to-date experience of Jesus as Lord and center of our faith.

Encountering Jesus Afresh

Much of what gets in the way of a true and life-altering encounter with Jesus can be traced to the problem of worldview. We have already seen how existential monotheism, reinterpreted christologically, radicalizes our understanding of things, but as much as a new application of worldview can change things and unify our world, another one can equally distort. This is because worldview is effectively the lens through which we engage and thus interpret the world. This issue of worldview plays itself out rather strangely in the Western spiritual and theological tradition when it comes to the understanding of knowledge, or apprehension, of God. The Western church is largely influenced by the more speculative and philosophical worldview ushered in by the Hellenistic world. The problem is that our Scriptures are formed by a significantly different way of seeing things—the Hebraic. We addressed this at length in *The Shaping of Things to Come*, which surprised some readers. Why introduce Hebraic thinking into a book on the missional church? For us, though, it goes to the heart of why the Western church has moved so far off course. The church is operating out of a Hellenistic worldview that makes it difficult to appropriate all that the New Testament is saying. If this is the case in the area of ecclesiology, it is all the more important in the study of Christology.

To try to get to the essential difference between Hellenistic and Hebraic worldview, some writers have called Greek thinking *step logic* and Hebraic thinking *block logic*. The Hellenists used a tightly contained step logic whereby one would argue from premise to conclusion; each step in the process is linked tightly to the next in a coherent, rational, linear fashion. "The conclusion, however, was usually limited to one point of view—the human being's perception of reality."[1] In contrast, Hebraic thinking tended to express concepts in self-contained units, or blocks, of thought. The blocks did not necessarily fit together in an obviously linear or harmonious pattern, particularly when one block represented a human perspective on truth and another the divine. "This way of thinking created a propensity for paradox, antinomy, or apparent contradiction, as one block stood in tension—and often illogical relation—to the other. Hence, polarity of thought or dialectic often characterized block thinking."[2] This creates problems for us, trained as we are in Hellenistic approach to thinking, when we try to grasp Scripture. In reading the Bible, in recalibrating, we need to "undergo a kind of intellectual conversion"[3] from the Hellenistic to the Hebraic mind.

It surprised us to learn recently that throughout the Apollo missions to the moon, spacecraft regularly drifted off course. In fact, more than 80 percent of their journey through space was slightly off course. To conserve fuel, the spaceships drift through space, moved by the gravitational pull of the earth. Jet engines are used occasionally only when the ship is getting too far off course to readjust their coordinates and get them back on track. The occasional burst of their massive engines completes the readjustment and keeps them heading toward their destination. We think this is a useful metaphor for the church today. Many people are claiming that the church has been drifting off course and needs a burst of renewed power to get back on track. However, for spacecraft, that surge of propulsion works only if the coordinates are accurate and the flight plan is properly conceived. Today, many voices are calling the church back on track, acting like power surges for a drifting church. But our contention is that the church needs to go back to the drawing board and work again on its flight plan. If the plan is wrong, all the bursts of renewed energy will only push us further into space.

One of those areas that need to be re-examined is that of worldview. Without an appreciation of the Hebraic worldview from which the New Testament was written, we can keep surging the church's engines and keep getting more and more lost, even though it looks like we're doing the right thing. By thinking in Hellenistic terms, we construct a highly philosophical approach to our world and indeed the Scriptures. Jacques Ellul notes that our fundamental problems in perception can be traced back to a change in the basic understanding of revelation, namely, the transition from history to philosophy:

> I *believe that all the errors in Christian thought go back to this* [italics added]. I might say that all the theologians I have named had correct thoughts, that their theology was true, that there was not heresy in the one and orthodoxy in the other, but that all of them are caught in the philosophical circle and pose metaphysical problems. All seek an answer by way of ontological thinking. All regard the biblical text or known revelation, as points of departure for philosophy, whether by translation into philosophical terms or as references of thought. They had intellectual, metaphysical, and epistemological questions, etc., and they adduced the biblical text with a view to providing a system of answers to their questions. They used the biblical text to meet their own needs instead of listening to what it really was [saying].[4]

In other words, as Ellul goes on to explain, the shift away from the existential and historical revelation of God toward philosophical formulations diluted the nature of the truth the church proclaimed. Even though the theologians Ellul refers to expressed a profound and authentic faith marked by a concern for truth, "all this was undermined and even falsified by the initial transition of the idea of revelation" in the first place. The die was cast. Very soon the developments in philosophical thinking became stronger than the biblical truth that they sought to retain. The theologians had forgotten the essential

Revolutionary Advocacy

Rigoberta Menchú

As a little Jesus, Rigoberta Menchú is undaunted in her advocacy for the poor and the rights of indigenous groups worldwide. She is noted to have said, "The work of revolutionary Christians is above all to condemn and denounce the injustices committed against the people." She was born in 1959 to a poor Indian family in Guatemala, and as a child Rigoberta Menchú would work alongside her family on local farms and large plantations picking coffee. In her teenage years, Menchú became involved in social reform activities through the Catholic Church and played a part in the women's rights movement. During a time of intense social upheaval between upper class landowners and the country's indigenous population, the oppressive Guatemalan regime accused Menchú's family of taking part in guerrilla activities. Her father, mother, and brother were all killed by security forces within only a couple years of each other. These horrors led the young Menchú to join the Committee of the Peasant Union, an activist group that campaigned against human rights violations. She later joined the more radical "31st of January Popular Front," through which she helped educate the indigenous Guatemalan population in resistance to massive military oppression. In 1981 Menchú fled the country, but still organized resistance to oppression in Guatemala. She has become known as an advocate for the rights of indigenous peasants, refusing to keep silent about their sufferings and struggles. Her autobiography, *I, Rigoberta Menchú,* attracted considerable international attention to her undertakings. Menchú has attempted at least three times to return to Guatemala to plead the cause of the Indian peasants, but death threats have forced her to return into exile each time. She has received several international awards for her efforts, including a Nobel Peace Prize in 1992.

point that God does not reveal himself by means of a philosophical system or a moral code or a metaphysical construction but rather enters human history and accompanies his people. Ellul concludes:

> The Hebrew Bible (even in the wisdom books) is not a philosophical construction or a *system* of knowledge. It is a series of stories that are not myths intended

to veil or unveil objective and abstract truths. These stories are one history, the history of the people of God, the history of God's agreements and disagreements with this people, the history of loyalty and disobedience. There is nothing else but history . . . a history that tells us that God is with and for us, but that does not speak about God in himself, or provide any theory about God.[5]

This history-anchored worldview values the action and word of God over a philosophical construct of his character. It also requires obedience in order to truly comprehend what is being revealed. In this worldview, the Bible is read as the history of God's self-revelation. It proves that God reveals himself in real life, in observable and distinct ways that defy neat explanation or simple formulation. Under the new Hellenistic worldview, the Bible is approached differently. God's revelation was interpreted as the climax of the teaching of Socrates, and the Bible was interpreted by the intellectual tools of Greek philosophy. The Torah, for example, is seen merely as a moral code, not unlike the Twelve Tablets, a Greco-Roman legal code. What resulted was of decisive importance. Instead of listening to the text as it was, theologians tried to draw from it a coherent philosophical system, whether modeled after Plato, Aristotle, Heraclitus, or Epicurus. It all came to the same thing. The biblical stories were treated as myths from which one had to draw some abstract, universal thought. And so the Christian theological tradition embraced a philosophical approach alien to Jewish epistemology (ways of knowing).[6] The Hebraic framework for the true comprehension of revelation was thus discarded in favor of the Hellenistic. Ellul continued,

> Some will tell me that we have no option but to use our available tools of knowledge even to understand a history. This is true. But I reply that Hebrew thought had its own tools of knowledge that are fully set forth in the language. We should bow and submit and convert to these instead of forcing God's revelation into the strait jacket of Greco-Roman thinking, instead of putting it in this cage of tigers. . . . To convert! This great word has been diluted. The people of the third century and later have been converted to Christianity in morality and religion, but they have kept intact their mode of thinking. Conversion is needed in the mode of thinking, too. . . . Now metaphysics, ethics, and law have radically transformed the meaning of revelation even though formally what is advanced seems to be right, the exposition is faithful, and the interpreters are serious and devout. The problem does not lie with their faith or piety or intelligence but with an integral falsity of meaning.[7]

If we hear Ellul correctly, this is part of the process by which Christianity was essentially subverted into something significantly less, if not entirely different, from the original way Jesus set down for us. Ellul therefore calls us to a new conversion if we are to reJesus, a conversion back to Hebraic thinking in order to rediscover Jesus afresh.

⟵ Letting the Bible Read Us, Not the Other Way Around

In order to reJesus our lives and communities, it is essential that we engage God through the revelation that he has given us in Jesus. And this will mean that we must take the Bible with utmost seriousness and must read it on its own terms if we are to truly comprehend its teachings. But the Bible should not in this process replace Jesus as the focus of our faith. In a way we are not really the "people of the Book," as we are so often called—as far as we can ascertain, it was the Muslims gave us this tag. In a far more fundamental way we can claim rather that we are truly Jesus' people before we are anything else. Our focal point remains the Messiah, and we must be guided by the Bible toward a true experience and understanding of Messiah. The Bible functions something like the wardrobe in C. S. Lewis's Narnia series—it is a gateway to another world; one goes through it in order to get into the knowledge, the love, and the wonder of God.[8] With this in mind, let us look at ways in which we can perhaps renew our love and understanding of Jesus with the Bible in hand.

Part of this journey will mean that we need to learn to value what philosophers call *subjectivity* in relation to truth. And here we find Søren Kierkegaard to be most useful. Kierkegaard stressed how important it was to move beyond mere objective understandings of truth to the subjective appropriation of that truth. He argued the case in one of his books that all truth means subjective change.[9] And he meant by this that if you believe something is really and objectively true (in this case statements about Jesus and the gospel), then it must somehow affect your life. It must become personal. It must become *your* truth, or it is by definition not true. Your values and your association with truth indicate what you really believe is true.

When we look at Jesus, we find that his approach to communicating kingdom truth squares with this very biblical idea of subjectivity in relation to truth. Jesus' method of communication is unbalancing. It destabilizes the smug complacency that stands between the individual and truth. Kierkegaard says,

> Jesus' method is essential to his goal. What Jesus "teaches" cannot be taught in some more objective manner. The listener is forced to confront the full para-

doxical power of "the lesson" and in doing so, is forced to confront himself or herself.[10]

With the previous discussion of the Hellenistic worldview in mind, we feel that so much of the way we approach the Scriptures are overly rationalistic. Perhaps some of our frustration with rationalist and overly modernist approaches to reading Scripture can be highlighted by taking a look at many of our standard commentaries. In writing a book like this, one has to refer to commentaries to glean more insight on a text. But trips to the commentary shelf often prove frustrating and useless when it came to integrating Jesus and his teachings into our lives. Biblical scholars who focus on the grammar, structure, and etymology of a passage and then carefully compare what other scholars have said couch their writings in a language laced with the assumptions of objectivity: the attempt becomes an exercise in investigating God rather than God investigating us. But following a purely rational, linear, historicist approach, we cannot hope to get at the true meaning of a text.

The problem is that the method dictates the outcomes! By not engaging the Jesus referred to in the text, scholars end up objectifying the Bible, making it into knowledge alone. In Martin Buber's terms, they move from an I-and-Thou stance toward an I-and-It in relation to the Scriptures. And herein lies many of our problems when it comes to engaging the God in and through Scripture; we lack the spiritual mechanisms to get beyond the written word to God's own self, and so we get stuck in the wardrobe. We have so attached ourselves to a Cartesian approach to knowledge (the viewpoint of the autonomous, objective, knower) that we have lost the art of participation in the text, of somehow finding ourselves in the text. James calls Scripture a mirror in which we see our true selves (Jas 1:22–25). To use it in an attempt to mine objective knowledge about God is to fall foul of the very thing he warns us about in this text. We think much of what goes by the name biblical exegesis (the critical explanation of a text of Scripture) does exactly this.

Our commitments to exegesis are now so one-dimensional that we no longer know how to connect with the Bible in a much more personally engaged manner. We suggest that alongside the task of exegesis (which we must do), we need to learn the spiritual art of *reading ourselves into the text*, participating in it, normally forbidden to the academic approach. We think that we have much to unlearn in regard to our approach to Scripture, and therefore the God of the Scriptures, and much to relearn as we seek to reJesus our lives and churches. This is not as far-fetched as it might seem at first. Any literature major at college is introduced to the art of reading himself or herself into the fictional text. The reader is invited to take the part of certain agents or players in a novel to try and assess the emotional and human richness of the material. When applied to our engagement with the Scriptures, this approach adds human warmth, pathos, perspective, and a generally richer reading of the text. And as we have already seen, this is part of what Ignatius Loyola demanded of his Jesuits.

One of the ways in which people have tried to overcome the distance between written text and dynamic Word as addressed to us is the use of the ancient practice of *lectio divina*, Latin for "divine reading." The Bible is the Word of God, which is always alive and active, always new. *Lectio divina* is a traditional way of combining prayer and reading the Scriptures so that the Word of God may penetrate our hearts and that we may grow in an intimate relationship with the Lord. It is a natural way of prayer and was developed and practiced by the early monks and then developed by the first Carmelite hermits. It involves a way of reading the Scriptures whereby we gradually let go of our own agenda and open ourselves to what God wants to say to us. It is a way of praying with Scripture that calls one to study, ponder, listen, and, finally, pray from God's Word. Any passage of Scripture can be encountered using *lectio divina*, as long as the passage is not too long. *Lectio divina* is not the same thing as exegesis but is a personal reading of the Scripture and application to one's life. After quieting our hearts and laying our cares aside, worshipers engage the text. *Lectio divina* involves the following four "moments" or readings.

1. *Lectio*: the worshipper is invited to read the passage out loud, per-haps several times. It is best to read the Word of God slowly and reflectively so that it sinks into us.

2. *Meditatio*: After the second reading, we think about the text we have chosen and ruminate upon it so that we take from it what God wants to give us. The reader is called to gravitate to any particular phrase or word that seems to be of particular importance.

3. *Oratio*: This involves a response to the passage. The worshipper opens his or her heart to God. This is not an intellectual exercise but an intuitive conversation or dialogue with God. Here we let our hearts speak to God. This response is directly inspired by our reflec-tion on the Word of God.

4. *Contemplatio*: This involves listening to God. We free ourselves from our own thoughts, both mundane and holy. We open our mind, heart,

and soul to the influence of God. We rest in the Word of God and wait quietly and listen at the deepest level of our being to God speaking within us with in a still small voice.

Any conversation must allow for both sides to communicate, and this most unfamiliar act is allowing oneself to be open to hearing God speak. One of the biases that we bring to the Bible, and one that blocks the possibility of true conversation, is the assumption that we read it. We are the active party. The Jewish approach to Scripture is that we don't read the Bible but rather that it reads us! Our standard practice is to assume we are its interpreter and therefore the arbiter of its meaning. Jewish approaches reverse this: we are not the interpreter, but rather it is the Torah that interprets us. This is because it is God who addresses us in Scripture; hence the idea of revelation that is so important to a biblical worldview. "It is not so much that we raise questions about him, but that that he raises questions of us."[11]

God addresses us and challenges us personally in and through Scripture. When it comes to the Word Become Flesh, Jesus as the incarnated *logos*, we see this whole questioning played out in dynamic ways. The kingdom presses itself upon the world in Jesus. The rule of God challenges the false claims to loyalty that so easily ensnare us. Jesus in his teachings and actions is constantly driving us back to our assumptions, forcing us to play our cards, bringing us to account, demanding that we respond to the redeeming love of God expressed through him. What is clear is that when we engage Jesus, we never get to objectively interpret him—he does not allow us that epistemological luxury. In Jesus, love is on the offensive, wooing us into the transforming encounter with God. Just try bringing Jesus and the Bible into conversation with any latent middle-class consumerism you might have. In any genuine encounter with Jesus, we can either respond in faith and obedience, cut and run, or take the fire out of the issue by reinterpreting the Bible to suit our understandings. Ever heard yourself saying, "Oh it's not what it means literally, Jesus is actually saying . . ." Just see what most preaching does with the kingdom way expressed in the Beatitudes, the Sermon on the Mount, or the rich young ruler—we emasculate the text by spiritualizing it or domesticating its direct implications.

⟶ Hebraic Ways of Knowing

We need to broaden our capacities to know God and to engage him through the text of Scripture. Because of issues relating to worldview, as previously discussed, we feel that we have to address this issue if we are to re-encounter the Jesus of the New Testament afresh.

The Hebraic approach to the knowledge of God includes the ways of the heart, of obedience, of wonder, of action, as well as the intellectual life of a person. We will look mainly at two, namely, the way of the heart and the way of action, because clearly these have implications when it comes to a mission that is funded by a sense of the immediacy of God. Jesus wants our hearts and our lives, and this he gets when we open ourselves to his invading love and when we act in his name.

Orthopathy, or the Way of the Heart

As we have seen, engagement with Jesus must move us beyond being spectators to participants. If we wish to become like him, we must learn to actively participate in Jesus, actively applying him and his teachings to our lives. We cannot be disinterested spectators when it comes to Jesus. In fact, in the encounters described in the New Testament, the desire of people to remain neutral observers is in a real sense the real sin (the rich young ruler, Pilate). It is those who allow Jesus to get at them who end up entering the kingdom. The Pharisees want to check him out, objectify him, line him up against their understandings of the faith, and because of this they are judged for their hardness of heart, for holding themselves back from what God is doing in Jesus.

And the heart is the issue. When the Bible uses the word "heart," it includes not only the source of emotion but of will, loyalty, and commitment. In many ways the heart determines our actions, not just our feelings, and it's critical to engage the heart when dealing with God (e.g., Ps 101:4; Isa 29:13; Matt 15:8). On this matter, the great revivalist Jonathan Edwards said:

> The Holy Scriptures every where place religion very much in the affection; such as fear, hope, love, hatred, desire, joy, sorrow, gratitude, compassion, and zeal. . . . It is an evidence that true religion lies very much in the affections, that the Scriptures place the sin of the heart very much in *hardness of heart*. . . . Now by a *hard* heart is plainly meant an *unaffected* heart, or a heart not easy to be moved with virtuous affections. . . .[12]

Without the heart, we cannot comprehend God. Besides, none of the really great things in human life spring only from the intellect but rather from the heart, which can embrace what the mind cannot. The great anonymous mystical work *The Cloud of Unknowing* says it this way: "Only to our mind is God incomprehensible, not to our heart." Following this spiritual logic, prayer affords us a certain kind of knowledge, one that cannot be attained through merely rational means.[13]

Most people reading this book would be aware of the distinctive meaning of the Hebrew word for knowledge, a word that is used for sexual intercourse, as well as for knowledge of God. The original meaning of the Hebrew verb "to recognize, to know," in distinction from Western languages, belongs not to the sphere of reflection but to that of personal contact.

In biblical Hebrew, in order to know something, one doesn't observe it, but one must come into contact with it. This basic difference is developed in the realm of a relation of the soul to other beings, where the fact of mutuality changes everything. At the center is not a perceiving of one another but a contact of being—intercourse. This theme of knowing rises to a remarkable and incomparable height in the relation of God to those he has chosen.[14]

Closely allied to this way of knowing is the role played by passion or affection in spirituality. Passion requires participation, involvement, faith. Søren Kierkegaard can say, "If passion is eliminated, faith no longer exists."[15] The truth of God can be found only by such a passionate search and by applying one's whole personality existentially. The criterion of the genuine search for truth is what Kierkegaard called *inwardness*, which requires an intense personal concern with it to be able to understand and assimilate it. Perhaps more widely known for this kind of approach was the American revivalist preacher Jonathan Edwards, made popular by his spiritual classic *The Religious Affections*. Edwards maintained that if the heart is left unmoved by God, no abiding action can, or will, take place. At its core, spirituality, what he called true religion, must redeem and direct our spiritual passion. It must involve the heart. And then he goes on to affirm that all great actions spring from the heart:

> I am bold in saying this, but I believe that no one is ever changed, either by doctrine, by hearing the word, or by the preaching or teaching of another, unless the affections are moved by these things. . . . In a word, there is never any great achievement by the things of religion without a heart deeply affected by those things. . . . True religion is placed in the affections.[16]

These are bases of motivation as well as the means to know God. Essentially what we are trying to say here is that we have to engage our heart to truly understand Jesus, but also to become like him and to follow him over the long haul. The emotional connection with God provides us with distinctive insights into God that cannot be gained from any other source.

In fact, prayer and worship grant to the worshipper a real, if highly subjective, knowledge of God. Prosper of Aquitaine (ca. 390–436) stated it this way: *lex orandi, lex credendi, lex vivendi*—how we worship reflects what we believe and determines how we will live. The law of prayer or worship is the law of life. Or, even more popularly rendered, as we worship, so will we live . . . and as we worship, so will we become! "Worship expresses the faith of the community, but it also helps form it. Doctrines grow out of people's actual life of prayer and worship, that is, their actual relationship with God."[17] Once again the function of orthopathy comes to the fore. Prayer is a form of knowledge that cannot be gained by any other means.

Orthopraxy, or the Way of Action

We have previously written of the idea that action is a form of sacrament,[18] so we will not repeat all that here, except to affirm the basic idea that when we respond to God in actions done in his name, we meet with him in a new and fresh way. The rabbis teach that we are never alone when we do a holy deed because we partner with God in the redemption of the world. In other words, a deed done in his name is a means of grace, a sacrament. As we state in *The Shaping of Things to Come*:

> . . . our actions, or more particularly our missional deeds, also confer grace. In fact, this could be the case even more so than the standard (somewhat abstracted) sacraments of the Christendom church. Humans have the freedom to protest against human suffering by *acting* to alleviate it. But it is the act itself, when done in the name of Jesus, that bestows something of the grace of God, not only to the beneficiary, but also to the benefactor. Grace goes two ways: such an action pulls a person away from their own self-involved concerns and directs them missionally toward other human beings in such a way that they, the person acted upon *and* the person acting, find God in a new way.[19]

Elie Wiesel, the Nobel laureate and luminous Jewish writer, has a character in one of his books affirm the sacramental value of the human, and humanizing, deed:

> If you could have seen yourself, framed in the doorway [Pedro once said to Michael], you would have believed in the richness of existence—as I do—in the possibility of having it and sharing it. It's so simple! You see a musician in

the street; you give him a thousand francs instead of ten; he'll believe in God. You see a woman weeping, smile at her tenderly, even if you don't know her; she'll believe in you. You see a forsaken old man; open your heart to him, and he'll believe in himself. You will have surprised them. Thanks to you, they will have trembled, and everything around them will vibrate. Blessed is he capable of surprising and of being surprised.[20]

Such deeds are not only sacramental but are themselves revelatory. That is, they reveal God in his goodness. There is a talmudic saying that may be interpreted as meaning that revelation resides within the deed itself: "From within his own deed, man as well as nation hears the voice of God."[21]

Hebraic faith puts such an emphasis on the sacramental nature of deeds that even if we don't understand why we should do it, or whether we doubt God, or don't wish to do a *mitzvah* (a holy deed), we are encouraged to do it anyway, because God will change us when we act in his name. The key to this form of knowledge is obedience. Helmut Thielicke says it like this, "Only conformity to God's will can open up access to knowledge of the figure of Christ."[22]

The New Testament epistle of James exhorts us to precisely such sacramental action in the world.

> Humbly accept the word planted in you, which can save you. Do not merely listen to the word, and so deceive yourselves. Do what it says. Anyone who listens to the word but does not do what it says is like a man who looks at his face in a mirror and, after looking at himself, goes away and immediately forgets what he looks like. But the man who looks intently into the perfect law that gives freedom, and continues to do this, not forgetting what he has heard, but doing it—he will be blessed in what he does. If anyone considers himself religious and yet does not keep a tight rein on his tongue, he deceives himself and his religion is worthless. Religion that God our Father accepts as pure and faultless is this: to look after orphans and widows in their distress and to keep oneself from being polluted by the world. (Jas 1:21–27, NIV)

Theoretical knowledge of spiritual truth is never commended in Scripture. In fact, as we can see, it is explicitly discouraged and condemned. As mediated through a Hebraic worldview, the understanding of Christian knowledge is indissolubly linked to experience. The follower of Jesus broadens his or her knowledge through experience or action, and his or her knowledge is to be expressed as experience or action. The Bible always aims at responsibility and responsiveness toward God. It is part of the conditions of God's covenant (e.g., Exod 24:7; Jer 11:3) as well as the momentous parting words of commission under which we live (Matt 28:18–20).

The command to obey is not because God wants to have it over us, but because, at least in terms of Hebraic worldview, it always confers knowledge of God that cannot be gained by any other means. Indeed, obedience is the

Transformative Suffering

Eva Price was a Midwestern American wife who in 1889 agreed to accompany her husband Charles into missionary service in the remote interior region of China. With their young sons, Donnie and Stewart, the Prices were sent to an isolated mission in Shansi. Located on a bare, windswept plateau, the mission was brutally hot in summer and freezing cold in winter. The area housed open sewers, piles of festering garbage, and contaminated wells that spread smallpox and typhoid, to which both Price sons succumbed within the first few years. The mission was not a successful one and the Prices returned to the United States in 1897 with little to show for their work but the deaths of their

Eva Price

beloved sons. Out of this sorrow and disappointment, however, Eva Price emerged a new person; although the first mission had taken their sons' lives, she later willingly returned to China with Charles, "stripped to the soul by the fires of suffering." She sensed that she was supported by the indescribable love of Jesus and wrote, "My capacity for loving has enlarged in all the discipline of sorrow. . . ." Eva Price was a little Jesus not simply because of the suffering she endured in her short life, but because she was able to transform her suffering into a rare ability for the deepest compassion. She had been awakened into life just in time to meet her death; both Price and her husband were killed in the Boxer Rebellion shortly after their return to China.

evidence that knowledge of God has been received and understood. In the Bible, the real test of what you know is how you live. Something goes seriously wrong with our capacity to integrate or even comprehend Scripture if we do not obey but just study it. This is so because the disciple is called beyond right belief (orthodoxy) to a direct relation to Jesus as well as to the Scriptures. But the Scriptures also point directly to Jesus Christ. So discipleship, as well as the Scriptures, find their true interpretive center in Jesus.

The surprising fact is that when one looks at the Gospel records, it is clear that "Jesus did not ask for homage but obedience. He always had much more to lose from his friends than from his enemies. Admiration has always blunted his sword. It serves to dull the original outrage of his mission. Veneration assumes that we know what kind of man he really was and that we approve of his demands. It blinds us to their radicalism and inoculates us against being wounded by them. In fact, our well-speaking makes him vulnerable to his own curse: 'Woe to you when all men speak well of you, for that is what their fathers did to the false prophets.'"[23] We think what is being pointed to here is true. Nowhere does Jesus call us to worship him in the Gospels; what is clear is that he does demand obedience. Understood from a Hebraic perspective, obedience is the worship we should render him. When we merely approve of Jesus, take his side as if we can agree intellectually with what he is saying, we can easily domesticate his demands, making them into mere sayings and aphorisms of a wise man. They are far more dangerous and demanding than that.

According to Bonhoeffer, any other approach to the Scripture serves only to provide the believer with an escape from the clear call to obedience. Bonhoeffer can therefore speak of discipleship as a "problem of exegesis" and goes on to say, "By eliminating simple obedience on principle, we drift into an unevangelical interpretation of the Bible."[24] So, orthodoxy is not enough. As followers of Jesus, we have to start obeying long before we know and understand much of him whom we obey. More than that, if we take obedience out of the equation, we cannot even hope to truly understand the Bible. Calvin can claim that only when the Scriptures are believed and obeyed do sinful people even begin to have an epistemological foundation for true knowledge: "all right knowledge of God is born in obedience."[25]

Along similar lines, Ellul writes:

> We are saved by grace, not by works. Hence we cannot glorify works. Yet doing them is indispensable, for they are prepared in advance by God, they are in his "plan," and we are created to do them (Eph 2:10). In Paul, then, practice (praxis) is the visible criterion that we have seriously received grace and also that we have entered effectively into God's plan. For Paul, as for Jesus, practice is the touchstone of authenticity. We are in the presence here of something that is constant across the centuries.[26]

⟿ Not Forgetting Orthodoxy

Ancient theologians came up with the potent slogan *lex seqendi, lex credendi,* which means that the law of following is the law of belief. This means that not only worship but also Christian life, ethics, and mission are centered in Jesus Christ and that following Jesus is a source for understanding him. This concept also suggests that Christian doctrines about Jesus arose in part out of the experience of following him. "Christians found themselves in a relationship of following and obedience to Jesus Christ and found life within this relationship. That believing flows out of following underscores the necessity that theology, like Christian life itself, must be Christ-centered."[27] We must remember this lest we slip into an ideology about Jesus rather than a true following of Jesus. Ideology is never enough.

We have noted that by itself orthodoxy, or mere creedal belief, is insufficient for a true knowledge of God. However, we are not suggesting that orthodoxy is unimportant. Far from it. We believe that right belief is an essential element of any discipleship in the way of Jesus. But we also believe that the church needs to reinterpret what it means by right belief and confession. The church nearly always sees orthodoxy as a commitment to propositional truth, assuming that the knowledge of God is received through purely the cognitive functions. We are convinced that our thinking about God must be right if we are to come to a full appreciation of God, but it must be complimented by othopraxy and orthopathy if we are to come to be in a full-orbed, biblical engagement with God. This can be depicted in the following way.[28]

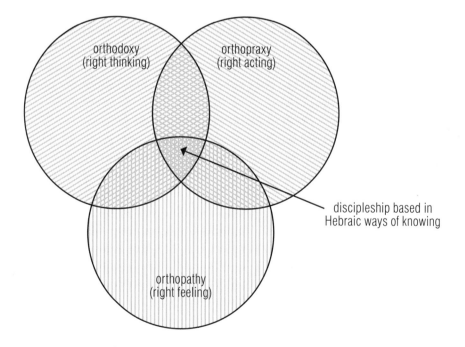

orthodoxy
(right thinking)

orthopraxy
(right acting)

discipleship based in
Hebraic ways of knowing

orthopathy
(right feeling)

As can be seen, it is in the nexus between orthopraxy, orthopathy, and orthodoxy that a true and full appreciation of God is to be found. In the place where all three intersect, we are less likely to make the mistakes that occur when we favor one over the others. If we adopt a commitment to orthopraxy alone at our worst we become tireless (and tired) activists, burning ourselves, and others, out while relying on our own efforts to please God. If we foster orthopathy to the exclusion of the others, we can end up as impractical mystics or experience junkies, so focused on contemplation and personal spiritual experience that we become of no use in the kingdom of God. But as we well know, if our primary or exclusive interest is in orthodoxy (as is the case in many churches today), at our worst we are arrogant bibliophiles, ideologues, no different from the Pharisees, worshipping our doctrine and our theological formulations over a genuine encounter with the Jesus revealed in Scripture. It is in the place where the ways of head, heart, and hand overlap that we find our way to Jesus. Or as John Wimber constantly reminds us in his writings, a true understanding of God required no less than Word, Works, and Wonders interacting together.

As we saw in the previous chapter, this is what the *Shema* (Deut 6:4–9) aims at and what Jesus directly affirms as being at the heart of discipleship and knowledge of God (Mark 12:28–34). We are to love God with all our heart, mind, will, and strength.

To illustrate this we can look to Luke 7, where Jesus encounters some Jewish elders sent by a Roman centurion to request that he heal the soldier's servant. When you read the Gospels and look to see who Jesus was personally impressed with, the number is not great. John the Baptist was one; Jesus called him the greatest of all prophets. And this centurion was another. It's a little disturbing to see what impresses Jesus: his cousin, a raving, ascetic lunatic in the wilderness, and a pagan soldier!

This soldier was a remarkable man, though. A military leader, probably garrisoned at Capernaum with a legion under his command, he was part of a conquering, occupying force that represented the crushing, superior, pagan imperial power of Caesar—everything the Jews despised. Romans tended to view their vanquished enemies as inferior barbarians. Israel must have seemed like a backwater to most centurions. These ancient peoples who worshipped one God and conducted ages-old rituals and embraced the strange ethical code of Moses must have appeared as foolish and childlike when compared with the sophistication of Rome.

But at some point this particular soldier had come to love Israel and its people. Using his personal resources and his ability to pull strings, he even manages to have a synagogue built in Capernaum. Surely, there would have been nothing in this for him. No one would go to such lengths to merely curry favor with the locals. Very likely he become interested in their God and their faith and their complex code of morality. The Jews of Capernaum came to say of him, "He loves our nation."

His involvement with Jesus is limited, as it turns out. They know of each other, though they don't meet. And yet the centurion has heard enough to put his complete faith in Jesus' power. His servant had fallen ill and had failed to recover in spite, one assumes, of even the finest quality health care. Knowing that a Gentile dare not speak face to face with a rabbi, and certainly not one of Jesus' standing, he asks the Capernaum elders to represent him. The small envoy rushes to Jesus' side and makes its request on the centurion's behalf. How bizarre. Jewish leaders, usually the enemies of Christ, representing a Gentile, usually an enemy of Israel, before the Messiah.

Jesus, no doubt intrigued by this request, agrees, as he does to many similar requests every day. But as they head to the centurion's home and to his dying slave, they are met by another emissary. The Roman has had second thoughts, not for his servant but about inviting the Christ into his home. The message from his friends reads, "I am not fit for you to come under my roof."

Jesus glances at the Jewish elders, "I thought you said he deserves my attention, because he built you a synagogue and he loves Israel? Now he tells me he deserves nothing, not even my presence in his home!"

The elders look furtively at each other. They are dumbfounded. What to say? They had assumed Jesus would be swayed to help the Roman if he knew he was a good man. Now Jesus feels betrayed. The Roman has told him he is not good at all! The Jews begin to suspect that Jesus, feeling duped, will not help them now.

"What, then, does he want from me?" Jesus asks the centurion's friends.

"He said that he knows about giving orders," they reply. "He is under the authority of his superior, and there are those who are under his authority. He simply sends out orders, and they are obeyed. So, he said you don't need to be physically present for your power to work. He says you transcend space and time. If you are who he thinks you are, then you are the master of the universe. Your power is universal. Just as Caesar can make decrees from Rome that are carried out around the empire, you can decree your will around the world."

An eerie hush descends upon the group. The Jewish elders blanch at this blasphemy. The Roman's friends await his response. A servant's life hangs in the balance. Jesus gazes at them in disbelief, before breaking the silence: "I'm impressed. And not just because he built a synagogue," he says, glaring at the embarrassed elders, who smile sheepishly. "But because I have never seen such faith in all Israel." And with that, far away, the servant was healed.

The centurion impresses Jesus because in him he finds that nexus between orthopraxy (the building of synagogues and other good works), orthodoxy (the right belief in the identity of Jesus), and orthopathy (the right sense of his own unworthiness and Jesus' holiness). Building synagogues doesn't guarantee Jesus' favor in itself, but it does indicate that the centurion recognizes the importance of good works, coupled with faith and humility. This man, in whom these things combine, evokes in Jesus an exclamation of joy. If a Gentile centurion can get it, then the kingdom is surely about to be unleashed across the empire.

⟻ReJesus, Take Three

By making Jesus the center or the norm, we are invited to embrace that same nexus between orthopraxy, orthodoxy, and orthopathy. And let's be clear about this, when we speak of Jesus Christ as primary norm, center, foundation, we mean the whole Christ. We do not refer only to the Jesus of history or Jesus of Nazareth prior to the events of the cross and resurrection. Nor do we mean some abstracted Christ figure cut apart from the Jesus of history. "The center and foundation of Christian faith is Jesus of Nazareth, the Messiah, crucified and risen, and present with us now in the power of the Spirit."[29] There must be no sundering of Jesus' person from his work and from what he has taught and modeled. It is all one of the same phenomenon. Anything less than this total understanding of our Lord is insufficient to fund the church's mission in the world or to sustain any vital faith. Since the beginning of the church's history, we have struggled between either making Jesus into either an otherworldly object of faith or limiting him to a mere figure of history.

As we have seen, the process of reJesusing the church involves in some sense a return to Hebraic perspectives. Much of recent scholarship has involved a re-examination of the historical Jesus and his Jewishness. But the Hellenistic worldview can lead us far astray in the study of the Gospels. Some approaches reject the Gospels as the historical revelation of the Christlike

God, as texts that read us and demand a response from us, and instead examine the Gospels simply as ancient texts. Now, we don't imagine that we can do justice to summarizing the history of New Testament interpretation here,

Explosive Storyteller

Harriet Beecher Stowe

When the writer Harriet Beecher Stowe visited President Lincoln in 1862, legend claims that he greeted her as "the little lady who made this big war." Whether this legend is true or not, Lincoln's words certainly illuminate Stowe's role as a catalyst of the American Civil War, which ended in the abolition of slavery in the United States. Stowe is credited with writing one of the most socially influential and politically explosive books in English literature: *Uncle Tom's Cabin.* Completed in 1852 at the height of the abolitionist movement, Stowe's novel provided many Americans with their first glimpse into the lives of slaves on a Southern plantation and is believed to have broadened abolitionist sentiment in the North. Begun as a serial for the Washington anti-slavery weekly *The National Era,* and based on Stowe's own exposure to slavery, herself having grown up across the Ohio River from the slave-owning state of Kentucky, her book gave the abolitionist movement a deeply human face. Stowe's portraits of local social life, particularly with minor characters, reflect an awareness of the complexity of the times. *Uncle Tom's Cabin* is not just a political tract; it is also a wonderfully written piece of realist literature presenting a social and political outlook within a remarkable story format. The beauty of her stories engaged a massive readership, but the truths they revealed also divided American society, energizing the efforts of the North, and infuriating the Southern states. After the book's publication, Stowe went on to speak out against slavery in the United States. After the end of the Civil War, she established several schools and homes for former slaves. Harriet Beecher Stowe passed away on July 1, 1896. She is a little Jesus because she advocated showing mercy and freedom to the powerless and marginalized through beautiful, socially relevant stories.

but we do believe it's fair to say that most of the recent innovations in New Testament interpretation—whether they are of the popular, and rather fanciful, variety like Dan Brown's *The Da Vinci Code*, or the more scholarly type like *The Historical Jesus*, by John Dominic Crossan, and *Jesus: Uncovering the Life, Teachings, and Relevance of a Religious Revolutionary*, by Marcus Borg, and the work of the Jesus Seminar—are indebted to the model championed by Rudolf Bultmann in the twentieth century. Called form criticism, Bultmann's approach involved the dismantling of the Gospels into their various pieces for the purpose of closer scrutiny. His assumption, and one followed by Wilson, Spong, Borg, Crossan, J. T. Robinson, and many more, was that the Gospels could, indeed should, be approached in the same way that contemporary literature studies approached ancient folklore such as Homer's *Odyssey* or *Iliad*. These folk stories were told and retold over an extended period of time. When finally written down, the texts were then edited and re-edited as they passed through the hands of various interpreters over the ages. The job of the modern literature scholar was to disassemble those parts, dicing them up into their various bite-sized portions according to literary style and historical sensibility for the purposes of clarity. Form critics do the same thing with the Gospels. Each piece, or *pericope*, whether a parable, a saying, or a riddle, is separated out, and judgments are made on their authorship, intention, and authenticity.

So, for instance, if you've ever met someone who believes in the resurrection but rejects the virgin birth, or who believes in the parables of grace but rejects the parables of judgment, chances are that person has been influenced by form criticism, or at the least operates under the assumptions that many theologically liberal interpreters adhere to. Even the atheist writer Richard Dawkins has no truck with this approach, which, to paraphrase him, is like cherry picking which doctrines you like from those you don't. Of course, Dawkins thinks all of the Gospel material is religious mumbo-jumbo, and he'd prefer you threw the lot out. But at least he sees the contradictions in people who consider themselves Christians choosing which bits are binding and which are negotiable.

With Bultmannian form criticism holding such sway, it has been interesting to watch the emergence of the British scholar N. T. Wright. He has been the leading light in the third quest for the historical Jesus (Bultmann launched the so-called second quest with his 1921 book, *History of the Synoptic Tradition*).[30] If Bultmann and the many varieties of his followers pull each tiny piece of the Gospels apart and examine them under a microscope, as it were, Wright does the opposite. He stands back from them, like a patron in an art gallery stands back from a massive Monet canvas, trying to take in the piece as a whole. Not unlike Jacques Ellul, Wright says we need to recognize that the Hebrew worldview—with its innate sense of the importance of history that gave rise to the Bible and the Gospels—provides us with the best tools for examining them.

Interestingly, Wright concludes his magisterial book, *Jesus and the Victory of God*, as he began it, with the parable of the prodigal son. Only this time the parable is related to the contemporary quest for the historical Jesus. Not only is Israel like the prodigal, who has experienced exile and has returned home to be restored by their Father (via the ministry of Jesus), but those of us who have followed the unhelpful leads offered by modern form critics have found ourselves in a far land, barely surviving on the non-nutritious results of their scholarship. Wright suggests we need to return home to a more Jewish appreciation of the Gospels and their inherent integrity. Referring to Albert Schweitzer, who had claimed that Jesus comes to us as one unknown, Wright concludes,

> We come to *him* as ones unknown, crawling back from the far country, where we had wasted our substance on riotous but ruinous historicism . . . But when we approached, as we have tried to do with this book, we found him running to us as one well known, whom we had spurned in the name of scholarship or even of faith, but who was still patiently waiting to be sought and found once more.[31]

We believe, with scholars like Wright, that we can have absolute confidence in the reliability of the Gospels, precisely by coming to them as their original Jewish hearers would. But we also believe that the Hebraic worldview invites us to come to the ancient texts in a different way to the approach taken by Hellenistic thinkers. That is, we believe rather than reading the Bible, we need to allow it to read us.

As difficult as it seems, we believe that a renewed engagement with Jesus requires a radical transformation in worldview as well as that of the heart. We need to recover a biblical epistemology (ways of knowing). In order to see Jesus truly, we need to saturate ourselves in the Hebraic perspectives that both originate and sustain the biblical worldview. And we believe we have to pickle ourselves in the Gospels. They must become our primary stories and reference point. There is no truer way to encounter Jesus afresh than prayerfully cycling through the Gospels and asking God to give us fresh insight into the remarkable person we find there. We must give our hearts, minds, souls, to the One around whom history turns.

Notes

1. Wilson, *Our Father Abraham*, 150. See also Thomas Cahill, *The Gifts of the Jews: How a Tribe of Desert Nomads Changed the Way Everyone Thinks and Feels* (Oxford: Lion, 1998).
2. Wilson, *Our Father Abraham*, 150.

3. R. Martin-Achard, *An Approach to the Old Testament* (trans. J. G. C. Greig; Edinburgh: Oliver & Boyd, 1965), 46.

4. Ellul, *Subversion of Christianity*, 23. Ellul's view is backed up by the analysis of Jewish theologian Michael Wyschogrod, *The Body of Faith: Judaism as Corporeal Election* (New York: Seabury, 1983), chs. 1–3.

5. Ellul, *Subversion of Christianity*, 24.

6. Wyschogrod, *Body of Faith*, ch. 2.

7. Ellul, *Subversion of Christianity*, 24.

8. This is not to say it is not authoritative for all matters of life and faith, but it is precisely because it is God's Word that it is authoritative. The Narnian metaphor was suggested by Bruxy Cavey from Toronto.

9. See Søren Kierkegaard, *Concluding Unscientific Postscript 2: Kierkegaard's Writings* (vol. 12.2; Princeton, N.J.: Princeton University Press, 1992), for a full exploration of the place of subjectivity in relation to truth.

10. Donald D. Palmer, *Kierkegaard for Beginners* (New York: Writers and Readers, 1996), 25.

11. Minear, *Eyes of Faith*, 16.

12. Jonathan Edwards, *On the Religious Affections*, in *The Works of Jonathan Edwards* (1834; repr., Peabody, Mass.: Hendrickson, 1993), I.II.4, 10.

13. Mystics often talk about the *via negative*, the way of negation, or unknowing, where one can but trust what is unknown. For example, "What can be learnt does not matter; what matters is the self-abandonment to that which is not known." Buber, *Mamre*, 87–88.

14. Martin Buber, *Good and Evil* (Englewood Cliffs, N.J.: Prentice Hall, 1953), 56.

15. Kierkegaard, *Concluding Unscientific Postscript*, 30.

16. Edwards, *On the Religious Affections*, 11.

17. Harold Wells, *The Christic Center: Life-Giving and Liberating* (Maryknoll, N.Y.: Orbis, 2004), 122.

18. Frost and Hirsch, *Shaping of Things to Come*, ch. 8.

19. Ibid., 137.

20. Elie Wiesel, *Twilight* (Suffolk: Viking, 1988), 69.

21. Martin Buber, *On Judaism* (New York: Schocken, 1967), 112.

22. Helmut Thielicke, *The Doctrine of God and of Christ* (vol. 2 of *The Evangelical Faith*; trans. and ed. Geoffrey W. Bromiley; Edinburgh: T&T Clark, 1977), 289.

23. Paul Minear, *Commands of Christ* (Nashville: Abingdon, 1972), 10. This does not mean that we believe that we should not worship Jesus, but it does force us to try understand what Jesus meant by worship. What it does mean is that our worship must be based on obedience and not just songs.

24. Dietrich Bonhoeffer, *The Cost of Discipleship* (New York: Macmillan, 1979), 83. Bonhoeffer always stressed the role of obedience in faith. He could say that "only he who believes is obedient and only he who is obedient believes." Quoted in J. A. Woelfel, *Bonhoeffer's Theology* (Nashville: Abingdon, 1970), 253.

25. John Calvin, *Institutes of the Christian Religion* (ed. John T. McNeill; Philadelphia: Westminster, 1960), 1.6.3, 73.

26. Ellul, *Subversion of Christianity*, 5.

27. Wells, *Christic Center*, 125–26.

28. We are indebted to the work of friend and colleague Stephen Said for this diagram.

29. Wells, *Christic Center*, 121.

30. The first quest for the historical Jesus was associated with the work of Albert Schweitzer and catalyzed by his best-known scholarly work, *The Quest of the Historical Jesus* (1910). Schweitzer proposed an understanding of Jesus as a primarily eschatological character, whose distinct mission was the institution of a messianic epoch. Bultmann and the second quest refuted this and consigned Jesus to the role of an earthly teacher of godly wisdom.

31. N. T. Wright, *Jesus and the Victory of God* (London: SPCK, 1996), 662.

Chapter Seven

The Church That Jesus Built

The ultimate problem, which has caused our theological
helplessness, lies in the separation between Jesus Christ
and the Church.
—D. Ritschl

The Indian is making an amazing discovery, namely
that Christianity and Jesus are not the same—that
they may have Jesus without the system that has been
built up around Him in the West.
—E. Stanley Jones

In 2006, a somewhat eccentric pastor, Jim Henderson, made national news
when he rented a soul for $504 on e-Bay after its owner offered an open
mind to the highest bidder. Henderson purchased Matt Casper's soul, and he
and Casper traveled around America critiquing various churches. The result
is Henderson's book, *Jim and Casper Go to Church*, a survey of the different approaches to church currently being tried in the United States, all presented
from the fresh point of view of an unbelieving outsider.[1] Jim and Casper visited
such diverse expressions as Rick Warren's Saddleback, Bill Hybel's Willow Creek,
Erwin McManus' Mosaic, Joel Osteen's Lakewood, as well as the Dream Center, First Presbyterian in Chicago, Lawndale, Jason's House, Imago Dei in Portland, Mars Hill in Seattle, The Bridge in Portland, and the Potter's House in
Dallas. You can't claim they weren't looking at churches from right across the
spectrum, from mega-churches to emergent churches (and a bit of everything
in between).

What did they find? Well, Matt Casper's perspective certainly is fresh,
uncluttered as it is by preconceptions and insider knowledge. And his com-

ments do heighten your sensitivity to showy, nonessential forms of church. He also highlights how churches can miss Jesus' message by focusing too much on raising money or by talking in indecipherable religious jargon. But the take-home point seems to be, "Why are there such glaring discrepancies among churches regarding what it means to be a follower of Christ?" If they're all talking about Jesus, why does the Jesus they're talking about look different in different churches?

This was similar to the question posed to us by a young man who had been raised by evangelical missionary parents but who had converted in the Eastern Orthodox church in California. While he took issue with a number of the practices of the Orthodox church, he preferred its unchanged seventeen-hundred-year message and liturgy to the multiplicity of Protestant versions. "With all the evangelicals telling me they were 'just preaching Jesus' I became confused when they were all preaching different Jesuses," he complained.

In *They Like Jesus but Not the Church*, Dan Kimball fires a similar shot across the church's bow. By interviewing a number of unchurched young people in California, Kimball discovered that, far from being antagonistic about faith in Jesus, his focus group was open to such faith but skeptical that the church as they knew it had anything to teach them about it. They believed the church is an organized religion with a political agenda, is negative and judgmental in outlook, and is generally male-dominated, homophobic, and fundamentalist.[2]

Kimball describes going onto a university campus with a video camera to interview students about their attitudes to the Christian faith. Instead of asking the usual questions that a lot of campus ministries ask ("Do you believe there is only one way to God? If you were to die tonight . . ."), Kimball asked just two: "What do you think of when you hear the name Jesus?" and "What comes to mind when you hear the word Christian?" The responses were interesting.[3]

Jesus	Christians
He is beautiful	The church messed things up
He is a wise man, like a shaman or a guru	They took the teachings of Jesus and turned them into dogmatic rules
He came to liberate women	Christians don't apply the message of love that Jesus gave
I want to be like him	They all should be taken out back and shot

In summing up their attitudes, Kimball quotes Gandhi's dictum: "I like your Christ. I do not like your Christians. Your Christians are so unlike your Christ."

As should be obvious by now, we believe that Christian faith must look to Jesus and must be well founded on him if it is to be authentic. If NASA was even .05 degrees off in launching a rocket to the moon, they would miss the moon by thousands of miles. And in many ways this is the same as it applies to the gospel. Because of the fundamental role that Jesus plays in Christian identity, ministry, and mission, we believe it is critical to get this right and to constantly keep checking. Church history makes it clear that such shifts take place. But these shifts are usually inadvertent and take place incrementally as other issues press in and traditions create their own overlay, obscuring the core of the faith. Whatever the process, it results in an insidious change in the resulting religion.

Therefore we propose that church should be recalibrated around its founder, Jesus. But what would that look like? Jesus didn't found any churches. He unleashed an army of little Jesuses who went forth and founded faith communities across the known world. But Jesus fashioned a temporary community, or a proto-church, if you will. Within the DNA of his itinerant community of disciples there exists the stuff of church, but it's not until we get to the apostle Paul that we see what it looks like to embody that DNA in a more stable, indigenous faith community. Paul takes the example of Jesus and, under the guidance of the Holy Spirit, unfurls those priorities and values into what we today call biblical ecclesiology.

Here is a curious question that will highlight the issue for us: If the church had only the four Gospels to go by, what would it look like? Certainly discipleship would be emphasized, as would the prominence on living in and under the kingdom of God. There would likely be a strong emphasis on uncluttered lifestyle and adventuresome community with lots of love, faithfulness, mercy, and justice going around. Would this be an adequate expression of Christianity? Now again, this somewhat tongue-in-cheek question is not meant to displace the canon of the New Testament or dislodge Paul's God-given apostleship in the church (God forbid), but as a mental exercise it should highlight the fact that all the basics would be in place—as they ought to be—when we focus on Jesus. Indeed, what we see Paul doing, in his epistles in particular, is working on developing the implications and logical conclusions of the stuff provided by Jesus in the example of his community. It's a relief that we are not just left with the four Gospels, because God has spoken through the rest of the New Testament to help us see the fullness of all that a community of Jesus' followers should look like. Our point is that there is no disjunction between Jesus' example and Paul's ecclesiology. One is the outworking of the other. But it's all seminally there in the Gospels themselves. The renewal of the church in our time is dependent on the renewal of the gospel. And the renewal of the gospel requires the recovery of the centrality of Jesus for faith and thought. We must reJesus our theology as well as our churches.

Paul's Vision of the Jesus Community

Let's take some time to explore Paul's ecclesiology and hold it up against the lens of Jesus' example from the Gospels. In his letter to the Ephesians, Paul addresses a number of what we might call generic church issues. Unlike his correspondence to the Corinthians or the Galatians, which specifically addresses particular issues with which each church was struggling, the letter to the Ephesians includes a lot of material applicable to all churches everywhere. This is probably because it was a circular letter that was sent around to various churches in Asia Minor. According to his Ephesian correspondence, Paul saw the notion of *ecclesia* being anchored on the foundation of a series of core truths.

Jesus Is "Head over All Things for the Church" (Eph 1:22)

Here we have an intriguing phrase regarding Jesus' pre-eminence. After noting that God has placed everything under the feet of Jesus, Paul then says that Jesus has been appointed head over everything for the church. That Jesus is head over all things is clear enough, but what did Paul mean by the phrase "for the church"? It seems that Paul is saying that Jesus exercises his supreme global authority over all things in the interest of the church. That is, the rule of Jesus is for the benefit of his church. It can sound arrogant of the church to suggest such a thing, as though Jesus rules in favor of Christians over all other people. Some church leaders have spoken this way to suggest that Jesus endorses them no matter what. However, a quick read of the seven letters to the seven churches found in the book of Revelation will show that Jesus doesn't mind standing against the church at times. It seems that what Paul is saying is that the future of Jesus' pre-eminent reign is inextricably linked with the future of the church. He has the church's interest at heart.

The Church "Is His Body" (Eph 1:23)

Paul makes much more of this metaphor in 1 Corinthians. Here, he is happy simply to introduce the idea. The church is the body of Jesus. It is his spiritual body, of which he is the head. In Ephesians 1, this implies intimacy and connectedness between Jesus and his followers. In Ephesians 4, Paul uses the metaphor to commend unity within the community of the followers of Jesus. And in 1 Corinthians 12, he expands it to discuss the diversity of gifts expressed by the followers of Jesus working together in harmony. The overall idea is one of teamwork, partnership, trust, respect, and intimacy. In both our previous books, we discuss the idea of *communitas*, the intimacy and devotion that develop between a group of people when faced with a common task or ordeal. Paul suggests as much in his use of body imagery in his letters.

The Church Is "the Fullness of Him Who Fills All in All" (Eph 1:23)

Now here is a big concept of the church—hardly a reduced idea of what Jesus intended! In the previous chapter we explored the centrality of the *Shema* in Hebrew thought and life. It was a declaration that Yahweh rules over all of life in every sphere. Here, Paul is identifying Jesus with such a rule by saying that he "fills all in all," that is, everything in the world. It is a statement of Jesus' omnipresence and sovereignty. But note how he refers to the church as Jesus' fullness. In other words, the community of Jesus' followers constitutes his fullness. In a sense Paul is saying, for example, "Look at the mountains and the sea. There you will see Jesus' presence on display. But if you really want to see the fullness of his presence, look at the church!" Now, often when church leaders say such a thing they implicitly (sometimes explicitly) refer to the institution of the church: "Look at our buildings and our church services! There you will see the fullness of Christ!" This isn't what Paul meant. There were no flashy church services to look at, and very few churches had their own buildings. Paul is saying that in the organic, messy, often troubled, sometimes harmonious webs of relationship found among Jesus' followers you can see the richness and beauty and power of the fullness of Jesus.

The Church Is Part of God's "Eternal Purpose" (Eph 3:10–11)

In this beautiful section of Ephesians 3, Paul declares that God has made his wisdom known in the heavenly realms through the church:

> Through the church the wisdom of God in its rich variety might now be made known to the rulers and authorities in the heavenly places. This was in accordance with the eternal purpose that he has carried out in Christ Jesus our Lord. (Eph 3:10–11)

Now that's saying something! It implies that throughout the ages God's manifold wisdom could never be quite appreciated by the heavenly community, because it seems that God doesn't have a true relationship with the rulers and authorities in heaven. They are excluded from the unique and intimate relationship God reserves himself for with humankind. It wasn't until the church was unleashed as a community of human beings in relationship with God through Jesus that the richness of God's wisdom could be appreciated. Therefore, to all the angelic beings God displays his wisdom through the church. Do we need a greater demonstration that God's wisdom is intrinsically relational than this? God's wisdom is not merely a matter of superior cognition or greater accumulated knowledge. The wisdom of God is displayed through the webs of relationships of Jesus' followers. In James 3:17, a similar idea is presented: "the wisdom from above is first pure, then peaceable, gentle, willing to yield, full of mercy and good fruits, without a trace of impartiality or hypocrisy."

If the wisdom of God is all these things—essentially relational things—then God is able to fully express such wisdom only through relationship with his people. This was God's plan, says Paul, throughout eternity. The followers of Jesus are essential for the expression of God's wisdom.

God Is to Be Glorified "in the Church and in Christ Jesus" (Eph 3:21)

In a somewhat premature benediction, Paul declares a closing prayer over the recipients of his letter (and yet he still has three more chapters up his sleeve):

> Now to him who by the power at work within us is able to accomplish abundantly far more than all we can ask or imagine, to him be glory in the church and in Christ Jesus to all generations, forever and ever. Amen. (Eph 3:20–21)

Certainly God is worthy of all glory, and Paul identifies two sources of his glory: his son, Jesus, and the church.

"Christ Is the Head of the Church, the Body of Which He Is the Savior" (Eph 5:23)

Paul returns to the body metaphor again, if only briefly, to re-emphasize Jesus' rule over his followers and to make explicit that he is its Savior as well. Having saved the church, he can then be its head or ruler. But this is not simply a matter of ownership. This text appears in the midst of a discussion about the relationship between husbands and wives. Jesus is the head and the savior of the church, but this is expressed in distinctly relational terms.

Jesus "Loved the Church and Gave Himself up for Her" (Eph 5:25)

Jesus loves his church, just as a good husband is to love his wife. His death on the cross is his supreme act of devotion and love.

Jesus' Design Is to Present It as a Holy, Blameless Church (Eph 5:26–27)

Paul has told us what Jesus has done for his church in a past sense: he has loved the church, saved the church, and rules the church. Now he turns his attention to the future and announces that the church is a work in progress. It is Jesus' work to improve us, to slowly but surely recreate us in his image. Jesus' future design for his followers is to

> make her holy by cleansing her with the washing with water by the word, so as to present the church to himself in splendor, without a spot or wrinkle or anything of the kind—yes, so that she may be holy and without blemish. (Eph 5:26–27)

Jesus Nourishes and Cares for the Church (Eph 5:29–30)

Says Paul, "No one ever hates his own body, but he nourishes and tenderly cares for it, just as Christ does for the church, because we are members of his body" (Eph 5:29–30). In another return to the body metaphor, Paul indicates that as part of his future orientation in presenting the church blameless and radiant, he nourishes and cares for the church, supplying its needs and attending to its concerns. It seems to us that Jesus is more than involved in it than what first appears to the casual observer.

⟵ If This Is Church, We Want In

And so, whatever the church is, we want to a part of it! We think that its true reality is far more than the religious institution it became. It is an intimate network of Jesus followers. It is saturated with Jesus.

Paul's favorite image for the church is that of a family, or to be more accurate, the household.[4] If you did a word search through his letters, you would find that he makes more references to body than to family, but if you include all Paul's use of family language (brothers, sisters, etc.), it is clear that the church as family is his favorite idea. Paul saw the church inextricably linked to Jesus and each other in a bond of deep interpersonal relationship. From this brief study of Ephesians, it becomes clear that Paul saw the church as something that issues forth from Jesus. It is a matter of what Jesus does for his followers and what they become in him doing it.

This table summarizes what we have explored so far.

What Jesus Does	What the Church Becomes
He reigns over the church	A Christlike community that reflects his character, life, and activity
He reigns over all the world	A holistic community that seeks to offer up all of life to the lordship of Jesus
His wisdom is relational	A peace-loving community that is considerate, submissive, merciful, fruitful, impartial, and sincere
He is glorified by the church	A worshipping community that exalts Jesus and declares his sovereignty
He loves the church	A devoted community that experiences intimacy with Jesus
He saves the church	A graced community that relies on the work of Jesus for salvation
He cleanses the church	A holy community that seeks after the righteousness of Jesus
He nourishes the church	A healthy community that feeds on God's Word and the ministry of his Spirit

In some of our previous books we have presented some rather pointed criticism of the way church is being done in the West.[5] This has riled some readers and led some critics to suggest that we don't love the church, but we submit to you that it is our very love for the church that motivates us to write what we do. And besides, there is a difference between liking the church and loving the church the way Jesus commands us to. To be sure, we do not *like* gatherings of strangers who never meet or know each other outside of Sundays, who sit passively while virtual strangers preach and lead singing, who put up with second-rate pseudo-community under the guise of connection with each other, who live different lives from Monday to Saturday than they do on Sunday, whose sole expression of worship is pop-style praise and worship, who rarely laugh together, fight injustice together, eat together, pray together, raise each others' children together, serve the poor together, or share Jesus with those who have not yet been set free. We do not *like* the church if it's a fractured organization with hundreds of competing creeds, names, and doctrines, teaching a multitude of contradictory beliefs and insisting on compliance with a raft of recently invented traditions. But if it's a family of Jesus followers striving, no matter how inadequately, to be Christlike, holistic, peace-loving, worshipful, devoted, graced, holy, and healthy, then we will love it with every ounce of physical and emotional strength we have.

There's a story told about a young soldier of the army of Alexander the Great who deserts his post and is tracked down and captured by Alexander's men. Normally deserters were summarily executed by these ancient bounty hunters, but according to this story, the young man was brought into the presence of the king. Alexander demanded that the deserter tell him his name. "I share the name of my king," said the soldier. "My name is Alexander." While the king went on to pardon the deserter, he did not do so before insisting, "Young man, you change your life, or you change your name."

This is as it was with the followers of Jesus. It was as if they took on his name as their own and their life had to mirror that marvelous name they now used. Likewise, the church today, we suggest. It's time to change its life or alternatively to change its name. The unconventional Christian musician Moby recently toyed with this idea in a journal entry on his website.[6] Beginning his comments with, "So, do you think that it's time to invent a new religion?" he playfully questioned whether the ways we perceive church or Christianity are so different from what Jesus had in mind that it's time to start a new Jesus-following religion all over. He said,

> I actually think that the teachings of Christ accommodate most of the new ways in which we perceive ourselves and our world.
>
> the problem is that although the teachings of Christ accommodate this,
>
> contemporary Christianity does not.
>
> here's more seriousness dressed up as flippancy:
>
> christ: acknowledging quantum realities.
>
> christianity: depressingly newtonian.
>
> Does that make any sense?[7]

He is echoing what Kimball's subjects told him, although as a Christian, Moby is more involved in the issue than are the non-Christian young people interviewed by Kimball. When many Christians hear comments like Moby's they react against what they see as a complete disregard, even disrespect,

Champion of the Poor

Dorothy Day

Dorothy Day was relentless in her commitment to social justice and peace and her devotion to the poor. Indeed, this little Jesus once said, "I firmly believe that our salvation depends on the poor." A bohemian living in New York City in the 1910s and 20s, Day began the spiritual journey that led her to the Catholic Church after the birth of her daughter. As a new Christian who had left behind the sexual mores of her contemporaries, Day retained her commitment to pacifism and the rights of the worker that were central to the bohemian culture, believing that these values were also central to the message of Jesus.

Together with Peter Maurin, in 1933 she founded the Catholic Worker movement (CW), a controversial organization dedicated to serving Christ by working for justice for those on the margins of society. The *Catholic Worker* newspaper promoted their mission, and the movement opened St. Joseph's, a house of hospitality in the slums of New York that provided the poor with accommodation and meals. Soon after, a series of farms in rural America were opened in which the poor could live in community. The movement spread quickly to other cities in the United States and then to Canada and the United Kingdom. By 1941, more than thirty independent affiliates of CW had been established, and the work continues today, with more than one hundred communities in operation. Though pilloried for her pacifism during World War II, and seen as outdated because of her opposition to the sexual revolution of the 1960s, she never budged an inch in her beliefs. Day did retain the respect of those in the antiwar movement, and she still attended protests up through the 1970s. Some hailed her as a saint, something she discouraged. "Don't call me a saint," she said. "I don't want to be dismissed so easily." Day lived at St. Joseph's, serving the poor, until her death in 1980.

for the tradition and history of the Christian church throughout the past two thousand years. But it is also worth noting that the church has seen the rise of hundreds of reforming and renewing movements from within its ranks throughout the Christian era. If we learn anything from church history, it's that raising questions about how we are to be and do church has never done the church any harm. Indeed, it has been the church's great strength that it has been able to listen to and accommodate such critique.

If we take Moby's critiques on the chin and go back to the Bible to re-discover our original DNA as a church, we find marvelous encouragement for renewal and transformation. What does it look like for a web or family of followers to become all that Jesus intends for them? What would a new religion of Jesus followers look like? This second table offers some clues.

What the Church Becomes	How
1. A Christlike community that reflects his character, life, and activity	1. by making an intentional corporate study of the Gospels to model our lives on the example of Jesus, preferring no lesser hero from our tradition
2. A holistic community that seeks to offer up all of life to the lordship of Jesus	2. by de-emphasizing Sunday and equipping all followers to hand over every sphere of their lives and every day of the week to Jesus
3. A peace-loving community that is considerate, submissive, merciful, fruitful, impartial, and sincere	3. by moving outward to serve others, knowing that community is forged by our collective commitment to a cause beyond ourselves
4. A worshipping community that exalts Jesus and declares his sovereignty	4. by understanding that worship includes singing but is never limited to it and involves a whole-of-life exaltation of Jesus
5. A devoted community that experiences intimacy with Jesus	5. by practicing the presence of Jesus in prayer, solitude, fasting, and missional action
6. A graced community that relies on the work of Jesus for salvation	6. by insisting continually that it is not by our own efforts that we are saved—that is, through a continual re-evangelization of believers
7. A holy community that seeks after the righteousness of Jesus	7. by learning and living the values of Jesus, as distinct from the piety of middle-class good-manners conventionality
8. A healthy community that feeds on God's Word and the ministry of his Spirit	8. by corporately devoting ourselves to the Scriptures and the exercise of the spiritual gifts

These eight action points don't require any significant collateral or specially designed facilities. They can be appropriated by any collective of believers devoted to following Jesus, and they can be lived out in the ordinary world.

⟵Getting Back to Jesus' Community

So far so good. But remember we have derived these points from Paul's words in Ephesians. Would Jesus agree with what Paul wrote in Ephesians? There's no doubt that Paul anchors the church steadfastly to the example of Jesus, but did Jesus teach or develop a community of followers that looks like this? Let's turn our attention back to the Gospels to find out. We will take the eight action points listed above and check them against the example of Jesus.

Jesus' Community Will Follow the Example of Jesus

As implied in the early sections of this book, our point is that we don't want Presbyterians to look more like John Knox or Methodists to look more like John Wesley or Salvationists to look more like William Booth. We want all believers to look more like Jesus. We don't discount the enormous contribution made to the Christian cause by people like Knox, Wesley, or Booth, and we recognize that there's much we can learn from such leaders, but let Jesus be our guide, our Lord, and our master. This was the crux of the Jesus community as found in the Gospels. Jesus is central. It is his example to which his followers continually turn. To them, Jesus is not merely some radical rabbi whose innovative take on Hebrew philosophy they had come to appreciate. He does more than conduct outdoor theology classes. He models an alternate lifestyle. He models itinerancy (Luke 9:57–62) and complete trust in the provision of God (Luke 12:22–31). He demonstrates how to treat children (Luke 18:15–17) and women (Luke 8:1–3; 10:38–42). He provides a template for how they are to pray (Luke 11:1–2). He sends them out to duplicate his ministry of healing and preaching (Luke 9:1–6). He allows them to question him on his parables (Luke 8:9). Some of them witness his transfiguration (Luke 9:28–29); all of them witness his resurrection (Luke 24:36–37).

This was the beginning of the conspiracy of the little Jesus. He replicates himself in the lives of his first followers. He allowed them to make an intensive study of his life and ministry and then unleashed them on an unsuspecting world like a tsunami of love and grace. Without the real thing in flesh and blood, we today have his Spirit within us and the Gospels as our guide and impetus. It would follow, then, that in order to replicate his life and ministry, we must make an intentional corporate study of the Gospels. They are the staple diet of Jesus followers. Rather than milk for Sunday school children, the Gospels should be the main course at every Christian meal.

Jesus' Community Will Equip All Followers

The examples of the de-emphasizing the Sabbath in Jesus' life and ministry are many. In Luke 14 we read,

> On one occasion when Jesus was going to the house of a leader of the Pharisees to eat a meal on the Sabbath, they were watching him closely. Just then, in front of him, there was a man who had dropsy. And Jesus asked the lawyers and Pharisees, "Is it lawful to cure people on the sabbath, or not?" But they were silent. So Jesus took him and healed him, and sent him away. Then he said to them, "If one of you has a child or an ox that has fallen into a well, will you not immediately pull it out on a Sabbath day?" And they could not reply to this. (Luke 14:1–6)

Jesus was picking up on a scholarly debate of the time. It had been a topic of much discussion by Jewish scholars as to whether it was lawful to save your dying son on the Sabbath. Surely, some argued, it would be unlawful to save an ox but legal to save your own son. Such debates always occur in rarefied academic contexts where neither child nor ox is thrashing for life in a watery well. Jesus throws their scholarly disconnection back in their faces. Before them lay a man who could not walk. Without work, he would have been starving to death, reduced to begging for scraps and alms. Knowing that their answer about the legalities of Sabbath keeping would directly bear on the livelihood of this poor soul, the Pharisees are silenced by their embarrassment. Jesus, though, is a man of action. He is a man of engagement and decisiveness. Sabbath or no Sabbath, the beggar needed his touch, and he refused to stand idly by, paralyzed by theological niceties.

How amazing that the religion that bears his name has become every bit as Sabbath-centric as Jesus' opponents! So much of the Christian church focuses on getting people into the pews on a Sunday morning as its highest goal. It has created its own legalism that defines holiness in terms of attendance instead of as communion with God in every area of their week and life. It has shifted its preference to Sunday, but it is no less paralyzed by the legalism that silenced the Pharisees. How could we have missed Jesus' words in Luke 6, where after the Pharisees rebuked his disciples for eating the kernels of grain on the Sabbath, he snapped,

"Have you not read what David did when he and his companions were hungry? He entered the house of God and took and ate the bread of the Presence, which it is not lawful for any but the priests to eat, and gave some to his companions?" Then he said to them, "The Son of Man is lord of the sabbath." (Luke 6:3–5)

Jesus is locating himself as the center of the religious cult of Judaism. As we've seen, he sees himself as the physical embodiment of the temple. He does what a temple is supposed to do. Now, he proclaims lordship over the Sabbath. It is *his* day now. He was not shifting the focus of Sabbath keeping from Yahweh to himself. He *is* Yahweh! It was always his day. What he is doing is declaring lordship over all of life, including the Sabbath. In Mark's version of the same episode, Jesus says, "The sabbath was made for humankind, and not humankind for the sabbath" (Mark 2:27). His point was that the Sabbath was made to serve people, instead of people being created to serve the Sabbath. The Sabbath was a servant, not a master. He was telling them that they should apply the law of the Sabbath with mercy and thought to human need. And he was telling them he had the authority to define how they should observe the Sabbath. In short, human need (the disciples' hunger, the ill man's dropsy) is more important than blind Sabbath keeping.

Jesus sets his friends free to enjoy snacking on the rolled husks of wheat. He attends to an ill man rather than be bound by legalism. Likewise, the church today must rediscover that while regular times of retreat and reflection are essential, they are tools for use by us as required. Michael has a friend who works in a downtown office in Sydney who takes his lunch two or three times a week to a nearby cathedral to reflect on Jesus and enjoy the serenity of the place. He is free to sabbath as he wills. Jesus is Lord of all of life, of every day and every place. Hallelujah!

Jesus' Community Will Move Outward to Serve Others

Jesus' community is not a static band of learners. They are a moving, living, breathing, organic team of little Jesuses. Far from setting up camp in Nazareth and downloading a whole new worldview framed in theoretical rhetoric, Jesus hits the road with his followers, showing that community is forged by the heat of action and joint cooperation in a cause beyond themselves. They are buffeted by criticism from opponents, confused by the reactions of others, and inspired by the example of Jesus. After he sends them (and fifty-eight others) out in pairs to preach, heal, and drive out demons, they return "with joy" to report on what they have seen (Luke 10:17). They are bound to each other as a band of brothers and sisters. Jesus even takes a tax collector (Levi/Matthew) and a zealot (Simon) into his troupe. No two people would have despised each other more than the nationalistic zealots who had vowed to slaughter the Romans and their collaborators and, well, collaborators like the tax collectors. This is not unlike the elf Legolas and the dwarf Gimli in *The Lord of the Rings*. Though avowed enemies, they are drawn together in their quest to return the ring to Mount Mordor. The political and theological differences that would have normally driven Simon and Matthew apart are overwhelmed by their joint commitment to the mission of Jesus.

To be sure, there are examples of occasional or casual observers enjoying the ministry of Jesus. At the Sermon on the Mount and the feeding of the thousands, Jesus attracted large audiences. However, John points out that most people weren't able to stomach Jesus' teaching. In John 6, after the feeding of five thousand, many turned away, offended by his uncompromising instruction (John 6:60, 66). Jesus is unfazed by this, though; he is aware that few will faithfully follow him (John 6:64b–65). Jesus' community is built not with casual observers but with those who have completely thrown in their lot with him. Listen to Peter's plaintive cry when Jesus offers him the chance to also turn away: "Lord, to whom can we go? You have the words of eternal life" (John 6:68).

How can churches today resist the pull to become a spectator sport? How can they fight against, instead of be caught up by, the spirit of consumerism? Churches wanting to grow sometimes end up desperately trying to attract a greater share of the market with advertising ploys and promises of greater luxury and better religious goods and services. We heard of a church in California that gives away a Harley-Davidson motorbike each year to the person who brings the most visitors to church on Sundays. Is this the way Jesus mobilized his followers? By appealing to their greed and self-interest? Jesus fashioned a community of devoted, selfless servants who had sought to model their lives on his selflessness and service. And in so doing they became bound to each in the bonds of a common cause.

Jesus' Community Understands That Worship Is a Whole-of-Life Exaltation of Jesus

Jesus' community was a decidedly missional one. It was defined and shaped by its founder's mission to usher in the kingdom of God. The term "missional church" gets bandied about by all sorts of folks from across different denominational backgrounds and from around the world. We suspect it might mean differing things to different people. We also fear that it might be becoming the latest buzz term along with such words and phrases as emerging, emergent, fresh expressions, new expressions, mission-shaped, and so on.

Caring for the Sick

Damien of Molokai

Born Jozef de Veuster in Belgium in 1840, Father Damien traveled as a member of a missionary order in 1873 to the Hawaiian island of Molokai in order to minister to those suffering from leprosy (known today as Hansen's Disease). Nearly 1,000 lepers had been quarantined at a settlement on Molokai that was surrounded by an impregnable mountain ridge. Neglected by the Hawaiian government, the settlement had declined into a lawless, filthy, immoral "Colony of Death." Although aware of the need for ministry in the settlement, the bishop of Honolulu hesitated to send a missionary into the colony, as the missionary would surely contract the contagious disease. Father Damien, however, requested the assignment, and the bishop introduced him to the colony as "one who will be a father to you, and who loves you so much that he does not hesitate to become one of you; to live and die with you." True to this introduction, Damien did not limit his role to that of a priest, and his arrival marked a turning point for the community. He dressed ulcers, built homes and beds, constructed coffins, and dug graves. Under his leadership, basic laws were enforced, shacks became painted houses, working farms were organized, schools were erected and even a girls' choir was formed. Also true to his bishop's words, however, Damien contracted the disease. In 1884, at the age of forty-nine, Damien died with his people. As a little Jesus, Father Damien was willing to give up his own life for those who suffer.

But the missional paradigm is a distinctly biblical framework for looking at the Jesus-given and Jesus-intended shape of the global Christian movement. When we refer to the missional church, we are using the term in the same way you might say the "biblical church."

For us, the phrase refers to those communities for whom mission has become the organizing principle of all they do and are. Of course, we recognize that the church has a variety of purposes or functions. These include worship, discipleship, formation, evangelism, and fellowship. Rather than seeing mission as one of the functions of the church, missional church people see it as its central and organizing purpose. For example, rather than seeing worship as central (as most conventional churches do), there is a growing movement of us who believe that worship is richer when organized around mission. We believe we do fellowship better when organized around mission. Likewise with discipleship, teaching, and the exercise of the gifts.[8]

And what is mission? It is the outward impulse of God's people. Above and beyond evangelism or social justice, it is the irresistible propulsion of the Spirit that sends his people out to declare the lordship of Jesus in all and over all. This can be manifest in sharing the Gospel, planting churches, feeding the hungry, agitating against injustice, and more. These are missional activities. But mission itself is the overarching sentness of God's people as they infiltrate all of society and stake a claim for the unending rule of Jesus in every sphere of life.

Missional churches understand that this sending impulse infuses all of church life. By contrast, conventional churches that make worship the organizing principle usually see evangelism, for example, as the recruiting of new people to attend worship and other organization-based services. They see Christian fellowship as the building up of the worshipping community. Missional churches understand that community is best built by those in league with each other in the creative task of mission. They worship like crazy because they see God's lordship over all of life. They disciple each other in order to be better missionaries. Mission is the spark, the catalyzing energy, that makes sense of everything the church was intended to be.

Someone once challenged us that in heaven there'll be no mission, only worship. We couldn't disagree more. Sure, we won't be feeding the poor or planting churches. Those missional activities will cease when every knee bows, every tongue confesses, and every tear is wiped away. But in the world to come, we will still be charged with the task of declaring Jesus' rule over all of life. We're looking forward to that unhindered mission of the new age and to worshipping through the process of offering our world back to God.

We never see Jesus' community at worship in the conventional sense of that word. They are always on mission, though. Their worship of God happens as they go. They have put worship at the service of mission and we do well to learn from Jesus' radical example in this matter.

Jesus' Community Practices the Presence of Jesus

Does this mean that if mission is the organizing principle for Jesus' community, there are never any times for private, silent, reflective worship and prayer? Far from it. Jesus commends this very thing to his community when he says,

> "And whenever you pray, do not be like the hypocrites; for they love to stand and pray in the synagogues and at the street corners, so that they may be seen by others. Truly I tell you, they have received their reward. But whenever you pray, go into your room and shut the door and pray to your Father who is in secret; and your Father who sees in secret will reward you. When you are praying, do not heap up empty phrases as the Gentiles do; for they think that they will be heard because of their many words. Do not be like them, for your Father knows what you need before you ask him." (Matt 6:5–8)

Personal prayer, solitude, and retreat are an intrinsic part of Jesus' community. In fact, Jesus models them as an essential part of his devotional life:

> in the morning, while it was still very dark, he got up and went out to a deserted place, and there he prayed. (Mark 1:35)

> But he would withdraw to deserted places and pray. (Luke 5:16)

Even at the lowest point of his life, in the Garden of Gethsemane, he withdraws from the others to pray. In fact, if we take his words to his community in Matthew 6 seriously, his preference is that prayer not be a showy display for the benefit of others but an intense and private connection between a disciple and his or her heavenly Father.

The question about fasting needs to be addressed as well, because it was noted at the time that Jesus' community did not participate in the devotional practice of fasting, unlike that of the disciples of John the Baptist:

> Then the disciples of John came to him, saying, "Why do we and the Pharisees fast often, but your disciples do not fast?" And Jesus said to them, "The wedding guests cannot mourn as long as the bridegroom is with them, can they? The days will come when the bridegroom is taken away from them, and then they will fast." (Matt 9:14–15)

For Jesus, his presence on earth was a time of celebration, of feasting, not fasting. He acknowledges that during his three days away from the disciples, they would fast as an expression of their grief and mourning. But after his resurrection, Jesus was returned to them, and he remains with his church to this very day. This is still the hour for feasting. So, is there any provision for the practice of fasting by Christians today? Well, frankly, not much. There seems to be no injunction to do so found on the lips of Jesus. We believe that while Christians might find fasting beneficial in building spiritual muscle by the discipline of self-denial and the creation of more time for personal prayer (during the time you'd normally prepare and eat food), we see it as merely that—helpful but not required. Of course, Jesus again cautions about showy displays even in the practice of fasting, when he commends us to do it in secret (Matt 6:16–18).

Jesus' Community Insists That We Need to Be Continually Re-Evangelized

The default by so many Christians toward earning their salvation by good works and dutiful church service has to be halted, and indeed, resisted. For this reason, the followers of Jesus need to be re-gospeled on a regular basis. We think this is why Jesus told his disciples to constantly remember his sacrificial and atoning death in the eating of the so-called communion meal. Far from intending it to be a sacramental or religious feast, we think Jesus intended to connect the gospel to an everyday occurrence like eating. It is not unlike the place of the *Shema* in Israel, as we saw earlier. The core of their belief system was so radical and so countercultural in its time that Israel was commanded to

> Recite them to your children and talk about them when are at home and when you are away, when you lie down and when you rise. Bind them as a sign on your hand, fix them as an emblem on your forehead, and write them on the doorposts of your house and on your gates. (Deut 6:7–9)

In a world of aggressive polytheism, you can understand how having reminders of their monotheistic faith tied to their hands or written on their doorframes was so important. Every time you left your home and re-entered it, you would be reminded again of the liberty of the existential monotheism of Israel. We are free from the fear of unknowingly offending some obscure god, they could say. All of life was now unified under Yahweh.

Likewise, the Lord's Supper was not intended to be a peculiar liturgical rite of a religious institution. Jesus was commanding his followers to remind themselves of the freedom that comes through his death every time they tore bread or sipped wine. It was a way of being re-gospeled every day, indeed, several times a day. When Paul does present certain words to the Corinthians that might accompany a collective love feast, he is not fixing it as a distinct Christian rite as much as he is reminding the wayward Corinthians of the true tone and belief that should undergird their meals together.

Jesus communities today must never lose sight of the essential work of the cross and celebrate that work as often as they meet together. It is not our pietism or our personal devotion that sets us free. It is the unconditional love of Jesus as demonstrated in his willingness to die for our sins.

Uncompromising Commitment

A98530

Simone Weil

T. S. Eliot described Simone Weil as "a woman of genius, of a kind of genius akin to that of the saints." Weil was a French philosopher, teacher, and activist whose precocious intellect and compassion for members of the working class were apparent even from an early age. As a six-year-old during the First World War, she refused to eat sugar because it was not rationed to French soldiers. In her early teens, she mastered several modern languages and often spoke with her brother in ancient Greek. Weil's espousal of Bolshevism and Marxism as a young woman led her to become known by some as the "Red Virgin." She was dedicated to bringing attention to the plight of manual laborers and factory workers, and alternated between teaching philosophy and performing manual labor in order to better understand the needs of workers. Preferring the company of the poor, she ate in their less-fashionable cafés and shared her salary with the unemployed. After the disillusioning outcome of the Spanish Civil War, Weil eventually abandoned communist and socialist ideologies. She later became interested in Christianity, although she refused to be baptized and never formally joined the church. In 1942 she fled from Nazi occupation and relocated in England, where she died at the age of 34 of tuberculosis and self-neglect in 1943, embodying her belief that one must "decreate" oneself to return to God. Her life was one of uncompromising commitment to her beliefs.

Jesus' Community Learns and Lives the Values of Jesus

For many suburban, middle-class churches, niceness is the supreme expression of discipleship. But any cursory reading of the Gospels will serve to remind you that Jesus wasn't all that nice. He was good. He was loving. He was compassionate. But he wasn't always nice. The church must abandon its preference for good-manners piety and adopt again the kingdom values as taught by Jesus. Allow us to give you an example. Some time ago Michael wrote an article for a Sydney newspaper, commenting on the influence of Sydney's largest church, Hillsong. In the article, he defended the church against various attacks in the media, but he also gently raised his concerns about Hillsong's emphasis on prosperity doctrine (the so-called health and wealth gospel). He received an avalanche of letters and email berating him for daring to be publicly critical of another church. A significant number of these angry correspondents claimed that it was un-Christlike to criticize the church in any way. Now, whether you agree with Michael's decision to write such a thing in the media or not is beside the point. But the point is that somehow these people, most of them ministers, failed to recognize that Jesus was regularly and scathingly critical of the religious leaders of his faith community. Furthermore, Jesus' seven messages to the seven churches in the book of Revelation (Rev 2:1–3:22) contain plenty of harshly critical comment directed at the church! To claim it is un-Christlike to criticize the church is to disregard the example of Jesus.

It seems to us that this is the exemplifying of politeness, courtesy, and niceness over the values taught by Jesus. We cannot boil his radical new vision for the kingdom of God down to an expression of conventionality and good behavior. It is so much more. And it is so *un*conventional that it landed Jesus and his followers in hot water on more than one occasion. And so what are those values? An incomplete list follows:

- meekness (Matt 5:5)

- mercy (Luke 15:4–10)

- peacefulness (Matt 5:9)

- sexual propriety in marriage (Matt 5:27)

- a non-anxious reliance on the provision of God (Matt 6:24–34)

- the love of enemies (Luke 6:27–30)

- forgiveness toward those who wrong you (Luke 6:31–36)

- reconciliation (Matt 5:21–24)

- truthfulness (Matt 5:37)

When Paul calls us to be a holy community, "without a spot or wrinkle or anything of the kind . . . holy and blameless" (Eph 5:26–27), he is not referring to our standards of behavior but to the salvific work of Jesus on our behalf. We cannot earn Jesus' love by politeness or niceness. It is offered freely, so we are free to embrace these kingdom values, liberated from any neurotic attempts to win Jesus over with our Sunday best. It is, however, these values mentioned above that should distinguish the followers of Jesus from the empire in which they find themselves. Rodney Stark, chronicler of the rise of Christianity, concludes his book with the following observations,

> Therefore as I conclude this study, I find it necessary to confront what appears to me to be the ultimate factor in the rise of Christianity. . . . The simple phrase, "For God so loved the world . . ." would have puzzled an educated pagan. And the notion that the gods care how we treat one another would have been dismissed as patently absurd. . . . This was the moral climate in which Christianity taught that mercy is one of the primary virtues—that a merciful God requires humans to be merciful. . . . This was revolutionary stuff. Indeed, it was the cultural basis for the revitalization of the Roman world groaning under a host of miseries . . .[9]

It is by our love that all people might know that we are Jesus' disciples. Any community of faith characterized by his name must be a community of peace, love, mercy, and freedom. Stark continues by exploring the ways this was manifest in the early period of the Christian era:

> In my judgment, a major way in which Christianity served as a revitalization movement within the empire was in offering a coherent culture that was entirely stripped of ethnicity. All were welcome without need to dispense with ethnic ties. . . . Christianity also prompted liberating social relations between the sexes and within the family . . . [and] greatly modulated class differences—more than rhetoric was involved when slave and noble greeted one another as brothers in Christ. Finally, what Christianity gave to its converts was nothing less than their humanity.[10]

Jesus' Community Devotes Itself to Scripture and the Exercise of Spiritual Gifts

Paul says, "No one ever hates his own body, but he nourishes and cares for it, just as Christ does for the church, because we are members of his body" (Eph 5:29–30). Jesus is therefore feeding and caring for his people throughout the ages. It is obvious the ways Jesus does this with his company in the Gospels. But how does he nourish and cherish us today? It seems to us that this is the reason why God gives spiritual gifts to the church—so that through the ministry of the Holy Spirit in our midst we are built up (nourished) and nurtured (cared for). How ingenious that the Jesus who dwells within each of us should use each of us to feed and care for each other.

In 1 Corinthians 11, Paul commends the harmonious expression of the gifts with each member playing his or her part in the building up of the church in the same way that different body parts operate as a united whole. It is no mistake that he then launches into his well-known description of love in 1 Corinthians 13, because without genuine love between the members of a church the differing expressions of giftedness would tear them apart. He is in effect commending a unity-in-diversity approach. We are better together, stronger for the ministries of each other in our lives, built up by all the gifts. When he turns his attention to the public gathering of the Corinthians he says,

> When you come together, each one has a hymn, a lesson, a revelation, a tongue, or an interpretation. Let all things be done for building up. If anyone speaks in a tongue, let there be only two or at most three, and each in turn, and let one interpret. But if there is no one to interpret, let them be silent in church and speak to themselves and to God. Let two or three prophets speak, and let the others weigh what is said. If a revelation is made to someone else sitting nearby, let the first person be silent. For you can all prophesy one by one so that all may learn and all be encouraged. (1 Cor 14:26–31)

Here is a picture of the church cooperating seamlessly with the Holy Spirit and each other, each playing their part, each making their contribution. What is one of the ways Jesus nourishes and cares for us? Via the other members of our faith community.

An example of someone who takes this seriously is Dan Kimball from Vintage Faith Church in Santa Cruz, to whom we referred earlier. He has developed a series of questions he asks of all his worship leaders as a regular way of reconnecting with the proper place of worship in the life of a faith community. Those questions are

1. Does our worship lift up Jesus as the center of our church community?

2. In our worship gathering, are the Scriptures read and taught as the normative wisdom for our church community?

3. When we gather to worship, is prayer an essential part of what we do?

4. Do our worship gatherings provide opportunities for us to express our togetherness as a community?

5. Is the communion meal a regular or central part of our worship?

6. Are the members of our church reminded of their obligations to live missional lives when they gather for worship?

7. Does the arrangement of our worship meeting allow for anyone or everyone to contribute to the whole as they see fit and according to their gifting?[11]

We wish all worship curators, rectors, ministers, and pastors were asked these questions more regularly.

↩A Photocopy of a Photocopy of a Photocopy

In the world to come, we will still be charged with the task of declaring Jesus' rule over all of life. Paul was intentionally seeking to replicate the model laid down by Jesus. It was as if he was taking the original Jesus community and seeking to translate it into various contexts across the world. The difficulty with the church today is that we are trying to make faded copies of Paul's copies. Try photocopying a document, then keep recopying the previous copy, and see what the image looks like after multiple generations of copying. Faded, illegible, unusable. How would you get back to the image you wanted? Why, you'd go back to the original document. Paul would hardly have been asking us to copy his copies. He was using the original as his template, and so should we. It's time to reJesus our churches so they look like copies of the pristine original.

At the beginning of this book, we shared about our visits to the great cathedrals of Rome and Moscow, and we asked how far has the religious institution of church moved from the dynamic, relational, countercultural collective first forged by the Nazarene rabbi. The eight characteristics just mentioned can be adopted by any group of Jesus followers today and lived out without any of the paraphernalia or property considered to be so indispensable by the mainstream church. We are not proposing some radical new ecclesiological model. We are not inventing some innovative new approach to being and doing church. We are calling faith communities of Jesus followers to rediscover the teaching, the example, the vision of our founder. We don't do so with contempt or disregard for the traditions developed by Christians over the centuries. Nor do we assume to have some higher or deeper insight into these matters. But we can hold up the models of church we find around us today—professionalized and institutionalized—against the example found in the Gospels and the New Testament, and we can ask some serious questions about the disjunction we find there. It us time to recalibrate the church around the person of Jesus rather than around marketing ploys developed for a shallow consumeristic age.

↶Notes

1. Jim Henderson, *Jim and Casper Go to Church* (Carol Stream, Ill.: Barna-Books, 2007).

2. Kimball, *They Like Jesus but Not the Church*, 79–89.

3. This graph doesn't occur in Kimball's book but is a summary of the responses made to him by his subjects.

4. There is a world of difference as to how we tend to interpret the word "family" and what the Bible means by "household." We tend to impose the nuclear idea of family on the Scriptures, but the Bible's idea of family is much broader and more inclusive.

5. Frost and Hirsch, *Shaping of Things to Come*; Hirsch, *Forgotten Ways*; and Frost, *Exiles*.

6. Moby, "Religion," August 12, 2005. Cited 25 September 2008. Online: http://www.moby.com/node/7007.

7. Ibid.

8. See Hirsch, *Forgotten Ways*, 40–42, 235.

9. Rodney Stark, *The Rise of Christianity* (New York: HarperCollins, 1997), 209–15.

10. Ibid.

11. See Dan Kimball, David Crowder, and Sally Morgenthaler, *Emerging Worship: Creating Worship Gatherings for New Generations* (Grand Rapids, Mich.: Zondervan, 2004), 87.

Conclusion: Read This Bit Last

*There is no Gospel at all if Christ be not God. It is no
news to me to tell me that a great prophet is born.
There have been great prophets before; but the world
has never been redeemed from evil by mere testimony
to the truth, and it never will be. But tell me that God
is born, that God Himself has espoused our nature,
and taken it into union with Himself, then the bells of
my heart ring merry peals, for now may I come to God
since God has come to me.*

—C. H. Spurgeon

Hey, we said to read this bit last, so if you've just bought this book and skipped right to our conclusion, turn back and start from the beginning. We need you to take the journey with us in rediscovering the alternate vision offered by Jesus; the journey of defragging all the pictures of Jesus you've accumulated over the years; the journey of reencountering a Hebraic framework for seeing and following Jesus as the visible presence of the one and only God; the journey of exploring what a Jesus-built church would look like.

Once you've walked that road with us, then we want you to turn your attention to the following image.

Two Men Walk into an Inn . . .

Two middle-aged men meet in an inn in a small, unremarkable village. They embrace, their heavy, solid hands slapping each others' broad backs affectionately. They kiss twice, on each cheek. They sit and eat, hunching over the shared table in a conspiratorial way. The dust that coats their faces highlights the deepening lines around their eyes. Their graying beards betray the years. They are like two old lions, warriors who've fought many a battle but live to fight another day.

Wiping crumbs from his mustache with the back of his hand, one says with a smirk, "You've gotten old quickly."

The other looks up and raises his eyebrows.

"I just mean," continues the first man, "I haven't seen you for a while, and you seem to have aged quite a bit in that time." Another smirk.

The other man starts to defend himself but instead waves his hand dismissively at his friend. "Why do I even bite at comments like that?" he smiles. "You're not exactly the strapping young fellow you used to be either, you know."

They both smile, and the first man reaches across and places his hand on his friend's arm. The tone turns serious. "It's the travel that wears me out," he confesses.

"Agreed. And the disappointment. I could bear the travel, the strange lodgings, the mishaps. But the disappointment of hearing about comrades turning from the cause or cells diverting from our doctrine, well, that's what wears me out the most. I've heard it makes me look old," he says, eyeing his friend warily.

"Very old, actually." They laugh. Silence.

After a while, the first man says, "The Corinthians still causing you a headache, Paul? Should I blame them for all your gray whiskers?"

"Headaches and whiskers are nothing, Peter. Have you heard the latest? You don't want to know. Jealousy, quarrels, and divisions. Some of them have even rejected me as an apostle. Apparently, they prefer more gifted leaders! Can you believe that? They don't understand that wisdom is from the Spirit. After even such a long time, they're still babies in Christ. Don't get me started on their list of crimes: sexual immorality, lawsuits among the comrades, abuse of freedom, tolerance of immoral brothers, taking pride in their spiritual gifts, chaotic and disorderly worship, improper theology on resurrection, and, well, just a complete lack of love. I've written them four letters about all this, and each one seems to get me into further trouble with them. I'm of a mind to stop writing and start fighting. Teach 'em a lesson with my fists that my letters obviously can't. Actually you're probably a better fighter than me. Fancy a trip to Corinth?"

"Clobbering Corinthians probably won't do the trick, comrade. Though I *am* inclined to join you," Peter smiles sympathetically.

"How is the cell at Galatia? Have you had contact with them?" Paul asks after downing a mouthful from his cup. Peter shakes his head slowly. Paul continues, "Their faith was not strong enough to resist the confusions stirred up by the teaching of the Jewish Christians about the circumcision requirement, and they doubted the gospel I preached to them. Like the Corinthians, they even doubt my authority, too."

And so it goes. Two tired men sharing back and forth, recounting stories of new cells in Asia Minor, new converts in Europe, new developments in Greece.

Finally Paul says, "Peter, I'm not sure when I'll see you again. . . ."

"You say that every time we get together."

"I know, and it's always true. But in case our paths never cross again, can you tell me about him one more time."

Peter smiles sadly, "Oh, Paul, you've heard me tell you those stories a million times. You tell them yourself better than I do."

Paul leans forward toward his friend. "Comrade, I've been beaten, abandoned, betrayed, shipwrecked, and left for dead. It's hard to think of a cell I've planted that isn't in the grip of some crisis, personal or doctrinal. I'm not well. I'm often hungry. And, well, according to some of my friends, I look like an old man. The revolution is unfolding, slowly but surely. Ah, the things we've seen. But at times it feels arduous. I long for the Lord as the watchman longs for the end of night. And there are times when I wonder whether these small, struggling cells we're planting will become the movement we dreamed of. Yes, I do wonder. Even after all I've seen and done. All *we've* seen and done . . ."

Then he fixes his eyes firmly on Peter's and says, pleading, "Tell me again."

⟵

We can imagine ourselves standing in the doorway of the ancient inn, looking into the darkened room and seeing two battle-weary warriors sharing stories of their hero, their standard, their inspiration. Would Paul and Peter have met like this and spoken in this way? Who can say? But there seems little doubt that it was the story of Jesus that inspired their work and ministry and was the lifeblood of their mission. Indeed, writing to the Romans, Paul introduces himself as "Paul, a servant of Christ Jesus, called to be an apostle, set apart for the gospel of God" (Rom 1:1). What is the "gospel of God" for which he felt set apart? Is it a set of doctrinal propositions, a revolutionary dogma, a collection of beliefs and practices centered on Jesus? In fact, it's far more. The gospel is not simply theological ideology. It is a historical event! Listen as he explains:

> |the gospel| he promised beforehand through his prophets in the holy scrip-tures, the gospel concerning his Son, who was descended from David accord-ing to the flesh and was declared to be Son of God with power according to the spirit of holiness by resurrection from the dead, Jesus Christ our Lord, through whom we have received grace and apostleship to bring about the obedience of faith among all the Gentiles for the sake of his name, including yourselves who are called to belong to Jesus Christ. (Rom 1:2–6)

When Paul explains the content of his gospel, it doesn't consist of propo-sitional statements about creation, sin, atonement, and redemption. It is a recapturing of the historical story of Jesus! For Paul, the gospel *is* Jesus—his messianic credentials, his physical descent from David, his vindication by the Spirit of God, and his resurrection from the dead. This looks identical to the gospel given to us in Matthew's Gospel. In effect, Romans 1:1–6 is a *Reader's Digest* version of the Gospels.

Later in Romans, Paul offers an even more truncated version of the same message, when he writes,

> But what does it say? "The word is near you, on your lips and in your heart" (that is, the word of faith that we proclaim); because if you confess with your lips that Jesus is Lord and believe in your heart that God raised him from the dead, you will be saved. (Rom 10:8–9)

Scholars believe that this was obviously the repetition of a well-known creed of the time. If it is a simple creedal statement, then note its trajectory. It is a super-summarized version of Matthew, Mark, or Luke. Compare it with the flowery Nicene Creed from the fourth century, which refers to Jesus as "light from light, true light from true light, begotten not made, of one being with the Father." Paul has nothing to do with this airy doctrinal language. In 2 Timothy he offers his preferred version of the gospel: "Remember Jesus Christ, raised from the dead, a descendant of David—that is my gospel" (2 Tim 2:8). Events. Facts. History. This is my gospel.

Probably nowhere is this expressed more urgently by him than in his advice to the Corinthians in the conduct of their public feast:

> Now, brothers and sisters, I want to remind you of the gospel I preached to you, which you received and on which you have taken your stand. By this gospel you are saved, if you hold firmly to the word I preached to you. Otherwise, you have

believed in vain. For what I received I passed on to you as of first importance: that Christ died for our sins according to the Scriptures, that he was buried, that he was raised on the third day according to the Scriptures, and that he appeared to Peter, and then to the Twelve. (1 Cor 15:1–5, TNIV)

Jesus died for our sins. He was the fulfillment of prophecy. He rose again. He appeared to witnesses. This is our gospel, anchored in the person and work of Jesus, "the gospel I preached to you," as Paul refers to it. In fact, there seems enough evidence to suggest that most of what Paul taught to his fledgling churches were the stories of Jesus, with an obvious emphasis on the death, resurrection, and appearances of Jesus. His epistles deal with specific pastoral and theological issues, but they should be read in the light of the fact that the gospel he preached to them, the doctrine he'd immersed them in, was the Christ event, the story of Jesus. Says John Dickson,

> The importance of [these] creedal statements should not be underestimated for they are rare glimpses into the missionary proclamation of the first Christians, and of the Pauline missionaries in particular. In his letters, Paul (and the other apostles) had no reason to repeat the missionary preaching at great length. The 'gospel' tends to be a shared assumption throughout the epistles, always in the background but rarely brought to the fore.[1]

Today, too many Christians are reading Romans as though it is Paul's exposition of the gospel—creation, sin, atonement. But Romans and the other epistles were applications of the gospel rather than expositions of it. Paul is assuming the Romans remember the amazing story of Jesus he had taught them. In fact, when Paul preaches the gospel it sounds more like Acts 13 than Romans 1–3:

> When he had removed him [Saul], he made David their king. In his testimony about him he said, "I have found David, son of Jesse, a man after my heart, who will carry out all my wishes.' Of this man's posterity God has brought to Israel a Savior, Jesus, as he promised; before his coming John had already proclaimed a baptism of repentance to all the people of Israel. And as John was finishing his work, he said, 'What do you suppose that I am? I am not he. No, but one is coming after me; I am not worthy to untie the thong of the sandals on his feet.' My brothers, you descendants of Abraham's family, and others who fear God, to us the message of this salvation has been sent. Because the residents of Jerusalem and their leaders did not recognize him or understand the words of the prophets that are read every sabbath, they fulfilled those words by condemning him. Even though they found no cause for a sentence of death, they asked Pilate to have him killed. When they had carried out everything that was written

about him, they took him down from the tree and laid him in a tomb. But God raised him from the dead, and for many days he appeared to those who came up with him from Galilee to Jerusalem, and they are now his witnesses to the people. And we bring you the good news that what God promised to our ancestors he has fulfilled for us, their children, by raising Jesus . . . Let it be known to you, therefore, my brothers, that through this man forgiveness of sins is proclaimed to you; By this Jesus everyone who believes is set free from all those sins from which you could not be freed by the law of Moses. (Acts 13:22–39)

Note the following three things: first, this sermon is a virtual summary of the Gospels, particularly Mark and Luke, focusing on the events of Jesus' life. Second, there is an unmistakable corollary between this sermon and the creedal statements we previously looked at in Romans and 2 Timothy, with their emphasis on the kingly rule of Jesus. And third, there is an explicit reference to the Pauline doctrine of justification by faith, rooting it firmly in the historic event of Jesus' messianic rule, his life, death, and resurrection.

We don't wish to imply that doctrinal statements are useless. But doctrinal purity for its own sake has riven churches apart and led to the current proliferation of denominations and competing Christian agencies. For Paul, as for Peter, the gospel is Jesus and Jesus alone. Any doctrine that emerges and is developed into propositional statement must find its locus in the story of Jesus.

Did Paul and Peter ever meet in a darkened inn, share a meal, and swap stories? We don't know, but if they did, we have little doubt that the stories they would have swapped wouldn't have been the trivial or the nostalgic. We are convinced that they clung to the gospel narrative as their sole reason for being. Try to imagine those battered old lions telling those stories, reJesusing each other. Then ask yourself how desperately you cling to the gospel—not the Four Spiritual Laws, not the Bridge to Life, not a doctrinal catechism, but Jesus. And if you do cling desperately to him, then join us in our quest to reJesus our churches in this day and age.

⟵ Notes

1. John Dickson, "Announcing the Christ Event: Aspects of the New Testament Gospel" (unpublished article, 2001).

Selected Resources

Bell, Rob. *Velvet Elvis: Repainting the Christian Faith*. Grand Rapids, Mich.: Zondervan, 2005.

Bonhoeffer, Dietrich. *Christ the Center*. Translated by Edwin Robertson. New York: Harper & Row, 1978.

Bosch, David Jacobus. *Transforming Mission: Paradigm Shifts in Theology of Mission*. American Society of Missiology Series 16. Maryknoll, N.Y.: Orbis, 1991.

Brunner, Emil. *The Mediator: A Study of the Central Doctrine of the Christian Faith*. Translated by Olive Wyon. London: Lutterworth, 1934.

Bryman, Alan. *Charisma and Leadership in Organizations*. Newbury, Calif.: Sage, 1992.

Bultmann, Rudolph. *Jesus and the Word*. New York: Fontana, 1958.

Burke, Spencer, and Barry Taylor. *A Heretic's Guide to Eternity*. San Francisco, Jossey-Bass, 2006.

Cave, Nick. *The Gospel according to Mark with an Introduction by Nick Cave*. Melbourne: Text, 1998.

Cavey, Bruxy. *The End of Religion: An Introduction to the Subversive Spirituality of Jesus*. Ottawa: Agora, 2005.

Chalke, Steve, and Alan Mann. *The Lost Message of Jesus*. Grand Rapids, Mich.: Zondervan, 2003.

Chesnut, Glenn. *Images of Christ: An Introduction to Christology*. Minneapolis: Seabury, 1984.

Clarke, Andrew, and Bruce Winter. *One God, One Lord: Christianity in a World of Religious Pluralism*. Grand Rapids, Mich.: Baker, 1992..

Conger, Jay Alden, and Rabindra Nath Kanungo. *Charismatic Leadership in Organizations*. Thousand Oaks, Calif.: Sage, 1998.

Dickson, John. *A Spectator's Guide to Jesus*. Sydney: Blue Bottle, 2005.

Ellul, Jacques. *The Subversion of Christianity*. Grand Rapids, Mich.: Eerdmans, 1986.

Erre, Mike. *The Jesus of Suburbia: Have We Tamed the Son of God to Fit Our Lifestyle?* Dallas: W, 2006.

Frei, Hans W. *The Identity of Jesus Christ: The Hermeneutical Bases of Dogmatic Theology*. Philadelphia: Fortress, 1975.

Frost, Michael. *Exiles: Living Missionally in a Post-Christian Culture*. Peabody, Mass.: Hendrickson, 2006.

———. *Jesus the Fool*. Peabody, Mass.: Hendrickson, forthcoming.

———. *Seeing God in the Ordinary: A Theology of the Everyday*. Peabody, Mass.: Hendrickson, 2000.

———, and Alan Hirsch. *The Shaping of Things to Come: Innovation and Mission for the 21st-Century Church*. Peabody, Mass.: Hendrickson, 2003.

Grempf, Conrad. *Mealtime Habits of the Messiah: 40 Encounters with Jesus*. Grand Rapids, Mich.: Zondervan, 2005.

Gruen, Anselm. *Images of Jesus*. Translated by John Bowden. New York: Continuum, 2002.

Heim, Karl. *Jesus the Lord: The Sovereign Authority of Jesus and God's Revelation in Christ*. Translated by D. H. van Daalen. Philadelphia: Muhlenberg, 1959.

Henderson, Jim, Matt Casper, and George Barna. *Jim and Casper Go to Church: Frank Conversations about Faith, Churches, and Well-Meaning Christians*. Carol Stream, Ill.: BarnaBooks, 2007.

Hirsch, Alan. *The Forgotten Ways: Reactivating the Missional Church*. Grand Rapids, Mich.: Brazos, 2007.

Houlden, J. Leslie, ed. *Jesus in History, Thought, and Culture: An Encyclopedia*. Santa Barbara, Calif.: ABC-CLIO, 2003.

Kimball, Dan. *They Like Jesus but Not the Church*. Grand Rapids, Mich.: Zondervan, 2007.

Kinlaw, Dennis F. *Let's Start with Jesus: A New Way of Doing Theology*. Grand Rapids, Mich.: Zondervan, 2005.

Men, Alexander. *Son of Man: The Story of Christianity and Christ*. Translated by Samuel Brown. Torrance, Calif.: Oakwood, 1992.

McLaren, Brian. *The Secret Message of Jesus: Uncovering the Truth that Could Change Everything*. Grand Rapids, Mich.: Nashville: W, 2006.

———. *The Voice of Luke: Not Even Sandals*. Nashville: Thomas Nelson, 2007.

Miguez Boniño, José, ed. *Faces of Jesus: Latin American Christologies*. Translated by Robert R. Barr. Maryknoll, N.Y.: 1984.

Minear, Paul. *Commands of Christ*. Nashville: Abingdon, 1972.

———. *Eyes of Faith: A Study in the Biblical Point of View*. Philadelphia: Westminster, 1946.

Moltmann, Jürgen. *The Way of Christ: Christology in Messianic Dimensions*. San Francisco: Harper, 1990.

Morgan, Alison. *The Wild Gospel: Bringing Truth to Life*. Oxford: Monarch, 2004.

Phillips, John A. *The Form of Christ in the World: A Study in Bonhoeffer's Christology*. London: Collins, 1967.

Ritschl, Dietrich. *Memory and Hope: An Inquiry Concerning the Presence of Christ*. New York: Macmillan, 1967.

Roberts, Dave. *Following Jesus: A Non-Religious Guide for the Spiritually Hungry*. Lake Mary, Fla.: Relevant, 2004.

Samuel, Vinay, and Chris Sugden, eds. *Sharing Jesus in the Two Thirds World: Evangelical Christologies from the Contexts of Poverty, Powerlessness, and Religious Pluralism*. Papers of the First Conference of Evangelical Mission Theologians from the Two Thirds World. Bangkok, Thailand, March 22–25, 1982. Grand Rapids, Mich.: Eerdmans, 1983.

Sayers, Dorothy L. *The Man Born to Be King*. London: Victor Gollancz, 1955.

Seay, Chris, Brian McLaren, David Capes, Lauren Winner, and Greg Garrett. *The Last Eyewitness: The Final Week*. Nashville: Thomas Nelson, 2006.

Shenk, Wilbert R., ed. *The Transfiguration of Mission: Biblical, Theological, and Historical Foundations*. Scottdale, Pa.: Herald, 1993.

Stark, Rodney. *One True God: Historical Consequences of Monotheism*. Princeton, N.J.: Princeton University Press, 2001.

———. *The Rise of Christianity*. New York: HarperCollins, 1997.

Stassen Glen H., and David P. Gushee. *Kingdom Ethics: Following Jesus in a Contemporary Context*. Downers Grove, Ill.: InterVarsity, 2003.

Taylor, John V. *The Christlike God*. London: SCM, 1992.

Taylor, Tom. *Paradoxy: Coming to Grips with the Contradictions of Jesus*. Grand Rapids, Mich.: Baker, 2006.

Walsh, Brian J., and Sylvia C. Keesmaat. *Colossians Remixed*. Downers Grove, Ill.: InterVarsity, 2004.

Ward, Keith. *Re-Thinking Christianity*. Oxford: Oneworld, 2007.

Wells, Harold. *The Christic Center: Life-Giving and Liberating*. Maryknoll, N.Y.: Orbis, 2004.

Wilson, Jonathan. *God So Loved the World: A Christology for Disciples*. Grand Rapids, Mich.: Baker, 2001.

Winner, Lauren. *The Voice of Matthew*. Nashville: Thomas Nelson, 2007.

Wright, N. T. *The Challenge of Jesus*. London: SPCK, 2000.

———. *Jesus and the Victory of God*. London: SPCK, 1996.

———. *Who Was Jesus?* London: SPCK, 1992.

Yancey, Philip. *The Jesus I Never Knew*. Grand Rapids, Mich.: Zondervan, 1995.

Illustration Credits

"Martin Luther King, Jr., 1964." Dick DeMarsico. Courtesy of the Library of Congress.

"Fannie Lou Hamer at the Democratic National Convention, Atlantic City, New Jersey, August 1964." U.S. News & World Report Magazine Photograph Collection. Courtesy of the Library of Congress.

"Sheila Cassidy." Reproduced with the permission of Darton, Longman & Todd.

Janani Luwum. Drawing by Edward S. Turner IV. Reproduced with the permission of the artist.

"Dietrich Bonhoeffer in London, 1939." Bildarchiv Preussicher Kulturbesitz. Reproduced with the permission of Art Resource/N.Y.

Søren Kierkegaard. Based on a sketch by Niels Christian Kierkegaard (1806–1882).

Alan Walker. Drawing by Edward S. Turner IV. Reproduced with the permission of the artist.

Jean Vanier. Drawing by Edward S. Turner IV. Reproduced with the permission of the artist.

Jesus. *The Light of the World*, William Holman Hunt. Ca. 1851–1853. Keble College, Oxford, Great Britain. Photo credit: HIP/ Art Resource, N.Y. Reproduced with permission.

Jesus. *Sacred Heart*, Pompeo Batoni. Il Gesu, Rome, Italy. Photo Credit: Scala/ Art Resouce, N.Y. Reproduced with permission.

Jesus. Film still from *Son of God*, directed by Jean Claude Bragand. British Broadcasting Company, April 2001. Reproduced with the permission of the BBC Photo Library.

Jesus. Film still from *Il Vangelo secondo Matteo* (*The Gospel According to Saint Matthew*), directed by Pier Paolo Pasolini. Arco Film, 1964. Every effort was made to obtain permission for the image used here. Concerned parties are welcome to contact Hendrickson Publishers.

Jesus. *Meek. Mild. As If*. Church of England poster, 1999. Church's Advertising Network (CAN). Reproduced with permission.

Jesus. *Christ Pantocrator.* St. Catherine's Monastery, Sinai. Photograph by Peter Brubacher. Reproduced with permission.

"William Wilberforce, with His Signature." Reproduced with the permission of North Wind Picture Archives.

"Mother Teresa." Evert Odekerken. Licensed under Creative Commons Attribution 2.5.

Rigoberta Menchú. Drawing by Edward S. Turner IV. Reproduced with the permission of the artist.

"Eva Price." Reproduced with the permission of the Oberlin College Archives, Oberlin, Ohio.

"Harriet Beecher Stowe." Reproduced with the permission of the Ohio Historical Society.

"Dorothy Day." Milwaukee Journal. Reproduced with the permission of the Marquette University Archives.

Damien of Molokai. Drawing by Edward S. Turner IV. Reproduced with the permission of the artist.

Simone Weil. Drawing by Edward S. Turner IV. Reproduced with the permission of the artist.

Index

LIKE A BLACK SHADOW THEY WERE MOVING ACROSS THE FACE OF THE LAND

The Revelationists. They were healthy, fresh-faced, and clean. They burned with a raging fervor—a mindless urgency to fulfill their mission.

They bought the brooding old asylum that crouched above the town. In a week they had fenced off two hundred acres of land. All the while their numbers grew.

They followed Michael . . . Michael, their leader . . . Michael, the Archangel . . . Michael, who was everywhere.

They published a message to the people of Hudson City. It read:

WOE TO THE INHABITERS OF THE EARTH. THE DEVIL IS AMONG YOU.

THE
TURNING

JUSTIN SCOTT

A DELL BOOK

Published by
Dell Publishing Co., Inc.
1 Dag Hammarskjold Plaza
New York, New York 10017

Copyright © 1978 by Justin Scott

Dell ® TM 681510, Dell Publishing Co., Inc.

ISBN: 0-440-17472-4

Printed in the United States of America
First printing—March 1978

For my mother, Lily K. Scott.
Whom can we turn to
in times like these?

"Whoever marries the spirit of the times will be a widow."
    —REVEREND RICHARD NEUHAUS

Prologue

A stone path led from the back door of the church to the rectory. Halfway there, the flat rocks split into a second path that led to the cemetery. The old minister hesitated at the fork. It was cold and dark, but sentiment prevailed. Tugging his coat around his frail frame, he groped his way along the dark left-hand path to his wife's grave. There he knelt, bowed his head, and offered a short prayer. It was only after he had ended his ceremony with a whispered "Good night" that he looked up and, high on the black of the mountain, far above the town, saw the faint, blue glow.

He stared, the cold forgotten. Strange. It was the color of a Christmas-tree light. And it looked as though it was in the old Spotting Asylum. He blinked and looked again. The blue light was still there, where it couldn't possibly be. The institution for the criminally insane had stood empty for fifteen years, its rows of broken windows mocking the town with a gap-toothed leer.

Suddenly, as he watched, the light disappeared, reappeared almost immediately, then repeated. A blue light, blackness, a blue light. It *was* in the abandoned asylum, passing from window to window as if someone were stalking the dismal corridors, pausing in each cell.

Why would anyone be up there so late at night, the minister wondered. And who? Perhaps the police, he told himself, in which case he would seem rather silly to report it. There was something quite bold about the way the blue glow moved from window to window. Then it disappeared. He waited awhile, shivering. When it didn't come back he hurried home to the warmth of his rectory, worrying that he had never seen the police use blue lights, wondering what it meant.

1

The kitchen telephone had a short wire and Alan Springer paced its limits. He was a tall, slim man, his angular hands and arms in constant motion, his thick brown hair touseled, his eyes restless. He finished his conversation and cradled the telephone.

"Some people just came into town. Our illustrious mayor thinks they're going to buy the old asylum."

His wife, Margaret, was cooking breakfast. "Why did he call you?"

"Tonsillitis, again. He's coming over for a shot."

Margaret's mouth tightened. She broke a yoke lifting an egg from the skillet to a plate. "Why can't he wait until you get to the hospital?"

Springer touched his lips to her shoulder. "Bob? He's practically family."

Margaret shrugged away from him. "He should know to respect our privacy. . . . Samantha," she called up the back staircase, "come down this instant!"

"She was up late reading," said Springer.

"She has to stop that, Alan. She never gets enough sleep."

Springer carried two plates across the old-fashioned kitchen to a scarred wooden table. He went back to the stove for the third and Margaret said, "The broken egg is mine."

"I'll take it."

"It's mine. Just sit down and eat."

"You all right?"

"Of course I'm all right."

Springer caressed her arm. "Good morning."

"Good morning. Samantha!"

"I'll get her."

"Your breakfast is getting cold. Will you please eat?"

Springer sat, arranged a napkin on his lap, and gazed out the window at the back lawn. It was still winter brown. The kitchen window, a large bay with water-stained woodwork, commanded a long view beyond the bare trees that marked the Springers' property line. Spotting Mountain was checkered black and green by stands of leafless oak and long-needled pine. Halfway up the slope, stone-gray on dead fields, crouched a brooding, empty-eyed visage, the abandoned Spotting Asylum for the Criminally Insane.

It had been built at the turn of the century to house the dangerous whose families could afford the deferential security of a private mental hospital. Like the other great sanitariums and institutions of the Adirondack region it had provided jobs and money for the residents of the lean and rugged land. Until the day, fifteen years ago, when the outdated asylum had closed and a heavily guarded cortege of locked ambulances and police wagons weaved down the mountain with its cargo of aging inmates. Hudson City had never recovered from the loss.

"Would you please tell me why Bob can't wait a half hour for a shot?" asked Margaret. She sat across from her husband and pushed a strand of honey-colored hair from her face. She was a handsome woman of thirty-eight, who alternately feasted herself plump and starved thin. She was thin now, too thin, Springer thought, her face sharp, her skin tight across her cheekbones.

He ate quickly, speaking between bites. "Yes, I can. Bob is my best friend. You know perfectly well that he's the only person in town I allow here for treatment. Besides, he's got a nine o'clock appointment that could have immense bearing on the town."

"You sound like the Chamber of Commerce, Alan."

Springer grinned. "Sorry."

"No one's going to buy that monstrosity," Margaret said scornfully.

"Bob says they have a letter of introduction from the bank."

"But what would anyone want a maximum security asylum for?"

Springer eyed the distant structure. "I think it's safe to say they couldn't use it as a mental hospital and nobody's building new schools these days, so what does that leave?"

"Your federal drug treatment center?" said Margaret, with a trace of a smile.

"No," said Springer. He had failed to convince the town fathers of the worth of that proposal and, two years later, the defeat still rankled. "What else could they want it for but a resort hotel?"

"In that creepy place?" She shivered. "It's hideous."

"But it's on a beautiful piece of land. It has a lake and room for riding trails. Obviously they'd have to renovate the building, but the walls and roof are solid."

Margaret spoke wistfully. "Wouldn't that be nice. We'd have such interesting people coming up here."

"We'd have jobs up here," replied Springer shortly. He did not like being reminded that his wife still felt like an outsider in his hometown.

Margaret continued her reverie. "It would be so nice to have a really good restaurant nearby. You know, the kind of place where we could just dress a little when you get home and just drive up the hill. You know?" She touched her hair. "Like a country club."

Springer took her hand. "So anyhow, Bob wants me to come along and show the place. Leading citizen and all that . . . talk about the hospital . . . good for ski injuries . . . enlightened government."

"You don't have the time," Margaret said, withdrawing her hand.

"I'll make the time. Selling— Good morning, sweetheart."

Samantha drifted from the stairs, which she had descended silently, touched her mother as if for reassurance, and sank into her breakfast chair. She was fifteen, a frail, softer version of Margaret, small for her age, her slender body as yet undeveloped. Springer put his arm around her and she brushed his cheek with her lips. Her flannel nightgown was still warm from her bed.

"And what were you doing last night?"

Samantha sipped a quarter inch of orange juice and snuggled against him. "I was reading." She yawned sleepily.

Springer loved the musical quality of her voice. "What were you reading, angel?"

"A book."

"I'm glad it wasn't a tree."

"Daddy!"

"Sit up, Samantha. You're going to be late for school. You're not even dressed."

"I don't feel too good, Mother." She touched her forehead. "I think I have a temperature."

Margaret reached across the table and placed her fingers on Samantha's brow. "You feel fine to me. Alan?"

He met his wife's worried glance. This was becoming a morning ritual two or three times a week. Always a quiet, shy child, Samantha had withdrawn more than ever in recent months and, mysteriously, school now seemed a painful experience. Unable to find the source of the problem, the Springers argued whether or not to let her stay home on mornings she seemed particularly unhappy. Margaret, recalling that Samantha had been a sickly baby, tended to be more indulgent than Alan, who, in spite of vivid memories of his own unhappy days at the Hudson City High School twenty-five years ago, hoped that Samantha would benefit most by comfronting her timidity.

Her pale skin felt cool to his lips. "You are fine," he pronounced, tapping her nose gently for emphasis.

"But I feel—"

"To school," he said with mock severity.

"Daddy," she pleaded, her eyes welling. Her body tensed as a sudden blast of cold air pushed into the drafty kitchen and Bob Kent thrust his head through the mud-room door.

"Knock, knock. Good morning, everybody."

"Come on in," said Springer. Samantha tucked her bare feet under her nightgown and stared at the table, her lips trembling.

Kent, fifty years old, short and stocky, wrapped in a nylon car coat over a sports jacket, white shirt, and wide necktie, was mayor of Hudson City, a position that dovetailed conveniently with his real estate business.

He was an enormously energetic man but this morning he seemed tired, and his cheerful, round face was pale and drawn. He took the tea that Margaret placed silently before him and, not noticing Samantha's glum expression, asked, "And how is the prettiest girl in town?"

She curled more tightly into her corner and mumbled an inaudible reply.

Springer took a tongue depressor from his bag by the

door and said to Kent, "Face the window, open wide, and say nothing."

"Ah?"

"Get your tongue out of the way. . . . Jesus Christ, when are you going to get these things out?"

"Any day now." He shrugged out of his coat and jacket. "Gimme a shot. We got work to do."

"You should be in bed. It's cold out there."

"After lunch, I promise. I can hardly think straight. You coming with me?"

"Sure."

"Keep a close eye on me. The way I feel I could knock sixty grand off the price just to get some sleep."

"Alan thought you needed a leading citizen to dazzle the buyer," said Margaret.

"That too," said Kent.

Springer grinned back at his friend and slipped a thermometer into his mouth. "Hold that under your tongue." He drew 600,000 units of penicillin into a hypodermic and rolled the mayor's sleeve up his fleshy arm. Samantha watched with big eyes as he dabbed his arm with alcohol. Kent winked and she looked away, flushing.

He winced when the needle punctured his skin and then removed the thermometer.

"Back in your mouth," said Springer.

Kent handed it to him. "I already know I have a temperature. I'm sweating."

"When are you going to get them out?"

"What out?"

"Tonsils. The ones you keep promising me you're going to get out."

"December," replied Kent, rolling down his sleeve.

"Why wait eight months?"

"I got an election coming up in November. I gotta campaign."

Springer laughed. "Uncontested, as usual. You're a shoo-in if they don't catch you molesting small boys."

"Alan!" snapped Margaret.

"It's a joke," Springer said. "Samantha, you know that's a joke, don't you?"

"Yes, Daddy," she replied mechanically.

"Can you keep me healthy till then?" asked Kent.

"I'll put you on Bicillin maintenance. It'll work awhile,

until the bugs get smart." He closed his bag. "Okay, let's get this show on the road. Young lady, if you're dressed in four minutes we'll drop you at school. Otherwise you walk and that's a bitter wind."

"I'll . . . take her later if she feels better," said Margaret. She taught art at the high school, but did not report until eleven o'clock, since, hard-pressed by a dwindling budget, the school had relegated nonessential courses to part-time status.

Rather than air Samantha's problems in front of Kent, Springer said, "Okay, if you feel that's best. . . . Drink some more tea, Bob. I'll warm up the car."

He kissed Margaret. For an instant she clung tightly.

2

The buyers, two fresh-faced blond men, were waiting outside their room at the Pines Motel a quarter mile south of town. Springer watched them as he paused for a yellow school bus.

"Who are these people?"

"Well, I'm not quite sure," said Kent. "I got a call from New York City real early. Before hours. The bank said show 'em the place. I asked if they were hotel people and the bank said, 'What do you think?' " Kent shrugged. "So I think they're hotel people."

As the bus blatted past with its load of children from the outlying farms, Springer turned off the two-lane highway into the motel parking lot. From here the two men looked very young.

They wore city topcoats over dark suits and, though it was cold, held their gloveless hands out of their pockets. Something about their expressions of remote courtesy, their watchful manner made Springer think of bodyguards. He was about to voice the thought, but Kent had already bounded from the car and was hurrying toward them, his right arm outstretched, a broad smile on his face. "Morning, fellas," he began, "hop in. I'll introduce—"

"Good morning, sir," said one, cutting him off smoothly. "We'll follow in our car." He thrust a long white envelope with the logo of the New York bank into Kent's extended hand, then wheeled in unison with his companion and climbed into a blue station wagon. While Kent scanned the letter of introduction, Springer waited until they got their engine started—a winter habit in the Adirondacks—then turned north toward Hudson City.

"Charming pair."

"Seem fine to me." Kent shrugged.

Springer grinned. "If Attila the Hun wanted an R and R resort for his hordes he'd seem fine to you."

Kent slipped the letter into his pocket. "You better believe it."

A tall, white Presbyterian Church dominated the view of Hudson City from the south, its blistered paint invisible at a distance. Possessing a visual significance far grander than its actual importance, it drew the eye away from the rutted mud sprawl of Moser's Lumberyard, the grim WPA-built high school, the garish Exxon station, and the double row of shabby mansions that lined Main Street like the musty ledgers of a once prosperous business.

"When are you going to paint your house?" asked Kent.

Springer glanced at his home. Though it was the best-kept on the street, the square, neo-Georgian porch columns were peeling noticeably, thanks to an ice-clogged gutter that had forced water under the soffits. "Soon as I get my consulting fee for your tonsillectomy."

"You ought to fix it up," groused Kent. "Or get a new place. I keep telling you that lot next to mine is yours anytime you want it." As had several other local businessmen, Kent had built a modern ranch house on Spotting Mountain Road a half mile out of town.

"You sound like Margaret."

"You can't blame her. These old barns are tough on a woman."

"I like my house."

The Main Street mansions, the more dilapidated flying forlorn TOURISTS signs, had been built before the turn of the century when lumbering, garnet mining, tourism, and the newly completed Spotting Asylum brought sudden wealth to Hudson City. The extravagant harmonies of Victorian-Gothic and neo-Georgian design had flourished with the town, and the ornaments—the spires, the gables, the great splayed half-moon lights—had sung Hudson City's self-delight.

But the hardwoods were lumbered off by the end of World War One. The garnet mines passed into receivership during the Great Depression. The asylum faltered and eventually closed. And just when it looked as if a wave of tourism might save the town, a new interstate highway sheered through the mountains ten miles to the east. Today, the cost of a regular coat of white paint, a trifling to the builders of the mansions, was beyond the means of the present owners, and the bold songs of the mansions' gleaming embellishments had long since faded to bitter whispers.

"Goddamn little vandals!" exploded Kent.

The contents of an overturned litter basket had spilled into the street in front of Rigby's Drugstore. Above it, a NO PARKING sign sagged drunkenly. "Why the hell do the kids have to do that? Makes the whole town look lousy."

"Calm down, Bob. They're not buying the town."

Kent looked anxiously behind them, but the men in the blue station wagon stared straight ahead as they drove through the commercial district, a short, double row of two-story attached buildings with tawdry aluminum and plastic storefronts. For more than a decade the town had subsisted upon the meager earnings of the local dairy farmers, small-scale lumbering operations, a scattering of summer residents from New York City, and welfare collected by its chronically unemployed, and Bob Kent's FOR RENT signs pleading in the gray windows of a half-dozen empty stores showed the strain.

The survivors included Rigby's Drugstore, a liquor store, a barber shop, the shabby offices of the Hudson City *Sun,* a branch of the First National Bank of Warington (the county seat, thirty miles away), a dry-cleaning pickup (also subsidiary to Warington), Lewis's General Store, a post office, and the IGA grocery and feed supply.

Kent looked back again as they passed an abandoned Shell station. Its windows were boarded. There were gaping holes where the pumps had been. Broken glass littered the tarmac.

"Relax," said Springer. "There isn't a town in New York State that doesn't own an empty gas station."

"Bastards," growled Kent. "First they knock down a perfectly good old stable, then they pull out a few years later and leave us with the mess."

"You sold it to them," Springer reminded him, with a smile.

"It looks like hell."

"Then look at the hospital."

Kent beamed happily at the Hudson City Hospital, a compact, modern, single-level glass and brick building with a brightly marked ambulance entrance.

"Much better."

The six-bed hospital was Springer's creation and a bright spot in Hudson City's bleak economic condition. He had conceived the idea while watching the wrecker from Grand's Gas Station, which employed a powerful receiver to scavenge accident reports from state police and citizen band radios, towing the blood-flecked remains of a station wagon in from the interstate. The driver had bled to death because the nearest hospital had been in Warington, thirty miles from where he had crashed, though only ten from Hudson City.

Springer hired a dirt-track stock-car racer, gave him a radio and a tightly sprung ambulance built for speed, and created a rescue unit that could bring a traffic casualty from the interstate to the converted den that served as his office within twenty minutes of the accident. By the time he had convinced the obstinately cautious town board to build a little hospital, the lemon-yellow ambulance was legend on the narrow, twisting Adirondack roads, a not-to-be-forgotten vision of blazing lights and howling sirens, the duty nurse cringing in the passenger seat as it roared past Grand's wrecker on a short straightaway.

The ambulance and the hospital saved lives and provided better local care in a clinic than a single country doctor could offer. And since vacationing motorists tended to carry comprehensive medical insurance, treating them was a profitable business that offset the losses sustained in the clinic and helped pay the salaries of Springer, an intern who covered the night shift, a head nurse, eight part-time nurses, a porter, two ambulance drivers, and a secretary.

At the church, Springer swung left onto Spotting Mountain Road, which bordered the cemetery, a neatly groomed fenced plot of modest headstones shaded by ancient trees. Just past the graveyard, Spotting Street connected with the road, making the turn confusing. Springer checked the mirror, but the young men were right behind, expressionless.

"Something's funny about them," he said.

"What?"

"They're not looking at anything. Like they couldn't care less, or they've been here already. They didn't even look down the side streets."

Kent swallowed painfully and massaged his throat. "Like you said, they're not buying the town."

"Remember Burger King?"

"Those bastards."

Two years before, Kent and some other Hudson City businessmen had formed a syndicate to buy a fast-food franchise, which, it was hoped, would provide jobs for the unemployed, profits for the investors, and taxes for the town. (Springer had counterproposed his drug treatment center, which would have been supported by federal funds, but no one wanted drug addicts on Spotting Mountain.) A contingent from the Burger King corporation had descended upon Hudson City, subjecting it to invasive scrutiny before deciding that the two-lane state highway didn't carry enough traffic to support a store.

"Burger King can go screw," said Kent. "If we get this hotel, McDonald's will be pounding on our door."

Spotting Mountain Road twisted back and forth as it scaled the four-thousand-foot mountain that dominated Hudson City and the surrounding valleys. Mounds of snow still rested in shadowy gullies. The road sparkled in the sunlight. Slag from the garnet mines was mixed into the macadam and fragments of the bright stones dotted its surface. White salt streaks radiated from the road's crown, evidence of the long winter struggle to keep it free of snow and ice.

When they passed a group of new homes clustered in a former alfalfa field, Kent reached over and blew the horn. His wife, a tiny round woman raking a bare lawn, waved back. Farther on, a hand-painted sign on a shabby farmhouse advertised a beauty shop within. A big hair drier stood forlornly in the kitchen window. The fields were empty, the earth still frozen. It would thaw soon. Already the spring sun muddied the surface, but the farmers would have to wait another week after the deep thaw for the mud to dry.

As the road climbed higher, the farmland grew rough, the stands of second-growth trees more frequent. Here and there abandoned barns paled into the landscape as cleared lands, untended for the first time in a hundred years, were overtaken by the weed trees, birch and poplar. They drove past a shack, hard by the road. Junked cars crowded the side yard. Plastic sheeting flapped from gaping black holes in the asphalt shingles.

"Jesus," Kent complained, jerking his head toward the buyers. "When you look at this from their point of view it must look like hell. That goddamn shack knocks five thousand dollars off the price of the next decent house."

Springer said nothing. Poverty was as much a part of the region as the bitter winter cold. He had vivid memories of it. Every October, when he was growing up and plastic sheeting was not available, he had collected newspaper to stuff the walls and keep the wind out of his father's shack. By March the papers had been soaked and dried so often that they were little more than brown dust. An April blizzard, not an uncommon occurrence in the mountains, where winter retreated fitfully behind a flurry of angry slaps, still reminded him of waking to snow on his blanket.

Tire tracks muddied the sparkling macadam where narrow dirt roads snaked out of the woods. A scalped hillock showed where Moser's men were cutting isolated stands of hardwood. Springer veered to the shoulder and signaled to the station wagon to do the same. A mill-bound truck careened past, its impossibly high load of logs swaying dangerously.

Another mile, halfway to the top of the mountain. The road turned and widened where it met a driveway. Flanked by thick shrubs, hanging from massive stone pillars, black iron gates blocked the entrance to the Spotting Asylum.

It was a bleak, gray-stone Victorian structure with a slate roof and barred windows. Three stories tall and two hundred feet wide, it reposed ominously on overgrown lawns. Behind it, Spotting Mountain loomed, bare of trees and scarred where quarry men had ripped stone away for the asylum walls. Surrounding it were several hundred acres of desolate field circled by rusting wire fences and stone walls. Few of its inmates had left cured. No one had ever escaped.

Robbie, the caretaker, a one-armed war veteran who had been given a cottage in exchange for protecting the broken-windowed property from further vandalism, greeted Kent and Springer at the gate. "I swept up, Mr. Kent. It's all squared away."

Kent thanked him and Robbie leaned closer to the window. "You think if they buy it they'll want me to stay on?"

"Sure," said Kent. "Besides, these deals take forever. Don't you worry."

Robbie fumbled open the locks and shoved the gate aside

with his empty shoulder. They drove up the curving drive to the front door. The blue station wagon followed.

"Look at those bars," said Kent. "I told the bank we should tear 'em out, but they wouldn't spend the money. Looks like a jail."

Springer stopped before the ornate front portico and the four men got out of their cars. When Kent tried to make introductions, the man who had spoken earlier said his name was Gabriel Fuller. The second man eyed the front door and said nothing.

Springer said he was pleased to meet them.

"You're director of the hospital," said Fuller. It was a statement of fact.

"So you know a bit about our town," Springer said politely.

"We want to see the interior, Mr. Kent."

"Sure thing."

Kent selected a key from his full ring and opened the massive front door. As it swung heavily into the dim light, a damp, musty odor blew into the warming air. "Now here's the thing," he began, pausing in the doorway. "Nobody's occupied the building for about ten, fifteen years." But Fuller and the second man had already brushed past him. Kent hurried after them. "But the roof is solid. No leaks."

Springer followed, his shoes crunching on broken glass.

"Not much water got in the windows," said Kent, adding, "The bank wouldn't pay to board them up. But Robbie—the fellow you saw at the gate—has taken good care of things."

Fuller and his companion ignored the mayor.

The front hall was paneled with oak and dominated by a staircase that curved grandly toward the second floor. On either side of it were large dayrooms where the less violent inmates had been allowed to receive visitors. Kent remarked that the wood and plaster work were unusually attractive, perhaps unique to the region.

"You'd have fantastic public rooms," he enthused.

"Elaborate," replied Fuller, weighing the word as if he meant "excessive."

The gloomy first floor had pretended elegance for the benefit of the visitors who had paid the bills, but the second and third floors, buffered from the grand stairway by soundproof doors, were chillingly functional machines for the control of the uncontrollable.

Strict security had been the asylum's prime concern. There were clear sight lines between regularly spaced guard stations in the wide, straight halls. Iron gates separated each group of ten cells, poised to slam shut and contain mass eruption. The cells themselves were grisly boxes, less than ten feet square, barred. Many were padded with stained and moldering canvas. They had oppressively low ceilings, heavy doors with tiny grilled windows, mesh-shielded overhead light bulbs, and open sinks and toilets. Though the doors were open, with a key in each lock, each room still seemed to cage a memory of fear and confusion.

Kent noted their single attribute. "Plumbing in every room. Kind of rare in a building of this age."

Springer came to his rescue. "If you knock out the connecting walls, two of these would make a very pleasant chamber."

Fuller did not respond. His blank face seemed to indicate he was as unmoved by Springer's suggestion as he had been by the agonies the cells implied. Springer concluded that he had never seen two people more devoid of imagination. Neither man reacted to the dreary atmosphere. Only when they paused to peer into a hideous hole deep in the cellar did a momentary flicker of interest cross Fuller's face.

A punishment cell, a dungeon for the most twisted inmate, or warder, it consisted of stone walls, a solid iron door, a drain in the floor, and manacles on the wall. Fuller gazed at it for several minutes, then tested the door to see if the hinges still worked. It swung with odd ease.

They inspected the kitchens, the furnace room, and the storerooms, and then as they were leaving discovered the chapel, where ornate stained glass and a decorative plaster altar looked as if they had been imported intact from a European church. Fuller and his silent companion stared reflectively.

"That's really something, isn't it?" said Kent.

"The best money can buy," said Fuller.

They turned away abruptly. Kent and Springer exchanged a "now what?" look and trailed after them to a concrete patio from which they surveyed the outbuildings, sheds, barns, and garages that had not been visible from the front of the asylum. Sweet woodsmoke rose from the caretaker's cottage. The sun was burning off the frost that glazed the ruins of the formal gardens.

"Mr. Mayor," said Fuller.

"Sir?"

Springer hid a smile. Kent had the country gentry's way of saying *sir* which clearly implied that he used the word at his pleasure.

Fuller asked about the water supply—a big spring-fed cistern farther up the hill—and electricity, public utility lines, and an old, possibly repairable emergency generator. He nodded at the building Kent indicated and his companion dog-trotted out to have a look. He asked if the water cistern were within the fenced property and seemed satisfied—even relieved, Springer thought—when Kent said it was. That the estate was self-contained was apparently important to the buyers.

"Garbage collection is handled by the town," said Kent. "We can work out a favorable arrangement, I'm sure."

"You say, town, Mr. Mayor. But it's called Hudson City."

"Town refers to the entire township of which Hudson City is the center. As mayor of the city, I'm *de facto* supervisor of the township, with my town board. Five board members. We—"

He was cut off by the return of the second man, who glanced at Fuller with a silent message. Fuller said, "You have your own police force?"

Kent nodded. "We have one man of our own plus any backup we need from the state police." He pointed north. "Their barracks is nine miles out of town. Of course if we were to get a big influx of tourists we'd hire more men. This property falls under our local police jurisdiction."

Springer added, "Even though it's beyond the city limits, it's our responsibility, not the state troopers'."

"Yes," said Fuller, and Springer thought he sounded as if he already knew that.

"Umm, would you be operating all year round?" asked Kent.

Fuller took a long look, turning a complete circle, then drew a wallet from his coat and handed Kent a check. "A binder, Mr. Mayor. We will negotiate with the bank in New York."

Kent squinted in the sunlight. "Ten thousand dollars. Revelations Incorporated. California."

Fuller and his companion were already headed for their car.

"Is there anything else I can do for you?" Kent called after them, clearly stunned by the speed of events.

Fuller paused, his expression bland. "Yes, Mr. Kent. As soon as the bank notifies you of the closing, see that the caretaker's cottage is vacated."

3

Pete Lewis was alone in his general store. There was no profit in paying a clerk these quiet weekdays. He polished the cluttered counter around the cash register until the air reeked of lemon oil, then sat on a stool and thumbed through a fancy-gift catalogue. Its contents were a far cry from the basic tools and supplies he sold his regular customers, but there might be a call for expensive gadgets and souvenirs when the hotel opened. If it opened. Nobody really knew what the Revelations company was going to do with their property, though Bob Kent, insisting it had to be a hotel, had already suggested that Lewis rent the empty store next door for a gift section.

The cowbell on the front door jangled hopefully. Lewis looked up and was surprised to see a fair, blond couple, a young man and woman. They were dressed in stiff, new blue jean overalls and, since he didn't recognize them, Lewis assumed they were summer people up for an early opening of their vacation home. Thank God for small favors. He often went a whole morning like this without a single customer.

"Hello," he called. "Help you folks?"

"We'll tell you when we need you," said the man. They made purposefully for the paint section. Lewis went over anyway, showed them the color charts, and hovered while they chose. It was not his habit to leave a customer unattended. He told his weekend clerk that service was what made Lewis's General Store different from the chain store in Warington, but the real reason was that he felt a kind of personal invasion whenever anyone walked through his door.

The cowbell jangled again. Three young men entered and went directly to the chain saws.

"Excuse me a moment," said Lewis. He left the couple

and joined the men, noticing that their blond hair was shorter than the local youths wore theirs. Nice, clean-cut types. "Help you, fellas?"

"Doing fine," said one, hefting a big McCulloch and testing it knowledgeably for balance. He was older than the others. A dull, heavy metal cross dangled from his neck. His companions watched silently.

"That's a powerful saw," said Lewis.

"Got a bigger one?"

"Sure. How about that one in the window."

Before Lewis could stop him, the smallest man stepped right into the window display and plucked the saw from its stand, which was surrounded by a forest of rake and hoe handles. If one of those rakes fell into the pyramid of red gasoline cans . . .

"Careful," said Lewis, but the young man climbed out easily without disrupting a thing and the three of them crowded around the saw. Lewis couldn't put his finger on it, but for some reason these people were different from the city people he was used to.

The bell jangled and four more strangers strode in and marched—a word he thought of later—to the dry-goods section.

"Be right back." He hurried after them, distracted by the sudden burst of activity. The couple at the paint rack were removing gallon cans from the stacks. He stopped to help them, but noticed that the new group was already pulling blankets out from under the counters. He excused himself and rushed toward dry goods.

"Help you?"

Two of the women were on their knees, sorting through the stock and handing blue blankets up to the men. "Any more blue?"

Lewis bent down and peered into the cupboard. His flashlight was at the cash register. The bell jangled. He started to straighten up, then thought better of it. One thing at a time. The new customers would have to wait. He crawled partway in and found another blue blanket.

"More," said the woman.

"I'll order them," said Lewis. "It'll take a week."

He backed out of the cupboard and stood up. Several men were clustered around the cash register. Brushing past the people who wanted the blankets, he hurried behind the counter and laid a protective hand on the register.

"Sorry, I was tied up. Can I help you?"

They were selecting screw drivers, pliers, and penknives from the paper paint-mixing buckets in which they were displayed. The bell jangled. Lewis strained unsuccessfully to see over their heads. He felt a moment of panic. He couldn't handle all these strangers. It wasn't like it was with his regular customers who would wait patiently or come back later or pick something out and sign for it.

The bell jangled again. Some girls crowded up to the counter with teetering stacks of open-stock dishes. Another arrived with his biggest iron skillet piled high with cooking utensils.

Again, the bell. Were some of them leaving, tired of waiting? Had they taken something? He darted around the counter so that he could see the front door. More people were coming in.

"Be right with you," he called.

His voice was the loudest sound in the store—a frightened noise against a steady shuffle of feet and rustle of goods being moved—and he suddenly realized what made these people different from the jabbering, laughing summer-home owners.

They were absolutely silent.

The men with the chain saws communicated solely with glances. The group with the blankets stood patiently, like draught animals, as one woman stacked them into their arms. The couple buying paint were walking cans to the counter in silent relays. The girls with the plates said nothing. Another girl he hadn't seen enter dragged an armload of brooms and mops to the counter, then waited with downcast eyes.

The man with the metal cross swung a pair of chain saws onto the counter, taking the last available space. He looked at Lewis with penetrating blue eyes and said, "Make a list. We'll load our cars."

"You're all together?" blurted Lewis. Of course, he realized. They all acted and looked the same. Their blue overalls, work shirts, and blond hair were like a uniform.

The man said nothing as he laid a check on one of the chain-saw blades. Lewis eyed it nervously. It was on a California bank. Then he spotted the name printed in the upper left-hand corner. Revelations Inc. His insides clutched for a second. They had come.

Lewis grinned jerkily, trying to think of something to say, but the man's steady gaze forestalled his questions. He started to enumerate the purchases in his order book. Responding to the man's silent nod, a pretty girl of about sixteen produced pen and notepad and proceeded to write her own list, repeating each item aloud in a curious monotone. Lewis, conscious of being monitored, worked carefully, his mind racing for a way to pump them about the hotel.

As the girl repeated each item, the customers picked up their purchases and filed out of the store. With the lemon-oiled counter empty again, Lewis was alone with the man and girl. Including the chain saws, the bill amounted to $463.38. He added the sales tax and the man made out the check.

"Thank you," said Lewis. "And welcome to Hudson City." He was burning to ask their plans, but he contented himself with an invitation. After all, the man was wearing a Christian cross. "I'm a deacon of the church," he said. "We hope you and your friends will stop by on Sunday."

The man leveled powerful eyes on Lewis's face. "We will visit your church soon, Deacon Lewis."

"The sooner the better," said Lewis. No one had ever called him Deacon Lewis before. He found himself pleased by the title.

"You did not have enough blankets," said the man.

"I'll order right away," Lewis said hastily. "How many?"

"Lots." The girl laughed. "We're camping in the main hall and it's so cold." The words tumbled out, an escape of enthusiasm that seemed to startle her. She stiffened visibly, then slowly, reluctantly, faced the man. Her face rigid, she whispered, "I'm sorry."

But the man spun on his heel and marched out the door. She stood rooted for a moment, quivering like a frightened puppy, then, with an audible whimper, broke and ran after him.

While the newcomers loaded their station wagons in front of Lewis's General Store, a girl with a pale complexion and deep, hollow eyes approached the grilled window of the Hudson City Post Office and dropped a blue envelope on the narrow marble counter. She waited nervously, pushing the letter in little circles, until Sophie Wilkins, the postmistress, levered her hefty frame out of her swivel chair and appeared at the window with a friendly smile.

"Yes, dear?"

"I want to mail a registered letter." The girl's voice sounded curiously flat, as if the words had been rehearsed.

"Where to?"

"The address is on the envelope." She turned it around until Sophie could see.

"San Mateo, California?" Sophie was surprised. Whenever she saw an unfamiliar face in Hudson City she automatically assumed it was a summer person from New York City.

"And I want a return receipt."

"One thing at a time," Sophie said. She weighed the letter. "The postage is thirteen cents."

"They said it would be more."

"Who said?" asked Sophie.

The girl did not reply, but her fingers turned white as she dug them into the marble counter. Sophie shrugged. "Well, they were right. Registration will cost two dollars and ten cents."

The girl relaxed.

"And, twenty-five cents for the return receipt." She penciled the numbers in a quick, neat hand, saying, "Let's see now—two thirty-five, two forty-five, two dollars and forty-eight cents."

The girl opened her left hand. Two folded singles, one quarter, two dimes, and three pennies fell on the counter.

"Well," said Sophie, smoothing out the bills, "just right. Now put your address on this stub and I'll do the rest."

The girl scribbled her address.

Sophie stamped the letter, the registration card, and the stub. Her eyes widened. "Two-two-O Spotting Mountain Road? The old asylum." She snapped her fingers. "You're with the Revelations company. Did you move in?"

The girl smiled mechanically and her eyes took on a faraway look as if she were gazing at a distant landscape.

Sophie reached under the grille and touched the girl's hand. She was the church organist and Bob Kent's sister-in-law as well as postmistress and was vitally interested in the business of Hudson City. Boldly, she asked, "Is it going to be a hotel?"

Without lowering her remote stare, the girl groped blindly on the counter, located the green postal receipt, then turned away and fled through the door, brushing past a young man and woman on their way in. They approached the grilled window. Like the first girl, each was wearing blue overalls. The man went first.

"I want to mail a registered letter."

It was a blue envelope.

"And I want a return receipt."

"One thing at a time," Sophie said irritably. Several more people were coming in, forming a line. Just when she wanted to telephone Bob Kent and tell him the news.

Shortly, it seemed, the newcomers would bring life to the old building on Spotting Mountain. They replaced some of the broken windows, boarded others, and painted the iron front gate. Though there was a sameness to the young people who came to town in their blue station wagons, the Hudson City merchants who sold them food, tools, and building supplies began to notice new faces, an observation confirmed by Sophie Wilkins, who reported that strangers were regularly sending registered letters to San Mateo, California.

They installed a telephone with an unlisted number, something almost unheard of in the area, and made a puzzling decision to repair the old diesel generator rather than hook into the electric company. The driver who made the first diesel fuel delivery was besieged with questions. But he couldn't answer them. A half-dozen silent young men had escorted him to the huge underground storage tanks and back to the gate. He had been to the asylum. But he had seen nothing.

All of them were polite, but maddeningly close-mouthed, and it was left to the local residents to speculate as to their intentions. It was generally agreed that the people arriving daily were architects and interior designers, sent ahead to plan the remodeling, and that the heavy flow of mail to California indicated close communications with Revelations Incorporated's main office. It was pointed out that many of them looked too young to be architects. The logical answer to that seemed to be that they were employed to cook and clean and do the heavy work.

Still, as spring quickened and the muds dried, people grew impatient. The new windows and the painted gate did nothing to soften the dismal face that brooded over the town. Even people who drove up the mountain for a closer look saw little change in the asylum's appearance. The lawns, greening in the late April rain, were still overgrown, and the driveway was a maze of deep ruts.

Then, one day, several strapping men with work-thickened arms and calloused palms descended on Moser's Lumberyard, which sold a wide range of building supplies, surveyed the operation with knowledgeable interest, and engaged old Ken Moser in brisk negotiations for an enormous purchase of ten-foot chain-link fence, poles, concrete, and barbed wire. They demanded immediate delivery and refused his offer to contract the installation.

Pete Lewis sold them ten post-hole diggers—his entire summer supply—all his wire cutters, and all his heavy work gloves. "What are you fellas doing up there?" he asked as he rang up the purchases.

"Fencing," said one with a laconic southern drawl.

Lewis smiled. He noticed himself being careful around these people who were buying so much. "Well, good neighbors, they say."

Two days later Moser's biggest truck, a straight-back International, ground up Spotting Mountain Road with the first rolls of a mile and a half of chain-link fencing. It was greeted by teams of husky, fresh-faced men and women. The driver, Ollie Fraser, Moser's nephew, took his lunch break at the soda fountain in Rigby's Drugstore.

"Damnedest thing I ever saw. I said I'd run the truck up the fence—there's a old dirt track 'long most of it—but they wouldn't let me in the gate. What them rolls weigh? Eighty-five pounds?"

"Ninety-five," said a carpenter hunched over his coffee down the counter.

"Number ten gauge?" said another. "Ninety-five, hell. Hundred-ten."

"Yeah," said Ollie. "Well, these kids hop on the truck the second I get stopped. Cut the ties. Boom! Off she goes. Hits the ground, three kids roll it in the gate and up the hill. Three more waitin' for the next roll. A ton of wire off and gone in five minutes. Like a mechanical loader. I didn't even get a chance to stretch. Back down the road. Load up. Back up the road. Wham. Bam. Thank you, ma'am."

The carpenter laughed. "They got you working, Ollie."

"Sure do."

A plumber farther down the counter spoke up. "I thought we was going to be building that place."

"The way I hear it," answered Ollie, "they wouldn't give Ken the contract and he bid real low."

"What does he care? He's already got the money for selling the fence."

The first carpenter said, "Fencing's one thing. Rebuilding that rock pile's something else. There'll be work."

"What the hell are they fencing the place for anyhow?"

The Cut was an old lumber road across the upper quadrant of the asylum property that Buster Crayton and some other dairy farmers on the far side of Spotting Mountain had reopened when the asylum had been abandoned. Now, as the newcomers tore down the old rusted fences, dug holes, poured cement for the new metal posts, and erected the shimmering sheets of wire links, Crayton grumbled that he suspected they intended to block the shortcut that saved the farmers five miles on the trip to Hudson City.

Crayton's neighbors were sure they would leave gates, but one afternoon he discovered that he had been right. The Cut was sealed by a gateless fence topped with five strands of barbed wire.

Seething, he stopped his Dodge Power Wagon, a massively bumpered, twenty-year-old vehicle with attributes of durability and brute strength similar to his own, and shouted at the people he saw completing the fence in the woods. They ignored him, inflaming his rage.

Crayton reacted characteristically.

He slammed his truck into low-low four-wheel drive, floored the accelerator, and blasted through the fence as if it were made of string.

Grinning happily, he sped through the asylum property and demolished a second fence on the way out. His satisfied chuckle died in his throat when he realized that he had torn off one of his side-view mirrors in the process. Angered by the loss, he stormed into Bob Kent's real estate office the instant he reached town and demanded that the mayor do something about the situation.

Kent waffled. "I think it's their property, Buster."

"That's been open road for fifteen years. And it was open road long before that nut house was ever built. You better make sure it stays open."

"Tell you what. Let's call Fred Zinser and see what he says."

"What for?" snapped Crayton.

Kent reached for his telephone. "It's a legal problem, right? That's why we pay a town attorney."

"Tell him he gotta keep it open or there's gonna be trouble."

Kent dialed. "Hiya, Fred." Glancing up at the irate farmer, he explained Crayton's complaint. "I got Buster Crayton here in my office. Buster says the new people are fencing the Cut."

"They already tried it," said Buster.

"He wonders what we can do about it," Kent said and listened with a thoughtful expression as Zinser advised against starting a row with the new neighbors. "No," said Kent. "We don't want to do that." He eyed Buster's impatient scowl. "What do you advise?"

"Up to you, Bob," Zinser answered softly. "But there's only about ten, twelve people that use the Cut."

"Thanks, Fred."

Kent hung up and shook his head. "Sorry, Buster. Fred says it's their property. They can do what they want with it."

Buster swept out the door with surprising speed. "We'll see about that."

He did his shopping, had a cup of coffee at Rigby's, and headed home, driving fast to get there before dark. As he approached the Cut he saw a line of young men and women in blue overalls spread out shoulder to shoulder across the road. Some of them were still holding the tools they had used to repair the fence, which stood behind them, straight and true as if nothing had happened. They watched silently as he rolled closer.

Goddamn nerve.

He stuck his head out his window, blew his horn, and shouted, "Listen, you people, that's a right-a-'way and you got no right blocking it. I'm warning you, every time you fence it, I'm knocking it down."

They regarded him with blank stares.

"You hear?"

No one answered. The darkening woods on either side of the road seemed to swallow up his voice. He glared, his face reddening. Did they think they could block him by just standing there? Maybe he ought to get out and bang a few heads. Then he saw a much better way.

He pointed at a large boulder next to his truck.

"I'm backing up. Then I'm coming through at thirty. When I pass this rock, I can't stop, so you better move."

He reversed the truck for two hundred yards, then started forward, winding through first and second. They stood steadfastly in front of the fence, their faces expressionless. Buster blasted the horn. The Power Wagon closed rapidly. If they didn't jump soon . . . He'd be damned if he'd stop. They'd jump. He roared by the boulder and they scattered away from the fence.

Then he saw it and a fearful yell leaped from his throat.

He slammed on the brakes. The truck slid, screaming, toward the fence, behind which they had dug a deep trench that straddled the road. If he hit it, his truck would be destroyed.

He twisted the steering wheel desperately, slewing into the trees. A couple of saplings slowed him, but he still hit a thick oak with jarring force. His chest slammed into the wheel and his head hit the windshield, starring the glass.

Dazed, he sat for several minutes, shook his head to clear it, and stepped out cautiously. His chest ached. It would be worse tomorrow. The front bumper was badly dented and it looked as though the grille had almost pierced the radiator. One of the headlights was smashed.

They were watching, expressionless as before.

He tightened with rage and frustration. The effort sent a wrenching pain through his chest. He had a strange feeling in his mind, something he had never known before. Rubbing the bruise on his head, he climbed back into his truck. The engine started reluctantly after a long grind. He backed out of the woods, acutely aware of their stares, and headed for Hudson City on the long way home.

Dusk was falling as he drove along Main Street worrying whether the creaking sounds from the front end meant he had bent the frame. Something odd caught his eyes. He stopped the truck and looked up at the mountain, which was a shade darker than the blackening sky.

He saw a blue light in the old asylum. Then another, and another. He looked around to point it out to somebody, but the street was empty. Blue lights were blossoming like burning flowers, mushrooming into the outer wings of the building until they shone in every window. Staring, he suddenly knew the new feeling in his mind. For the first time in his life Buster Crayton felt helpless.

4

"Your wife on line two, Doctor."

Springer looked at his watch. Three o'clock. His back hurt; he'd been working steadily in the clinic since one, attending to spring colds, minor injuries, an early poison oak rash, and a slew of intestinal virus attacks. "I'll take it in the office."

In pleasant contrast to the bright examination room, his office had dark wood paneling, a brown carpet, book-shelves, and a large brown couch. A window behind his neat desk overlooked the emergency-room entrance where Reggie, the day driver, was polishing the yellow Cadillac ambulance.

Springer lowered himself comfortably into his posture-back chair. "Hello, dear."

"I'm on my way home. What would you like for din-ner?"

"I won't be home in time for dinner. I have to go up the hill for Mrs. Cook and—"

"Why can't that woman come to the clinic like every-body else?"

Mrs. Cook lived on the far side of Spotting Mountain on an isolated farm with neither telephone nor electricity. "She's ninety-three years old," said Springer. "She can hardly drag herself to the outhouse."

"Okay. I'll have a snack with Samantha. You and I can eat later."

"You better not wait. I have a meeting at Bob's at eight. I'll bum a sandwich from Mary."

"Why didn't you tell me?" Margaret complained.

"I meant to call you as soon as I had a chance. Bob thinks that with the hotel coming we should make another try for a fast-food franchise. He asked me in on it."

She wasn't interested. "When will I see you?"

"I'll shoot for eleven."

He went back to the clinic. Angela Gallagher, his head nurse, was sitting on the examination table, her pretty legs crossed. She was a statuesque, raven-haired beauty, three years out of nursing school, well organized, and good in a crisis.

"Who's next?" asked Springer.

"Believe it or not the waiting room is empty." She lighted a cigarette.

"They'll kill you," said Springer.

Angela inhaled deeply. "I'm quitting. Promise."

Springer sat down on a stool and poured a shot of bourbon into a paper cup.

"That will kill you too," said Angela.

Springer smiled over the rim of the cup. "My dear lady. Man and woman have been drinking for ten thousand years. The species has survived. Since they started smoking cigarettes, they're dying of lung diseases. Why don't you concentrate on your other vices?"

Angela uncrossed her legs. "Is that—" she began and was cut off as a tall, spindly seventeen-year-old boy, his face rutted with acne, pushed through the door. The sleeves of his worn red- and black-checked lumber jacket were inches short, exposing bony wrists. He looked frightened.

"Doc?"

"Danny? What's the matter?"

Danny Moser limped in; a bloody rag on his right foot spotted the gray floor red. "I got hurt, Doc."

Springer was on his feet, his active hands gripping the boy, helping him across the room, lifting his lanky body onto the examination table. Angela snuffed out her cigarette in the sink and filled a metal basin with warm water.

"Lie down," said Springer. "Before you keel over."

Danny's voice was a nasal, cocky whine. "I'm okay, Doc. Hurts like hell." At seventeen, Danny Moser had already established a reputation as the town's prime troublemaker. His father, the black sheep of the Moser family, had deserted Danny's mother years ago, and since the boy had quit school he had been arrested twice for peddling pills and marijuana to his former classmates. He lived with his mother, a semi-invalid, in a shack at the end of Spotting Street, and Springer was the only man in Hudson City he could call his friend.

"What happened?"

"I was working in the woods. The ax slipped, Doc. Almost took my toe off."

Springer and Angela unwound the crusted bandage. "Where were you working?"

"Up the hill," Danny replied vaguely. "Off Rock Road."

Springer continued unwrapping until he reached a dirty sock. Angela gave him a scissors; he cut the sock away and gently washed the boy's foot until he reached the wound, a deep furrow that ran from the instep to the space between his larger toes. Danny winced and pulled away when Springer put his foot in the basin.

"Easy, son. I've got to get it clean."

"Hurts like a m—" He met Springer's warning glance. "Hurts like hell, Doc."

Angela brought fresh water and sponges. Springer inspected the ragged furrow, puzzled. "Where's your shoe?"

"Uh . . . I left it up the hill. It was totaled."

Springer surveyed the wound and shook his head. "You did this with an ax?"

"It slipped," Danny whined. "Right into my foot."

"What were you cutting?"

"A tree. Whad'ya think? Why all the questions?"

Springer stared at the wound; the boy grew nervous. "I got a job. This guy wanted firewood. I knew where a tree blew down last summer."

"What guy?"

"A guy on Spotting Street."

"Angela," said Springer. "Would you please close the waiting room? I'll finish up here."

"What about Mrs. Cook?"

"Later."

Danny stared longingly at her strong, full hips as she left the room. He looked away when Springer caught his eye.

"Danny, I never heard such utter bullshit in my life. There must be a hundred dead trees within a five-minute walk of Spotting Street, if the guy doesn't have one in his back yard."

"You think I'm lying, Doc? We're friends, right?"

Springer answered mildly. "My friends don't tell me phony stories. Your foot isn't cut."

"Isn't cut?" Danny howled. "Look at it, Doc. I'm still bleeding."

Near his big toe, where the furrow was deepest, the blood oozed slowly. Springer sponged it with sterile gauze. "So you are. But no ax did that to you. It looks like you were gouged by something. But I can't figure out what and I certainly can't treat you until I know."

Danny wet his lips. "What do you mean?"

"I don't know what kind of infection you might have picked up. You'll have real trouble if I don't get to the cause of it. What happened?"

"You won't tell nobody?"

"That depends."

"I saw on TV where doctors can't tell on their patients."

"Tell what?"

Danny stared at the ceiling. "I got shot."

"Oh, for Christ's sake. Who shot you?"

The boy sought Springer with lonely eyes. "I did it myself, Doc. I was fooling with this gun and it went off and —"

"What gun?"

Danny nodded at the knapsack he had dropped by the door. "In there."

The knapsack contained a pair of sneakers—Springer recalled that the boy had done well at track—some chocolate bars, a bottle of pills he didn't care to see, and a small .22-caliber revolver. He opened the cylinder and removed four cartridges. "Where'd you get this?"

"I traded it from a guy in Warington. I gave him some grass. There's nothing wrong with having a gun."

"Okay, over here. I want an X ray. Make sure you didn't break something."

Danny swung his legs off the table and hobbled to the X-ray machine. "I can move my toes, Doc."

"Good."

"You won't tell nobody, will you?"

Springer grinned in spite of himself. "What? That you're packing a gun or using your toes for target practice?"

Danny's ravaged cheeks turned fiery red. "Both."

"No, I won't tell anybody." He took an X ray, disinfected the wound, deadened the flesh with a shot of Provacaine, and drew the ragged skin together with a half-dozen stitches.

"Weird," said the boy. "I could feel the stitches and I *couldn't* feel them. Know what I mean?"

"Like watching yourself in a movie?"

"Yeah," he exclaimed. "Just like that."

Sometimes the boy responded so hungrily to the slightest communication that Springer thought that his mind must be a turmoil of unanswered questions and uncompleted thoughts. Most of the time, though, he wouldn't open up at all, even with Springer.

"How's it been going, Danny," he said now, "still at the gas station?"

Danny lowered his head. "Old man Grand fired me."

Springer dropped the needle and scissors into the sterilizer. "What happened?"

"Aw, I was late a couple of times."

"When you work for somebody you got to show up on time. He's counting on you. . . . You know how to paint?"

"Sure."

"As soon as it gets a little warmer you can paint my porch." He bandaged the wound and helped him on with his sneakers. "We'll change the dressing Friday and take the stitches out next week."

"Can I have my gun back?"

"I'll take it for payment. Ten bucks for the office visit and ten for the X rays."

"I'll pay you out of the paint job."

Springer dropped the gun in a drawer and swept the bullets in on top of it. "I don't want you carrying this."

Danny sneered. "I can get another one."

Springer stepped very close. Danny tensed. "I kept you out of jail twice—look at me—you get in trouble with a gun in your pocket and there's no way I can help."

Danny looked at the floor.

"You don't need a gun," Springer said softly.

"What if I want to go hunting?"

"Not with a handgun. Hey, tell you what. Mayor Kent is setting up an archery range at his place. Want to learn how to shoot a bow?"

"Can we go hunting?" Danny asked eagerly.

"When you get good enough you can go with Mayor Kent. I don't hunt."

"He wouldn't want me."

"He'd love it. We'll start next week on my bow."

"Thanks, Doc." He picked up his knapsack, then

stopped by the door. "Hey, Doc, can you get me a job at the hotel?"

"Sure. As soon as—"

"Excuse me, Doctor," Angela said from the doorway, "we have a broken leg."

"Whose?"

"One of the youngsters from the asylum. He's in the O.R."

"Really?" They'd been around for a month now, but he had yet to meet one. "Be right there. Take care, Danny," he said, placing a reassuring hand briefly on the boy's shoulder as he strode from the examining room. "See you Friday."

"Doctor?"

Springer was halfway down the hall. Something in her voice stopped him. "What's wrong, Angela?"

"His friends won't leave him."

"What do you mean won't leave him?"

"You better see for yourself."

Four young men were standing around the operating table talking in low voices to the ashen-faced victim when Springer burst into the room. A big man with intense eyes said, "He fell from a window. His leg is broken."

"Thank you," said Springer. "Please wait outside and we'll take care of him."

"We will stay," said the man.

"The hell you will. Out." He waved impatiently at the door.

"We will help you."

"Are you a doctor?"

"I was a medic in Nam. We will tend to our friend while you set his leg."

Springer crossed his arms. "My nurse will do the tending. Please leave."

The man stepped closer. "Doctor," he said firmly. "We intend to stay with our friend while you set his leg. Will you please begin?"

Baffled, Springer said, "This is ridiculous. You can't stay here. If you were a medic you know damn well you're infecting the hell out of this place."

"There's no open wound," replied the man. "It seems to be a simple fracture, so you can do a closed reduction."

Springer flushed. "If it's that simple," he snapped angrily, "what are you bothering me for?"

"We need an X ray," was the bland reply.

The other three men were ignoring the exchange and muttering to the man on the table. All five wore identical blue work shirts and overalls. The injured man's pants leg was cut open to the thigh; he lay rigid with pain, his lower leg slightly swollen. He looked up at Springer with appealing eyes.

"Listen, son," said Springer. "I can't work on you until your friends leave. Would you ask them to wait outside?"

He shook his head, his lips compressed with pain.

"Trust us," said the spokesman. "We know what we're doing."

They watched gravely, waiting for an answer. Springer considered and swiftly rejected calling for help. The minimal swelling indicated no blood vessels had been pierced, which meant it would likely be a simple operation to reduce the fracture. Though he didn't like it, it didn't matter if they stayed.

"Okay. I'll take an X ray. Keep out of my way."

They stood aside while Angela helped him with the X-ray machine and waited quietly until she returned minutes later from the darkroom. As predicted, the break was a simple fracture of the lower tibia. Springer prepared a needle.

The man who had said he was a medic plucked the hypo from his hand.

"No drugs, Doctor."

"What?"

"We don't need drugs."

Springer snapped it back with a lightning move.

"You may not need drugs, but your friend does. He's too tight to work on. And he hurts. And he's going to hurt a lot more when I perform a closed reduction, which, if you've ever seen one, Mr. Medic from Vietnam, goes like this—I yank his leg into alignment. Without narcotics he would scream his head off and compound the fracture trying to escape the pain. He needs Valium to relax his muscles and morphine to make the pain bearable."

"We will prepare him."

"You what?"

At a nod from the medic, they shouldered past Springer, gathered around the table, and placed their hands on the injured man's body. Murmuring to himself, the medic touched the broken leg with the tips of his fingers. The man winced. The others touched his temples, his chest, his thighs. The medic resumed his murmuring, louder now, the others joining him, until the sounds took on the cadence of a chant.

"What are you doing?" asked Springer.

They closed their eyes. The songlike moan went on.

"Look!" whispered Angela.

The man on the table started to sag. His pain-arched back fell flat to the table. His mouth, so tense a moment before, relaxed into a half smile. His eyes closed as if in sleep. The chant quickened. Astonished, Springer watched the corded leg muscles melt liquid before his eyes.

The medic drew forth a small metal cross that hung from a chain around his neck. He fingered it lovingly and prayed to the music of the chant.

"Dear God, we beseech you to attend your suffering servant. Michael needs your sympathy, dear God. Please help him, in the name of your Son, Jesus. Amen."

He opened his piercing eyes. "You may set the bone, Doctor."

Fascinated, Springer peeled back the lid and shined a light in the patient's eye. The pupil was constricted as if he were narcotized. He placed his stethoscope on the chest. The heart was beating easily, slow and steady. Tentatively, he touched the leg. The victim lay still.

He positioned himself and gripped the foot. All the while the chanters continued to stroke the boy's body. Springer tugged once, his hands quick and sure.

The X ray showed a perfect reduction.

When he finished the cast, the medic looked at him with respect. "You're very good, Doctor."

Springer grinned. "You guys aren't too bad yourselves. Okay, let's get him to bed."

Angela wheeled in a table, and she and Springer transferred the patient to the six-bed ward. His friends trooped along and though the boy was beginning to wake up, Springer said, "Let him get some rest. You can visit him tomorrow morning."

The men exchanged glances, murmured inaudibly to their friend, and left the hospital. Springer and Angela walked back to the clinic.

"That was incredible," she said. "Like faith healing."

"No such thing."

"Then how'd they do it?"

"Acupressure points, I'd guess. The chanting was a bunch of malarkey. Anybody in the waiting room?"

Angela led in a young whittler who had received a new knife for his birthday. The boy's mother was with him, so Angela went out to the ward. Springer was tying off the stitches and distracting the victim with an involved story about carving a totem pole when Angela burst into the examination room.

"Alan—Doctor! They took him."

"What?"

"They took the man with the broken leg. He's gone."

Springer patted the boy's head and told his mother to bring him back Tuesday; he contained his anger until they were gone.

"Who the hell let him out of here? Who's the duty nurse?"

"Jenny took a break and when she came back he was gone. The porter saw them put him into their station wagon. He didn't think anything of it."

"Brilliant. Okay, cancel the afternoon. Tell 'em I have an emergency." He stripped off his lab coat and put on his tweed jacket.

Angela asked, "Where are you going?"

"I'm getting my patient back, dammit." He stormed out the emergency-room entrance. Reggie was still polishing the ambulance. He took one look at Springer's face, dropped his rag, and jumped behind the wheel. Springer sat next to him and buckled in. "The old asylum."

"Fast?"

"Very!"

Reggie flipped on the whooper siren. The custom-built ambulance shot across Main Street and onto Spotting Mountain Road. It was powered by an enormous fuel-injected engine and suspended on a rare set of tightly tuned Packard electric-load levelers, and Reggie, the man who had done the custom work, proudly claimed that it had the climbing and cornering abilities of a rocket on rails. Accelerating out of the turns, cracking ninety on the steep straightaways, he drove with both hands on the wheel, eyes everywhere but the rearview mirror.

When the ambulance squealed to a stop outside the locked asylum gates, Reggie apologized for the three minutes the two-and-a-half-mile trip had taken. "Tough climb, Doc."

Springer unbuckled his shoulder harness. "Wait here."

He found a bell next to the freshly painted gates and pushed it. He waited a few minutes, conscious of Reggie's eyes on him, but no one answered. Standing alone at the side of the road, the big building looming inaccessibly in the distance, he felt small and ineffectual and that rekindled his anger. He pressed down on the bell button, holding his fist on the buzzer until, finally, the front door opened and the medic strolled down the drive, his face a mask of indifference.

"What's the problem, Doctor?"

"Return my patient or I'll call the police."

"He is perfectly comfortable here. Why waste a bed in your hospital?"

"I'll worry about wasting my beds. He'll be released when I say so."

"Doctor—"

"Dammit," snapped Springer. "I don't want to argue about this. You had no right to drag that man out of my hospital."

"He wanted to come home. We can care for him."

Springer gripped the iron bars. "That is not the point."

"What is the point?"

"The point is he is in my care until I release him."

The medic spoke with smug self-assurance. "Isn't it really that you did't get your way, Doctor? And is that worth dragging your police up here and forcing yourself onto private property?"

Springer's neck tightened painfully. As a professional among working people he was accustomed to a certain grudging deference and to having his orders obeyed. The fact was, the medic was right: the patient could recover at home and Springer was furious that he had been defied. He took several deep breaths and rubbed the back of his neck.

"All right, Mr. Medic. You've got him, keep him. But goddammit if his temperature goes up or there's any other indication of infection you get him down to me right away. And check his toes. If they're cold it means he's swelling under the cast, cutting circulation."

"We know," said the medic. He turned and strolled up the drive.

Springer stared helplessly at his back until he disappeared inside the building. Feeling baffled, violated, and furious, he climbed back into the ambulance, crossed his arms, and glared at the passing landscape. By the time they reached the hospital, he was chuckling ruefully. He had to admit that there was something ludicrous about a doctor chasing a patient with a broken leg.

Angela was waiting in his office. "What happened?"

Springer dropped into his chair and put his feet on his desk. "He got away."

She gave him a paper cup of bourbon and lighted a cigarette. "There's something strange about this."

"Strange? What's so strange about operating without pain killers and abducting patients from their beds?"

"No, seriously." She pointed to an open folder on his desk.

"Look at the admittance form. See the name?"

Springer picked it up. " 'Joseph Malley, Spotting Mountain Road, Hudson City, New York. Blue Cross-Blue Shield Group, Revelations Inc.' Well, that's something, we can get paid."

"The name," said Angela. "Joseph. Remember when they prayed they said Michael?"

"Marvelous," said Springer. "If they used a phony name we can't bill Blue Cross."

"His name was Joseph on the card."

"So who's Michael?"

"Good question," said Angela, drawing the drapes.

"A minor problem in an otherwise insane day," said Springer.

"Do we still have time for Mrs. Cook?" asked Angela.

Springer took her in his arms. She smelled of the Madame Rochas he had given her for her birthday. "Plenty of time," he whispered, backing her strong body toward the couch.

Springer awakened and felt around on the floor for his watch. Seven-thirty. Plenty of time. Angela was beside him, her head nestled against his shoulder. He gazed down at her taut, white hip flung high by her bent knee. A hot tear splashed on his chest.

He propped himself up on one elbow. "Are you crying?"

"No."

More tears trickled down her cheek, warm against his skin. "What's wrong?"

She turned her face away.

Springer sat up and pulled her to him. "What's wrong?"

Angela wiped her eyes. "I'm leaving, Alan."

His stomach clutched painfully. "What are you talking about? Why?"

"You're playing and I'm not."

"I'm not playing."

"It's starting to hurt too much, Alan. Please." She pulled away, her heavy breasts bobbing.

"I'm not playing," Springer repeated.

"I'm in love with you. I want a life with you. If you don't want a life with me, then you're playing."

"I . . ." He did not know what to say. They had shared a warm, easy camaraderie in the two years she had worked at the hospital, but their affair was a recent explosion that tinged his life with rich shades of joy and guilt.

"I'm not blaming you," said Angela. "But you're not going to leave Margaret—why, I don't know, but I know you won't—so I have to leave."

"But we're friends. You make working here special for me. We talk. I can tell you about things. It isn't only bed."

"Bed?" Angela said with a trace of bitterness. She kicked at the tangle of clothes on the floor. "This isn't a bed. . . . You know what I wish?"

"What?"

"I wish we'd had one full night and awakened together in the morning."

"I couldn't do that."

"Of course you couldn't. That's why I'm leaving."

They shared a long look, a final search for a decision that Springer would not make. Angela turned away, new tears rising.

"You really mean it?" he asked.

"Yes."

"You can still work here."

She shook her head, rippling her black hair. "No. There isn't much for a single woman to do around here." She smiled. "Other than you. It wouldn't work."

He took her hand and tried to pull her to him, but she stood her ground. "No."

"I'll miss you a lot."

She pressed his fingers to her breast, then backed away, touching the red marks. "If I don't find a replacement for you, Doctor, I'll be back with a net."

6

"Dicky Lewis says there's a secret room in the cellar where they run around without clothes."

"Samantha," said Margaret, "eat your breakfast."

Springer laughed. "Dicky's been there?"

"I think he's making it up," said Samantha. "He says it's a commune, but I don't think a commune could afford to buy such a big place, do you?"

"No." It was a warm morning. The back door was open and a heavy scent of flowers and cut grass flowed into the kitchen. Springer put his arm around Samantha. "Are you making friends with Dicky?"

Samantha stared at her cereal. "I heard him talking to some kids in the lunchroom," she mumbled.

Springer could imagine the lunchroom, a group of children eating and laughing at one table, Samantha alone at another. He kissed her hair. "Hey. I told Danny Moser I'd teach him archery up at Uncle Bob's. Why don't we ask Dicky and some other kids to come along? You want to learn how to shoot?"

"That can get a little dangerous," said Margaret.

"Not at all," Springer said firmly.

"And I don't like the idea of Samantha playing with that boy."

"I can handle Danny. . . . What do you say, darling?"

"I don't know how," Samantha mumbled.

"Do you think those lummoxes do?" Lummox had always been a giggle word, but it didn't work this morning. "You'll all be beginners. But you'll have the greatest teacher in the world."

"Uncle Bob?"

"Me, dummy."

This time she giggled.

"Want to do that?"

"Umm."

"I'll ask Dicky's father if it's all right. Who else?"

"I don't know."

"Think of a girl," he said, hoping he had not given her too painful a task. "We'll talk about it tonight."

He spent the morning doing preliminary telephone interviews for a new nurse. They called through the same Albany agency that had sent him Angela and their youthful, wondering voices piping over the line kept reminding him of her first call. The hospital seemed quiet and empty. She had offered to break in her replacement, but he had declined because he saw how badly she wanted to be away. Already he regretted those few extra days.

Missing their shared sandwich at his desk, he took a walk at lunch hour and picked up his mail—bills and *Time* magazine. Sophie Wilkins was busy at the window, writing registered-mail forms for a line of people from the asylum. How common a sight their blue shirts and overalls were becoming on the streets of the town. He thought he recognized one of the men who had been at the hospital.

"How's your friend's leg?" he asked.

The man smiled noncommittally. Springer shrugged; they all looked so much alike. Leafing through the magazine while he walked, looking up to see his way and exchange pleasantries with other people on the sidewalk, he noticed an attractive woman with shoulder-length black hair gazing out the drugstore window. She was a stranger; she was quite beautiful; and she was obviously going to be around awhile since she was wearing an apron and working behind the soda fountain.

Springer went into the drugstore and sat down at the Formica counter. The soda fountain occupied the right side of the store. To the left were display racks of notions, cosmetics, and nonprescription remedies. In the back, Dwight Rigby presided over the prescription counter, dispensing medicines from a tiny alcove lined with shelves of bottles and boxes. Fluorescent lights hung incongruously from the high, old-fashioned tin ceiling, casting garish light on the polished black and white tile floor.

At close hand she was even more lovely. Springer said hello and asked for a cup of coffee and a tuna-fish sandwich.

"Would you like your coffee first?" Her voice was pleasant but somber.

"Please."

He watched her draw the coffee from the urn with quick, awkward movements as if she were trying to hide the fact that she was unfamiliar with the machine; it overflowed onto the saucer. She groped for a rag, wiped the china, and placed it on the counter. Then she went to the sandwich board and searched the iced containers for tuna-fish salad. Springer opened his magazine and read until she brought his sandwich with a nervous smile. After he assured her it looked perfect, she picked up a rag and began polishing the coffee machine, her gaze fixed on the front window.

Alfred Potter, a big, red-faced plumber wearing greasy overalls, lumbered in and ordered a large Coke. He guzzled it noisily. Tipping his head back for a mouthful of ice, he noticed Springer in the cloudy mirror.

"Hey, Doc, heard you lost a patient."

Springer gave him a rueful grin. "You heard right, Alfie. Fastest one-legged man you ever saw."

Alfie laughed, a hearty noise like kettle drums. "When I heard about it I said, 'Son of a gun, there's a man who had the good sense to clear out before Doc Springer set the wrong leg.'"

"Did they pull your truck out of Fowler's septic tank yet?"

Alfie laughed louder. "Haven't even found it yet."

"Well, next time, Alfie, you just tie a bobber on it."

"A bobber? Shoot, Doc." He laughed and wiped tears from his eyes. Springer took another bite of his sandwich.

"Hey, Doc?"

"What, Alfie?"

Alfie jerked his head in the general direction of the old asylum. "What the hell is going on up there? Are we building a hotel or not?"

"Got me," said Springer. Out of the corner of his eye he noticed that the woman behind the counter seemed to be listening intently, though her gaze remained fixed on the window. "What do you think?"

Alfie swallowed some ice. "Moser sold 'em a pile of Orangeburg pipe. Sounds to me like they're fixing their sewers themselves."

"Any damn fool can lay sewer pipe, Alfie. Wait'll they

put pressure on that old plumbing. You'll be driving a Cadillac."

Alfie laughed. "You're okay, Doc. Cheerfulest son of a bitch I ever saw."

Springer grinned appreciation for the compliment and went back to his sandwich. Alfie's *you're okay* was followed by an unspoken *in spite of your pushing* and both men knew it. Back in 1972, Springer had organized McGovern's primary bid for the presidency in the Adirondacks and had gone to Florida as a delegate. His coup had gained him the enmity of the local Democratic and Republican organizations as well as a reputation for activism, which, in this conservative area, was considered synonymous with fire-breathing radicalism. They'd taken their revenge by squelching his drug treatment center and his proposal, last year, to build low-income housing on Spotting Street. There had even been talk of stripping him of his directorship of the hospital, but Bob Kent had blocked it—at what cost the mayor had never said.

Alfie finished chewing his ice, paid, and left. Springer opened his magazine. A graceful hand crept into his field of vision and carefully removed the empty plate. The heavy gold bracelet on her wrist looked out of place on a soda-fountain waitress. Springer raised his gaze from her hand and met her eyes. They were liquid brown, sad, and large in a striking, fine-boned face.

"You're new here, aren't you?"

"I just started today."

"I mean you're new in town."

"Yes." She put the plate in the sink under the counter. Her straight hair swayed from side to side as she wiped the Formica.

"Permit me to welcome you. I'm Alan Springer."

"Ellen Barbar," she replied. "I heard that man call you 'Doc.' Medical doctor?"

"Partner in crime with your new boss."

A small smile curled her mouth. There was something appealingly waiflike about her big eyes and thin, graceful body. Though she wasn't as richly developed as Angela, her face and eyes hinted at a similar combination of vulnerability and strength. He had come to love Angela's power and her occasional desire to surrender it. Margaret, less sure of her power, clutched it with obstinate tenacity. He sometimes wondered if he had done something that made her afraid.

As Ellen held his gaze for a moment, he saw something cool and purposeful he had missed at first. He had a feeling that she was assessing him, calculating his value.

"Are you going to be around here long?" he asked.

"I might be," she said just as Dwight Rigby stepped up behind the lunch counter.

"Hi, Alan, did you meet my new girl?" He had scraggly hair and a long lantern jaw.

"Just now," said Springer, sharing a smile with Ellen Barbar over Rigby's patronizing phrase. "Why don't you and Margy bring her to the Wrights's party?"

The druggist said, "I guess we could."

"Matt Wright is the high school principal," Springer explained. "It's a kind of thank-God-school-is-almost-over party. Good way to meet people."

"Thank you. I'd like that. Is that all right with you, Mr. Rigby?"

"Sure."

"Great," said Springer. "See you then. Take care, Dwight."

He walked slowly back to the hospital, enjoying the warm May day. The air was still and for a moment he wished he could go home, sit in the back yard, and read. That would have to wait until the weekend—provided the black flies held off for a few more days. He satisfied his lazy desire by looking in the shop windows and stopping at Lewis's to ask Pete if his son might like to join in the archery lessons.

He had to wait while Lewis scurried back and forth between several of the newcomers who were dragging long coils of line from the Manila rope spools and another group who were taking rakes and hoes out of the window display.

"Hi, Al," he called. "Be with you in a minute."

He rang up their purchases and Springer was a little surprised to see that Lewis was giving them credit already. As soon as they left, the shopkeeper began to rearrange the tangled rope spools. "What's up?" he asked briskly.

Springer told him.

"Good idea. Dicky might like that. Give him something to do when school's out." The cowbell jangled noisily, announcing the entrance of yet another group of fresh-faced young men. Lewis glanced up hastily and, for a moment, Springer thought he looked stricken. "Uh oh, excuse me, Al," he muttered, turning away. "Busy today."

The newcomers crowded through the door and spread among the racks and counters. Lewis darted nervously about, as if unable to decide which of them to serve first.

"I'll see you, Pete," said Springer. "Talk to Dicky."

Lewis nodded distractedly and bent to pick up a white apron that a woman had knocked to the floor as she rushed through the dry-goods section. When Springer opened the door, he whirled toward the sound of the jangling cowbell.

That evening at dinner Springer told Samantha that Dicky Lewis's father thought the archery lessons were a good idea, and he asked if she had invited anyone. Samantha reddened.

"Not yet," she said in a small voice, looking down at the table.

"Time's a-wasting."

"I will, Daddy."

Margaret said, "You don't have to, sweetheart. Your father can do that with the boys."

"I think," Springer said evenly, "that Samantha will enjoy it very much."

"Just don't push her," said Margaret.

"May I be excused?" asked Samantha, her mouth quivering.

Springer felt sick. She was so unhappy. "Homework?"

"I finished it."

"What are you going to do?"

"Read." She took her plate to the dishwasher and fled upstairs.

Springer turned angrily on Margaret, but kept his voice low. "Listen. Will you stop encouraging that child to hide?"

"I am not encouraging her to hide," said Margaret. "I just don't want you forcing her."

"To do what?"

"To grab at people. She'll make friends when she wants to."

"Grab? The child has no friends. She does nothing but read and hide in her room. I know it's a hard age for some kids, but it's also a time when they learn to be social, to interact with people, and you're not helping her."

"Forcing her isn't helping."

"Margaret, you have to support the child at least."

"She is fifteen years old," said Margaret. "She's old enough to make those decisions by herself."

"I want her to have the opportunity to learn to enjoy people."

"Not everybody's like you, Alan. A lot of us prefer not to run around throwing ourselves at everybody."

"What the hell is that supposed to mean?"

"Nothing. Just, oh, stop forcing her."

"What is she going to do this summer?"

Margaret looked alarmed. "What do you mean, do?"

"Should we try a camp?"

"Absolutely not. That was horrible last year."

"Wait a minute. Let's contain the drama. She got home-sick. We brought her home. Is she going to stay here forever?"

"She doesn't have to go away to camp. You're always saying how great the country is for kids. Let her enjoy it. She can go walking, and climbing, and swimming, and anything she wants to."

"Alone?"

Margaret slammed her hand on the table. "If she wants to. Leave her alone, Alan."

"Stop shouting."

"You make me so upset." Tears lapped at her eyes. Springer stood up, put his napkin on his chair, and placed his hands on her shoulders. She pulled away. "That's your answer to everything, isn't it? Just grab me and everything's fine."

Stung, he stepped back. "Touching happens to be a way I show how I feel."

"Well I don't feel like it." She gripped the edge of the table, staring at her half-eaten dinner.

"Sorry," said Springer.

"I have to clean up." Keeping her head down, she stood up and began stacking the dishwasher. Springer started to help, but she brushed him impatiently aside. He watched her for a moment, then stepped out on the back porch and breathed the chilly night air.

It was very clear and the stars, thousands of them, seemed as close as the blue lights in the old asylum. Margaret, Margaret, Margaret. What had he done? What had happened? They had had a love match once. And now they were just two people with not very much to say, bound together by an unhappy child. A lot of it had to do with Hudson City. Springer loved the Adirondacks and still reveled in his triumphant return to the town where his family had dwelt in a shack. Margaret hated it. Once, during a terrible fight, she had said she never would have come if she had known they were going to stay. Springer pointed out that they had not known—he was filling in temporarily, right after his internship, when Margaret was pregnant with Samantha and he'd needed the job. And now he was too involved professionally to leave.

When he went back inside, the kitchen was empty and he heard a tub being drawn in the upstairs bathroom. He settled into his chair in the den and tried to escape into *Time* magazine. Under "Medicine," he skimmed what had to be the sixth article this year on lithium, learned nothing new, and browsed the back pages, saving the political news for last. He was debating whether to read a three-page article in "Religion" when, suddenly, he sat up straight, gripping the magazine tightly with both hands.

A new religious sect was the subject of the article, but what caught Springer's attention was a photograph of a group of people locked in prayer. He stared in disbelief. One of the worshipers was the big blond medic who had abducted the man with the broken leg.

"Clean for Christ," said the caption. "A Revelationist Prayer Session."

Beneath the subheading, "The Advance Guard," *Time* described a fast-growing fundamentalist sect called the Revelationists. The Revelationists worshiped the Archangel Michael, God's militant angel who drove the Devil from heaven. They believed that the warring archangel was soon to visit the earth to cleanse it for Christ's second coming.

"Revelationists?" said Springer aloud. Revelationists. Revelations Inc. He looked closely at the picture. It *was* the same man. He devoured the rest of the article.

Militantly puritanical, the Revelationists had converted thousands of young people on the West Coast and were preparing to carry their message eastward. The sect's supporters spoke of the love and understanding and simple heartfelt faith promoted among its members. Numerous former drug addicts and runaways attested to the beneficial changes that the Revvies, as they were nicknamed, had effected in their lives.

Its detractors accused the sect of brainwashing its converts, destroying their will, and forcing them to surrender their lives and possessions to the movement. Several scions of wealthy families had turned over their inheritances and in one case the sect had gone to court and won the right to keep what had been bequeathed.

Supporters and detractors agreed on one thing. The zealots were remarkably successful in obtaining converts and raising large sums of money to further their mission. The sect owned considerable property in California, Oregon, and Washington State, preferring rural to urban properties, though it normally canvassed urban areas for new converts. The leader of the Revelationists was a shadowy, seldom-seen figure known only as Michael.

Now Springer remembered that while the boy, Joseph, lay on the operating table, his companions had asked God to ease Michael's suffering. Jesus Christ, a bunch of fanatics. Wait until the town heard about it. Poor Bob. No hotel. Springer chuckled with perverse amusement. The crazies were back. And this time they had the key to the front gate.

Bob Kent purpled. "Sons of bitches! Why didn't they say who they were?"

Springer sipped his bourbon. "Wouldn't have made any difference. The bank would have sold it anyway."

"Tell that to the voters," said Kent. "Jesus Christ, they'll blame me that there's not going to be any hotel. Goddamned bank must've known all along."

"They'll forget about it by November."

"Do you realize what this means?" roared Kent. "Besides no hotel?"

"It means a lot of things," Springer replied mildly. "But I know which one's bugging you. They're off the tax rolls."

"Goddamned right," said Kent. "Two hundred prime acres and the biggest goddamned building in the township. Do you know that down in the Catskills some of those counties have lost a third of their taxable property to free-loading fanatics—meditators, gurus, what-have-you? Well, they're not getting off the tax rolls in this town."

"Good luck."

"Revelationists," moaned Kent. "Why us?" He glared at Springer, who was smiling affably. "Are you enjoying this, Alan?"

Springer shrugged. "I told you so. We could have had a real money-maker with a drug center."

"I don't want to hear about it. A hotel would've saved our asses."

"Sorry, Bob. I didn't come up to gloat. Just thought you'd like to know before the rest of them do."

"Yeah." Kent sighed. "Well, we've got new neighbors. Better make the best of it. They'll need clothes and food and supplies and if we remain on good terms they'll continue to buy local." He levered his stocky frame out of his armchair and splashed more bourbon into their glasses. His round face brightened. "I think they're making a deliberate effort to fit in and contribute. At the volume they're buying they could do a lot better over in Warington or down in Saratoga."

"True," said Springer.

Kent rubbed his fleshy hands. "Yeah. We'll do okay."

Springer stood up and walked across Kent's wood-paneled living room. He looked at his reflection in the gleaming night-black plate-glass window that occupied the entire south wall of the room, then switched on the outdoor floodlights. A young deer, a doe, was nibbling the shrubs at the edge of Kent's redwood deck; it leaped high in the sudden glare and bounded into the dark. "You know what bothers me?"

"What?" asked Kent.

Springer stared through the circle of light to the night beyond. "What do these people want in Hudson City?"

7

Tom House, the publisher, editor, and sole reporter of the weekly Hudson City *Sun*, was out looking for Revelationists. He was in his late fifties, a handsome, white-maned pedant who wore the same black suit summer and winter, a white shirt and a string tie, and lived alone in a room behind his office.

A Hudson City native, he had started out working for his father on the *Sun*, but quickly pushed on to write for the Binghamton *Press*, then the St. Louis *Post-Dispatch*, and finally the New York *Herald Tribune*, striding a career route well trod by the better journalists of his day.

Of all his triumphs he remembered most vividly a single afternoon at the St. Regis Hotel, the crowning moment before it had all slipped away. Passing through the brightly lighted bar to meet a publisher who wanted to do a book of his "City Lights" columns, he had stopped to greet men he had worked with, people he had met at parties, others who praised his columns, a beautiful woman. He had basked in the recognition, enjoying the unique reward for having met and conquered—belonging—that only New York could bestow, when all the great buildings, the rich streets, and the striving millions were rendered briefly ordinary by the admiration of a few special people in a special place.

But the book deal fell through and shortly afterward the *Trib*, flailing about like a wounded scorpion, dropped his column. Then suddenly it folded altogether and he was out competing for work. Reeling from a year of disappointments, he'd drifted home and revived the defunct *Sun*, which had died with his father. He wrote school news, legal notices, synopses of town board meetings, accounts of automobile accidents, and a social column, "At Home in Hudson City." What remained of his advertising revenues after he paid his printer, his rent, and repairs on his second-hand Buick provided a thin existence.

His poverty was a grinding reminder of what he had lost, but over the years it had narrowed his vision to the point where a small check and a page-six by-line in the New York *Daily News*, for which he was the Adirondack stringer, were the limits of his dreams.

He looked to the Revelationists for a salable story. He didn't have to look very hard. Three of them, two men and a woman, were mailing registered letters at the post office. The moment he introduced himself, the woman, perhaps twenty-eight and a trifle older than her male companions, took charge. She was not particularly attractive, but she had a bright smile.

"We're happy to meet you."

"Thank you, ma'am. I want to welcome you to Hudson City and I would appreciate the opportunity to ask a few questions."

Her smile changed, focused, and locked with the fixed quality of a photograph. "For what purpose?"

"I want to write about you."

She and her companions walked shoulder to shoulder out to the sidewalk. House hurried after them. "Can you tell me something about your organization?"

The men flanked her so that House had to walk ahead and look back for her answer. "We are a movement, Mr. House. Not an organization."

House dutifully wrote in his notebook. It was expected and it kept people talking. "What is the purpose of your movement?"

"We are disciples of the Archangel Michael. His purpose is our purpose."

"And what is his purpose?" House tripped on the curb crossing Grand Street. One of the men thrust out a strong hand and steadied his arm.

"His purpose," said the woman, still walking, ignoring the curious looks they were receiving, "is to cleanse the earth for the coming of our Lord, Jesus Christ."

"And how do you propose to do that?"

"We will do that," she said matter-of-factly.

House waited for elaboration, but there was none. "How?" he asked.

"We support people in their efforts to cleanse themselves."

"Specifically, how do you do that?"

"We teach people who have declared their intention to cleanse themselves." She turned on him suddenly. "Have you?"

House was startled by the power of her gaze. "I'm just asking questions," he said hurriedly. "Specifically, just how would you teach someone?"

"A person who has declared himself ready to cleanse his soul, his body, his mind, for the purposes of Michael and the glories of Christ needs only our support." She stopped walking and pointed at the man who was still holding House's arm. "Mark," she said, "Just arrived from the Coast. He's leading a Rev session tonight. Mark can tell you about the help he received while I go into this store a moment."

She disappeared into Lewis's General Store while House scribbled furiously in his notebook. "Rev session? Spell that please."

"R-E-V."

"What's a Rev session?"

Mark smiled mechanically, his eyes fixed in their sockets as if he were watching movement at a great distance. "When I found Michael I was lost."

"What's your last name, Mark?" House interrupted, pencil ready.

"I was high on drugs all the time. I was perverse, degraded, filthy. I was broken. I had no goals, no desires beyond immediate pleasure. And no happiness. Michael gave me everything I need."

"What did you do for him?"

"I renounced the Devil. And now I serve Michael."

"What do you do for him?"

"What is asked. Only through service can we really love."

Mark's companion nodded assent.

"I thought we were talking about cleansing," said House.

"Cleansing is love," said Mark.

"And love is cleansing," said his companion. "We love those who are clean and we love those who are not clean . . . yet."

House bridled at their simplicity, but he tried to retain his detachment. "You mean you love everybody. You love me right now?"

"Of course. You are God's child. I love you."

"What if I don't get clean?"

"You will."

House searched the man's face for humor or a glint of irony. He found neither, only an innocent smile beneath curiously empty eyes. "Listen, Mark," he said, lowering his voice to a conspiratorial whisper, "before what's-her-name comes back, just fill me in a little on the mechanics of this thing. What exactly do you people do?"

Mark laughed and addressed the other man. "He'll be with us soon."

"I know."

"What do you mean?" asked House.

"You're so curious, so alive. You're almost ready."

"Bullshit," snapped House, "I'm a reporter. I'm doing my job."

The woman returned. She had overheard the last exchange and she said, "Everyone has a reason at first. They say they want to tell a friend or they want to write about us. They really want to join Michael, but they're afraid of giving up their empty lives. You see, as empty as they are, they are familiar and, therefore, comfortable."

"Ridiculous," said House.

"You're right," said Mark. "He's almost ready." They surrounded House, gently patting his arms and shoulders, laughing and talking. He drew away, busying himself with pad and pencil. To his relief, the Revelationists' blue station wagon pulled up to the curb and they scrambled in. The woman rolled down her window and handed him a pile of printed matter. "You'll find what you need for your story here."

House leafed through the papers. Handouts. A press-pack.

"Wait. This PR stuff isn't any use to me." He read aloud from the top sheet, " 'Over five thousand people have joined the Revelationist effort to cleanse the earth for Christ.' I doubt they just walked in and signed up."

"They underwent a conversion experience," said the woman.

"It's the conversion experience I'm asking about," House said patiently.

She gave him her bland smile. "Conversion is an experience, Mr. House. Not a story. You cannot tell people about something you know nothing about."

"How do you convert them?" insisted House. "What do you do to them?"

"As water seeks its own level, so does the soul rise to love."

"Gravity makes water seek its own level," said House.

"And God draws the soul to love," replied the woman.

House took a deep, frustrated breath. "Okay. You don't want to talk about conversion. How about this Michael? Is he around?"

"Michael is everywhere."

"No, no, no. I don't mean the angel. I mean your leader."

"*Arch*angel. Michael is everywhere."

"Can't you give me one straight answer. What are you trying to hide?"

The man driving said something House couldn't hear and the woman pulled a wallet from her overall pocket. "We would like to buy an advertisement in your newspaper. How much is a full page?"

"What kind of ad?" House asked warily.

"A message to the people of Hudson City. How much will it cost?"

"Seventy-five dollars."

She gave him the money. "Please write this down." Her voice took on the tremulous tone of a preacher nearing the climax of his sermon:

"And there was war in heaven. Michael and his angels fought against the dragon; and the great dragon was cast out, that old serpent, called the Devil, and Satan, which deceived the whole world. Woe to the inhabiters of the earth. The Devil is among you."

House read it back. "That's it?"

But the car had pulled away. He watched it go up Main Street and turn onto Spotting Mountain Road. Then he went to his office and wrote a story on the Revelationists, larding his account of the interview with facts from *Time* magazine. Few of his readers subscribed to *Time* and by the *Sun*'s standards it was a good piece—the *Daily News* wouldn't touch it with a rake.

He fingered the $75. He would get his television fixed and maybe buy a shirt.

8

Matthew Wright was the principal of Hudson City High School, his party an annual June event. Wright was a plodder whose tight accounting was applauded by the school board and property owners; his parties, featuring cheap New York State wines and prepackaged cheddar cheese, evoked less enthusiasm. Knowing what to expect in the way of libation, Springer had fortified himself at home before he and Margaret set out across the street.

Like the Springers, the Wrights lived in an old mansion on Main Street. The party was held in the living room and the dining room, the windows open to the night air. All the teachers were there as well as the merchants and their wives, the men in open shirts and sport coats, the women in bright dresses. The Revelationists were the main topic of conversation. Most of the guests had had no contact with the sect and they turned to Tom House, since he'd interviewed them, and Springer, because he had treated the man with the broken leg.

House was enjoying the attention. He stroked his white mane with nervous sweeps of his bony fingers. "Simpleminded drivel," he answered when Wright's wife, Jeannie, a pretty grade-school teacher, asked what they had talked about. "They don't talk, they preach. Fanatics."

Jeannie Wright pursed her lips. "Do *you* think they're fanatics, Alan?"

Springer swirled his wine and smiled at her. "I didn't have the chance to talk with them. I was kind of busy."

Wright was a tense, muscular man who had once taught physical education and still coached the basketball team. He was ill at ease at parties, particularly when Jeannie talked to other men. "Yes, Alan," he chimed in now, "what exactly happened?"

As Springer described the incident in detail others gathered to listen. House fidgeted, irritated that Springer had captured center stage. "Why did you let them stay?" he demanded.

"I wondered about that too," said Jeannie Wright. "You're usually so much in command at the hospital."

Wright, catching the mildly flirtatious note in her voice, put a possessive arm around her. "It seemed to me like an unusual lapse for a doctor." Jeannie pulled away. Wright dropped his arm and rubbed his close-cropped hair.

Springer smiled at the byplay, smiled some more at Margaret, whose cheeks were flushed with wine, and said, "Not at all, Matt. I try to handle each situation on its merits. There was no reason why the man's friends couldn't stay, so I let them."

Dwight and Margy Rigby appeared in the doorway as Springer paused. They had Ellen Barbar in tow. She looked beautiful in a simple black dress. Margaret, ever sensitive to his reactions when they were with other people, glanced where he had. Springer continued smoothly, "I never saw anything like it. That man was a knot of pain-tensed muscle. Then his friends went to work on him. Relaxed him just as if they'd shot him full of Demerol. It was quite impressive."

"That may be so," intoned House, "but we can't have people walking in and out of our hospital at whim. I'm surprised you didn't take some action."

Springer shrugged. "It didn't seem worth the trouble."

"Alan's right," said Margaret. "He's got better things to do than chase after patients who want to go home."

"Hi, Dwight," called Springer.

Dwight and Margy pressed into the group, ushering Ellen Barbar between them. Margy was as lantern-jawed as her husband and with Ellen between them they looked like a pair of battle-hardened Crusaders returning from the Levant with an exotic captive. Dwight introduced her as "My new girl at the store." The men greeted her carefully under the watchful eyes of their wives.

"And you already met Alan, didn't you?"

Springer noticed the merest flicker of Ellen's eye toward Margaret. "I think so," she said vaguely. "I've met so many people this week. Everyone's been so friendly."

"Yes, we did meet," said Springer.

Tom House responded with pompous gallantry. "A woman as lovely as you, my dear, will always meet friendly people."

Springer sensed, rather than saw, her gaze meet House's and predicted to himself exactly what she would do. Assessing the group with a sweep of her dark, liquid eyes, she concluded, correctly, that House was the only man without a wife and went straight to him, as if to assure the other women that she did not intend to be a threat.

House asked her if she would like some wine.

"I'd love some," Ellen said, letting him take her arm. The group watched as House steered her to the dining room.

Jeannie Wright said, "Do you suppose our bachelor publisher has found a friend?"

"I don't think he can afford her," said Donna Lewis, Pete's dowdy, pinch-faced wife. "Did you see that dress?"

"I sure did," said Jeannie. "How much are you paying that girl, Dwight?"

"Not enough to buy a dress like that," Margy said.

Her husband nodded agreement. "I was sort of surprised when she asked for the job. She said she needed money."

"Well, she won't find it with Tom House," Donna Lewis declared.

"I think he's swish," muttered Wright.

Several people laughed and looked over their shoulders.

"Oh, Matt," said Jeannie. "You think everybody is gay."

"You can't be sure of anybody these days."

"Jesus Christ," said Jeannie.

"Do you want a dress like that?" asked Matt. "Is that what's bothering you?"

Jeannie glanced at the uncomfortable expressions in the group and deftly changed the subject. "What I want to know is what the Revelationists' being here will mean to the children."

"What do you mean?" asked Springer.

"According to what Tom wrote they're missionaries. Are they going to approach our children?"

Margaret looked alarmed. "You mean try to convert them?"

"They wouldn't come to a little town like Hudson City just for our children," said Pete Lewis. "I've met a lot of them. They're really very nice people."

Bob Kent was passing by, drink in hand. As mayor, he assumed the role of cheerful host at any party he attended. "Of course they're nice people," he boomed magnanimously. "We're lucky to have them here."

"As long as they keep buying," said Springer.

Pete Lewis's mouth set in a hard line. Kent punched him lightly in the ribs. "Don't mind Alan. Every community needs its cynic. Thank God ours is a competent doctor as well." Springer smiled at his friend's gentle rebuke.

Fred Zinser, the town attorney, said, "From what I've read, they get their converts in the big cities where children are alienated and confused."

"You don't think they are here?" asked Margaret.

"Of course not," said Matthew Wright. "They enjoy the closeness of a small town and stable families."

Margaret and Jeannie Wright exchanged a doubtful glance, but Matt smacked his fist in his palm. "The kids here are under constant supervision. They have teams and sports and some damned good teachers, including you, Margaret, and a church."

"Church?" snorted Sophie Wilkins, who had just joined the group. "If you'd bring that baritone back, Matt, we'd have a heck of a good choir again."

"I can't make it every week," said Wright. "You know how busy I am since the budget cuts."

"Time was around here," Sophie Wilkins went on, "when school employees went to church or they lost a job."

"Times are different," said Bob Kent, edging her away.

Margaret said, "What about all the children who don't get on your teams?"

"They get plenty of help in the regular phys. ed. classes," replied Wright, adding firmly, "Our school is small enough to look after each student."

"Then how come so many drop out?" asked Margaret.

"You're exaggerating," said Wright. He was becoming irritated now. "We graduate a higher percentage each year . . . except last year, which was an exception."

Springer said, "Margaret may exaggerate slightly, but her point is a good one. There is a condition of poverty and ignorance in this area that the school can't always cope with. I treat people with diseases that supposedly haven't existed in the civilized world for fifty years. I have a woman with pellagra, for Christ's sake. A niacin deficiency.

You know why? She's living on beer. That's all. Beer. Too bombed out to even remember to take the vitamin supplements I give her. She's a mother of one of your students," he added pointedly, though that wasn't entirely true. Danny Moser had already quit school. But there were others in similar straits.

"So?" said Wright. "Is that woman our fault?"

"My point is that there are children whom the school has not been able to help."

"Right," said Margaret. "If those Revelationists come after our children they'll find just as many unhappy, alienated children here as in any big city, and then what do we do?"

"It can't happen here," said Wright.

Margaret continued to lace into Wright, who was growing more red-faced by the moment. Springer, knowing his wife's was a lost cause, detached himself from the group and drifted around the room until he ran into Ed Stratton. The automobile dealer was drinking wine with the look of a man who wished it were rye.

"Springer," he said coolly. "How you doing?"

"Hi, Ed. Pretty good, pretty good." They had tangled over the low-income housing issue and the memory was fresh.

Springer nodded at Stratton's waist. "You lost some weight."

Stratton shifted his cigar in his mouth. "When you're talking like a doctor I listen to you. I feel much better."

"Next the smoking."

"Fat chance."

"Where's Janet?"

"Home with the kids. We don't like baby-sitters. Let 'em get away with murder."

Springer looked around the room. Most of the guests had gathered around the large cheese table, but Margaret and Wright were still in the middle of the room. She was gesticulating with her empty glass while Wright nodded mechanically and stared at the floor.

"I better go rescue Margaret before Matt fires her. See you, Ed."

"Right," said Stratton.

Springer caught Kent's eye as he crossed the room. Together they disengaged Margaret and Wright and eased them toward the buffet table, where House, Ellen Barbar, the Lewises, the Rigbys, the Spencers—who owned the IGA grocery—the Zinsers, and others were talking and picking at the remains of the cheese.

Kent interrupted with a hearty laugh. "Got to hand it to these Revelationists, they sure do make for conversation. Maybe we ought to invite them to our next party."

Pete Lewis took him seriously. "That's a good idea, Bob. Let's invite them to the fair in August."

"Sure," boomed Kent. "Why not?"

"I already asked them to come to church," said Lewis. "Maybe all of us, every time we see 'em, should do that. Get 'em to join in."

"Right." Kent laughed. "Hell, we'll convert them before they convert us." He winked at Springer.

Springer said, "Beat 'em to the punch."

"Make 'em all Hudson City Presbyterians," bantered Kent. "When we get through with them we'll start in on the Moonies."

"And the Jesus Freaks."

"Yeah," said Kent. "We'll put Hudson City on the map. Send us your alienated youth. We'll straighten them out. Make everybody a Hudson City Presbyterian. The whole world."

"It's not funny," said Ellen Barbar loudly.

Kent stopped laughing. "What's not funny?"

"It's nothing to joke about. I know all about them and what they do."

The group faced her, uneasy with her earnest tone. "And what do they do?" asked Kent.

Her face was as grave as her voice:

"They steal souls."

Springer and Kent exchanged puzzled glances. Gary Spencer smirked. His wife and Margy Rigby nodded as if politely encouraging a poor joke teller to keep talking. Tom House's watery blue eyes turned attentive, and Margaret, peering owlishly into her glass, repeated, "Steal souls?"

Matthew Wright said, "That's rather strong language."

"They have my sister."

"I beg your pardon?"

"They're holding her."

"The Revvies?"

"Don't call them that. It makes them sound innocent, and the Revelationists are not innocent. They're very dangerous. They brainwashed her."

"Come on," said Bob Kent.

"Do you think I'm kidding?" She regarded him with a steady, open gaze, but her voice trembled. "They've had her for four months."

They listened anxiously, uncomfortable with the sudden shift from party banter to sober talk. Isolated in their small town, realities beyond life and death and the cost of living tended to touch them only lightly, arriving as a form of entertainment from magazines and television. Old people took sick and died; youngsters perished in automobile accidents; food and fuel cost more every day; people married, children were born, families fragmented; but the pulse of the age—wars, changing life-styles, politics, the urban upheavals, the rendings and tearings of the modern societal fabric—flickered distantly like lightning beyond the mountains.

"Do you mean," asked Springer, "that they're holding her against her will?"

She bit her lips, nodded.

"There are laws against that. Why don't you go to the police?"

"I—"

"Wait a minute," said Kent. "Is she here? Up there?"

"Yes," said Ellen.

"Are you sure? Do you know that for a fact?"

"I know she's there."

"Have you seen her?" Kent persisted.

"No. That's why I came here. To find her."

"But you have no proof she's here."

"I *know* she's here."

"Well, that's not good enough."

"Hold on, Bob," said Springer. "Give her a chance."

"Bob's right," said Pete Lewis. "Charlie Daniels can't go barging in there on her say-so. That's private property."

"She didn't ask for help from your cop," snapped Springer, annoyed by the way they discounted her story.

"Can I say something?" asked Ellen.

"Go right ahead," said Kent. "But our police—"

"I know they can't do anything," said Ellen. "I've already tried that."

"How did your sister get hooked up with them?" asked Tom House.

Ellen began her story. At first she seemed reluctant to talk, but soon the words poured forth, an emotional torrent that engulfed the party; the room grew quiet.

Her sister's name was Rose. She was twenty-one. She had graduated from college the year before and had traveled to the West Coast, where she drifted around San Francisco, studying Zen, practicing Yoga, living on odd jobs, searching.

"She got a job as a ticket taker in a pornographic movie theater."

Several people smirked.

One night a band of Revelationists invaded the theater. They stopped the projector, turned up the lights, and harangued the audience until the police arrived to disperse them. Rose, impressed by their fervor, attended a Revelationist rally, a Rev session, in Golden Gate Park.

Caught up by their enthusiastic discipline, she joined a weekend training retreat in Big Sur, returned for a week-long instruction period, and shortly after became a Revelationist; she renounced the Devil, pledged her life to Michael, and signed over her car and her small savings account.

Ellen learned of this when Rose telephoned her in New York, where she worked as a computer programmer, and announced breathlessly that Michael the Archangel was coming to earth to prepare it for Christ's return. Rose demanded that Ellen join with her before it was too late.

"She sounded crazy," Ellen said with a shudder. "I tried to talk to her, but she just ranted about Michael and Christ and sin. Crazy talk. So crazy that I took my vacation early and flew out to San Francisco."

She closed her eyes and shook her head. "I found her begging in the streets."

The music stopped; it was the last record on the stack and the stereo shut down with an audible click. "Begging?" asked someone.

"Begging," Ellen said fiercely. "They lived outside the

city on a big farm. Every morning they drove them in to beg. Rose said she sometimes made over a hundred dollars. She sounded proud of it, but she was so confused and so tired and pale. I tried to persuade her to leave them, but it was very hard to get her alone because they worked in groups and they kept an eye on each other. A couple of times when the streets were very crowded I managed to take her aside but she was afraid, looking around all the time, afraid they would see us. She begged me to join. But her face and eyes were so strange . . . as if she were hypnotized; I knew she wasn't in control of herself. The last time I saw her she suddenly burst into tears. I held her and then I started to lead her away and she came, but the others saw us. One of them commanded her to stay with them. They pushed me away and before I could do anything they put her in a car and drove off.

"That's when I went to the police. They were"— she looked up, as if tracking the proper word, speared it with her eyes—"sympathetic. Other relatives had complained too, but they said they couldn't search the Revelationists' farm without a warrant. I took a leave of absence from my job and hired an attorney. We got a judge to issue a warrant."

The police had searched the farm. The Revelationists denied that Rose Barbar had ever been there. Within an hour the sect's lawyers, top San Francisco attorneys, produced a restraining order. The police gave up and Ellen was left alone.

Questioning Revelationists who had dropped out of the movement, she learned that Rose had been taken to another West Coast retreat. "They moved her north, then to Oregon and then Washington State." A note of steely purpose edged her voice as she described the way she had followed. It had taken her three months and now she was certain that Rose was in Hudson City.

"What will you do now?" asked Springer.

Ellen shrugged wearily. "I'm not sure. Even my parents have given up. They can't give me any more money. They say they have to abide by Rose's decision."

"Maybe they're right," said Kent.

"She didn't make a decision," Ellen said fiercely. "They brainwashed her. I have to save her."

"Maybe she doesn't want to be saved," said Kent.

"What does she look like?" asked Pete Lewis. "I get a lot of 'em in my store. Maybe I've seen her."

Ellen fumbled in her bag and produced a photograph. "She has red hair. She's about my height and looks a lot like me."

Springer looked at a snapshot of a baby-faced girl in a graduation cap. She didn't have Ellen's fine bone structure, but the wide, wistful eyes were similar. He handed it to Tom House. No one recognized the girl.

Margaret said, "You must know more about them than we do. Why do you think they're here?"

"They're expanding. They're moving over the entire country," Ellen said ominously.

A long, worried silence greeted her prediction. Finally, Bob Kent said, "I'll tell you why they're here. They got plenty of room and plenty of privacy."

"Right," said Pete Lewis. "They're not going to bother us, Margaret. They just want to be left alone. They're sure as the dickens not going to beg on our streets. Charlie Daniels would toss 'em in the clink before you could say 'Howdy-do.'"

The group laughed. Someone turned the records over and the music resumed. Ellen turned to Tom House and Springer heard him say, "I'll walk you home."

When they left, the party picked up again, the guests relieved that the outsider and her problems were gone. Though Springer asked several people what they thought of Ellen's story, no one really wanted to talk about it beyond speculating that a girl who worked in a pornographic theater probably couldn't be very stable to begin with.

"Her parents are right," said Matthew Wright, his arm tightly around Jeannie. "Some kids just don't work out."

"She's really determined," said Springer.

"And *so* attractive," said Jeannie. "Come on, Coach. Let's break out some more wine."

Springer wandered around the party. Margaret was talking on the couch with Fred and Betty Zinser. He found the front porch empty, put his glass on a table, and stared out at the night. His house was diagonally across Main Street. The light was on in Samantha's bedroom. He looked at his watch. Almost midnight, but no school tomorrow, so it didn't matter. A bottle shattered musically near the stores, followed by loud laughter and pounding feet. Then it was quiet.

Samantha's light went out. Springer blew a silent kiss in her direction and turned back inside to collect Margaret. On the top step he paused and looked again at the night. It was cloudy and few stars shone. But, high above the town, from the windows of the old asylum, blue lights burned.

9

"Run!" yelled Danny Moser.

He limped along the sidewalk as fast as his aching foot would allow. Smothering their laughter, the Stratton brothers, Jackie and Roscoe, tore past him and raced for the dark safety of the abandoned Shell station. Danny struggled after them, the crash of the breaking bottle ringing in his ears.

He looked back as the square of light that shone from the window in the police-station door lengthened and Chief Daniels sprang through the open door, looking up and down Main Street. Danny pressed against the wall and eased forward until he reached the protective shadows of the garage.

He found Jackie and Roscoe giggling behind the cinder-block building. Danny leaned against the cold concrete and caught his breath. "Nice catch, turkey."

Roscoe broke up.

"Shhh," said Jackie. He was only fifteen, excited to be with his older brother—and terrified what their father would do if they were caught raising hell with Danny Moser.

"Butt me," snapped Danny. He'd heard the expression in a war movie he'd seen on television. Roscoe dutifully produced a pack of Camels.

"Light," said Danny.

Jackie lighted Danny and Roscoe's cigarettes and brought the match to his own. Danny slapped it out in his hand. "Three on a match. Youngest one dies."

Roscoe gave Jackie his cigarette and he lighted it from the burning tip.

Danny waited until the youngster had drawn the smoke into his lungs. Then he said, casually, "Chief Daniels is coming."

"What?" The smoke caught in Jackie's throat and he coughed.

"Shhh," said Roscoe, looking wildly about. "Let's go."

"He saw Jackie," said Danny.

"What?" cried Jackie. "No he didn't. You were last."

"He's going to call your father."

"Bullshit," said Roscoe. But his voice cracked.

"We better go home," said Jackie.

"No," growled Danny. "I was kidding. He went the other way. Relax, turkey."

Roscoe laughed.

Danny tossed his butt into the dark. "Got any more grass?"

"A little."

"Well, what are you waiting for?"

Roscoe whispered, "I think Jackie's had enough."

"You his mother?"

"Come on," said Jackie. "I can take it."

Roscoe pulled a skinny joint from his shirt pocket. Danny snapped it out of his hand, lighted the twisted paper, and drew deeply. "Where'd you get this garbage?"

Roscoe laughed. "From you."

"Great stuff," said Danny.

Jackie laughed. He inhaled on the joint and put his hands over his mouth to stop from coughing. They passed it back and forth until it was too short to hold. Danny fastened the burning roach in a surgical scissors clip and drew the last smoke.

"Neat," said Roscoe. "Where'd you get that?"

"Borrowed it from Doc Springer."

"He *gave* it to you?"

"What do you think, turkey?"

"You *stole* it?" asked Jackie.

"So?"

"Is that where you got those pills?"

Danny pushed Roscoe's shoulder hard with his open palm. "Watch your mouth, Roscoe."

"Hey, I only—"

"Watch it, Roscoe. The Doc doesn't give me any pills and you better not say he does. You'd get him in trouble."

"So?"

Danny pushed him again. "I don't want to hear that shit."

"Where do you get them?"

"There's a guy in Warington."

"Who?"

"You want pills, you come to me. But watch it about the Doc."

"Okay, man."

"That goes for you, too, Jackie."

Jackie looked fearfully at the older boy. "Okay, Danny, I didn't say nothing."

"Just remember." Danny stared the brothers down. Then he laughed. "Okay, no big deal. Now what do you wanna do?"

Jackie yawned.

"Come on," said Danny. "Let's hear something."

"I don't know," said Roscoe.

"Okay." Danny grinned. "Follow me."

"Where?"

He eased around the garage, checked that Chief Daniels wasn't about, and started up Main toward the church. Moments later, the Stratton boys caught up. "Where you going, Danny?"

"You'll see." He turned off Main onto Spotting Mountain Road. As they came to Spotting Street, Roscoe said, "You going home?"

"Do I look like I'm going home?"

Answering his own question, he continued along the road. When they reached the last streetlight, Jackie said, "Hey, where you going?"

"Come on." He walked faster, enjoying his secret. They followed, whispering to each other. Finally, when they had gone a quarter mile on the dark road, Danny announced, "We're gonna check out the Revvies."

"What?" said Roscoe.

"The nut house?" Jackie asked fearfully.

"Let's see what they're doing up there." He started walking again. Jackie and Roscoe whispered fiercely and ran after him.

"Wait a minute."

"What's the matter?"

"We don't wanna walk two miles to look at the nut house."

"Up close," explained Danny. "Find out what's going on."

"Inside?" asked Jackie.

"Chicken, turkey?" Danny laughed. "Chicken, turkey."

Roscoe giggled. "We can't go in, man. They got a fence."

"You can't climb?"

"What if they catch us?" said Jackie.

"I been in there a million times."

"Not since the Revvies came," said Roscoe.

"They're not stopping me."

"I don't want to." Jackie was whimpering now, close to tears.

"Shut up, turkey."

Roscoe hesitated. "I don't think we should."

"What's with you guys?" A car bore around a curve in the road, headlights blazing. The boys jumped aside and turned their faces from the light.

"I want to go home," whined Jackie. "Daddy might—"

"Christ on a crutch," sneered Danny. "You guys still putting up with that father shit? Anyhow, he's at old man Wright's party."

"It's kinda late," said Roscoe. "If he catches us sneaking out like this we're in real trouble. We better go."

"I don't believe you turkeys."

"You coming back?"

"No way, man. I'm going in."

"You better not, Danny."

"Butt me, turkey. I'll tell you all about it tomorrow."

"Bullshit," said Roscoe. "You're not going in alone."

"Oh yeah?" Danny lighted the cigarette, jammed it in his mouth, and limped up the road. When he looked back, the Strattons were gone. Turkeys. He walked quickly, his foot throbbing. The road was very dark. Now and then a house cast faint lights into the night and occasionally a car raced past. Otherwise he was alone.

Half an hour later he came to the Revelationists' main gate. A few blue lights glowed in the brooding building. The gate and driveway were dark. He shivered in the cool night air and wished he'd taken another cigarette from Roscoe. The blue lights beckoned hypnotically. He saw two people standing by a window, talking. They looked like women, but he couldn't be sure at that distance. One put her arm around the other and they moved slowly out of sight.

When he was sure that no one could see him, Danny

planted his foot in the ornamental iron cross piece and hoisted himself up. The gate shook with the trembling in his legs. He paused at the top and shifted his weight from his injured foot. Then, careful that the barbed wire didn't tear his clothes, he eased over the top strand and lowered himself to the ground.

He crouched in the dust, ready to hurl himself back over, but nothing changed. The night was quiet. A figure passed by one of the distant windows. Danny shrank into the shadow of the stone pillar and hid there. The perspiration he had worked up on the walk was cold and damp now. He stood stiffly and hurried along the grass verge next to the driveway, pausing where it curved toward the front door, until, positive he wasn't observed, he scrambled across the lawn to the right wing, dodging the light falls from the windows.

Sidling along the building, he crept to the nearest window and looked in on a large unfurnished room. Its wood floor gleamed in the soft light of candles. Several men and women were sitting cross-legged on the floor, hands clasped, heads bobbing up and down. He heard a thin murmuring sound, chanting. Fascinated, he drew closer to the glass.

A powerful hand crushed his biceps and yanked him away from the window. Squealing in terror, Danny wrested free and ran. A shadow sprang out of the dark. He braked and swerved, but a second shadow loomed suddenly in front of him. He twisted away and blundered into a third shadow.

A dreadful blow smashed into his midriff; he collapsed to the ground, his legs and arms paralyzed. Strong hands hauled him to his feet. He tried to open his mouth and gasp air, but he couldn't. The shadows converged from all sides. Half-conscious, he saw the front door open. They dragged him toward it. His feet bumped on the steps.

The heavy door closed behind them.

10

Spotting Street, the shabby neighborhood of tiny frame houses built for the asylum attendants, bordered the cemetery. Springer was about to turn onto Main when he noticed Reverend Davies arranging flowers on his wife's grave. It was Saturday, hot and clear.

Davies sensed the intrusion and straightened up. He peered about myopically through thick lenses, focused on Springer, and approached the fence. Recognition lighted his face as he drew close.

"Good afternoon, Doctor. I thought that was you."

He was a formal man who preferred titles to given names. Springer responded in kind. "Reverend Davies. How are you?"

"Well enough," Davies answered in his reedy tenor voice. He looked around the immaculate churchyard. "A lovely day, isn't it?"

"Beautiful," Springer agreed. "It's a joy to be outdoors."

Davies hesitated, as if wanting to talk but afraid to pry. He smoothed his white mustache. "Were you making a house call?" He nodded up the street. "I understand Mrs. Francis isn't well."

"She's much better," said Springer. "Actually, I was at Mrs. Moser's."

"Is she ill?"

"No. No more than usual. I was looking for Danny. Have you seen him?" Springer had made the arrangements for the first archery lesson tomorrow afternoon, but he couldn't find Danny.

"No, I haven't. I do hope he's not in trouble again," said Davies.

"Me too," said Springer. "Me too."

Davies nodded at the folded copy of the *Sun* under Springer's arm. "Have you seen the advertisement?"

Springer grinned. "Yes. Our new neighbors." He opened the paper to the full-page ad. The text was centered and House had set a cross in each corner. "Obviously from the Bible," said Springer. "But what book?"

"The Book of the Revelation of St. John the Divine. Revelations as it is commonly known. The last book. Odd."

"How so?"

"It is a compilation of several verses of Chapter Twelve. Not only that, they've edited it." The minister looked surprised. "Most unusual, don't you see? Fundamentalists ordinarily view the scriptures as literal truth and the King James version as sacrosanct. Have you a minute?" He waited anxiously, as if certain of rejection.

Springer glanced at his watch. "Sure."

"Come in. I'll show you what I mean."

They strolled on either side of the fence to the driveway, then around the church and through the garden to the rectory in back. Since his wife had died the year before, the old man had closed up most of the house, rarely venturing beyond the kitchen, the den, and a small downstairs bedroom.

They went into the den, a dark, shuttered room lined with books, an anchorage for meticulously wrought model sailing ships—clippers, whalers, barks, cutters, sloops, and yawls—the output of a lifelong hobby. Old navigational charts hung on one wall and the lamps were ship lights, brass with red and green glass. The room seemed more the haunt of a retired sea captain than the study of a minister. The curious thing was that Davies had never been to sea or even lived near the coast.

Since he had been widowed, his main activity, other than preaching a desultory sermon each Sunday, was the pursuit of his hobby. In one corner, on a worktable with a fluorescent draftsman's lamp, was his latest project, a half-finished model of the racing yacht *America,* the winner of the cup which bore its name. Davies had built it from scratch, using the original shipwright's plans and re-creating in miniature the schooner's every board and screw.

Springer bent over for a closer look and Davies switched on the light. Tiny ribs, like the bones of a trout, inclined upward from a pencil-thin keel. The planking was half finished. "Beautiful," said Springer. "Really beautiful."

Davies smiled his pride. "Another two or three months and I'll begin the decking."

"How often do you work on this?"

Davies looked away, as if ashamed to answer. "I try to put in four hours a day—after I've done my regular duties, of course. Would you like some sherry?"

"If it's no trouble."

Davies turned off the fluorescent and a soft glow from the ship lights returned to the room. He poured two glasses from a bottle in the bookcase and indicated a chair for Springer. Then, after they raised their glasses to each other and took the first sip, he laid an open Bible on the table and showed Springer Chapter Twelve of the Book of the Revelation of St. John the Divine.

The old man breathed heavily as he leaned over the table and pointed out the passages in the dim light. Springer noticed a sweet, not unpleasant, odor of dried perspiration.

"It begins here, verse seven," Davies said, indicating the place with his finger. " 'And there was war in heaven: Michael and his angels fought against the dragon.' Then it skips to verse nine. 'And the great dragon was cast out,' and then farther down they go to verse twelve. Very unusual."

Springer read the intervening passages. "It's meaning is clear."

"Certainly," said Davies. "The *meaning* is intact . . . except . . ."

"What?"

"The emphasis is different. It's been subtly altered. You see, they left out verse ten." He read the verse, tracing the words with his spindly finger. " 'And I heard a loud voice saying in heaven, Now is come salvation, and strength, and the kingdom of our God, and the power of his Christ.' By omitting the verse, they've made the Archangel Michael seem of primary importance, whereas, in fact, he is only one of God's and His Son's many servants.

"It's a small point, perhaps, but here in verse twelve they leave out the first line. 'Therefore rejoice, *ye* heavens, and ye that dwell in them.' Instead, they go directly to 'Woe to the inhabiters of the earth.' "

He smiled abruptly, and gave his mustache a satisfied tug.

"I'm not sure I follow you," said Springer.

"Well, don't you see, it indicates the worldly interests of these people. These Revelationists are less concerned with the state of heaven or the afterlife than with what is happening right here and now."

"I see."

"They are telling their converts that life on earth can be altered and that the Archangel Michael will direct the changes. It's rather American, you know."

"American?"

"Pragmatic."

Springer nodded. "Direct action here and now."

"Precisely." Davies chuckled mirthlessly. "I can tell you one thing, they're promising more than we are." He closed the Bible and gazed at his ships over the rim of his sherry glass. When he spoke again, his voice was full of foreboding. He said, "I wish I knew what they want here."

Springer stopped at the police station on the way home. It was little more than a storefront, a small room with a bench and an officer at a desk behind a partition. The single cell was visible at the end of a short hall. It was empty, as it usually was, though for Springer it would always hold the ghost of his father sleeping off a binge on the wooden bunk.

Charlie Daniels said, "Hello." He was a stringy-looking man in his late twenties, a local boy who had learned his trade in the military police. He wore an open khaki shirt with a large badge and a small-caliber gun at the waist of his khaki pants.

"How's it going, Charlie?"

"Good. What's up?"

"I'm looking for Danny Moser."

Daniels' eyes narrowed. "Now what did he do?"

"Nothing. I just want to find him. His mother says he hasn't been home in a few nights."

"Lost cause, Al."

"Not yet," said Springer.

"Well, I'll bet you he hitchhiked to Saratoga again to buy drugs."

"He promised me he wouldn't anymore." Springer ignored the police officer's doubtfully raised eyebrows. "Anyway, I'm just wondering if something happened to the kid."

"Al? You know something? If that little punk just disappeared it wouldn't be the worst news we ever had in this town. But I'll keep my eye on the ticker. He might have been picked up someplace. If he doesn't show up in a week or so we'll issue a missing persons. Okay?"

"Thanks, Charlie."

"He'll show up," said Daniels. "Sure as black flies and twice the bother."

11

A single pleading note pealed over and over from the bell tower of the Presbyterian church. It was a strident sound and it carried far in the hot, still air. Those who heeded it quickened their pace, hurrying out of the side streets onto Main toward the white church at the curve in the road, which was lined on either side with old cars and trucks from the outlying areas.

Springer grinned at his reflection in Lewis's store window. Flanked by Margaret and Samantha in pretty cotton dresses and clad in a gray summer suit he ordinarily reserved for business trips to Albany, he looked like an old *Saturday Evening Post* illustration of dutiful husband, loving father, substantial citizen, and dependable churchgoer.

Waving to Charlie Daniels, who was directing traffic, they entered the church to the organ music of a Bach prelude. Bob Kent and Pete Lewis were ushering. Kent kissed Margaret's cheek and patted Samantha's head. He handed Springer the programs.

"Will wonders never cease?"

"Morning, Deacon," whispered Springer. "How they hanging?"

"Piously," muttered Kent. "Just behave yourself in there."

"Good morning," Pete Lewis whispered solemnly. Lewis was a deacon out of conscience; Kent, because the mayor had to be. Lewis's son, Dicky, hurried up with extra programs. He piped greetings to the Springers and said, "Hi," to Samantha, who buried her hand in her father's and murmured, "Hi," at the floor. Margaret led them to her customary seat at the end of the rear right pew. Springer put Samantha between them and relaxed into the timeless, peaceful scene.

The walls and the vaulted ceiling were painted white, a

clean setting for the bright stained-glass windows, the sprays of spring flowers, the gold of the altar and the red velvet behind it. Each window bore the name of the family that had donated it when the church was built eighty years before: Moser, Kent, Grand, Lewis, Whalen, Rigby, Spencer, and a new window, Springer. An old Moser glass, the legacy of a branch of the family that had since fared poorly (of whom young Danny was the last male), had blown out in a blizzard and Springer had paid for a new one. He told himself he had done it for Margaret, who loved the church, but like the mansion on Main Street it was a symbol of belonging in the town in which he had grown up feeling like an outsider.

A farm family, the father in an old, loose-fitting suit, his wife and three small daughters in clean, worn dresses, hurried in just as Pete Lewis and Bob Kent were shutting the massive double doors. Kent ushered them to an empty pew with smiles and whispers, while Lewis, with a final glance into the foyer to see that no one else was coming, closed the doors.

Reverend Davies entered the church through a small door next to the pulpit. He smiled hesitantly, as if startled to find people waiting for him, tugged his white mustache, and stepped up to the altar. Sophie Wilkins shifted from Bach to the opening chords of the introit, which the choir —eight sopranos lilting above Alfie Potter's deep bass— rose and sang. Then Davies invoked the call to worship in a thin tenor voice and the congregation sang the first hymn, "Let There Be Light."

Margaret sang beautifully. Springer followed her lead, an octave lower. He felt Samantha shrinking beside him. She mouthed the words, but made no sound, and when they sat down she opened the Bible she carried with her and turned to the scripture that was posted on the wall above the organ. Following the dialogue of Confession of Sin and Declaration of Pardon, Davies read the scripture from the second chapter of the General Epistle of James, verses fourteen, fifteen, and sixteen:

" 'What *doth* it profit, my brethren, though a man say he hath faith, and have not works? can faith save him?

" 'If a brother or sister be naked, and destitute of daily food,

" 'And one of you say unto them, Depart in peace, be *ye*

warmed and filled; notwithstanding ye give them not those things which are needful to the body; what *doth it* profit?' "

It was hot in the church with the doors closed. Reverend Davies smiled bleakly and launched into his favorite sermon theme.

"Christian men and woman represent the strongest, most effective force in the world today to alleviate suffering, misery, and hunger. Because, as the Bible tells them, they must *demonstrate* their faith, their love of God, they must contribute to the well-being of those less fortunate than they.

"God cannot look happily on His earth when human beings suffer. Thus the people of this church sent food and medicine to Biafra, thus several families offered to provide homes for Vietnamese orphans at the conclusion of that unhappy conflict. Thus we prepare our Christmas baskets for the needy and contribute to the breakfast program at the school. But we can do more. . . ."

The little minister's soft tenor voice lulled more than it stimulated. Springer stifled a yawn and glanced around. Margaret was paying rapt attention to the sermon, but Samantha, catching his eye, stirred. Her Bible was open to James. She gave Springer a small smile and pointed at the verses that followed the ones Davies had read.

"Was not Abraham our father justified by works, when he had offered Isaac his son upon the altar?"

She looked up at him inquiringly. Springer bent close. "What?"

"Christmas baskets?"

Springer bit his lip to keep from laughing. "It's open to various interpretations, smarty," he muttered.

"Shhh," said Margaret.

"Sorry, dear." He nudged Samantha with his elbow and pressed a finger to his lips. When she acted this way, which was rare, it was easy to hope that she would explode one day into a delightful maturity.

Reverend Davies was asking a series of rhetorical questions, pausing for several moments between each. The hard surfaces of the wooden pews, the plaster walls, and the high ceiling made the church acoustically harsh, and during a pause, a cough crackled dry and loud and tiny whispers rustled sharply. The heavy doors blocked the noise of automobiles and in its serenity it might have been the year

1900 were it not for the fact that the church was half empty.

"Who are the faithful?" asked Davies. His eyes darted myopically about the silent church.

Three loud knocks shattered the quiet.

The parishioners turned in their pews, looking back at the doors. Bob Kent and Pete Lewis, who were standing solemnly on either side of them, exchanged looks. Reverend Davies peered inquiringly down the aisle. After a moment's hesitation and another look, Kent opened the doors a crack and peeked out.

A warm smile replaced his puzzled expression. He flung the door open and waved to the minister to wait. A double line of men and women wearing clean, ironed work shirts and overalls led up the steps and into the foyer. Sweeping past Kent, they marched silently into the church and stood in the last five pews on both sides of the aisle, women on the left, the men on the right. When they were all in place—fifty of them, Springer estimated—they sat in unison at some invisible sign and stared mutely at the altar.

An approving murmur rose among the regular members of the congregation as they faced back with friendly smiles. Reverend Davies tugged his mustache and cleared his throat. "Welcome," he called. "Welcome to our church. How wonderful to see so many new faces."

The Revelationists fixed their eyes on Davies. Not one of them smiled back or nodded or made any sign at all acknowledging that the minister and people of Hudson City had welcomed them into their presence. A deathly silence filled the church, a silence so tangible that it might have been a solid object that the intruders had brought with them.

The parishioners turned back to the altar with troubled faces. Reverend Davies hesitated, looking from his text to the silent Revelationists, and the ominous hush settled more deeply over the congregation. At last he spoke.

"The scripture, for the benefit of our new brethren, is from James. 'What *doth* it profit, my brethren, though a man say he hath faith, and have not works? can faith save him?' "

He smiled nervously and probed his text. The parishioners waited anxiously and expelled sighs of relief when he located his place and continued his sermon.

One of the Revelationists, a boy who could not have been more than seventeen, had taken a seat next to Springer. He sat rigidly. His hands lay still on his stiff overalls. His hair was short and neatly combed, his face immobile, his eyes blank—aimed unblinkingly at the pulpit.

Springer leaned forward and glanced down the pew. Four men with shorn necks and squared shoulders, so similar as to be one, were sitting in identical repose, watching Davies. Across the aisle six women with scrubbed faces and short, straight hair sat similarly, looking starched and sexless as they stared at the minister.

Davies droned on like a reedy clarinet. His eyes moved restively over the group in the back of his church and something in their silent, implicit reproach galvanized him to theatrics. He began tapping the pulpit with his fingers, then beating it lightly with his open palm.

It proved as distracting to him as to his listeners. He faltered a couple of times and once lost his train of thought for a full ten seconds. The Hudson City parishioners sat on the edge of their seats, bodies tensed in mute sympathy for the struggling minister, fearing what would happen next.

When he concluded at last, Sophie Wilkins had the presence of mind to introduce the next hymn with a resounding burst of chords. The congregation, rising, responded vigorously, releasing its distress in bold song. But, almost immediately, the hymn faltered and died away as one by one the members of the congregation realized that their visitors had stayed in their seats, stock-still, silent, expressionless as mannequins.

Sophie Wilkins pulled them back with the organ, pounding the keys, vibrating the ceiling with the power of its sound. As the final chords expired, they resumed their seats uncertainly. A tense silence smothered the church.

In a tremulous voice, Reverend Davies made the regular announcements of church business and then, with practiced routine, the deacons began passing the plate for the morning offering. Kent and Lewis commanded the center aisle, handing the velvet-lined brass plates to the nearest person, who dropped in his envelope and passed it to his neighbor. When they reached the other end, the plates were taken by Spencer and a boy from the Bible class and sent back along the next row. Davies sat in a chair to the left of the pulpit with his head bowed, his cheeks flaming.

The offering went smoothly until Kent reached the forwardmost row of Revelationists and extended the gleaming plate. The blond Revelationist at the end of the pew stared straight ahead. Kent leaned forward and whispered something, his face reddening. The Revelationist ignored him. Kent stepped back and tried the next row. He met the same cold-faced response. Lewis was undergoing a similar ordeal on the women's side.

Kent tried each row in succession and was rebuffed at each. When he reached the last pew, at the other end of which sat Springer, he tried once more. Again nothing. His lips set in a tight line, but his eyes were confused.

Springer reached for his wallet.

Margaret stared at him with alarm, but he ignored her and extracted a five-dollar bill.

"Excuse me, son," he asked loudly of the boy next to him. "Would you please pass my offering to the deacon?"

The Revelationist gazed stonily ahead.

"I said," Springer repeated, "please pass my offering to the deacon."

There was dead silence in the church. The people in front craned their necks and stared. The Revelationists stared back. Springer took a deep breath. Then Kent said, "Thank you, Doctor. I'll be glad to come for it."

He walked behind the pew and held out the plate. Springer dropped in the five and winked. Kent looked away, his mouth tugging nervously. Holding the plate before him, he joined Lewis at the center aisle. The people of Hudson City rose and sang, "Praise God from whom all blessings flow . . ." and the deacons marched to the altar to present the offering to Reverend Davies.

"Did you have to make a scene?" Margaret hissed when they sat down.

"Yes," said Springer. He glanced at Samantha for approval, but she was hunched over her Bible, her back stiff with mortification. He tugged her sleeve. "Kitten?"

She shrank from him.

"It's not that bad." He noticed the boy next to him was watching.

"Yes, Daddy."

A tear splashed on the pages of the open book. The boy stared.

Davies laid the plates on the altar and faced his congregation. His mouth worked and he seemed on the verge of trying to speak, but Sophie Wilkins piped out the opening chords of the final hymn and the congregation rose hesitantly to sing. Again, the Revelationists stayed seated— silent, immobile, sinister.

The hymn over, Reverend Davies delivered a short benediction and walked stiffly down the aisle, his eyes retreating from the stony gaze of the Revelationists as he took up his customary position at the front door for a word with his departing flock.

Sophie Wilkins rang up the postlude—Corelli, achingly beautiful. People rose, whispering, and began edging down the aisle. They stopped at the invisible dividing line where the Revelationists were sitting as if afraid to cross it, afraid to step too near them.

At no visible signal, the Revelationists stood *en masse* and filed out of the church, brushing past Davies with neither word nor look. Marching in two columns, they went up Spotting Mountain Road toward their retreat, fifty silent people acting as one.

12

"It was sacrilege!"

Sophie Wilkins' plump frame shook with indignation. Still attired in her flowered Sunday dress, she had kicked off her shoes and her nylon-clad toes clawed angrily at the thick grass in Bob Kent's back yard. "They deliberately waited till the service started."

"Now, Sophie," soothed Kent, freshening his drink at his portable bar, a hideous plastic affair on oversized wheels.

"Don't 'now, Sophie' me, Bob Kent."

Springer grinned at Mary Kent, Sophie's sister, and took a long pull from his gin and tonic. They were sitting in a circle of oak chairs behind the house. The sun was hot, the sky cobalt blue. A charcoal grill waited on the redwood deck for a cookout later on. Springer had begun to relax, though the morning's incident still nagged.

As far as Margaret was concerned, he had committed an offense as awful as the Revelationists' by making a scene in the church. She had gone to bed with a headache and would stay there until Monday morning, nursing her anger, reliving her humiliation over and over until she had proved herself so wronged that he could not possibly be right. Screw. He gazed at the mountain, soft and green in the afternoon light. The nice thing about Bob's view was that you couldn't see the old asylum. If only Samantha had understood. He had attempted to explain as they walked home, but she had remained silent, her lips set like Margaret's, and had said nothing when Margaret angrily accused him of making matters worse.

Since Danny Moser had not reappeared, Springer had canceled the archery lessons and come alone, only to find a similar argument raging at the mayor's house. As Sophie continued to lace into him, Kent looked to his wife, a silent appeal in his eyes. Mary was smaller than her sister and lacked her forthright manner. She spoke in a slight, girlish voice. "There wasn't much that Bob could do."

Sophie would not be mollified. "Is that so, Mary? Well. Dr. Springer did something. I thought you were wonderful, Doctor."

Springer grinned lazily. "I was inspired by your angelic music."

Kent tugged at his Bermuda shorts, smoothed the hair on his white legs, tinkled the ice in his glass. "It might have been better to ignore them."

"Ignore them?" cried Sophie. "Just sit like sheep and allow them to do that to us?"

"They had already done it," snapped Kent. "It was over. They came to church and they showed us they didn't approve. I'm not saying I like their tactics, but they're becoming important around here. You and the good doctor might not care about the business they bring into town, but the store owners sure as hell do."

"Business," sniffed Sophie, "is no excuse for bad manners."

"We're going to have to learn to live with them."

"We may have to learn to live with them," said Springer, "but they're sure as hell going to have to learn to live with me."

"Don't be so damned high-handed," said Kent. "As the doctor you sort of represent the town, you know. Try to take it easy."

"I'm not taking it easy so Pete Lewis can sell post-hole diggers."

Sophie laughed. Kent gave her a sour smile and Mary jumped up like a startled chicken. "Sophie, why don't you help me with the steaks? You better start the fire soon, Bob."

"Right."

"Alan? Are you sure you don't want to call Margaret? It would be so nice if she joined us."

"Thanks, but no, Mary. Margaret had a busy afternoon planned."

None of them looked as though they believed the lie.

After Sophie and Mary went into the house, Kent said moodily, "The merchants are having a good year, Alan. Give 'em a break, for Christ's sake. Next thing you know you'll be launching another one of your crusades."

Springer admired Kent more than he would admit, which made it hard to bear his criticism. "Sorry. It's not that important and it's too beautiful a day to worry about it. Right?"

"Right." Kent grinned. "Another drink?"

"Right."

Samantha had a secret place.

When she was tired of reading or very sad—as she was today because everyone in church had looked at her with eyes like hungry snakes—she would look out her window across the street, beyond the school, all the way to the back of the playing fields. And if she saw them by the wooden fence that separated the fields from the old railroad tracks, she would slip quietly down the stairs and walk to her secret place where she would hide behind the fence and listen to the kids singing and playing their guitars on the other side.

Lost in the music, she didn't see the Revelationist until he was standing over her. She covered her mouth, startled, wondering how he could have come so quietly. He was the one who'd sat next to Daddy in church. Two more of them were standing across the tracks, watching. She was terrified that the kids would hear them talking and find out she was there.

But he put his fingers to his lips as if he knew her secret. It made her smile. He knew.

He crouched easily and brought his face close to hers. She didn't like people so close. She wanted to look away, but she couldn't. His eyes were so steady. He beckoned her to lean closer.

Bob Kent had heard enough.

"This is all going to blow over," he announced to the members of the town board who had stayed on for a private discussion after the regular Monday night meeting. "They haven't made a single move at anybody, other than that bull at the church. They don't want to get us mad at them. They just want to be left alone and" —he grinned— "allowed to spend money in Hudson City."

"Hear, hear," said Gary Spencer with an easy smile. "I

just don't want some hothead scaring them off. They're buying a lot of groceries."

"And tools and lumber," said Kent, nodding at Pete Lewis and old Ken Moser. "It'll blow over. You wait and see."

Joe Preston, the president of the Hudson City branch of the Warington First National Bank, raised his hand. He had been sitting quietly through the discussion, a distant look on his face. "I'd like to say something, Bob."

Preston was a beefy, red-faced man who might have looked more at home on a tractor than in a bank. He glanced conspiratorially at his fellow board members and lowered his voice.

"There's a little bit of an ethics problem here. I shouldn't be saying this, 'cause it's privileged information, but you're going to find out soon enough anyway. Just don't say it came from me."

Pete Lewis, Gary Spencer, Moser, and Kent nodded, faces lighting with interest. "What's up, Joe?"

"You know that we hold the mortgage on the old Shell station."

"Sure," said Kent. "I'm still trying to sell it for you."

Preston looked uncomfortable. "Well, you know, Bob, since our main office is in Warington, we also had to list that property with Ray Peters over there."

Kent shrugged. "Ray Peters couldn't sell air conditioning to Arabs."

"Maybe so, but he sold the station."

"He did? Son of a gun. . . . Who bought it?"

"The Revelationists."

"What?"

"You heard me. They bought it last week. The closing is tomorrow."

The board members sat in mystified silence. Then Kent exploded. "Damnation! That property brought in four thousand dollars a year in taxes. Shot to hell!"

Preston raised a meaty palm. "Only while it was still in business, Bob. Hadn't brought in a nickle in two years now."

"Yeah, I know. But it would've."

"You seen any new gas stations being built lately?"

"We would have gotten something in there," Kent said doggedly.

"We didn't," said Preston. "Anyway, it's theirs. Just wanted to warn you."

"What the dickens do they want with an old gas station?"

An hour after the sale of the Shell station was closed in Warington, twenty men and women marched down Spotting Mountain Road with tools, paint, brooms, and mops. They set to work tearing off the plywood that covered the windows, swept up the broken glass, and started painting the derelict building. Several men made measurements and walked across town to Moser's, where they ordered plate glass, lighting fixtures, and lumber. Others dug up earth behind the station and dumped it into the holes where the pumps had been.

When people stopped and asked what they were doing, they received pleasant smiles and a promise that all would be welcome. Welcome to what? The Revelationists smiled some more and went back to work. From inside, loud hammering pounded and an electric saw whined busily. They worked into the night, then marched back up the mountain, singing, by the light of blue-shaded lanterns.

Work continued the next day. They planted flowers— apparently grown at the retreat—in the earth-filled pump holes, installed new plate-glass windows, and finished painting the outside bright blue. Unmarked trucks with Albany license plates rolled up, and ranks of Revelationists descended upon them, working in practiced relays to transfer their contents—heavy objects shrouded in shape-concealing tarpaulins—inside.

Speculation ran high among those who gathered to watch the strange proceedings from the sidewalk. But the doors remained closed, the workers silent as, laboring from early morning to midnight, twenty to thirty Revelationists at a time swarmed about the old garage.

Dusk was falling on the day of the high school graduation when work ceased abruptly. Matt Wright had just concluded the ceremonies in the stifling gymnasium, and people were still milling about the streets taking advantage of a slight breeze, when the garage bay doors of the former Shell station flew open. A brilliant spotlight trained on an enormous sign hand-painted in bold blue Day-Glo letters:

REVELATIONS SOCIAL CENTER

ALL ARE WELCOME

Teen-agers flocked to the commotion, gathered at the side of the road, and watched as dozens of blue lights suddenly flared to life in the windows. They gaped at the dazzling sight.

There at the end of town, backdropped by the black mountain, the transformed building glowed like a miniature city, an outpost of light and gaiety in the dark, boring night. Like animals drawn to the circle of a campfire, the teen-agers crept closer, sharing their wonderment in soft voices and sudden bursts of loud laughter. The Revelationists were inside, shadowy forms briskly moving about behind the lights and the windows.

The teen-agers came closer, their numbers swelling, and suddenly, punctuated by a deep, booming bass, a jukebox roared to life, pounding out the sweet and melancholy strains of country and western music. Revelationists flooded outside and flanked the entrance. They were smiling.

"Come in!" they called. "All are welcome."

Hesitantly, led by a swaggering boy whose bold stance almost hid his trepidation, the children of Hudson City approached the open door.

13

Springer found his home in an uproar when he got back from the clinic the next evening. Margaret was standing in the kitchen, her arms crossed, her lips tight. Samantha, tears streaming down her face, threw herself into his arms. Springer hugged her and mouthed "What?" to Margaret over the child's head.

"No," said Margaret, ignoring her husband's question, "under no circumstances are you going there."

"The social center?" Springer asked incredulously. He'd heard about it all day at the clinic, but his immediate reaction that Samantha wanted to go was amazed delight. What had happened to make the child forsake her safe room and her books?

"Please, Daddy," sobbed Samantha. "Can't I go?"

"Run upstairs a minute, sweetheart. Your mother and I have to talk about it."

"But Dicky asked me. He really did, Daddy. Can't I go?"

Springer felt a spasm of joy and relief. Could a skinny, bespectacled fifteen-year-old boy who had hardly yet learned to comb his hair bring Samantha into the world?

"It'll be okay, sweetheart. Just go up. I'll be there in a minute."

Samantha squeezed him tightly and ran up the back stairs, not looking at her mother.

Margaret hadn't moved. "No, Alan. I won't allow it."

"Margaret, didn't you see her face? She actually wants to go out with other children. It's wonderful. I swear when I see that boy I'll kiss him."

"He's a very nice boy and he can take her someplace else."

"He's a fifteen-year-old kid and there's no place else around here a fifteen-year-old kid can take a date."

"They can have a picnic."

"He didn't ask her on a picnic. Now what's wrong with the social center?"

"Those people, Alan. I'm not having her exposed to them."

"Exposed? They're offering music and some free soda. What the hell is wrong with that?"

"No."

"You're going to have to do better than just 'no,' Margaret. I'm not disappointing that child for no reason. Wait—listen, dammit," he said as Margaret began to protest, "I've been hearing about the place all day. Everyone who came in was talking about it. The kids who went last night had a good time. They don't allow drinking, smoking, or drugs. They just let them have some fun. And it worked, somehow. The kids enjoyed themselves. It's the kind of place we should have started ourselves and didn't."

"It's a trick," said Margaret.

"A trick? Come on, dear."

"How do you know what they want?"

"We'll see what they want. If it's out of line then we won't allow her to go anymore. But she can go tonight. Darling, we've hoped and prayed she would come out of her shell. If you stop her, she'll go back into that shell and never come out."

"But what if they—"

"What? Sell her into white slavery? Dammit, Margaret, they're a religious organization."

"Exactly!" snapped Margaret. "They've converted five thousand people in two years. They're not just giving this dance out of kindness."

"Okay, now we're down to it." He glanced up the back stairs and lowered his voice. "For all her shyness, Samantha is a very sophisticated child. She gets a lot out of all that reading. She's bright and aware. She reads the paper more than you do, for Christ's sake. She watches the news and you and I talk to her like an adult. She's been taught to think for herself, and if some zealot comes on to her she'll be perfectly able to see him for what he is."

"She's a frightened, confused child," whispered Margaret. "She's exactly the kind of child those people get."

"I know she can take care of herself," said Springer. "It's her first date, Margaret. Her first. Remember yours? You can't stop that. It would be cruel. No reason in the world would make sense to her. Let her go, dear. She'll be too excited about being out to give a damn about religion. Let her be with the other kids and have some fun."

Margaret unfolded her arms. "I'm so afraid."

Springer held her close. "I've always been afraid of what would happen if the wrong boy asked her out. But Dicky's perfect for her." Again he lowered his voice. "From what Pete tells me, it's probably his first date too. They're just right for each other."

"Eleven o'clock," said Margaret.

Springer grinned. "Not a minute later. That would be funny, wouldn't it? We're worried about her getting converted and she comes home pregnant."

"Alan!"

"Just kidding." He bounded up the stairs. When Samantha opened the door and saw his expression, her face broke into a big smile.

"You can go," said Springer. "Home at eleven."

"Thank you, thank you, thank you."

"Have a good time, kitten. Your mother loves you, you know. She wasn't being mean, just a mother."

"Daddy?"

"What, dear?"

"Which should I wear?" She led him into her room. Margaret had overdecorated it with ruffles of white eyelet, embroidered pillows, and diaphanous curtains despite Samantha's complaints that she barely had room for her books and stuffed animals. Three dresses were laid out on the canopy bed. Springer looked at her, put his chin in his hand, and looked at the dresses.

"The middle one."

"Really?"

"No?"

"I don't think so."

"How about the yellow one?"

"I don't think so."

"Hmmm. How about the green one?"

"Daddy! It makes me look twelve years old."

Springer stroked his chin, enjoying the closest feeling he had had with Samantha in months. "Well, where does that leave us?"

Samantha threw open the closet door. "Nowhere. I have

no clothes." She looked at the bed. "Do you really like the middle one?"

"I sure do. Here. Hold it up."

It was blue and not as childish as the other two, sleeveless with a slight scoop neck. She held it up in front of her and gave him an anxious smile. Springer regarded it thoughtfully. "I think that without your dungarees it's going to be beautiful. Absolutely beautiful."

"Do you mean it?"

"I mean it. Look in the mirror."

She stood before the glass and made doubtful faces.

"Beautiful, angel. Just right."

Samantha smiled. "You really like it?"

"I do."

She looked at him quizzically. "Daddy?"

"What?"

"Why do you suppose Dicky asked me to the dance?"

Springer swallowed hard and waited until he could trust his voice. "Because you're so very lovely, angel."

When she looked back at the mirror, he turned away. Tears were rising in his eyes.

"Should I put my hair up like this, Daddy?"

She was holding the dress with one hand and her hair up in the back with the other. For a second, Springer saw her as she would look when she was twenty. He picked up her Snoopy dog.

"No," he said firmly. "It's much prettier down. You better get dressed now. Your mother has dinner ready."

The mantel clock chimed eleven.

"Where is she?" asked Margaret.

"Relax," said Springer. "Let's not worry until five after."

They were sitting at their dining-room table drinking coffee. They had baked oatmeal cookies, which were heaped on a plate next to a pitcher of icy lemonade.

"She grew up so fast," said Margaret. "I can hardly believe it. Do you realize that she might be gone in three or four years?"

"A comfort in our old age."

"Can't you ever be serious?"

"I'm sorry. I am serious. It's sad. But it's not the end of the world—or of us."

Margaret regarded him reflectively. "We're so different, aren't we?"

Springer gave her a bleak smile. Her mood was getting to him, his happiness over Samantha's date souring into a melancholy appreciation of times past and energies spent. "Sometimes," he said, "I think we're not so different as we are distant."

"What is that supposed to mean?"

"I don't know." He felt very tired. "I suppose I wish we shared more. Talked more. Told more." He laughed, trying to shake the solemnity of the moment, but stopped when he saw tears forming in Margaret's eyes.

"I just wish—oh, Alan, I'm so tired of being alone."

Springer stood up and pulled her into his arms. Her body stiffened and he could feel her effort as she tried to relax. He kissed her neck, gently, slowly, and now when she stiffened it was with a hint of desire. She pressed herself against his chest, her hands moving hesitantly around his waist. Suddenly she broke away.

"What's wrong?"

"The door. Samantha." Her face was flushed. She smoothed her hair and brushed his cheek with her lips. "Later. Promise." She touched his mouth and called, "In here, darling."

Footsteps approached and then Samantha and Dicky Lewis were standing in the doorway.

"Hey, how was it?" asked Springer.

"It was all right, Daddy," said Samantha. She looked tired.

"Real nice, Dr. Springer," said Dicky Lewis. His tie was askew and his shirt bunched around his waist like a deflated flotation belt. He shifted uncomfortably from one foot to the other.

"Come in," said Springer. "We just happen to have some cookies."

"And lemonade," said Margaret. "Sit down, Samantha. Can you stay, Dicky? Do you want to call home?"

"I guess I better."

"Use the phone in the living room," said Springer. "Here, I'll show you." He led the boy to the telephone. When he returned to the dining room Samantha's cheeks were flushed and she was telling her mother about the dance.

"They had free soda, all you could drink. Billy Wright had eight Cokes and six hot dogs."

"I'll be hearing from him in the morning," said Springer.

"And they have this really neat jukebox. You don't have to put any money in it. You can play anything you want."

"Did you dance?" asked Margaret.

"A little. I'm not very good, but they showed me how."

"Who, your friends?"

"No. The Revvies. Dicky and I were kind of standing there—he doesn't know much either—and a couple of them came over right away and showed us how."

"Was it fun?"

"Sure. They made it easy." She looked up with a shy smile as Dicky returned. "He stepped on my foot."

"We'll get you some lumberjack boots," said Springer. "With steel toes. Sit down, Dicky."

By Hudson City standards, the Springer dining room was rather formal and the boy looked slightly awed. The table, an Empire piece in rosewood and oak, shone in the light of a sparkling chandelier. The chandelier had come with the house; the table, in mint condition, from an auction in Saratoga. Margaret spent a lot of time doing handwork and had covered the dining-room chairs with beautiful needlepoint. As Dicky sat down stiffly, a bell rang in the kitchen. Samantha giggled at his dismay.

"The family who used to live here had a cook," explained Springer. "We never took the bell out. It's right under your foot, beneath the carpet."

"Oh," said Dicky.

"Samantha rings it for seconds."

"I do not, Daddy."

"Speaking of which, how many hot dogs did you have, Dicky?"

Dicky straightened his glasses. "Just a couple."

"You better eat some cookies before you fall over."

Margaret passed him the plate. He chose one, brought it to his mouth, and then, as an afterthought, offered it to Samantha. She smiled happily and took it. Dicky picked up another and nibbled the edge.

"What did you do besides dance?" asked Springer.

"Some of the guys played pool," said Dicky. "The ones who didn't bring somebody."

"I told him to play," said Samantha, "but he wouldn't."

"What about the people who ran it?" asked Margaret. "What were they like?"

"Oh, real nice," said Samantha. "Weren't they, Dicky?"

"Yeah. They really know what's it like."

"What what's like?" asked Springer.

"Uh, you know, being a kid." He shook his head with amazement. "They really know."

"Well, what do you mean?" asked Margaret. "Did they talk to you?"

"Yeah," said Samantha. "They had a whole bunch of people, old people in their twenties, and they were walking around and anytime they saw you alone or not having fun they came over and talked. They were really nice."

"Well, what did they talk about?"

"Stuff. You know. Things."

"I wonder"—Springer smiled—"if you could be slightly more specific than 'stuff.' "

"Did they talk about religion?" asked Margaret.

"They prayed. We all did."

"Prayed? At a dance?"

"Sure. Like in church. We closed our eyes and one of them said a prayer."

"Yeah," said Dicky. "It was kind of cool."

"How?" asked Springer.

Samantha and Dicky exchanged a glance. She said, "It was like we were just talking with Him."

"God?"

"Michael. The angel."

"Archangel," corrected Dicky.

"What do you mean talking to him?"

"Well, they just said, 'Dear Michael, please help all the children have a nice time at the dance.' That's all."

"Yeah," said Dicky. "It was like he was next door or something."

Margaret picked at some crumbs on the table. "Did they make you do anything?"

"What do you mean?" asked Samantha.

"Well, do they . . . well, just be careful."

"What do you mean, Mother?" she repeated with a puzzled smile.

"Your mother means did they ask you to do anything for their organization?"

"It's not an organization, Daddy. It's a movement."

14

Ed Stratton figured he was the richest man in Hudson City. He owned the Chevrolet dealership and his lots and showroom occupied both sides of the state highway a quarter mile north of town. He had inherited the business from his father, who had started it in 1931, and something else: he was known to be as hard-nosed a son of a bitch as the old man, and he relished the reputation. The Strattons had a family motto: if anybody within seventy miles wants to buy a Chevy and doesn't want to buy it from Ed Stratton he can buy a Ford.

He was at his desk in the corner of his showroom chewing his first cigar of the day when he saw a pair of men in work shirts and overalls walking up the road from town. The sun glinted on the big iron crosses that dangled from their necks. Revelationists, he thought sourly, recalling the houseful of sullen offspring he had left with his wife. He had forbidden them to set foot inside the social center. Child-raising was a simple matter of keeping them out of trouble until they could fend for themselves, and from what he had heard at Matt Wright's party, the Revelationists were trouble.

Stratton frowned. The bastards were turning onto his property, heading for the showroom. Their old Chrysler station wagon must have broken down. He smiled grimly; they were in for a disappointment if they thought he'd allow his mechanic to waste time on that heap.

They entered soundlessly, passed his display vehicles without a glance, and stopped at his desk. Both men were on the smallish side, neat, precise, and looking a little uncomfortable in their work clothes.

One said, "We want four panel trucks, one pickup, and three hatchback cars."

"What color?" asked Stratton.

"Blue."

Stratton put down his cigar. They weren't kidding; eight units equaled a good month's gross sales. "All of them?"

"Standard equipment. No radios, no air conditioning."

Stratton took a closer look at their expressionless faces. They reminded him of the General Motors auditors who dropped in now and then without an appointment—men with fathomless eyes and no time to spare.

"I have two panel trucks in blue and one hatchback. I'll get the rest of 'em by tomorrow afternoon."

"Price."

Stratton scribbled on a scratch pad with a chewed wooden pencil. "Even numbers, seeing as how it's volume. Forty-five hundred for the panel trucks. Five thousand for the pickup. Forty-three for the hatchbacks. Comes to thirty-five thousand nine hundred."

"Discount."

"That includes the discount."

"Ten percent."

Stratton put down his pencil, picked up his cigar, and chewed it thoughtfully. A discount on volume was fair enough, but he didn't like being pushed. On the other hand, the Ford dealer in Warington was close enough to make the ride worth thirty-six hundred dollars. Besides, if the Revelationists were going to be around for long—and it sure looked like they would—they'd be back for more.

"All right. Knock off thirty-six hundred. That makes it thirty-two thousand three hundred dollars, plus sales tax. That's thirty-four thousand two hundred and thirty-eight dollars. You want GMAC or bank financing?"

"We'll pay now," said the one who had done all the talking. He wrote a check and passed it to Stratton.

"Wait a minute. I said thirty-four, two, three, eight. This is only thirty-two, three."

"We don't intend to pay the tax."

Stratton flushed. He wanted very much to rip their check into small pieces. He knew he wouldn't.

The Revelationists' fleet of blue cars and trucks became a familiar sight, a constant reminder of their presence. They plied the streets and local roads and before long people gave little notice when they saw one of them parked outside the grocery or loaded high with lumber and driven by two or three smiling young men and women. When people did notice, they watched with anxious expressions. There seemed to be so many of them now.

Every day new faces appeared at the post office. Every day two or three cars were parked outside the social center. It opened in the afternoon and its gaily lighted windows were bright until midnight. Though the sign said all were welcome, it was the bored, restless teen-agers who drifted in and out at will and flocked there each Saturday night for the regular dance. Many took to wearing blue work shirts and overalls—the uniform of the Revelationists.

It was assumed that there were anywhere from two to three hundred people living at Revelations, a name which was gradually replacing "the old asylum" in the local parlance. Two to three hundred religious zealots was a sizable addition to the population of Hudson City, which numbered around a thousand. At one time the asylum had housed five hundred inmates. What would the Revelationists use the room for? Were more of them on the way?

On a Saturday morning in the middle of July three long-distance charter buses brought an answer. They ground slowly through town, lumbered left onto Spotting Mountain Road, and could be heard for some time laboring up the mountain in low gear.

Later that morning, Springer was having coffee with Ellen Barbar at the drugstore, as he did several times a week. He found himself drawn to her beauty and her obsession. She had taken to prowling the hills around Revelations, hoping for a glimpse of her sister, and the sun had tanned her healthily, lending a gypsy cast to her exotic face.

The bus drivers parked their silver behemoths on Main Street, came into the drugstore, and ordered breakfast. They wore dark green gabardine suits, black bow ties, and khaki shirts. One of them, a husky black man, sat next to Springer, who asked, "Long trip?"

"Not too bad. Up from New York."

"Until we left the Northway," said another man. "What you call roads we put in Coney Island and call roller coasters."

"What a load of nuts," said the third. All three men had New York City accents.

"Nuts?" asked Springer.

"The passengers," said the black man. "You should have seen them. What is that joint up the mountain?"

"It used to be a mental institution."

The drivers laughed. "Just right," said one of them. They glanced at Ellen and exchanged approving nods. Springer met their grins. "What do you mean, nuts?"

"Ever hear of the Revelationists?"

"They live up there," said Springer. "New neighbors."

"Yeah? Well, you're welcome to 'em."

Ellen brought their coffee, and while they were adding sugar and milk Dwight Rigby came over to the lunch counter and asked Springer to verify a prescription dosage.

"You the doctor?" asked the black man.

"Yes."

"That's what I need." He shifted uncomfortably on the stool. "My leg's killing me."

"Right leg?" asked Springer.

"Yeah. How'd you know? Sciatica. Kills me when I'm driving. I got these pills but I'm afraid to take 'em on the road."

"Take your wallet out of your back pocket."

"What?"

"I said—"

"I heard you, Doc. I don't get it."

"Take it out. It presses against the nerve in your hip. Creates the symptoms of sciatica."

The driver reached back and extracted a bulky wallet from his rear pocket. "Yeah?" he asked dubiously.

"Yeah."

"I'll try it."

"Where should I send the bill?"

The black man grinned. "I'll be back next week. We got a long-term charter for these nuts. When I stop hurting I'll buy you a cup of coffee."

"Fair enough. How come you keep calling them 'nuts'?"

Ellen brought plates of eggs and sausage, toast, home-fried potatoes, and more coffee. The man with the bad leg chewed a sausage link and washed it down with coffee.

"They're nuts. Screaming, shouting, crying, singing, howling nuts. And praying their asses off. They prayed more than forty Baptists in a sinking rowboat. Prayed for each other, prayed for the bus, prayed for the road, even prayed for me."

The driver next to him chuckled. "I told one of them I'd knock an hour off the run if they'd pray the troopers away. He didn't think it was very funny."

While they ate, the men swapped stories about their passengers. Springer and Ellen and several customers who had come into the drugstore listened attentively. One hundred and fifty initiates, first-timers, had come up in the buses. They were mostly New York City people in their teens and early twenties. Many seemed nervous, but the Revelationist chaperones kept them occupied with hymn singing, rousing sermons, and long prayer sessions.

The loud and frantic activity had started at the Port Authority Bus Terminal in New York City and did not stop until they had reached the iron gates of Revelations. None of them had carried luggage and all the drivers knew about their plans was that they were supposed to pick them up late Sunday night and take them back to New York. They agreed that though the passengers had been loud, they had been a lot less trouble than a bunch of drunken ski bums. The chaperones had even swept out the buses when they disembarked.

"Did you get inside?" Ellen asked eagerly.

"No, ma'am. They stopped us at the gate. Wouldn't even let us take a—use the bathroom."

"What do you think they're doing up there?" asked one of the drivers.

"That's what we've been wondering," said Springer.

"What are you people *wondering* about?" Ellen said sharply. "They're having training weekends to convert people they signed up at rallies. They're moving their street work into New York. Right?"

"You're right," said the black driver. "They been stopping people on Forty-second Street. Had a big rally in the Park."

"Hudson City is their new training camp," said Ellen. "That's why they came here. This is their East Coast center."

The drivers broke the silence that followed. "See you

folks next week. Thanks for the advice, Doc." As they headed for the door a small boy ran in, a quarter in his hand. He saw the black man and stopped stock-still, his mouth agape. Then he turned and ran out.

"What the hell's wrong with him?" asked the driver.

Rigby and the customers who'd been listening looked away in embarrassment. Springer smiled. "You're probably the first black man he's ever seen outside of television."

The driver laughed heartily, but the mirth took several long moments to light his eyes. When it did, he took a dollar from his wallet and gave it to Ellen.

"Buy him a soda on me if he comes back."

He grinned at Springer, limped out, and climbed aboard his bus. The three engines started simultaneously. Minutes later their roar faded to the south.

"Well," said someone finally, "I guess we know what they're doing here."

"Fine with me," said Rigby. "All they want is a quiet place to do their work. They won't bother us."

"You'll wish they never came," said Ellen Barbar.

"Alan? This is Ellen Barbar. I hope you don't mind me calling you at home."

Springer did mind, but he kept it light. "Mind? Why should I mind if my wife answers the telephone and hears your beautiful voice asking for me?"

Ellen sounded surprised. "You *do* mind. I'm sorry. I don't think of our friendship that way." Her voice turned brisk again. "I tried your hospital first, but they said you'd gone home. It's important, otherwise—"

"Don't worry about it. What's important?"

"There's someone waiting to meet you at Henry's Tavern."

"Who?"

She said she could not discuss it on the telephone. When he met the person he would know why she wanted him to. Springer was curious; anything with which Ellen was concerned had to relate to the Revelationists. He asked if she would be there.

"No," she said sharply. "We can't be seen together."

That cinched it; he had a hunch who, or more correctly, what, the person would be.

He told Margaret he had to go to the hospital and told the hospital he would be at Henry's Tavern. The bar occupied the front half of a small frame house on the state highway a mile south of town. Springer eased into the rutted parking lot that had been the front lawn when Henry's was a private dwelling and parked between an old Ford and a white Cadillac Eldorado with California plates.

The owner of the Ford was asleep at a corner table and Henry was frying a hamburger on a greasy stove in the yellow kitchen behind the bar—which made the big man in the expensive tweed jacket playing bumper pool the owner of the Eldorado and most probably the person Springer had come to see.

Springer walked up to him and extended his hand. "Mysterious stranger, I presume?"

He put down his cue stick, flashed a startling white grin, and took Springer's hand in a powerful grasp. "Sorry about my circuitous approach. I'd appreciate it if my visit to Hudson City were between us and our mutual lady friend. Name's Frank Bissel."

"I had a feeling you'd be a deprogrammer. I read about you in *Time* magazine."

"Exaggerations, I assure you."

"Did Ellen hire you?"

"Nope. Recognized me at the motel. We got to talking. She told me about you and I figured you'd make a good contact. Nice of you to join me."

Bissel looked about fifty. He had thinning black hair and warm brown eyes that softened his rugged face. He might have been a football player thirty years ago, before the giants had taken over the game.

"You picked the right place for privacy," said Springer.

Bissel eyed the dimly lighted room, the low cork-tile ceiling pocked with cue-stick blue holes, the plastic-paneled walls and the cracked linoleum floor, worn down to the wood in a circle around the bumper pool table.

"I imagine folks in these parts drink at home."

Springer chuckled. "They have some good fights here on Friday night."

"Those aren't fights," said Bissel. "Just a panicked exodus. Let me buy you a drink."

They found a pair of stools that looked cleaner and more stable than the rest and sat down. Henry shuffled out of the kitchen. He was unshaven and wore bedroom slippers. "Hi, Doc."

"Hello, Henry. How's business?"

Henry shrugged gloomily.

"How about a couple of Depth Charges?" asked Bissel.

Henry cast a dubious eye over his meager stock. "Never heard of 'em."

"Simple," said Bissel. "Start with a big mug of beer."

"Genny?" asked Henry.

It was Bissel's turn to look dubious.

"Genesee," said Springer. "Local stuff. Very good."

"I'll take your word for it."

Henry opened two bottles and poured the beer into the mugs that Bissel indicated. He wiped his hands on his gray apron.

"Now," said Bissel. "Two shots of your worst rye."

"I got Seagrams."

"Save it for Friday night. That one looks fine, in the shot glass. Now watch closely."

Bissel dropped the brimming shot glass into the beer; it settled to the bottom of the mug, landing upright. He did the same to Springer's.

"Ready?"

"You're kidding."

"There are things a man doesn't kid about. Watch your teeth and don't swallow the glass."

Bissel chugged the mug and caught the falling shot glass on his lips. He sat back, wiped his mouth, and said, "You planning to absorb yours by osmosis?"

"I'm a sipper."

"Doesn't work the same if you sip it. You see the alcohol is heavier than the beer and—"

"They told me that in organic chemistry."

"So?"

"So, I'm a sipper. Cheers." Springer sipped.

"It's a Pennsylvania steelworker drink."

"I'll remember it if I change professions."

Bissel laughed. "Another beer, Henry, *sans* booze."

"What kind?"

"Just a Genny."

Springer waited until Henry went back to the kitchen. "What do you mean you figured I'd be a good contact?"

Bissel glanced toward the kitchen, then at the sleeping man in the corner. "Excuse me." He got up and stuffed a handful of coins into the red and green jukebox on the far wall. Arlo Guthrie began singing "The City of New Orleans."

Bissel returned to the bar. "Obviously, I'm here on business. I have a contract to locate, capture, and deprogram the son of a Detroit automobile executive. I *think* they've got him here. There's a lot about this area you can tell me. Ellen said you were born here."

"Did Ellen say she thought I would help?"

"She said you were sympathetic to the cause."

Springer fixed his gaze on Bissel's craggy face until he drew the man's eyes to his. "I'm not all that sure I approve of your work, Mr. Bissel. And as far as the 'cause' is concerned, you've seen the lady. Any man in his right mind would be sympathetic."

Bissel grinned. "For sure. However, before I change your mind about my work, I'd like to pass along the words of a great and wise man, a fellow Chicagoan, the writer Nelson Algren. They apply." He sipped his beer. "Three rules of life. Nevers." He ticked them off on his fingers, which were powerful-looking, the nails well cared for.

"Never eat at a diner called Mom's. Never play cards with a man named Doc. And never, ever, sleep with a woman who's got more troubles than you do."

"Beautiful," said Springer.

"And she's got 'em, my friend. Want to hear Bissel's Corollary?"

"Okay."

"Bissel's Corollary—'Every great-looking piece of ass is attached to a person.' "

Springer smiled ruefully. "What do you mean Ellen's got troubles?"

Bissel eyed him closely. When he spoke, his voice was somber. "While I admire her perseverance, I suspect the motivation. As far as life is concerned, Ellen is out to lunch. She's using her sister as an excuse for not living."

"What do you mean not living?"

"I mean, specifically, what is a bright, young, educated woman who had a good profession doing in this one-horse town jerking sodas? Listen, Springer. I meet a lot of people. I've met parents like her. People with empty marriages and boring lives. All of a sudden a kid they've never really done a damned thing for gets hooked up with the Revvies or the Moonies and now they have a goal, something to live for—save the kid. It becomes their whole life. Just like it's become Ellen's."

"Whose side are you on?" asked Springer.

"The kids'. They're right in the middle. Which brings us back to you. What don't you approve of?"

"The force involved and, frankly, the fact that you seem to be making a living off those people's problems."

Bissel laughed. "A living? My lawyers are making a living. I'm under indictment in two states for assault and forcible restraint. The Revvies have a permanent injunction against me in Oregon—I'm not allowed within a half mile of them. On top of that, some poor mixed-up little girl who went back to them is accusing me of rape. There are easier ways to make a living."

Bissel took another long swallow of beer, draining the mug. "As far as force is concerned, getting somebody to sit still is a lamentably necessary first step to talking some sense into them. The Revvies get a real tight hold on them. I have to show the kid how crazy they've made him in order to reverse the brainwashing—to deprogram the program the Revvies have filled him with. That takes time and isolation." He grinned. "Brainrinsing gets kinda rough. I had one kid locked up with me for six days before I cracked him."

"How was he afterwards?" asked Springer.

"Fine. Now he's a law student at Stanford. Listen to this, I'll tell you how I knew he was cured. Six days, right? All of a sudden, his face changes. He blinks like he's coming awake. Then he says, 'Thanks, Frank. Thanks for bringing me back.' Both of us unshaven, filthy, looking like a couple of bums. The motel room a wreck from us rassling around, food wrappers all over the place, and we're standing there hugging each other and he's saying 'thank you, thank you.' Best one I ever had. Makes it all worthwhile. Now, you going to give me a hand?"

Arlo Guthrie stopped singing. The jukebox clicked into a new cycle. Guthrie resumed his song. Springer said, "I'm not convinced that what you're doing is right. I know nothing about the boy you're supposed to be rescuing."

"All I'm asking for is some information."

Springer hesitated and Bissel rubbed his jaw. "Got any kids, Springer?"

"We have a daughter, which Ellen must have told you."

"Eighty years ago there was hardly a family in America that hadn't lost a child to disease. In the sixties we started losing them to drugs. Today, the mind benders are after them. How old is your daughter?"

"Fifteen."

"The kid I'm looking for is sixteen."

"Get off that," said Springer.

"It's not beyond the realm of possibility that I or someone like me might be looking for your child one of these days."

Springer eyed him calculatingly. In spite of his objections, he liked what he saw. "You really believe in what you're doing, don't you?"

"I do."

"What do you want to know?"

"Right," said Bissel, slapping his hands together. "Now you're talking. I've been reading the terrain map for this area. There's a gully under the Revvies' west fence about a hundred yards south of that old access road. You can't see it from the road, according to the map. Is it dry?"

"Right now it is," said Springer. "But it'll run four feet of water an hour after a rain. It's not the best way in. You'd land right in the midst of some very rugged rock. Nothing to hold onto. The gully drops fifty feet."

Bissel nodded. "I didn't like the look of the map."

"It's almost impassable by day. At night, forget it."

"How about if I drop down on a line?"

"If you're good, sure. I imagine you are. But how would you get back dragging a prisoner?"

"Client," said Bissel with a small smile.

Springer shook his head. "There's a culvert under the road, Spotting Mountain Road, at the northeast corner of the fence diagonally across their property. The fence runs over it, but they must have left the culvert open because wiring it would catch debris and stop it up and the water would flood the road."

"You sure about that?"

"Positive," said Springer. "It's about a quarter mile through the woods from the buildings. I used to sneak in there when I was a kid."

Danny Moser was a sneak, a practiced shoplifter, and one opportunity was all his sharp eye and quick hands needed. He palmed a fork, hid it in the foul drain in the floor of his cell, and bent the tines into picks with which he painstakingly probed the secrets of the crude lock in the heavy iron door.

He had no idea how long it took him. He didn't think of time anymore. Three or four meals passed and several sessions with the trainer. He had fainted during the last session, and when he awakened in his cell he was terrified that he had talked about the fork. He looked in the drain. The picks were still there. Gagging from the smell, he pulled them out and resumed his work.

When the lock opened, he was so startled that he almost blew it by racing blindly down the hall like some dumb kid. He stopped himself, leaned against the door, and tried to figure his next step. His head felt fuzzy. The training sessions were making it harder to think. He clenched his fists until the pain of his fingernails biting into his palms cleared his mind.

He had his fork, the handle of which he had sharpened by rubbing it on the stone. And they'd given his clothes back. A reward, the trainer had said. He'd been good. Even though he hated the trainer fiercely enough to kill him, he had felt a spasm of joy at his approval. It was crazy. He put on his sneakers. What else? He looked around his cell, which he had dubbed "the hole" from the prison movies he'd seen on TV.

His rope!

He'd almost forgotten his rope. It was hidden behind the shredded canvas walls. He'd braided it from strips of the canvas. It had taken a long time to tear off pieces that were strong enough. At first it was for his escape, but later he had knotted a loop at one end. It gave him a different kind of comfort to know he could hang himself when he couldn't stand it anymore.

Now he had a better way out.

Trembling, he eased the door open a crack. The hall looked empty. He opened it wider and looked the other way. Empty. His weapon in his back pocket, and his rope looped over his shoulder, he inched down the hall past locked doors, past the training room, the sight of which sickened him, to the far end of the long corridor, where he found a narrow, unlit stairwell.

On the first floor, the sharp, delicious odor of varnish and wax pierced his nostrils, so accustomed to the stink of the cell. They were chanting on the other side of the stairwell door. The sound chilled him to the bone. It was part of his worst memories.

He scampered to the second floor, heard footsteps, and ran for the third. There it was quiet. Cautiously, he opened the stairwell door and saw a freshly painted hall illuminated by strings of naked bulbs.

Some of the doors were open. He slipped into a dark cell and looked out the window. It was night. The window slid up easily, but bars sealed the opening. He closed it and tried the next room. It was barred, as was the next and the next. Every room was barred. The doors seemed endless, and he was so frantic that when he finally found an open window he almost passed it by.

He tied his braided rope to an exposed beam and lowered it carefully out of the window, climbed over the sill and slowly down the stone wall. It was hard because his hands felt weak. A window on the second floor spilled light on him, blinding his eyes. He slid quickly past it, burning his hands. Stopping abruptly to ease the pain, he jerked his full weight on the rope.

It snapped.

He fell, his foot flailing, breaking glass.

The ground stopped him suddenly, knocking the wind from his lungs, but terror whisked him to his feet and into the night. Footsteps pounded behind him. He ran into a field, gasping deep breaths of the cool, clean night air.

Old Man Wright, who coached track, had kicked him off the team for smoking even though he was the fastest runner in Hudson City High. His heart surged. He hadn't had a smoke since they'd caught him a long time ago. They'd never catch him again.

He ran the long way down the mountain on secret paths no one but a boy born there could know. Only when he stopped to rest and think near the edge of town did fright overtake him. It felt like they had chopped out a hunk of his brain. Thoughts came to him slowly as his laboring lungs recovered. Doc Springer. The hospital. Check it out from the shadows of the old Shell station. Make sure the coast was clear then make a run for it. The emergency-entrance doors were always open.

He struggled to his feet and forced his aching legs into a shambling trot. Doc Springer would take care of him. Protect him, hide him. He ran faster, almost there.

Something was wrong. All that light. What happened to the Shell station? He stumbled to the edge of the frightening circle of light that probed right into the woods and watched for a long time, trying to digest the change. He couldn't understand. How could the town change so much? What had they done to him? How long had they had him?

He backed away from the strange building, hurried through the woods and across Spotting Mountain Road into the cemetery, sneaked behind the church, over the highway, and worked his way through dark back yards until he was behind the hospital.

A man in white passed by a window. Danny's heart dropped. The intern. It was night. The Doc wasn't there. He felt his lips begin to tremble. Hot tears burned his eyes. He shook them away. Idiot! The Doc was at home. Silently, he headed for the other end of town.

He never saw the Revelationists who were waiting in the shadows around the hospital.

Danny lay in the musty earth under Old Man Wright's front porch and watched Doc Springer's house through the lattice-work screen that concealed the supports. He had a clear view between two of the boxwood shrubs that lined the street side of Wright's property. The Doc's house was less than a hundred yards away across the street, but his car wasn't in the driveway. The front-porch light was on and there were bright lights on the second floor.

Danny waited a long time, tensing whenever a car came down Main. Suddenly the Doc's car swung into the driveway. Danny's heart began to pound. The Doc was getting out. He backed out of the hole in the lattice, scrambled to his feet, and broke into a dead run as Springer climbed his front-porch steps. He'd planned the path: straight across Wright's lawn, jump the flower bed between the boxwood shrubs, cross the street, and run like hell up the Doc's walk.

He jumped the flowers.

Hands, white blurs in the night, closed over his mouth, pinned his arms, pulled him deeper into the shadows of the shrubs. Danny struggled, his eyes locked on Springer's back as the doctor opened his screen door and stepped into his house. He screamed futilely against the flesh that blocked his mouth. The porch light went out.

"Bissel's gone," Ellen said quietly, her big eyes flicking cautiously at the people seated nearby at the counter.

"Where?" asked Springer.

"He just said we'd see him again. And he said you were really great."

"He's really a character," said Springer.

"I appreciate what you did, Alan."

"I didn't do anything. Did you ask him to help you?"

"We discussed it. He said he might be able to do it for less than usual. . . . Did you hear the buses this morning?"

Springer had seen them from his bedroom. He was still sipping coffee, enjoying the hot summer morning and talking with Ellen, when the bus drivers returned from the mountain and came into the drugstore.

The black driver saw him and waved. "Give that man a cup of coffee."

"Leg all better?" asked Springer.

"Stopped hurting Wednesday. Threw away the pills and tore up my doctor's bill." He and his companions ordered breakfast. One of them said, "Brought you some more nuts."

"New group?" asked Springer.

"Yeah. Jesus, you should have seen the old ones Sunday night. Right up the wall."

The black man nodded emphatically. "Zombies. Great big eyes and smiles like paralyzed beavers. The chaperones said pray and the zombies prayed. Chaperones said sing and the zombies sang. Unreal. I don't know what they did to them but they did it good.

"You never saw anything like it. Shrieking, screaming . . . then it gets real quiet and everybody starts crying. Gnashing their teeth, howling, and the chaperones start running up and down the aisle yelling they should cry some more. They cry and carry on and then the chaperones start laughing and then the zombies are laughing. They laugh their asses off and then they sing another song."

"Same thing on my bus," said another driver. "Whole trip."

"Yeah," said the third. "Then all of a sudden they start hugging and kissing like they're going to have this huge orgy, only the boys are kissing boys and the girls are kissing girls 'cause they got them separated, girls on one side of the bus and boys on the other."

"But it wasn't sex," said the black man. "Just patting. Like you'd hold your kids on your lap. Know what I mean?"

"Friendly," said Springer.

"Not exactly. More like they were comforting each other."

"Congratulating," said the man next to him. "Like when we drive the winning team home from a football game."

"Right. They even looked like they played a big game. Really beat. But look out, if one of them nodded out those chaperones landed on him with all four feet. Fire him up again and away they go."

"They looked like they hadn't slept in a week."

The black man spread jam on a wedge of toast. "I wonder what happened to the no-shows?"

"Who?" asked Springer.

"Twenty of 'em didn't come back."

That evening Springer decided to look in on the Revelationists' dance. The bright lights of the social center were an oasis in the dark and even from a distance the pulse of the jukebox promised excitement for the young people hurrying up on foot and arriving from the farms in battered jalopies and dusty pickups. As Springer drew nearer, he felt a knot form in his stomach. Margaret had applauded his going, but declined to join him on the grounds that their combined presence might make Samantha uncomfortable.

Hearing the music and the shouts of the teen-agers, he was reminded of the teen-age dances he'd gone to, alone, hoping that something special would happen to change his life, hoping he might meet a girl, hoping someone might offer a ride in his car, and hoping that if any of it happened his father wouldn't ruin it all by lurching past the school, insensibly drunk.

The garage bay door was open to the warm night. Springer entered in the midst of a laughing group. If the smiling young man who immediately accosted him had objections to adults attending, he did not express them.

"Welcome!" he said heartily. "Would you like a soda?"

Springer shook off the memories and followed the young man across the jammed dance floor toward the soda fountain. The walls of the brightly lighted room were painted white, the concrete floor blue. Most of the teen-agers wore the same overalls and work shirts as their hosts, who were distinguished by their fixed smiles and the metal crosses that dangled from their necks.

Positioned throughout the room, the Revelationists were busily talking to the kids, carrying trays of soda and cookies, cajoling the wall flowers to join in. Unlike adult chaperones at a school dance, they were personally attending to every child, guiding each one into participation. The music was loud and seemed like any of a number of country and western songs he'd heard until Springer caught the chorus. The nasal singers whined:

> "I know not how that Calvary's cross,
> "A world from sin could free;
> "I only know its matchless love
> "Has brought God's love to me."

The verse told a story of sin abandoned for righteous living; when the chorus resumed the dancers sang with it. Clutching a paper cup of Coke, Springer shouted over the din, "They seem to be having a good time."

"We're glad you came, Dr. Springer," said the Revelationist who had welcomed him. "God's will that you would be here tonight."

"What's special about tonight?"

"We'll have a surprise for you later on."

"What kind of surprise?"

"It wouldn't be a surprise if we told you." The young man smiled. "Samantha is a wonderful child. We like her very much."

"Where is she?"

"Dancing with her friends. Why don't you go look for her?"

Springer moved slowly around the perimeter of the crowded room. Many of the teen-agers called "Hello" to him, while the Revelationists watched with fixed smiles. He noticed that the sizes of the crosses they wore seemed to indicate rank and felt a minor victory in penetrating their shield of sameness. Eventually he spotted Samantha dancing with Dicky, her face alight with enjoyment.

Curious about the music, he wandered toward the juke-box and read the titles on the songs. They were all religious. Many bore the label of a recording company called Sounds of Revelations. Samantha was closer. He tried to catch her eye, but at that moment one of the chaperones, a man in his twenties, put his arms around her and Dicky and guided them to a corner. He was talking earnestly, concentrating on Samantha and turning now and then to Dicky, apparently for agreement. The boy nodded and spoke to Samantha. Springer could see her shoulders tensing.

He started toward her, but the Revelationist who had greeted him reappeared and casually blocked his way. He had with him a big man, tall as Springer and much broader, whom he introduced, reverently, as a trainer.

Springer bristled. "Does he have a name?"

He had a penetrating gaze and a smiling face that expressed utter confidence. A large metal cross hung from his neck. "You can call me John. . . . The word 'trainer' bother you?"

"Yes. Animals have trainers; people don't."

John smiled smugly. "God works in many ways. All practical. He achieves His will. That's really all that matters, isn't it?"

"Can I ask you something?" said Springer, watching Samantha from the corner of his eye.

"Of course."

"Fundamentalists usually frown upon the enjoyment of worldly pleasures like popular music and dance and pool. How come you don't?"

"Without debating whether or not the Revelationists are a fundamentalist sect—which we are not, we are a movement—I can refer you to the Bible. The first book of Corinthians, Chapter Nine, verse twenty-two—'To the weak became I as weak, that I might gain the weak: I am made all things to all *men,* that I might by all means save some.' "

Springer nodded at the dancing couples. "Slumming?"

" 'Give none offence. . . . Even as I please all *men* in all *things,* not seeking mine own profit, but the *profit* of many, that they may be saved.' "

"Speaking of saved," said Springer. "Do you have a person up there named Rose Barbar?"

"Someone you know?"

"A friend of a friend."

"That disturbed young woman at the drugstore?"

"Then you do know who I mean?"

"No, I don't. We have many Roses, many Johns, many . . . Alans. And more every day, Doctor. Have you considered where *you* will stand when the Messiah comes?"

"At a distance," said Springer. "So I can see who's propping him up."

"Humor is a formidable shield, Doctor. It will protect you from everything . . . except yourself."

"I can deal with myself," said Springer. "A devil I know."

John's smile vanished. "We do not joke about the Devil in Michael's house."

"Then I apologize, John. I didn't come here to offend. I wanted to see the place where my daughter's spending so much time."

"Do you doubt our intentions?"

"Frankly, I wonder about them. This social center is a great place for the kids to go. But some of us in town are concerned with the goings-on at Revelations."

"Revelations is a place for those who seek God."

"We're a little worried about what Revelations is seeking," Springer replied. "I gather you're training converts."

John smiled. "A convert can do little for Michael's cause until he has been trained and initiated."

"I advise you not to try the same thing here in the social center," said Springer. "Don't try to convert our children." His words hung emptily in the noisy room and he felt a little foolish for having uttered them.

John seemed to sense his confusion. "First you say that your children need a social center, then you say we shouldn't have anything to do with them."

"I didn't say that. I just—"

"Would you prefer to run this place? How many parents in your town would give the necessary time to help the children?"

"I'm not saying we're not grateful."

"What *are* you saying?"

"Just that it would be better if you didn't insinuate yourselves too deeply into our lives. We can get along well with each other if you leave us alone." Again his words sounded bellicose and he grew uncomfortable under John's steady gaze.

The trainer remained as unemotional as Springer had tried to be. "Michael has given the Revelationists a mission. We shall cleanse the earth for Christ. Who could possibly be threatened? The unclean? The wrongdoer?"

"As soon as you decide who's unclean and who's doing wrong, then we're all threatened."

"It is not our mission to *punish* the unclean," said John. "They are God's creation too, and even Michael himself wouldn't presume to judge God's creation. We intend to cleanse them."

" 'Cleanse' is a chillingly vague word," said Springer.

"Would you prefer 'convert'?"

"It's clearer."

"And do you object to our converting people to Christ?"

Springer considered the question. Emotionally, he didn't like the idea and couldn't imagine it happening to himself, but intellectually, he believed that people had a right to try to persuade others to agree with them. He incorporated the paradox into his answer. "Not if you do it fairly."

"Fairly?"

"If you can persuade a person with reason and logic, fine. But if you force him, I'm against it."

"Are you talking about brainwashing?" asked John.

Springer was surprised by his candor. "Your word."

"We know what people say. We don't let it interfere with our mission. . . . So it's all right with you if we convert with logic?"

For the first time, Springer sensed some emotion behind the steady smile. Triumph?

"One of our trainers holds his Ph.D. in philosophy, Dr. Springer. He wrote his dissertation on general semantics. Would you care to debate with him?"

Springer grinned. "I'll sooner box with Muhammed Ali."

"You get my point, Doctor."

"Your point is specious. Your Ph.D. might talk me in circles, but he can't make me agree with him as long as I control my faculties. That is not the same as brainwashing."

The music stopped. As if on signal, the teen-agers hurried from the dance floor and crowded against the walls. John vanished in the confusion and Springer watched over their heads as a young woman began playing the piano. Two men with fiddles accompanied her and the spectators clapped time to the music. Samantha and Dicky were still talking with the Revelationist. As Springer watched, Dicky stood aside and the man put his hands on Samantha's temples. He spoke and she closed her eyes.

Then, to Springer's astonishment, she stepped boldly into the middle of the room, clasped her hands before her, and looked at the piano. Her face was flushed with excitement. The piano player vamped a few bars. Samantha took a deep breath and sang:

"Nearer, my God, to Thee,
  "Nearer to Thee!
"E'en though it be a cross
  "That raiseth me . . ."

Her voice was a strong contralto and the listeners seemed hypnotized by its sweet beauty. Springer was delighted by her poise and he thought, as she continued the song, that she had never looked so pretty. If only Margaret could see her.

> "Still all my songs shall be,
> "Nearer, my God, to Thee . . .
> "Nearer to thee."

He rushed across the room when it was over and hugged her.

"That was beautiful, darling. Wonderful."

Samantha blinked, as if coming out of a trance. She shook her head from side to side and spoke in a monotone. "Thank you. Thank you." She turned to the other people who were crowding around and repeated, "Thank you."

Springer stepped back to let the children near her, but that night, as he raved to Margaret about Samantha's performance, he was troubled by a memory of the child's blank stare when he tried to congratulate her. He had an awful, only half-formed fear that whatever had given Samantha the strength to perform had taken something in return.

The Revelationists were going to have a picnic, Samantha announced at dinner a few days later.

"Up there?" asked Margaret.

"Yes, Mother." She pushed a piece of paper across the table. "They said everybody under eighteen has to have permission. Please sign this, Daddy."

Springer hesitated. "Is Dicky going?"

"Sure," said Samantha. "Mr. Lewis sold them some grills for cooking out."

"Could we come?" asked Margaret.

"Sorry, Mother. It's just for kids. Maybe next time."

"I want to hear you sing, dear."

"You will. You just sign at the bottom, Daddy. I already filled in my name."

"Okay, sweetheart. Let me read it." The form was similar to the one the high school used for class trips. Samantha gave him a pen and leaned on his shoulder while he read aloud, " 'I hereby give permission for Samantha Springer'—the golden-throated warbler—'to attend a picnic at Revelations on Saturday, July seventeenth, beginning at noon. I understand my child will return to the Main Street Hudson City Revelations Social Center at six o'clock.' "

He signed his name and gave her the paper. She looked unhappy. "What's wrong, kitten?"

"You shouldn't make fun of my singing."

"Fun? Oh, baby, I'm sorry. I was just teasing. I'm so proud of your singing. It's wonderful."

"You should join the church choir," said Margaret.

"No, Mother. I'd rather not."

"But if you sing so well . . ."

"I can sing at the social center anytime I want to. Can I be excused?"

"Go ahead, dear. We'll have dessert later."

Samantha bounded up the stairs. Springer nodded after her. "She's really getting energetic. Prancing around like a colt."

"I hate the idea of her going up there," said Margaret. "Out of town and in that awful building. Are you sure we should let her?"

"I drove past Revelations today. They're pitching a big tent on the front lawn. It's in plain view of the gates. I don't think there'll be any problem."

"But she's getting so involved with them, Alan. They take up a lot of her time—homework from the Bible classes and then those dances and she's been there twice this week already." Margaret pushed a strand of hair from her forehead. "I'm worried, Alan. They've made themselves part of our town. They're all over and the children—"

"I know," said Springer. "It bothers me too. But I can't really object to anything they've done."

"What about when they invaded the church?"

"That was wrong. But it doesn't have anything to do with the kids. And when they took that man from the ward, well, it didn't matter that much. Since then, they've been giving the kids a hell of a good summer. When's the last time you saw any of them hanging out on street corners?"

"I'm afraid, Alan."

Springer took her cold hand in his. "I know what you mean. Let's see what happens after the picnic. Maybe we'll have to do something."

"What can we do?"

"Let's see what they do."

As Springer guessed, the Revelationists held their picnic under the bright blue tent in front of the asylum. There were tables under the tent and games on the lawn, all in full view of the road. Occasionally, children entered the stone building, but the majority of the hundred Hudson City children and the crowds of Revelationists who hosted them were always visible on the front lawn, although, as some of the people who watched remarked, it was difficult to tell them apart from a distance, so many of the children had taken to wearing the blue work shirts and overalls. When the picnic was over, the children marched the two miles down the road and arrived, as promised, at the social center at precisely six o'clock. Each child clutched a memento of the day, a small, blue pamphlet.

Samantha reported a wonderful time. Her nose was sunburned and there were grass stains on her knees, sustained, she said, while losing a tug of war.

"Did Dicky have a good time?" asked Margaret.

"I guess so. I didn't see him much."

"Oh? Did you have an argument?"

"No. We just did our own thing. He was playing baseball."

"Who'd you play with?" asked Springer.

"Everybody. Can I take a shower, Mom? I'm all dirty." She charged up the stairs and moments later they heard her singing in the shower.

Margaret smiled. "I've never seen her so happy. Maybe it's all for the best."

"She looks healthy," Springer conceded.

Dinner was pleasant that night as Samantha regaled them with animated accounts of the day's activity. She went to bed early, but at midnight, when Springer went upstairs, her light was still on. She was reading the blue pamphlet.

"To bed," said Springer. "You've had a long day." He kissed her brow.

"You've been drinking," said Samantha.

"We had a glass of wine," said Springer. "Go to sleep, dear." As he backed out of her darkened room, he heard her pray aloud. She asked God to cleanse the world and she begged for the salvation of her mother and father. She ended her worship, "In the name of Jesus and his protector, Michael. Amen."

Springer awakened early; on his way downstairs he slipped quietly into Samantha's room and took the blue pamphlet from her night table. It was a modern English version of the Book of Revelations. He read it over a cup of coffee in the kitchen and finished by the time Margaret and Samantha came down. Margaret was wearing a dress, Samantha was in jeans.

"Samantha doesn't want to come to church," said Margaret.

"Why not, angel?"

"I don't feel like it today."

"But your mother will be all by herself."

"You can take her."

"Not today," said Springer. "All week I've been promis-

ing myself a walk in the hills." He lifted his foot to show
the walking shoes that covered his ankles.

"That's all right," said Margaret.

"I'm going to read my Bible at home," said Samantha.

"This?" asked Springer, holding up the pamphlet.

"Did you read it?" asked Samantha, challenging him
with her eyes.

Springer was startled by the look. A stranger had sallied
forth from the girl she was. "Yes, I did. Tell me something,
sweetheart. Is the Michael who says he wrote this version
the same Michael you were praying to last night?"

Margaret looked up sharply. She hadn't heard the
prayer.

Samantha drank her orange juice in one long swallow.
"There are two Michaels, Daddy. Michael the Archangel
and Michael the founder of the Revelationists."

"Handy coincidence of names," bantered Springer.

Samantha's eyes went blank as they had the night she
sang. She spoke in a monotone, reciting, "Just as there is a
Trinity of Father, Son, and Holy Ghost, so too there is a
Duality of Michael the Archangel and Michael of the Revelationists."

"But you don't think that Michael is an angel, do you?"

Samantha flushed. "Michael is an *Arch*angel."

"Did you meet him at the picnic?" asked Margaret.

The child hesitated. She closed her eyes. "I sensed him."

"Was he there?" asked Springer.

"No. But I'll meet him soon," she added with a rush. "I
know I will." Her face and voice became animated again.
"They say he's wonderful, Daddy. Really wonderful."

"I'm sure he is," said Springer. "But try to remember,
dear, that he is just a man. Perhaps wonderful, perhaps not.
That will be for you to judge. Please don't let others persuade you ahead of time. Wait until you meet him."

"He's an archangel," Samantha retorted stubbornly.
"And I know he's wonderful."

"Listen to what your father is saying," said Margaret.

"He's wonderful," repeated Samantha. "He will save us.
You must believe that, Mother. He'll save you and he'll
save Daddy and he'll save me."

A sarcastic retort formed on Springer's tongue, but he
assessed Samantha's stone-faced determination and re-

strained himself. He had no intention of driving the child closer to the Revelationists.

"When do you think you'll meet him?" he asked gently. Samantha relaxed. "When he comes. They said soon."

Springer stepped off the front porch into a beautiful morning. A Canadian high-pressure system had blown in overnight bringing a cool north breeze and crystal-clear air. He walked quickly toward Spotting Mountain Road. Reverend Davies was in the cemetery, his head bent, lost in thought, rehearsing his sermon, Springer guessed.

As the road inclined upward, Springer slowed his pace. The initial burst of speed had done its job; the tensions of the week, the work at the hospital, and some of the worries about Samantha were run out now. He began to forget, to empty his mind. He grew aware of his surroundings.

The sun was hot, but the breeze kept him comfortable. Birds sang from the bushes in the gullies along the road. A corn field rustled richly, the new crop glistening in the sharp light. He kicked a beer can off the road and looked up at the mountain. Part of its green face was still dark in the shadow of the peak. It hadn't rained in two weeks and dust coated the road, dulling the garnets.

When he passed Bob Kent's place he saw him shooting his bow in the back yard, getting in a few shots before church. Springer kept going, hoping he hadn't been seen. He passed two men who were working on a '64 Cadillac in the front yard of their shack. The car's hood and trunk were open and it rested on cement blocks, the wheels tireless.

Springer said "Hello" and kept climbing, pausing now and then to look at a wild flower or a feeding bird. Once he heard the drum of a big flicker. He searched, but the bird was deep in a wood. He stopped again when he came to an overlook just before a hairpin turn. From there he could see Hudson City.

The church steeple rose sharp and white from a cluster of trees. Main Street was visible from the stores on south. He could see his own house and the broad green patch of the playing fields behind the school. The old railroad track to the garnet mines skipped a dotted line behind the town.

Moser's Lumberyard stood out like a brown spot on a green lawn.

A sound intruded. It was rhythmic. It grew louder. It seemed to come from beyond the bend in the road. Springer cocked his head and listened, curious. The sound was measured, but not quite mechanical. Tramping, people walking. He watched the bend in the road. The sound grew nearer.

Like an army on the march, the Revelationists rounded the turn in two tight columns. Men were on the left, women on the right; the leaders wore large iron crosses and the dull metal glinted, swinging from side to side with the marchers' gaits. They occupied the crown of the road; when the end of the column appeared at the turn, Springer saw there were at least a hundred of them.

They bore down on him, silent but for the tramp of their feet, and passed by as if he were not standing six feet away with a quizzical expression on his face. He searched their wooden faces looking for John, the trainer, or the medic, but saw no one he recognized. Refusing to accept the absurdity of a hundred people ignoring one man on a country road, Springer waved and called loudly, "Good morning."

None of them answered.

"Hi there," said Springer. "Good morning. Well, hello. Really? You don't say?"

They filed past in solemn isolation.

"Enjoy the service," Springer called after them. He knew instinctively that they were heading for the church and he wondered if he should go back. But what could he do other than sound a breathless warning moments ahead of their arrival? With or without him, Davies and his deacons would still have to confront the invaders. The tramping feet faded toward the town. Springer shrugged and resumed walking.

A quarter mile along he came to Revelations. The flower boxes in the windows did little to relieve the building's brooding countenance. There were no people on the front lawn and the gates were locked, the center pieces wrapped with a stout chain.

Beyond the entrance, Spotting Mountain Road inclined steeply. Springer walked more slowly now, pausing to catch his breath. The road paralleled the shiny new fence for another quarter mile, then veered sharply away to the right, its surface changing from macadam to gravel; if he had continued on it for another mile, Springer could have walked to a parking area several hundred yards from the final peak of Spotting Mountain. Instead, he climbed down and up a gully and crossed a field thick with young cedars, walking parallel to the fence's top or west leg. To his right was a high ridge that joined the mountain. He jumped over a stream and continued along the fence until he reached another wide meadow. Then he turned away from the fence toward a secondary ridge.

Walking carefully through high grass, his eyes alert for holes, briars, and poison ivy, Springer forged up the slight incline until he reached a smooth, grassy knoll that was backed by a rock face. At one end of the face, screened by cedars and invisible from any distance, a cut in the rock provided a steep path. Springer climbed it hand over hand until he reached a cool, green glade ten feet above the knoll.

The glade was sheltered on three sides by the next ridge. From the open side, at the edge of which he had entered, there was a view of the pretty meadow below. In the distance, a half mile beyond the fence and woods, were the gables and outbuildings behind Revelations. Though the building had seemed deserted when he'd passed the main gate, from this angle Springer could see tiny blue figures moving about the open ground.

The glade was almost flat, a tiny circle no more than twenty feet across. It was covered with smooth moss and low grass and a blanket upon which lay Ellen Barbar, wearing cut-off blue jean shorts and a red bandanna halter. She was on her stomach, propped up on her elbows, her eyes glued to high-power binoculars.

18

The double doors flew open and banged against the church walls. The parishioners whirled about, startled by the sudden explosive sound. Three grim-faced Revelationists stood on the threshold; they were the cutting edge of a phalanx that stretched to the street.

Reverend Davies gripped his pulpit. "Welcome," he quaked. He cleared his throat and repeated, "Welcome to our church."

The Revelationists marched up the aisle in lock step, halted at the very edge of the pulpit, and raked the minister with contemptuous eyes. Davies flinched. He retreated a step, wet his lips, and looked pleadingly at the deacons in the back.

"Please," he murmured, his nervous little hands playing at his sides as if the fingers were searching a hiding place in the folds of his robe.

A man in the congregation stood up angrily. The movement drew no attention from the Revelationists, whose eyes remained on the minister. He looked around at the frightened faces in the congregation; he saw no support and he sat back down. The parishioners whispered anxiously and still the Revelationists just stared. A deep hush fell over the church. When it was absolutely silent, the Revelationists sang:

"Nearer, my God, to Thee,
"Nearer to Thee!
"E'en though it be a cross
"That raiseth me . . ."

They sang hard and fast, a battle song, a challenge, a condemnation of the parishioners in their Sunday clothes, the stained-glass windows, the gold on the altar, the red velvet, the minister's gentle call to faith.

> "Though like the wanderer,
> "The sun gone down,
> "Darkness be over me . . ."

The deacons argued in angry whispers at the back of the church.

"We can't allow this," said Bob Kent.

"How can we stop them?" asked Gary Spencer.

"Maybe I better get Charlie Daniels over here," Kent suggested. The voices were pounding in his ears, mocking his helplessness and his indecision.

"No," hissed Pete Lewis. "You can't do that. Let's try to talk to them."

"They won't listen."

"Then what can we do?"

Kent was spared having to answer. At that moment Charlie Daniels hurried into the church carrying an electric bullhorn. His quick eyes took in the singing Revelationists, the dumbfounded congregation, and the cringing minister.

"Sorry, Mr. Kent. They waited until I went back to the station. I'll take care of this."

He raised the bullhorn to his mouth. Kent grabbed it. "No, wait."

Daniels looked askance. "What do you want me to do, sir?"

"You can't use that in the church," said Pete Lewis.

"What are you going to say to them, Charlie?" asked Spencer.

Daniels squinted at the nervous storekeeper as if he hadn't quite understood the question. "I'm going to tell 'em to cease and desist and haul ass out of here."

"What if they don't go?"

"I'll worry about that when it happens." He raised the bullhorn.

"No," said Spencer. "We can't do that to them."

"Look what they're doing to you," said Daniels. He turned to Kent. "Mr. Mayor, I want your permission to handle this situation. They're disturbing the peace and disrupting a legal public gathering."

Kent looked at the backs of the singers. "We can't risk a confrontation in here. Somebody might get hurt or they'll just end up making you look silly."

"I'll call the state police."

"No," said Kent.

"You going to let them take over your church?"

Kent would not meet the officer's eye. "I don't know. Maybe they'll go soon."

Contempt edged Daniels' voice. "It's your church and your town. You do what you want. I'll be at the station if you need me . . . sir." He spun on his heel and stalked out.

> "Or if, on joyful wing
> "Cleaving the sky,
> "Sun, moon, and stars forgot,
> "Upward I fly . . ."

"We have to do something," said Kent. He had been aware for some time of Sophie Wilkins' icy gaze from the organ. He looked the length of the church, caught her eye, and nodded reassuringly. "What if we ask them to pray with us after they finish singing?"

"Great idea," said Pete Lewis. "They couldn't refuse to join a prayer."

Quickly, Kent rehearsed what he would say. He hurried up the side aisle toward the altar.

> "Nearer, my God, to Thee,
> "Nearer to Thee! . . ."

The last words echoed into silence. Kent raised both hands and opened his mouth to speak. But the Revelationists had turned their backs. They were already marching out of the church.

19

"You found me," said Ellen as Springer knelt beside her, her eyes still glued to the glasses.

"I used to come up here when I was a kid," said Springer, looking around. "See anything?"

"The usual. Some of them are gardening. . . . They're building something in the barn. . . . Laundry."

"No sign of Rose?"

"No."

She lowered the glasses and blinked wearily.

"How long have you been watching?"

"I don't know." She flopped onto her back and stared at the overhanging leaves. "I left town at dawn." Gesturing at her canvas knapsack, she said, "Since you said you'd come I brought some wine and cheese."

Springer rummaged through the pack, opened the wine, and laid out the cheese with the fruit and nuts he carried in his own knapsack. He poured the wine into the plastic cups he found in her pack and handed her one.

"Cheers."

Ellen took a small drink and put down her cup. "I'm going crazy," she said. "Watching is almost worse than not doing anything. I keep seeing the same faces. They wouldn't let her out. Oh, Alan." She looked him in the eye for the first time since he had arrived. "I'm glad you came."

"Me, too," said Springer. He extended the nuts and fruit. "Have some protein."

They ate and talked while Ellen scanned the Revelationists' property with the powerful glasses. She watched awhile longer, then put the glasses down with a resigned sigh.

"Why'd you come?" she asked.

Springer shrugged. "It's a nice day. And I like you."

Her eyes darkened and her expression grew soft and vulnerable. "I appreciate the way you talk with me and listen. A lot of people think I'm crazy doing this. It's very lonely."

Springer smiled.

"You're lonely too, Alan."

"Sometimes."

"Why?"

He started to put her off with a joke, but suddenly the memory of Angela assailed him and he heard himself describing how she had filled a bigger gap in his life than he had ever before admitted. "She was young and loved medicine. Bright. I liked being her mentor, I suppose. She was my protégé. More than my poor intern, who should be, but I hardly ever see him. He's nights, I'm days." He laughed. "She was a lot prettier." His laughter died as he told Ellen how their friendship had started, grown, changed. Ellen listened more attentively than was her custom. It was rare, he had noticed, that she concentrated long on any topic that did not have to do with her obsession.

"So you're still lonely," she said when he was done. "Or lonely again."

"Sometimes."

She rolled onto her stomach, picked up the glasses, and sighted in on Revelations.

"What are you going to do about it? Another nurse?"

"I don't have a plan, if that's what you mean."

"I think you're looking."

"It shows?"

"Only to someone who's used to seeing it."

"And you are?"

"I've been what a lot of men thought they were looking for." The absence of emotion in her voice made the statement sound like an invitation. Her smile, if she was smiling, was hidden by her hair.

"Speaking from personal observation," Springer said lightly, "I must say I can understand their desire."

He leaned over, swept her hair aside, and kissed the corner of her mouth. Slowly, lowering the binoculars, she turned her face until their lips joined in a long, trembling kiss.

Springer lay on his back, watching the cloudless sky through the lacework of the leaves. His thoughts were blurred behind a soft screen of bird calls and insect noises. His body remembered. It pulsed and quivered, playing the physical memories.

Something tugged at the screen.

Ellen stirred next to him and he remembered the way he had been in her control. She had taken pleasure and given pleasure. He had never experienced his body so cherished nor his soul so empty.

The screen tore.

Springer bolted upright at the loud sound of nearby voices, frightened, thinking that the Revelationists had wandered beyond their property, then angry that they could make him afraid. Ellen scanned the glade with wide fearful eyes. They were alone, but the voices were getting louder.

"Down in the meadow," said Springer. They crept forward and peered over the rim of the ridge.

Two couples were spreading picnic blankets on the grass ten feet below and twenty yards away. Springer saw the trail they had trampled through the high grass as they had walked from the west along the Revelationists' fence. "Summer people," he said. "There are some homes on Rock Road about a mile that way."

Ellen nodded, her hair brushing the moss on which they lay naked. "I walked up there last week."

The picnickers stripped down to bathing suits. One of them played softly on a guitar while the others laid out food and wine, working with the easy comfort of close friends. Springer and Ellen watched for several minutes from their high vantage point until they were certain that the picnickers were not going wandering. Then they crept back to their own blanket.

The guitar music and the distant laughing voices were a pleasant addition to the summer sounds of birds and insects and the rustle of the wind in the trees. Springer's spirits rose. Ellen came to him again, insistent on satisfying him first.

"You'll spoil me," he protested.

"You think too much," she said.

He thought she was beautiful. Even as they drifted into another sleep, visions of her beauty burst before his closed eyes and he had to open them to confirm what he thought he remembered.

The sun was lower when he awakened again, his head on Ellen's shoulder. He blinked, wondering what had coaxed him out of sleep. The guitar had stopped. And the voices were different, sounds instead of words. He heard a moan. Ellen's eyes opened. "What is it?"

"I don't know," said Springer. "Come on." They crawled to the edge of the glade and looked down at the meadow.

"Now that's what I call a picnic," said Springer.

Amid empty wine bottles and the remains of lunch, the summer people had wrapped themselves into an undulating, writhing heap of naked bodies. One of the men sat up, freed an arm long enough to take a deep drag on a smoldering pipe, and resubmerged himself in the orgy. The sweet smell of marijuana drifted up to the glade.

Springer watched critically, sliding his fingers down Ellen's back. "Amateurs."

"Ummm," Ellen murmured. Then: "*Look!*"

Startled by the sudden change in her voice, Springer looked where she pointed. "Oh, my God." He flattened himself against the moss and pulled her down next to him. She was trembling.

The Revelationists were climbing their fence.

Thirty or forty strong, they set out across the meadow in a wide, ragged line. They stalked like African hunters, crouched low and moving so quietly that the picnickers didn't hear them even after they were surrounded.

"Oh, God," whispered Ellen. "What are they going to do?"

The Revelationists' faces were fathomless masks. They moved closer and closer and suddenly the people on the blankets realized they were not alone. They gaped in frightened disbelief at the blank-faced people who crowded around them. Slowly they disengaged, the women reaching tentatively for their clothing, the men drawing into defensive crouches.

One of the Revelationists, a stern, buxom woman with a harsh voice cried, "Fear God, and give glory to Him; for the hour of his judgment is come."

Several others, equally harsh-voiced, chorused with her. "Babylon is fallen because she made all nations drink of the wine of the wrath of her fornication. You shall hate the whore and shall eat her flesh and burn her with fire."

One of the men sprang to his feet. He was tall, with a swimmer's wide shoulders. His face was red with anger. *"Get the fuck out of here!"*

The Revelationists regarded him silently.

His entire body flushed red. He clenched his fists. "Fuck off, you freaks. Leave us alone."

He charged the circle and straight-armed one of the men. The circle bulged but held. The naked man threw a punch, but the Revelationist at whom he'd aimed it stepped aside and the blow went wild. Enraged, he plowed into the circle, flailing madly with both fists.

The women on the blanket screamed and the other man ran after his friend and tried to stop him. The circle blocked him and closed in on the attacker. Baiting him, drawing close behind and falling back in front, the Revelationists performed an agile self-defense, a swaying, dancing motion that kept them beyond the reach of his furious blows. He swung more wildly as his frustration grew, and now that he was tiring, the Revelationists moved in, goading him beyond endurance until, exhausted, he sank to his knees, his sobbing gasps audible to Springer and Ellen on the glade.

The Revelationists closed their circle and waited. One of the women on the blanket brought the naked man pants and shoes. He argued, shaking his sweat-drenched head, but she prevailed and he put them on. The Revelationists watched silently as the couples rolled up their blankets, filled their baskets, and started to walk away. Only then did the circle open, just wide enough to let them pass.

20

People were snickering the next day about the summer people's picnic. Two teen-age boys had spied on the love-making and its untimely interruption by the Revelationists. Springer spent a ticklish afternoon until the absence of knowing looks in his direction convinced him that he and Ellen had gone unobserved. Because it involved group sex and city people the incident was considered amusing and it diverted attention from the disruption of the church service.

Some people, Springer included, compared the incidents and found them disturbing for the same reasons—the frightening tendencies of the Revelationists to act as one, to do whatever they pleased, to be so determined and purpose-ful. What next would they do in concert? What limits did they impose upon themselves? Were they getting bolder?

Springer was beginning to wonder if some sort of action should be taken against the sect. He had no clear idea what action or even what its purposes should be, merely a vague feeling that a defense should be considered. Thus he was in a receptive mood when Frank Bissel telephoned after din-ner that night and asked him to come to Ellen's motel room.

Bissel greeted him briskly. He was dressed entirely in black from his close-fitting pullover to his ankle-high boots. Ellen sat on the bed. She smiled at Springer and patted the mattress for him to sit with her.

A lineman's utility belt was spread out on the bed. Hooked to it were a coiled nylon line, wire cutters, three sets of handcuffs, a black plastic flashlight, a plastic quart bottle filled with clear liquid, and a short machete. Springer lifted the machete from its sheath; the metal was dull gray, the cutting edge razor-sharp.

"Brush," said Bissel. "Not people."

"I don't suppose this is just a rehearsal tonight," said Springer.

Bissel gave him a tight smile. He looked tense. "The boy is definitely there. I've got a way in and another out, thanks to you. And I rented a house down in Utica for the deprogramming."

"So tonight's the night," said Springer. He heard himself saying silly things, but he couldn't stop them. He found it hard to believe that this was happening, that this cheerful middle-aged man was about to penetrate Revelations, sliding down rope and wielding a machete, slapping handcuffs on a boy whose father thought he was brainwashed.

"Alan," said Ellen. "I need a big favor." She placed cool fingers on his wrist. It was electrifying; she sought him with burning eyes.

"What?" asked Springer.

"Money. Frank wants a thousand dollars to find Rose. I only have six hundred."

Bissel met Springer's eye. "The man whose kid I'm after is paying ten thousand. I'm nearly broke, Alan. Money goes through my lawyers like shit through a goose. The car has sixty-three thousand miles on it. I can't afford favors."

"One thousand sounds like a favor in itself," said Springer.

Bissel shrugged. "I'm sorry it can't be free."

"I don't have it with me."

Bissel said, "Don't worry about it. Ellen can give me a check if you'll lend her the money to cover it. If I don't find her sister I'll tear the check up and mail her the pieces."

"I'll pay you back," said Ellen.

"I'll cover it," said Springer, thinking he would have even if they had not made love and wondering if it was why they had.

She squeezed his wrist. "Thank you, Alan. Thank you so much." She wrote a check and Bissel slipped it into his shirt pocket.

"I got another favor," he said.

"What?"

He unfolded a terrain map on the floor. Springer was familiar with it; a copy hung on the wall of his den. Bissel had outlined the borders of Revelations with a felt-tip pen. His thick fingers jabbed at the sites he discussed. "I'm leaving my car here, below the culvert. And I want to get in here, by the access road."

Springer nodded. "And you want me to drive you around the mountain."

"It would save me walking from here to here."

Ellen said, "I offered to take him."

"I'd rather have you," said Bissel.

Ellen smiled strangely. "He doesn't trust me. He thinks I'm a little whacko."

"Flakey." Bissel grinned. "Not whacko— Seriously, Alan knows the territory."

Ellen shrugged.

"I don't care," said Springer. "I'll take you if you want."

"I want."

"Okay. But if we go up Spotting Mountain Road they might see your car when we pass the social center."

Bissel traced Spotting Mountain Road on the map. "I don't see any other way to get up there. The road dead-ends on this plateau."

Springer pointed at the church. "There's a dirt path wide enough for a car behind the cemetery. We can drive out of town, past the church, then double back onto Spotting Mountain Road."

"I don't see any road."

"It's not on the map. I'll ride with you. Ellen can take my car straight to the culvert and meet us there."

"If Mr. Bissel thinks I can be trusted," said Ellen.

Bissel leaned over and gently cupped her chin in his hand. "I know you're nervous, Ellen. I promise I'll get your little sister, straighten her out, and hand her back to you. I'll call you as soon as I get to Utica and you can come flying. Okay?"

Ellen's face turned childlike. She answered in a small voice. "Okay."

Springer and Bissel went first. The deprogrammer had parked behind the motel out of sight of the road. The car's interior lights did not go on when they opened the doors, but in the glow from the motel windows Springer saw manacle rings in the back seat. Bissel tossed his utility belt on the floor and started the engine. Springer buckled his seat belt.

Bissel drove at fifty until they reached town, then at a steady thirty on Main Street. When they passed the busy social center he jerked his head at the bright lights. "What are you people going to do about that?"

"Not much we can do," said Springer. "Anyhow, it seems that they're keeping hands off local kids."

"Really," said Bissel without conviction. They rounded the bend.

"The turn is right past the back of the church—see it?" Bissel kept on the main road.

"You missed it."

"I saw it. I want to take it from the other way." He floored the accelerator and the big car shot forward. He ran at seventy for two miles, braked on a straightaway, and turned back to town. Two hundred yards from the church Bissel shut off his lights and rolled slowly toward the dirt path. Murmuring quietly, the car drifted behind the cemetery. Springer saw a light in Reverend Davies' den. White fluorescent light; he was fashioning his model boat.

They reached Spotting Mountain Road and Bissel stopped with the emergency brake to avoid blinking the tail lights. The way was clear. He coaxed the car onto the macadam and drove a quarter mile before turning on his headlights. The garnets winked back, as if condoning their stealth.

"Did Ellen know you were coming today?" asked Springer.

"Yes."

"When did she know?"

"I telephoned last week. Why?"

"Just wondering." Bissel's eyes flashed toward him; Springer stared at the road. A mile or so farther on, Bissel braked to a stop and backed the car, lights out, onto the shoulder.

"Careful of the ditch," Springer warned.

"Don't worry about it." Bissel steered away from the road. The car lurched.

"Look out," said Springer, "you're heading right for it."

The car rumbled over some heavy boards and came to rest in the woods. Bissel chuckled in the dark. "Built a little bridge last night."

"How'd you find this hole?"

"Chopped it out of the brush. Let's go."

The stars cast dim light that barely showed the ground. Bissel took Springer's arm and led him out of the cut over the boards to the road. The bridge was little more than two sturdy timbers and Springer marveled how Bissel had managed to position the wheels so accurately. Had he been off a foot either way the car would be lying on its side in the ditch waiting for Grand's wrecker to pull it out.

From ten feet away the white car was all but invisible. they walked up the road to the culvert. "Wait here," said Bissel. "Watch for Ellen."

"Where are you going?"

"You were wrong about the culvert. They barbed-wired it." He drifted into the dark and a minute later Springer heard the sharp click of wire cutters. It was brighter on the road than it had been in the trees and he was growing accustomed to the night.

Car lights lanced into his eyes. Instinctively, Springer hid in the ditch until the car slowed and he could see Ellen at the wheel. Bissel was back from the culvert. Springer hadn't heard him coming.

"You drive."

Springer slipped behind the wheel. Ellen stayed close as Bissel came in the other side. She said nothing, but her face still wore the childlike expression that had formed at the motel.

"Lights," said Bissel.

Springer turned them off until he had reversed the car. Then he backtracked down the mountain and through the town until he reached the base of Rock Road, which skirted the south side of Spotting Mountain. There were clusters of vacation homes here, readily identified by the rich amber glow of their big windows, thinning out as the road began to climb the far side of the mountain. Finally, after a mile of uninterrupted darkness, Springer turned onto the lumber road, a dirt and gravel affair that snaked through deep woods.

"How close to the fence?" asked Bissel.

"Quarter mile."

"Stop. Lights off."

Springer stopped. Bissel unscrewed the dome light, dropped the bulb in Ellen's lap, and climbed out of the car. "Thanks. I'll call you as soon as I'm on the road."

Ellen reached through the open window and held his arm. "If she resists, it's not her fault. Tell her I sent you."

"I can handle her," said Bissel. He took two steps along

the road and vanished. Ellen stared after him into the black night. Springer waited several moments. He patted her knee soothingly.

She said, "I can't believe it's almost over."

Bissel ran like an animal, quick and sure, his feet sliding over the ground automatically testing the footing. Now that he had recovered from the glare of the car lights he could see clearly the twin walls of trees that blocked the sky on either side of the road.

The utility belt thumped softly on his thighs. He spotted the gleam of the Revelationists' fence when it was twenty feet ahead and bore left, sliding his hands along the links until he felt them bend downward.

The gully. He lowered himself to the bottom and sat on a flat rock, listening to his own breathing. When it slowed to the point where he could hear the night sounds again, he waited and listened. A wind was rising in the trees, making it difficult to hear. Five minutes passed. He was alone. He cut a line of links from the bottom up and to the side, bent open the cut, slipped through the fence, and pulled it closed behind him. On his belly, he slithered along the gully until he sensed he had come to the edge of the drop. Again he listened, straining his ears, peering into the yawning darkness. Alone.

He released the tie on his coil of rope, secured it to a tree on the edge of the gully, and dropped it over the edge. It fell hissing against the rocks. Aiming his flashlight down after the rope, he blinked it on for an instant. Before it blinded him he saw the bottom. The line reached. He waited several minutes until he could see again then climbed down the rope, pushing off the rocks with his feet. He ignored the ache in his arms when he reached the bottom and groped for several yards along the gully until he came to a clearing.

The open field was bright in the starlight. Bissel hugged its border, following the downward slant of the land. He passed from one field to another and then he saw the blue lights of the building several more fields below.

He walked toward it, checking frequently to be sure he wasn't silhouetted against a break in the high land behind him. He crossed two more fields, paused to get his bearings, and entered a small wood several hundred yards above the building. He unscrewed the cap from the plastic jar and spilled its contents in a wide circle among the leaves. He moved upwind of the circle, lighted a match, threw it, and ran.

"Stay with me?" Ellen asked when they got to the motel. Springer's dashboard clock read ten-thirty. "Sure. I'll just call the hospital."

He parked in the back and they went to her room. Ellen closed the door and leaned against it. "I'm glad I'm leaving. I don't think I could stand one of these small-town affairs."

"Big-city affairs are better?"

"Wives live in the suburbs," said Ellen. "There's the phone." She knelt beside the bed and pulled out two matching suitcases while Springer called the hospital. When he put down the telephone she said, "I'm sorry. I didn't mean that. I'm so nervous."

Springer took her hands in his. "I'm sorry you're leaving."

"Thank you, Alan. You've been a nice friend. I don't know how I would have made it without you to talk to."

"Don't be silly."

"I mean it. I was falling apart when I came here." She shuddered. "God, I'm glad it's over." She let Springer draw her into his arms. He caressed her, but when he kissed her neck she pulled away. "Gotta pack."

She opened the dresser and the closet and began transferring her clothes to the suitcases, folding each item with practiced ease. Springer looked around the tiny room. The dresser, the single armchair, and the bed practically filled it.

"You wouldn't have anything to drink, would you?" he asked.

"No, I'm sorry. Maybe the night clerk could get it for you."

"Doesn't matter."

She straightened up from the suitcases, her face anxious. "I hope Frank is okay."

"It's not the first time he's done this," Springer said lightly. "He acted as if he was born to slither on his belly with a knife in his teeth."

"He told me he was in an intelligence unit in the Korean War."

"It wouldn't surprise me," said Springer. He sat down in the armchair and watched her pack. He was depressed that she was leaving and he didn't know why. All they had ever talked about was her sister Rose and the Revelationists and last Sunday on the mountain was the only time they had made love. Perhaps it was that Ellen shared his fear of the Revelationists. With her gone he would stand alone.

"What are you going to do?" he asked.

Ellen looked across the bed. "Do?"

"You know. When it's over, what are your plans?"

"Oh. Well, I'll take Rose home and take care of her until she's all right."

"Have you considered what you'll do if the deprogramming doesn't work?"

Ellen's face hardened. "It will work. If Frank Bissel can't do it I'll do it myself. She'll be all right."

"I'm sure Frank can do it."

"Yes," she snapped, her eyes burning fiercely.

"What will you do after Rose is cured?"

"I don't know. I guess I'll go back to work. Maybe she'll stay with me. We could be roommates. I think she'd like that."

"I'm sure," said Springer.

Ellen fished a piece of paper from her handbag. "Alan, here's a deposit slip for my checking account. Could you possibly mail the four hundred dollars tomorrow? I'll send it back as soon as I can. To the hospital?"

"To the hospital is fine. I'll mail a bank check so it clears immediately."

"Thank you." She drummed her long fingers on the almost full suitcases and looked around the room. "Medicine cabinet."

"I'll help," said Springer.

They reached for her shower cap at the same time. Springer laughed. "We think alike. I'll hold it, you fill."

Ellen smiled back. "Two very efficient people. A rare breed." Springer carried the shower cap to the bed and held it while she unloaded the tubes and bottles. "When you send me the money—and there is absolutely no rush—put in your address and telephone number. I go down to New York sometimes."

"Alone?"

"I can."

Ellen smiled. "That would be nice."

"I'll phone ahead in case you're involved. Give you a chance to kick him out."

"I don't plan to be involved."

"Things happen."

"I told you, they've happened too much for me. I'm being very careful these days." She kept her eyes down and busied herself unloading the toiletries.

"What are you talking about?"

"Will you stop asking me questions," she said coldly.

"One more. How did I happen to slip through the filter?"

"You really want to know?"

Springer recoiled from her empty stare. "No, thank you. I can guess." He started to turn away, but he saw puzzlement fill her eyes, then recognition, and, with it, shock.

"No," she cried, grasping his arm. "No. Not the money."

"You said it, not me."

She shook her head. "No, Alan. I'm sorry. I knew I was leaving eventually and I wouldn't have to get involved. I can't handle that. I can't have a man needing me."

Springer nodded, unsure what he believed. "Didn't you think I might need you after you left, *if* I needed you."

"That wouldn't be my problem when I left. I'm sorry, Alan, but that's the way I am."

Springer smiled. "I've seen worse." He cocked his head. "Did you hear something?"

Ellen listened. "Wind. It's blowing harder. . . . Will you visit us in New York?"

"Us?"

"Rose and me."

"Sounds great. . . . I want you to know something. You didn't—"

Three loud knocks drummed urgently at the door.

Springer and Ellen looked at each other. *Who?* he mouthed.

She whispered, "Frank?"

Springer shook his head. "See who it is. I'll wait in the bathroom."

They heard a car grate across the gravel parking lot.

Springer stepped into the bathroom, leaving the door open a crack. "Who is it?" Ellen called.

No one answered.

She looked back at Springer, shrugged, and turned the knob. The catch let go with a sharp click and the door blew open. Frank Bissel stood stiffly in the doorway, his back to the room as if he were watching the parking lot while he waited. He was wearing his tweed sport jacket and twill pants. Ellen stepped aside. "Frank?"

Bissel swayed, then, gathering speed like a whipsawed oak, he toppled backwards into the room and crashed full length on the floor. His head lolled at an impossible angle to his still body; his wide, staring eyes saw nothing.

Ellen's check fluttered from his breast pocket like a dead leaf.

21

Ellen shut the door. She had to push one of Bissel's feet aside to do it. She moved mechanically, her eyes wide, her mouth rigid. Springer knelt next to the body. No breath. No heartbeat. Bissel was dead.

Ellen keened into her hands. She had cupped them over her mouth; they muffled the sound, but the horror seemed to pour from her eyes. Springer pressed her to his body. A moment later she pulled away. Her voice was almost normal.

"Listen. Go to the hospital."

Springer's mind was spinning. "Why?"

"I'll call there and say he's hurt. Then I'll call the police. You come back with your ambulance as if you were answering a call."

"Why?" Questions were roaring through him now. What happened to Bissel's clothes? The way Bissel had fallen told him he was dead before he hit the floor. That the Revelationists had killed him was beyond doubt. Why had they dumped him this grisly way? He shook his head, trying to clear it of assumptions. He didn't know what had happened and he didn't know what Ellen was talking about.

"Why?" he mumbled again.

"You can't have been here, Alan. It will cause all kinds of trouble for you. Go. I'll tell them I drove him to the mountain." She pushed him toward the door. "Hurry. I'll call in five minutes. Make sure no one is watching."

Springer opened the door, looked out. Bissel's Eldorado was parked next to Ellen's car; he hadn't seen it when Bissel had tumbled through the door. Everything had happened so fast. He saw no one in the lot so he walked quickly around the end of the long, low building and got into his car.

On the way to the hospital his head began to clear. He

was grateful to Ellen. Her quick thinking had saved him a lot of problems, provided she didn't fall apart. He doubted she would; she had recovered too quickly for that.

The intern was surprised to see him. Springer had hired him so he wouldn't have to work at night and he rarely wasted the privacy he had gained.

"It's okay, Mel," he said as the young man dropped his magazine and scrambled to his feet. "Just thought I'd check out our trucker." The driver had jackknifed his rig on the interstate that afternoon and had a mild concussion.

"He's sleeping," said Mel.

"Didn't he wake up at all?"

"He ate dinner at seven and watched some TV."

"Thanks. I'll have a look."

The telephone rang as he turned toward the ward. Mel answered, listened. Springer stopped, waited curiously.

"What's up?" he asked as the intern hung up.

"Somebody's been hurt at the motel. Woman sounded hysterical."

"Stay comfortable," said Springer. "I'll go."

Five minutes later he was sitting next to Reggie as the ambulance careened down Main Street, lights flashing, siren off.

Ellen was standing in the open doorway of her room. Her small body looked fragile in the harsh headlights. "That's the drugstore chick," Reggie said as he braked to a stop. Springer leaped out with his bag and Reggie backed the ambulance to the door.

"Did you call the police?" Springer whispered as he knelt next to the body.

"Yes. Are you all right?"

"As good as can be expected. How about you?"

"I'm okay," she said brittlely. "Remember, we know each other and you met Frank a couple of weeks ago."

Springer looked up as Reggie crouched next to him. "Oxygen?" the driver asked. Then he saw Bissel's broken neck. "Oh, guess not."

"Guess not," Springer agreed. He looked up at Ellen, who had folded her arms into a tight embrace. "What happened?"

They were spared further charade by the noisy arrival of the state police, followed hard on by Charlie Daniels, who had no jurisdiction this far from town but felt obliged to put in a protocol appearance. Within minutes, the parking lot took on the eerie look and din of police action—the ceaseless sweep of red and white lights, the crackling of radios like snapping branches, the curious motel guests clustering in their doorways in their robes and pajamas.

Springer watched Bissel's face flash white in the police photographer's camera lights. He felt a sudden sharp grief. The deprogrammer's massive body seemed to be shrinking in death. He wanted him covered and taken away before he got any smaller. The photographer finished taking pictures. A lab man outlined the body's position with thick white chalk. A plainclothes homicide detective squatted close for a final look, then helped the lab man spread a blanket. He covered the staring eyes, stood, and lighted a cigarette.

Springer exchanged small talk with the state troopers as he would at any accident scene. They shared an easy camaraderie based on years of serving life and death in the circling lights. But while he talked, he watched Captain McNelty questioning Ellen a few yards away. She looked shaky and he was relieved when the police captain nodded him over.

"Miss Barbar says she knows you."

"Right. How are you feeling, Ellen? Do you want a Valium?"

"I'm all right." A tiny vein pulsed in her temple.

McNelty was the youngest captain in the state, his uniform immaculate, his shoes polished. A Smokey Bear hat added several inches to his six-foot height. Puzzlement showed on his intelligent face.

"I gather you also knew Bissel."

Springer looked at the body.

"We met. Had a few at Henry's. Hell of a nice guy."

"You know what he was doing here?"

"I presume he was trying to break into Revelations to rescue somebody."

"Is that what you talked about?" asked McNelty.

"Yeah."

"Why, Al?"

Springer shrugged. "I liked him. I agreed with what he was doing. I didn't expect him to get killed."

"What makes you think he was killed?"

"Ellen said he fell backwards through the door when she opened it. Nobody ever broke a neck like that falling like that. Besides, he was kind of cold when I got here. Dead for an hour or two at least, I'd guess."

"It's a cool night," said McNelty. "The M.E.'ll check it."

"Of course he was murdered," Ellen said harshly. "He had my check in his pocket. They're trying to frighten me away."

"We don't even know he was up there," said McNelty.

"I told you I drove him," said Ellen. "I dropped him on that old lumber road off Rock Road."

"That's where I suggested he enter," said Springer.

McNelty shook his head. "I don't see how you could get mixed up in this, Al."

"Well, I did, and I'd appreciate it if my name could be kept out of it as much as possible."

"I imagine you would," said the captain.

"What are you going to do about it?" Ellen broke in. "Bissel's dead and my sister is still there, I hope to God alive."

"Just relax," said McNelty. "First things first."

"He was wearing different clothes when he went up there," said Ellen.

"Yes, ma'am."

"And his car was parked on Spotting Mountain Road. Miles from where I dropped him."

"Yes, ma'am." McNelty guided Ellen into the back of the police car. Then he shut the door and took Springer aside. He spoke quietly. The red lights flashed in his eyes. "Listen to me, Al. I could get fired for talking like this, but I'm asking you, do you know any reason why I should believe her story?"

"Yes," said Springer.

"Goddamnit, I thought you were there."

"I'm not saying that," said Springer. "I'm saying you know me and I know she's telling the truth. She took him up there. He must have gone in and they caught him."

McNelty shook his head. "Unless my lab man finds something—and he hasn't so far—there's no sign of a struggle. No evidence of murder. Nothing. For all we could prove, he fell in the door when she opened it."

"Maybe you'll find where he went into Revelations."

"Maybe. And we'll dust his car and his clothes. And we'll see what happens at the post." He grinned. "Maybe we'll get lucky and find a slug in him."

Springer smiled bleakly. "If I have to say I was with her I will." The admission put him deeply in McNelty's debt. He would pay for it sometime, probably by patching up a prisoner who had "tripped."

"Save your heroics," said McNelty. "Unless you actually saw him climb the fence your testimony wouldn't be worth a hell of a lot."

"I did not actually see him enter Revelations."

"Then I don't think we have a case." The captain reached for his door handle.

"Do you want me to ride along?" asked Springer. Ellen looked small in the back seat of the highway cruiser.

"No," said McNelty. "Just do your death certificate and ship him to the morgue when my boys are through." He climbed into the car and it raced south on the highway toward Rock Road.

Someone had uncovered Bissel. Other official cars had arrived. Springer waited while a forensic man did his work and additional photographs were taken. Finally the technicians signaled they were through and Springer supervised the loading of the body into the ambulance. Reggie drove to the Warington morgue, his radio open for emergency calls from the hospital. Springer watched him go. He didn't like his ambulance operating as a morgue wagon, but double duty was normal in the sparsely populated area. Minutes later, McNelty returned.

The captain helped Ellen out of the car. She was trembling, on the brink of hysteria. Springer led her to her room. McNelty followed.

"They won't believe me," Ellen mumbled, digging her nails into Springer's arm.

"Just lie down," he said soothingly. "I'll get you something."

McNelty was waiting at the door. He signaled Springer with a jerk of his head. They conversed in low whispers. "Nothing," said McNelty. "We couldn't find anyplace he might have gone in. We'll check it out in daylight. Better give her something, she's raving about her sister."

"I'll take care of her." He had been wrong earlier about her calmness. Hysteria had hidden behind a veil of shock. Springer closed the door. He brought Ellen a Valium and a glass of water. She sat up jerkily, her eyes wild. "Rose. They won't help her. They said—"

"Shhh. Take this."

He put his arm around her shoulders and tried to slip the Valium between her lips. Ellen drew back and cried, "Don't you understand? She's up there. What are they doing to her?"

"Easy, Ellen."

"She's up there. What are they doing to her? We can't leave her there now." She swung her feet off the bed. "Come on, before it's too late."

Springer grabbed her arm. "No, Ellen. Swallow the pill. Take it."

She stared at the pill, which rested in his fingertips. "We have to save her." Her voice was shrill.

"Take the pill, Ellen."

She knocked it to the bed. As Springer tried to pick it out of the tufted spread, Ellen leaped up suddenly and ran from the room. Springer dashed out the door after her. The parking lot was quiet and empty, the police cars gone, the motel guests in their rooms. Ellen was racing toward her car.

"Wait!" yelled Springer. He ran after her, but by the time he reached the car she had locked herself inside. He pounded on the glass and shouted to her to open the window. In the shadowy light from a streetlamp, he saw her levering her body up from the seat, searching her tight dungaree pockets for her keys. He tugged on the door handle, pleading with her to open it.

Ellen found her keys, jammed them into the ignition, and started the engine with a roar. Springer jumped aside as the car ground furiously backward, flinging dirt and gravel.

"Wait," he yelled.

Ellen slammed the gears into forward and shot out of the lot onto the highway. She went several hundred yards before her lights came on, then she skidded around a turn and was gone.

Springer darted for his own car before he remembered he had come in the ambulance. Clawing a dime from his pocket, he went to the pay telephone and dialed Charlie Daniels.

"Hudson City Police."

"Charlie, Alan Springer. Ellen Barbar just ran out of the motel. She's hysterical. She's heading for Revelations."

"Driving?"

"Yes. Stop her."

"Right—son of a bitch, she just blew down Main like a bat out of hell. I'll get her." The telephone banged dead. Springer slammed down the pay phone and trotted toward town.

Ten minutes later, his heart pounding with exertion, he reached the hospital, retrieved his car, and drove up Spotting Mountain Road. At every bend he expected to find Daniels standing by the wreckage of Ellen's car, but he didn't see the policeman until he reached the front gates of Revelations.

Daniels was alone, inspecting the ground around the gate in the glare of his headlights. Springer was out of his car before it stopped rocking. A single blue light burned high in the building.

"Where is she?"

"I don't know," said Daniels.

"What do you mean you don't know?" snapped Springer.

Daniels' lean frame stiffened. "Take it easy, Doc. I *thought* I saw her turn onto Spotting Mountain Road. I *thought,* when I got up here, that I saw some dust in my lights. Now I'm not so sure. She could have turned off on one of the lumber roads farther down."

"What would she do that for? She doesn't know anybody out here."

Daniels glanced at the mountain, which was faintly darker than the sky. "Maybe she went farther up."

They got into the police car and drove past Revelations and up the gravel extension to the parking area beneath the final peak of Spotting Mountain. Daniels flashed his spotlight at the single car there. Two startled white faces popped into view. Daniels flicked on his dome lights to show they weren't bumper jumping and asked if they had seen another car. They had not.

As they drove back down to Springer's car, Daniels radioed the state police and told them that the woman who had found the dead man at the Pines Motel had left town suddenly.

"But she might be in there," said Springer.

"I didn't see her go in. You didn't see her go in. I'm not

even sure I saw her on this road. Don't worry, the troopers will find her."

"What makes you so sure of that?" asked Springer.

Daniels said, "Because the county medical examiner and the D.A. will be very unhappy if the lady who found the body isn't at the inquest."

22

"And *what* happened to this woman?" the Warington County medical examiner asked sarcastically.

Captain James McNelty glared from the witness box like an offended wolf. It was hot—the air conditioning in the County Office Building had broken down—and the medical examiner was posturing at his expense.

McNelty replied that the police had not yet located the witness. The medical examiner, a pathologist in his middle thirties who had held his post several years too long for the logical advancement of his career, postured some more, then led McNelty through testimony concerning Frank Bissel's whereabouts before his death.

The state police had searched the lumber road in the daylight. There was no evidence that Bissel had either cut the Revelationists' fence or used the rope Ellen Barbar said he had to climb down the gully. Her claims were further impugned by the absence of fingerprints, other than Bissel's own, on his Cadillac, his shoes and belt.

Springer testified as the attending physician after McNelty stepped down. He insisted that body temperature indicated that Bissel had died earlier and elsewhere. According to the autopsy, the medical examiner replied, that was debatable. He entered his post-mortem report in the record: Bissel's neck had been broken by a powerful lateral force; while the body bore no marks of a fall, neither was there physical evidence of a struggle. He concluded that Frank Bissel had died of a broken neck—possibly from a fall, possibly at the hands of unknown assailants—and recommended, with a malicious nod at McNelty, that the state police investigate all leads and bring any new evidence to the attention of the Warington district attorney.

Springer sat seething as the room emptied out, then trailed the Warington district attorney through the shiny halls of the County Office Building and cornered him in his office. The D.A. looked pointedly at his watch, remarked upon the stifling heat, and agreed to give Springer five minutes. They had locked horns years ago in the '72 campaign and each felt that sense of wary obligation shared by former opponents.

Springer said, "We know Frank Bissel was murdered. We know he was intending to rescue two people from Revelations. I think we can assume that it was the Revelationists who caught him and murdered him."

The D.A. was a bantam of a man. He raised a miniature pink hand admonishingly. "We *suppose* Frank Bissel may have been murdered. An unhappy, and now vanished, young woman with an ax to grind *said* Bissel was intending to rescue two people from Revelations—I know, you say it too.

"*No one* saw him enter the property. *No one* saw him trespassing on the property. Therefore, we can assume anything we want to, but we sure as hell can't *prove* that the Revelationists caught and murdered him, particularly now that our witness has split."

Springer made an exasperated gesture. "I told you that the last I saw of her she was heading up there. I think she's still there."

"And I told you," said the D.A., "that the Ohio State Police found her car in a motel parking lot four hundred miles from here. The transmission was shot and it looked like she'd abandoned it and hitched a ride with somebody."

"A setup," said Springer.

"What do you want me to do that I haven't done already?" asked the D.A.

"Search the grounds. The case is still open."

"We can't do that without a warrant, and the court, as you know, has turned down our request."

"The court," snapped Springer, "is Judge Lester Strunk, whose cousin Wilber represents the Revelationists."

Now the D.A. looked exasperated. "Come on, Springer. Wilber Strunk doesn't need any help from his cousin. He presented a perfectly reasonable argument why his clients shouldn't be bothered by the police. Unless we come up with better evidence linking your friend Bissel with the Revelationists' property, we can't get a warrant."

Springer growled his disgust and headed for the door.

The D.A. hopped up from his desk and blocked him. He kicked the door shut with a backward flick of his tiny foot and craned his neck to speak to the tall doctor.

"Springer, I'd *love* to prosecute. The Revvies are news. I'd have every TV station in the state up here. I could run for state senate. If I got a conviction I could run for Congress."

"Get a warrant from another judge," said Springer.

The district attorney lowered his voice. "I already tried. They blocked me in Albany. The Revvies have some good contacts there. . . . Surprised?"

Springer recomposed his face. "Not really. I just never considered it."

The D.A. reached for the door knob. "It's tough dealing with a group like them. If you don't do it hot pursuit, you can't just bust into an estate the way you'd kick down a shack door, or even a house like yours or mine. All that land and fencing puts them in another category. And now it's too late to search. They've had plenty of time to clean up." He closed the door, which he had opened slightly. "Just between you and me, McNelty blew it. He should have busted in there that night. Legally he did the careful thing. Too bad. No case."

"What about the woman?"

The D.A. opened the door again. "What about her?"

"She's a prisoner, or dead."

"Springer, you got a little too involved with all this. Back off and take a look at what you're saying. No one even saw her near the estate. Talk to your man Daniels. He'll explain it to you." The D.A. walked quickly down the hall. Springer listened to his heels click on the shiny tiles.

The clinic was jammed that afternoon because he had gotten back late from Warington, so Springer said that they would have to wait when the nurse brought the message that Jackie and Roscoe Stratton wanted to talk to him. Each time he walked a patient to the waiting-room door, he saw them sitting there, squirming anxiously, faces forlorn. Finally, at a quarter to six, the last patient had gone and Springer went out to the waiting room. He knew them, as he did most of the children in town.

"You guys sick?"

"No," said Jackie, the younger one. He nudged his brother.

"Can we talk to you, Dr. Springer?" asked Roscoe.

"Sure. What about?"

Roscoe glanced at the receptionist, who was tidying her desk, preparing to go home. "It's kinda private. . . ."

Springer grinned at the woman. "Don't worry. This is a doctor's office. Nobody's going to tell your father you're here. Come on." He led them into his office, shut the door, and pointed at the couch. "Sit. What's up?"

Stripping off his coat while they hemmed and hawed, he thought that they were immature for their ages, which wasn't surprising considering the tight rein Ed Stratton kept on them. What he couldn't imagine was how such a pair of innocents could have a problem they'd need him for. They squirmed and murmured.

"Let's hear it, guys. I'm getting hungry."

"It's about Danny Moser," said Roscoe.

"Oh?" asked Springer with quickened interest. "Is he back?"

The boy shook his head. Springer approached him, concerned by the tears in his eyes.

"That happened?"

"We think the Revvies got him."

"They were afraid to say anything because they're not allowed to play with Danny, but when they heard about Bissel and Ellen Barbar they got really scared and came to me. They knew I looked out for the kid. They chickened out—being a little brighter than that idiot and having Ed to worry about—but the last they saw of him Danny was heading up the road to sneak into Revelations. Nobody's seen him since."

Charlie Daniels reached across his desk and handed Springer a sheet of teletype paper.

"This came in on the ticker this morning. I haven't even told his mother, yet. There's an all points out on him from New York City."

Springer scanned the cryptic sheet.

"I phoned right away. They found his knapsack at a drug bust. Some kids got away. He was one of them."

"They sure?"

"His food-stamp card was in it. Along with a bottle of Quaaludes and some other crap."

"Oh, Christ." Springer shuddered at a mental image of Danny Moser wandering the New York streets like a stray dog.

"Lost cause, Al."

He was surprised, the next day, to see Frank Bissel's white Cadillac parked in front of Rigby's drugstore and recalled with sadness the way the deprogrammer had pushed the big car lovingly to its limits. It was washed and polished and gleamed like a ghostly chariot. Curious, Springer went into the drugstore, fancying he would find Bissel cheerily relating recent adventures in the nether regions.

The soda-fountain counter was full and Margy Rigby, looking dismayed that she'd been chosen to fill in for Ellen Barbar, was scrambling to keep up with the lunch rush. When she saw Springer, she pointed him out to a young man who spun around on his stool, stood up, and thrust out his hand.

"I'm Rod Dwyer, Dr. Springer. Frank was a friend."

Dwyer had short, curly black hair and a weak, gentle face.

Springer took his hand. "I think I saw you at the inquest."

"Yes, sir. I didn't want to bother you then, but I want to thank you for your kindness."

"I didn't do anything," said Springer.

"The troopers told me you tried to get an investigation."

"You're taking his car?" asked Springer.

Dwyer smiled sadly. "Frank's lawyers called me. He willed me the car. It was the only thing he owned. I flew out to . . . to make the arrangements." Dwyer's eyes darkened. "I sent him to Chicago. He had a sister there."

Springer studied the young man. "You're a law student at Stanford, aren't you?"

"Yes. Frank deprogrammed me."

Springer nodded. "He was very proud of you. He said you were his best case and made it all worthwhile."

"I don't suppose that included dying," said Dwyer.

"He didn't sound like he intended to," replied Springer.

"He gave me back my life." Tears rose in Dwyer's eyes. "He wasn't the kind of person you can imagine dead."

"I know," said Springer. "When I saw the car I half expected to find him here."

Dwyer blinked at his tears. "I'm scared shitless. If a guy like him can die we can all die."

Springer watched the tears, listened to the clatter of plates and cutlery, the cars swishing past the open door on Main Street, the sizzle of meat on the grill, and recalled his feelings when he was an intern, Dwyer's age, and had lost his first patient. The man had died suddenly, in the midst of what had seemed a perfect recovery from surgery.

Death had seemed ferocious then.

"What did he get for all his work?" Dwyer said bitterly.

Springer measured him. "I suppose that depends upon what you do with your life."

Dwyer shivered. "You know something crazy? I can feel them up there."

"The Revelationists?"

"There's a fascination. I feel like a junkie who knows where to get a hit. I've been free for a year, and still I'm tempted to drive up there and have a look."

"Why?"

Dwyer looked out the plate-glass window. Several Revelationists were walking briskly by; a blue pickup truck zipped past, the tailgate down. Three people sat on the bed, their legs dangling over the edge. The truck swerved to avoid a car. The Revelationists grabbed each other and held on, laughing.

"Why?" Springer repeated harshly.

Dwyer returned his gaze to the busy drugstore. "Purpose," he said. "They have purpose."

Springer was angry. "Get your own purpose, sonny."

Dwyer laughed unexpectedly. "That's what Frank used to say."

"Frank was right. You don't miss purpose, you miss them *giving* you purpose. You miss them doing everything for you. You miss the simplicity of doing what you were told."

"It was more than that," said Dwyer. "It was like having a family. You knew where you were at."

"Goddamnit," snapped Springer. "You sound like you wish you were still there."

"I do," said Dwyer. He blinked rapidly, as if surprised by the conviction in his voice, and quickly added, "Sometimes. When I'm lonely, or frightened, or hurt. I know, I know, you don't have to say it. I know it's crazy, but the pull is there. I feel it now. I'm lonely and frightened. I've lost a friend. I feel as empty as when I first met the Revvies."

Springer restrained his retort. Dwyer's mouth was weakening and his eyes kept darting toward the window. "What did they do for you, Rod?" he asked gently.

"They made it all go away. All the bad stuff."

"How? How do they do that?"

"Technically? They overload your mind with so much information about Michael and Christ and God and sin and their mission to save the world that you don't have the room for your own problems. They don't let you sleep. You don't have the energy to do anything but what they tell you to do. They wear you down."

"How can you possibly consider going through that again?"

"That's technically," said Dwyer. "That's an explanation of how it happens. Actually, what happens is that you find meaning in your life. You see your own problems for the selfish, empty things they are. To replace them, you find something to believe in—God. And you find something to do—serve Michael. It's not a bad life."

"It's not any life at all." said Springer.

"Sure," said Dwyer. "That's easy for you to say. You're not"—he groped for the word—"not vulnerable. I am."

"You *were* vulnerable."

"*Am*," said Dwyer. "Frank notwithstanding." His mouth was working again. "I don't know what will happen to me with Frank gone. He told me he'd shoot me if I ever went back and I believed him."

Springer smiled grimly. "I'm glad we met, Rod. Let's go." He gripped the young man's arm, noting it was poorly developed, and turned him toward the door.

"Where are we going?" asked Dwyer. "I didn't pay for my coffee."

"On me," said Springer, marching him across the sidewalk. He stopped next to the white car, which shimmered in the noonday sun. "Get in."

"What?"

"Consider me your new Frank Bissel." He opened the door and guided Dwyer into the driver's seat. Springer scribbled his number on a piece of notepaper. "If you ever want to visit the Revelationists—anytime, anywhere—call me first."

Dwyer took the paper. "I doubt I—"

"As my first Frank Bissel act I have put you in his car and am sending you directly across the United States to Stanford University. Do not pass Go. Do not collect two hundred dollars. Do not talk to any Revelationists."

Dwyer stared at the telephone number and took a deep breath. "Thank you. I'm okay now. Honestly, that's the only time I've felt like that since he saved me."

"Start the engine."

Dwyer closed the door and started the engine. His window hissed down. He punched another button and Boz Scaggs roared to life on the tape deck. Dwyer lowered the volume and smiled approvingly at the car's sleek, long hood.

"Just like Frank. Flashy on the outside and full of piss and vinegar underneath."

"Maybe that's why he left it to you."

The window hissed up and the car pulled out into the busy summer traffic. Dwyer waved once, an insubstantial figure behind the tinted glass.

Springer felt suddenly depressed. Who would be there the next time the young man weakened?

He looked up and down Main Street, counting them.

A blue panel truck was parked in front of Lewis's. The pickup was returning from Moser's, the Revelationists perched on a stack of lumber. A blue car disgorged six occupants at the post office. Up toward the church, a blue hatchback pulled into the social center. The sidewalks were filled with them, many with their arms full of packages, conspicuous among the local shoppers.

He wondered how many people Bissel had rescued. Fifty? A hundred? What difference had he made? Each weekend saw the arrival of another three busloads of new converts.

The Revelationists were growing. They had the energy, the drive, and—he smiled wryly—the purpose. All they needed were people whose sole life-force was a primitive search for meaning—any meaning, no matter how simple—

the Rod Dwyers and Danny Mosers of the world. The lonely, the ignorant, the weak, the wanters.

Bob Kent hurried across Main Street, his elbows pumping. The long-acting Bicillin was working well. The mayor hadn't had tonsillitis since the spring and his energy was back up to the level of a hungry squirrel. He bustled up to Springer, his hairy forearms bristling from his short-sleeved shirt. His tie was loose.

"I've been watching you for five minutes. You're loitering."

"Just waiting for someone to invite me into his air-conditioned real estate office for a drink."

"Did you sell the hospital?"

"Lunch hour."

Kent looked at his watch. "Come on. We can have a short one."

They crossed Main Street through a gap in the traffic. "Wasn't that white Caddy the deprogrammer's?" asked Kent.

"I'm glad that's all over," said Kent. He ushered Springer into the storefront office. "Did you see my interview in *The New York Times*?"

"Since when do you read *The New York Times*?"

"Since they interviewed me on the Revelationists." Kent beamed. "I got in a hell of a pitch for summer property."

"Congratulations."

"What are you so miserable about?"

"I don't know. Bissel . . . everything."

Kent poured two shots of bourbon. "I don't have any ice."

"No sweat. Cheers." Springer tossed it back and held out his glass for more. Kent raised his eyebrows. "Lunch?"

"Weekend coming up."

"It's Wednesday."

Springer sipped the second shot. "What are we going to do about those sons of bitches?"

"Which sons of bitches?"

"The Revelationists."

"Do?" Kent asked cautiously. "What do you mean 'do'?"

"I think they're getting out of hand. That was a murder up there, Bob. And now that girl is missing. They killed that man up there as sure as I'm talking to you. And God knows what they did to Ellen Barbar."

"We don't know any of that's true," said Kent. "Remember, he was attacking them. That was between him and them and that woman, though I heard a little rumor about you that sounded mighty weird."

"Don't believe everything you hear."

"Good," said Kent. "I didn't like the sound of it one bit."

Springer waved him aside impatiently. "It's not just the murder and the girl. They're all over us, Bob. I counted twenty of them while I was standing there."

"Each with a dollar in his pocket," said Kent.

"And I don't like what's going on at the social center."

"What's going on?" Kent asked.

"They're running our children's lives. Samantha goes to Bible class three days a week, songfests twice, a dance every Saturday, and now she's begging us to let her hang out there a few more nights."

"Beats street corners," said Kent.

"Samantha was not hanging out on street corners, Uncle Bob."

"Not Samantha, but a lot of kids I could mention. I don't see what's so worrisome about her spending time there." Kent laughed. "You afraid she's going to convert?"

"Shouldn't I be?"

"Samantha? She's too much your daughter to fall for that Holy Roller nonsense."

"It's not just Samantha," Springer insisted.

Kent smiled easily. "If it's not Bissel and that woman and it's not Samantha, what is it?"

"We've been invaded."

"Bull," Kent said cheerfully. "Go operate on somebody, I have work to do." He bent over his desk, shuffled papers, and looked up with a wink. Springer had not moved. Kent looked down again, his brow knitting with concentration.

"Do you think I'm exaggerating?" asked Springer.

Kent eyed him calculatingly. "You want an argument or an opinion?"

"Opinion."

"You're exaggerating."

Springer stared miserably at his friend. Kent put his papers down and waited patiently. Springer said, "Maybe I'm just upset about Bissel. He was a good guy. You would have liked him."

"It's over, Alan."

"I suppose. Thanks for the drink."

Springer walked to the hospital. He quickened his pace when he reached the emergency entrance. A blue station wagon had backed up to the loading bay. Several grim-faced Revelationists were standing by the tailgate staring at the flapping doors to the emergency room.

Springer ran in a side entrance. One of his nurses spotted him with obvious relief. "It's one of the Revvies. They just brought him in."

"Call Charlie Daniels," he told the woman. "This one's going to stay here until I let him go."

"They won't take this one, Doctor."

Springer took note of her subdued voice and hurried down the hall. The attending nurse looked sick. Springer nudged her aside. A young boy, perhaps seventeen, lay on the stretcher, motionless. Someone had put a blanket under his head. It was soaked with blood.

Springer knelt for a closer look. The back of the boy's skull had been flattened like a stop-action photograph of a tennis ball leaving the racket.

"No pulse," said the nurse.

"Let's get him on the table for a better look."

"He couldn't survive such a massive fracture."

"I would like to confirm your diagnosis," Springer said icily. He stepped back and let the chastened nurses wheel the stretcher into the operating room, where he examined the boy and tried to get his heart going.

It was hopeless.

Charlie Daniels was waiting when Springer emerged, shaking his head.

"D.O.A. What happened?"

"They said he fell from a window. Three stories. He was painting flower boxes."

Springer tried to knead the tension out of his neck. "Thanks for coming over."

"They called me," said Daniels.

"Where are they?"

"They left. They knew he was dead."

"Oh. What do I do with him? What's his name?"

"I'll bring you a copy of my report." Daniels closed his notebook and tapped the imitation leather cover against his jaw. "Funny thing."

"What?"

"The kid was from Detroit. He's the one Bissel was looking for."

23

Ed Stratton, the Chevy dealer, was a man with a fine sense of the subtleties of power.

"Too many of them," he stated flatly. "They could turn us on our ear one of these days."

"How?" asked Springer.

"I don't know how. It doesn't matter how. They've got the numbers."

"Have you discussed this at the town board meetings?"

Stratton snorted. "I tried a few times. They won't listen. None of them get it. Lewis and Spencer and Moser rattle on about all the money the sons of bitches are spending. Joe Preston wouldn't leave a burning barn unless his bosses in Warington told him to and your buddy Bob Kent smiles and tells anybody who says anything how interesting it is."

"What do you think we should do?" asked Springer.

"I'd shut 'em down if I could," said Stratton. "But there's no way you could do that without the town board declaring war on the bastards. And that ain't gonna happen until the Revelationists start hanging old ladies from lampposts."

"I'm worried about my child," said Springer. He was feeling Stratton out, hoping the automobile dealer might be an ally, but Stratton wasn't interested in Springer's family problems, and when Springer related his conflicts between letting his child make up her own mind and wanting to protect her, Stratton made it clear that he had little use for permissive parents.

"My kids got strict orders. They're not allowed near that social center, no way, no how. If I catch one of them talking to a Revvie he'll get a hiding."

Springer dropped the subject. Stratton's approach was in violation of everything he had taught Samantha.

Stratton was a loner by nature and he refused to join Springer in organizing a resistance, but both he and Springer continued independently to air their misgivings until slowly the town stirred under their prodding. Within a day everyone had heard the story of the dead boy from Detroit. Now, a week later, many were arguing whether or not the religious sect was a danger to Hudson City.

The new mood emboldened Reverend Davies to query parishioners whose children no longer attended his church. From the pulpit, at the farewell in the foyer, and on the telephone, he asked if the children might not be better served by traditional Presbyterian worship than by the fanatical Revelationists. But despite their fears people thought Davies' attack too forward. Some took offense, others were embarrassed that they could not persuade their children to return. They had found themselves in an indefensible position when their children insisted that no teenager who attended the Bible and singing classes at the Revelations social center was starving for godly attention.

Church attendance declined. But criticism of the sect continued until the Revelationists responded in a way that quieted debate and warned their critics to consider the consequences.

On a hot, gray, sultry afternoon when heat lightning flickered over the mountain and noises seemed muted by the heat, a screaming siren pierced the stillness. Springer thought at first it was a fire alarm, but the sound was sharper than the volunteer's siren at the firehouse, a wail that reached a painful summit of loudness and pitch and stayed there.

Springer gritted his teeth and tried to concentrate on the state Medicaid forms that littered his desk. The noise was too much. Unable to stand it after five minutes, he stormed out of the hospital, angrily hunting its source.

A crowd of people had already come out of their homes and stores and were massed in front of the hospital. Those not holding their hands over their ears were pointing across the street at the social center. Springer edged through them until he could see what they were watching. The siren screamed relentlessly.

A dozen older Revelationists, sporting the large crosses of the leaders, were gathered around a gleaming, lemon-yellow fire truck parked in front of the social center. It was a pumper, its polished side studded with shiny chrome connections and white-faced dials. A piece of cardboard was taped over the driver's door. The Revelationists were smiling as if unaware of the ear-splitting racket.

Mayor Kent hurried up Main Street with Charlie Daniels at his side. Kent looked worried. Daniels had a hand on his belted night stick, the long one, which, Springer noticed, the lanky policeman had taken to carrying all the time now. The scream abated as they reached the pumper. The siren wound down to a low-throated growl, a rumble, a mutter, then silence.

The Revelationists waved to the townspeople.

"Come on over!" they shouted. "Take a look!"

The popping of soda-can tops accompanied the invitation and as the crowd converged on the truck the Revelationists pressed beaded cold containers into their hands. Springer accepted a Coke from a smiling woman with blank eyes. The scream of the siren still echoed in his head.

A Revelationist climbed the truck and perched atop the cab. Smiling beneficently, he stood with arrogant grace, waiting until everyone had a soda. Then he raised his arms for silence. The curious chattering subsided immediately. He threw back his golden head and spoke in a powerful voice, a remarkable baritone with just a hint of the preacher's quaver.

"Michael is grateful to our friends in Hudson City. He knows how long and hard you've tried to raise money for a new pumper for your volunteer firemen. He knows how difficult you've found it to be. Michael hopes you can use the money you have raised for another worthy purpose, because Michael bestows this gift to you with love and hope of continued friendship. May God protect you and keep you in the name of Jesus and Michael. Amen."

Two women ripped the cardboard from the pumper's door, revealing brilliant blue letters that read:

HUDSON CITY VOLUNTEER FIRE DEPARTMENT

Bob Kent started the applause. Others put their sodas on the ground and joined in, clapping and cheering. Whistles followed, and several shivery backwoods yells. They crowded around the new pumper, mingling with the Revelationists. Many of the men in the crowd were volunteers and they swarmed over the truck lavishing praise on its modern fittings. In the rural areas they served, the pumper, the machine used to suck water from storage ponds, was the most important apparatus in their station.

The Revelationist who had presented the gift leaned over the cab and handed a ring of keys to Bob Kent. Kent waved them over his head and bellowed for Archie Lewis, the chief of the volunteer fire company. The big plumber waded through the crowd, his face alight. Kent hopped up on the running board so they could all see him. He yelled for quiet.

"I want to thank Michael and his people for this great truck. I'm giving the keys to Archie Lewis, who knows what to do with them. Here you go, Archie"—he tossed the ring—"see you at the next fire."

Lewis caught the keys and climbed aboard. There was a hush as he engaged the starter. The big diesel cranked over and fired up with a precise authority that drew admiring grins from the other firemen. Archie let loose a blast on the air horn. The volunteers grabbed the chrome handholds and scrambled on. The big truck rumbled away from the curb and rolled down Main Street at a ceremonious pace.

Ed Stratton watched the truck leave. He was tight-lipped, his cigar dangling from his fingers. Springer approached.

"What did that thing cost?" asked the doctor.

"I don't know. Thirty grand, maybe."

"Didn't they buy through you?"

"No."

"I thought you always handled fire trucks for this area."

"Not this time."

Stratton crammed his cigar in his mouth, stalked to his car, and drove home. He wondered what price he was expected to pay to get the Revelationists to do business with him again. Would shutting up be enough? Or would they demand his kids at the social center?

Screw them.

The Strattons had been around a long time and they did not kowtow to outsiders. His grandfather hadn't kowtowed when the Vanderbilts tried to take his farm for a vacation site. The rich people had finally forced him off, but a year after he had moved to Hudson City his grandfather went back and dynamited the dam—reducing lake and farm to swamp. Nor, during the Depression, had his father kowtowed to the National Recovery Act dodos who'd tried to make him run his business their way. And Ed Stratton was sure as hell not going to kowtow to a gang of Jesus freaks.

They could take their message and shove it sideways. . . . Still, he was worried because he knew that the others, Pete and Spence and Joe, were probably shaking in their boots. Which was exactly what the Revelationists wanted.

Springer had just stalked back to his office when the Revelationists' message arrived for him in the form of a telephone call from the director of the Warington Hospital, a private institution which was his chief competitor for the traffic-accident trade. Could Springer spare any flu vaccine?

"How many?"

"Two hundred?" the Warington man asked hopefully.

"I suppose. How come so much?"

"The Revvies are coming down here for inoculation."

"All of them?"

"They said five hundred. Is that all of them?"

Five hundred? Springer was amazed. He had no idea there were so many of them. "Is Social Services picking up the tab?"

"Nope," the director said cheerfully. "They're paying privately. Pretty good deal for us. We're borrowing from every hospital in the area. How come they didn't come to you, Springer?"

Springer didn't bother to answer. "I think I can let you have two hundred," he said. "I'll send it over in the morning."

"That's all right. We've got a car out making pickups. Thank you, Doctor."

He hung up, deep in reflection.

There was a lot of profit in five hundred vaccinations. But it wasn't lost revenue that rankled. It was the warning: Shut up.

He'd be damned if he would.

"But the Doc was really good to me," mumbled Danny Moser.

"Are you sure?"

Danny's burning eyes closed. His head slumped to his chest.

"Wake him!"

The trainer squeezed the nerve between his neck and shoulder until the boy regained consciousness, cringing from the pain.

Danny focused blearily on the tattered walls.

The trainer's voice was the same strong drone, chipping away at Danny's spirit. It was a sound that dominated his life. He could hardly remember a time when he hadn't heard it. But the words were wrong. He knew they were wrong.

"The Doc didn't do anything to me," he protested.

"Are you sure?"

"He was really good to me."

The trainer leaned closer, forcing him to meet his awful gaze. Danny's skin prickled. The trainer's eyes seemed to bore into his head like a dentist's drill. His voice droned on as steadily as a stream at spring flood, his questions endless.

Danny's body sagged toward the sleep it screamed for. The trainer's grip shot pain through his arm to the tips of his fingers. He opened his eyes.

"Are you sure?" the trainer asked again.

Dwight Rigby was pleading.

"I don't want to happen to me what happened to you and Stratton, so would you please stop using my store as a soapbox? You're exaggerating what's going on anyway."

"They are dangerous," said Springer. "And they'll get more dangerous if you show them you're afraid."

Rigby thrust out his bony jaw. "You're making an ass of yourself, Al. People don't think the Revvies are as bad as all that."

"Bull," said Springer.

But Rigby was right. The fire truck was merely the opening salvo of a good-will blitz that pounded the townspeople into reassessing their feelings about the newcomers.

The Revelationists opened a large checking account at Joe Preston's bank. The first check they wrote on it was a five-hundred-dollar donation for the upcoming Hudson

City Fair. The fair benefited several local charities including the church's Christmas baskets program, intramural sports at the high school, and the fire department, which was discussing the need for a larger firehouse to garage the vehicles displaced by the new pumper.

Even as one delegation of Revelationists was ceremoniously delivering the contribution to Mayor Kent, another larger group was trekking toward the town dump with thousands of feet of stockade fence purchased at Moser's Lumberyard. They enclosed the unsightly dump in a single afternoon and were back at the social center in time for the regular teen-agers' dance.

Tom House chronicled the generosity in the *Sun* and "Religious Sect Plays Santa" finally got him his by-lined story in the New York *Daily News*. He fired off a follow-up piece about the Revelationists roofing an old widow's house and another when droves of them descended with rakes and hoes upon an injured farmer's neglected truck gardens.

The *News* slipped the roofing story into a desultory bulldog edition on a quiet Thursday night. The weeding piece earned House a telephone call from the regional editor, who said he was more interested in body counts than benevolence. Had anyone else connected with the Revvies died lately? No? Keep in touch.

Locally, however, the contributions had a calming effect, and as the hot summer lurched heavily toward a stifling August, Springer had to concede that Bob Kent and Dwight Rigby were right. Though Hudson City was increasingly entwined with the Revelationists, most of the townspeople did not seem to mind. They appreciated the new fire truck, the busy shops, the smiling faces at the social center, and the publicized donations, and if they felt misgivings about the deaths of the deprogrammer and the boy from Detroit or the mysterious disappearance of Ellen Barbar they did not voice them.

Three weeks after those incidents Springer was drawing cool responses and outright snubs. Finally, he stopped talking. They wouldn't listen until the Revelationists did something that frightened them again. That the sect would, he never doubted. But what happened next frightened him much more than anybody else.

* * *

He was alone in his office, working late. It was night. The lights were dim. A metallic jingling sound intruded upon the soft hum of the air conditioner and he looked up, blinking to refocus from the papers in the pool of light on his desk to the shadowy figure that was moving into the room. The jingling repeated. Springer stared.

"Danny?"

Danny Moser stepped into the light, his hands balled at his sides. He had changed. His hair was short and neatly combed, and his clothes, the overalls and work-shirt uniform of the Revelationists, fit perfectly. He stood erect, looking Springer in the eye as the doctor rose from his desk.

"Where have you been?"

"I'm living with 'em, Doc."

"Who?"

"The Revvies. They saved me."

"The Revelationists?"

Danny's eyes sparkled unnaturally. "Christ is coming," he said with fervor. His face was pale and he looked very tired.

"What do you mean? Is that where you've been all this time?"

"They saved me."

"You've been living there?"

"Sure."

"I've been worried about you. So's your mother. You should have told her where you were."

Danny's eyes went blank. "They told me I wasn't ready."

"Who told you?"

"My trainers."

"Do you mean that they wouldn't *let* you tell her?"

"God knew I wasn't ready."

Springer grasped the boy's thin shoulders. "Danny? Did they hold you up there? Did they keep you there against your will?"

"It was God's will."

"Who told you that?"

"God told me. I'm saved, Doc. I don't smoke and I don't drink and I don't take dope. I'm God's servant now." His voice assumed a repetitive, singsong tone like a chant. "We have so much work to do. Christ is coming. We must prepare the earth to turn to Him."

"Listen to me, Danny. They did something to you. You're not the same."

The boy looked at him with dead eyes. "So?"

Springer stared back, then snapped angrily, "Cut the crap! They held you prisoner. I'm calling Chief Daniels." He reached for the telephone. "Sit down!"

"I'm not a prisoner, Doc. I turned to God and He gave me a job."

"A job?" Springer released the telephone. "What are you talking about?"

"I have a job at the social center."

"Doing what?"

Danny's hands flew open. Chained to his quick fingers, jingling like wind chimes, were dozens of shiny metal crosses. He clapped his hands with the speed of a magician. The crosses disappeared. He smiled at his empty palms. "I'll be working with the children."

Springer couldn't get anyone to understand the seriousness of what had happened to Danny Moser.

"The kid was a pain in the ass," said Charlie Daniels. "Now he's fine."

"They did something to him."

"Goddamned right," said Daniels. "Somehow they turned a punk into a decent kid."

"It was illegal restraint," snapped Springer.

"Not if he doesn't make a charge," said Daniels.

"What about the charges in New York City?"

"N.Y.P.D. caught a kid who said he'd stolen Danny's bag. I don't know what's going on. All I know is he's no longer wanted by the police."

"Wait a minute," said Springer. "Doesn't it sound like the Revelationists manufactured a cover story? Duped the New York police into charging Danny when he wasn't even there?"

Daniels shrugged. "Maybe."

"They could have done the same with Ellen Barbar with that story about her car."

"Maybe, maybe not. You're talking to the wrong man, Al. I'm not a detective. I'm a town cop."

"We should search the place," said Springer.

"Forget it. If McNelty can't get a warrant, how the hell can I?"

"She could be a prisoner, like Danny was."

"No," Daniels said irritably. "I didn't see her go in there. Who is she? Some girl riding around between New York and California? The police said they got her car. All I know is Danny Moser came back and he's conducting himself like a decent citizen at the social center. How he got that way is his business. Whatever happened to him, I'd like to see it happen to a few more punks around town."

Everyone agreed, even those who had misgivings about the Revelationists: in the matter of Danny Moser the sect had done the town a favor. Gloomily, Springer perceived that he had repeated an old pattern in his relationship with Hudson City. Once again, as with the primary campaign, the low-income housing, and the drug facility, he had drifted too far from the mainstream of local attitudes to change people's minds.

The failure took its toll on his nerves and he began arguing with Margaret, who suffered in the heat, becoming moody and discontent. It was a simple matter of replying to her jibes, which he ordinarily ignored. Soon they were fighting mechanically, each chafing to say *no* to the other's *yes*.

The tension in their house drove Samantha to the Revelationists. And the more Springer protested it, having seen what they had done to Danny Moser, the more Margaret defended it. She, who had always cocooned Samantha, was practically pushing her into their arms. Springer couldn't understand it: was she simply being perverse? Or was she afraid of her own child?

He came home one evening to find his daughter perched defiantly on the kitchen table amidst the wreckage of her long, golden hair. She was still holding the black shears she had used to chop it short and ragged the way the Revelationist women wore theirs. The cut hair covered her overalls like strands of sunlight.

Margaret watched him apprehensively. Springer met her hurt gaze, then looked away. "Why'd you let her?" he snapped.

"*I* did it," said Samantha. "I didn't need Mom's permission."

"But why?" he pleaded. "It was so pretty."

"Why shouldn't she?" said Margaret. "Its her hair."

"I asked Samantha."

"It's my right, Daddy. Michael says women shouldn't tempt men with bodily excess."

"Bodily excess!" Springer exploded. "Jesus H. Christ, what the hell does a—"

"Don't bully her," Margaret shouted and another fight began. Samantha fled to her room. Minutes later the front door banged. Springer ran to the window. Samantha was running up Main toward the social center. Margaret had followed him into the living room. The fight was long and bitter and ended only when Springer raged out of the house and holed up in Henry's Bar, where he drank himself blind.

He awakened in his driveway with the rising sun glancing off his rearview mirror into his eyes and spent five of the most terrifying minutes of his life looking for dents in his car. Finding none, he resolved gratefully to walk next time he got so angry.

He was still nursing his hangover late that afternoon, stepping into the operating room for an occasional restorative whiff of pure oxygen, when Bob Kent bustled into the clinic wearing his best sport jacket and a bright tie.

"How you doing?" asked Springer. Things had become a little strained between them since Springer had been railing against the Revelationists and he was glad to see him.

"Fine, fine." Kent slapped his hands together and paced about in his usual energetic fashion. "Just had lunch up at Revelations."

"Up there?" asked Springer.

"Yeah. They gave a little lunch for the town board."

"What did they want?"

"It was first-class," said Kent. "Steaks on the back lawn."

"What did they want?" Springer repeated.

"No booze. You wouldn't happen . . ."

Springer pulled his bourbon bottle from his desk drawer and poured a single drink. Kent tossed it back. He sat down abruptly, his expression serious.

"What's up?" asked Springer.

"They want the kids to come up there for a weekend retreat."

24

"No way," said Springer.

"Well . . ."

Springer waited. Then: "Well, what?"

"They pitched it real cute."

"Did you *buy* it?" asked Springer, genuinely amazed.

"Well, I don't know if I did."

"You don't have any kids."

"I *know* that. . . . They made it very hard for the guys to say no. They talked about what they're spending up there for food and clothes and how happy they are with the way we've welcomed all six hundred of them."

"*Six* hundred?"

"That's what they said, and from what Sophie tells me about their mail they probably do have six hundred people."

Springer shook his head. "That's a lot of people." He recalled Stratton's comment on their ability to turn the town on its collective ear. "What did Ed Stratton say about the retreat?"

Kent looked uncomfortable. "Umm, Ed walked out."

Springer chuckled. "That's beautiful."

Kent scuffed the rug. "I don't know. It was embarrassing as hell for the rest of us. You know, we've having a nice lunch and they pop the question and Stratton says, 'Not my kids,' and walks out."

"What did Pete Lewis do?"

"He thought it was a great idea."

"He's letting Dicky go?"

"With his blessing."

"Oh, Christ, I'm going to have my hands full with Samantha."

"I didn't think you'd want her to."

"Absolutely not. What did you say about it?"

Kent made vague gestures with his hands. "You know, I . . . just listened and—"

"What are they doing, Bob?"

"Umm, they said it would be like going to the social center except the kids would sleep over. They'll have a picnic and all that and singing and praying . . . whatever. Didn't sound terrible."

"The 'whatever' sounds terrible. In other words they didn't tell you what they're going to do to the kids."

"They didn't give us a schedule, if that's what you mean."

"I can't believe you guys fell for it."

"It was kind of hard not to," Kent admitted. "They made it sound so . . . ordinary. Kids go on religious retreats in other churches. Why not this one? It's no big deal."

"If you're so relaxed how come you look so worried?"

"I'm not relaxed. I kinda wish we hadn't gotten snookered into it."

"Screw 'em. You didn't sign anything."

"The others agreed. Pete promised Dicky would be there. Preston's sending three of his."

"Even Laura? She's only fourteen."

"Even Laura," said Kent. "The Revvies run fifty thousand dollars a month through that checking account. And Spencer is sending his kids—all five of 'em. When the other kids in town hear that they'll be howling to go and there won't be any stopping them."

Springer said, "I don't want my child in their hands for a whole weekend. It's crazy, Bob. Two nights up there."

"One night. They're starting Saturday morning."

Springer looked out the window at his ambulance. "Thanks for the warning. Maybe we'll go down to Saratoga this weekend. Catch some dance. You and Mary want to come along?"

"Sounds great, but I got a feeling I'd better stick around just in case."

"Sure you're relaxed."

But as he walked home, pondering how to handle Samantha, Springer rejected the idea of leaving for the weekend. That was underhanded and unfair; Samantha would be excited about the retreat and he owed her an honest discussion.

He didn't have long to wait. The moment they sat down at dinner, Samantha said, "Guess what?"

"I heard," said Springer.

"What?" asked Margaret.

"We've having a special retreat at Revelations," said Samantha, watching Springer's expression.

"What kind of retreat, dear?" asked Margaret. She looked tired, wearied by the summer heat.

"It's overnight," said Springer. These were the first direct words he had spoken to his wife since their argument the night before.

Margaret seemed grateful that the fight was declared over, but then the meaning sunk in. "Up there?"

"Just one night, Mom. Can I go?"

"*May* I go."

"May I go?"

"I don't think it's a good idea," said Springer.

"Daddy? Why not?" Defiance rang in her voice and blazed in her eyes. She shook her cropped head impatiently. "Why not?" she repeated, harshly, her diffidence vanished.

Springer felt as if he were talking to a stranger, another man's child. "We don't think you should stay overnight."

"Do you feel that way too, Mother?"

Margaret hesitated.

Samantha attacked. "You haven't even talked about it," she said accusingly.

"We just—"

"We've talked a lot about the Revelationists," Springer interrupted. "We don't think you're old enough to stay there."

Samantha laughed, a brittle, menacing sound. "What do you think they're going to do to me?"

"I don't know," said Margaret.

"We'd be less worried if we knew," said Springer.

"I can't believe this," said Samantha. "They're my friends. I've spent the summer with them. Why can't I go to their place? You'd let me go to the Presbyterian retreat if I wanted."

"Do you?" asked Margaret. "I'll ask Reverend Davies—"

"No, Mom," she said exasperatedly. "I want to go to *my* retreat."

"Kitten," Springer said gently. "I think this is really one

time when your mother and I know what's best. I hate to
be authoritarian about it, but—"

"But you *are* being authoritarian about it," Samantha retorted. "You're treating me like a helpless child. I'm nearly
sixteen."

"Which is not old enough to protect yourself."

"From what?" she cried. "You're pushing your bigotry
about the Revvies on me, Daddy. I've experienced them. I
know what they're like."

"I've seen what they do," said Springer.

"And what do they do?" Samantha asked scornfully.

"I've spoken to people who've been through their training, their so-called retreats. They take people's minds, Samantha. People who aren't strong enough or old enough to
protect themselves."

"Come on, Daddy. You sound like Ellen Barbar."

"Who?" asked Margaret.

"Daddy's friend at the drugstore."

"Didn't I meet her at the Wrights' party?" asked Margaret. "I didn't know you were friends."

"We weren't," said Springer.

"She worked for Mr. Rigby," said Samantha. "I just
thought she was Daddy's friend too." She smiled strangely
at Springer. "She's gone away, hasn't she?"

"I guess so," said Springer. "Mrs. Rigby is working the
soda fountain."

Samantha said, "She was always saying mean things
about the Revvies."

"What about the way they invaded the church?" said
Springer. "You can't condone that kind of behavior."

Samantha hesitated.

"They were wrong to do that," said Margaret.

"So?" said Samantha. "Maybe they were. But they've
done a lot of good things, too."

"That's true," said Margaret.

Springer snapped, "And Mussolini made the trains run
on time."

"What?" asked Margaret.

"Daddy's being clever," said Samantha. "He means that
the Revvies are fascists."

"They *act* like fascists," said Springer.

"They don't," cried Samantha. "They love and they're
gentle. They don't hurt anybody who doesn't hurt them

and they don't drink and curse and smoke and lie and steal and they live quietly and grow their food and don't abuse the land."

"That's quite a mouthful."

"They love God, Daddy. They're in tune with the Universe."

"I could forgive them everything but their clichés."

"They're right, Daddy. They are the future."

"Oh, for Christ's sake."

"Don't curse them." She clenched her fists and glared across the table.

"Don't yell at me, young lady."

"Alan," Margaret cautioned.

"She's not going."

"Yes I am," Samantha shouted.

"Shhh," said Margaret. "Alan, you've always said that Samantha has to learn to think for herself. She has spent a lot of time with the Revelationists and she's had a chance to see them for what they are. So if she says she likes what she sees maybe we have to accept that."

"I don't believe you," said Springer. "You've always said I pushed her too much."

"Don't talk as if I'm not here," said Samantha. "Mom's right. I'm old enough to make my own decisions. I'm going."

"You're not," said Springer.

"Mom?" asked Samantha.

Margaret nodded wearily. "We'll talk later."

"We will not," said Springer. He was angered and confused by Margaret's attitude. "I'm not allowing her to go there and that's final."

"You can't stop me," said Samantha.

Margaret brushed Samantha's hair from her forehead. "Go upstairs, dear. Please. I'll take care of this."

Samantha fled with an angry backward glance at Springer. He said, "She's not going."

"Yes she is, Alan."

"How can you say that?"

"I'm afraid we'll lose her if we try to stop her."

"We have to say no," said Springer.

"I won't take that chance," said Margaret. "Sometimes I think she's all I have."

"Come on."

"I don't want to talk about it anymore. She's going and she'll have my blessing."

"She won't have mine."

He shoved through the screen door, headed for the car, thought better of it, and walked blindly down Main, with no real destination in mind. It was a sticky evening and by the time he reached the edge of town he was perspiring and some of his anger had dissipated. He turned back toward town, moving more slowly now, and wandered Hudson City's root-cracked sidewalks, through dark tree shadows and yellow pools of lamplight, past bright windows and open doors in homes he had known all his life, lulled by a familiar cacophony of nighttime noises, the sleepy calls of children, the murmur of front-porch conversation, the tinny blat of television, the pounding of a teen-ager's records.

He paused outside Sophie Wilkins' white shingled house and listened to guitar music, an adagio movement from a Baroque concerto. The lighted windows became fewer as people went to bed, and still he walked, thinking, wondering. When he passed Sophie's house again she was still playing her guitar. He listened, and when she paused he squeezed between her front hedges and her big, shiny custom Blazer truck, an oversized all-terrain station wagon, climbed her porch and knocked on her screen door.

Sophie appeared in Bermuda shorts and a print blouse, holding her guitar by the neck and squinting into the dark. "Who's that? Alan? What are you doing there? Come on in."

"I know it's late. . . ."

"Come in, come in." She opened the door and led him into her comfortable, old-fashioned parlor, a room full of overstuffed furniture covered with lace doilies, dominated by a gleaming mahogany Steinway baby grand.

"I was just going to open a beer. Want one?"

"Great."

She went to the kitchen and returned with two cans, opened them, and pressed one into Springer's hand. He drank thirstily.

"What were you playing?" he asked. "Bach?"

"Vivaldi. 'Concerto for Two Guitars and String Orchestra.'"

"I always get them confused."

Sophie touched a strand of her gray hair. "I remember a church organist once told me how to tell them apart. Bach is for the body. Order. Vivaldi for the soul. Beauty."

"How about Corelli?"

Sophie smiled. "Corelli is tears. Angel music. Too lovely for us to bear."

She sat next to her guitar on her couch, put her hands on her plump knees, and regarded him directly. "What's wrong?"

Springer told her about the weekend retreat.

When he was finished, she said, "You're damned if you do and damned if you don't."

"I'm scared, Sophie. She's only fifteen."

"I never had my own kids, as you know," said Sophie. "But I was in on Bob and Mary's from diapers to sheepskins and I learned one thing. It's not much consolation, but what it all comes down to in the end is that character will out. . . . I remember you when you were a ragged little boy, Alan. Now look at you. Samantha's your daughter. She's got what you have."

Comforted, Springer returned to his own house on a back path through the woods, a route he hadn't walked in years. Margaret awakened when he crept into bed.

"Where were you?"

"Walking. How's Samantha?"

"She's all right. You're the one I'm worried about."

"I'll give her my blessing. I won't mean it, but you're right. I can't shut her out that way."

But when he apologized to her in the morning he realized, to his surprise, that he did mean it. The wedge he had driven between them had left him with an emptiness he could not bear. Samantha let him hold her.

"Thank you, Daddy."

"Just take good care of yourself, darling. Keep your head on straight."

"There's nothing to worry about."

Springer ran his fingers through her hair. He was still unused to its new length.

"I love you, Angel. Have a good time."

Eighty teen-aged children, with the notable exception of the Strattons, assembled at the social center early Saturday morning and marched under the direction of the Revelationists up Spotting Mountain Road. The Revelationists who shepherded them were unusually somber and their mood affected the children, who grew quiet and pensive.

Samantha walked at the end of the line. She looked back at her father. He was standing in front of his hospital like a lone, tall tree in a empty field. She had an awful sudden vision of a cedar blown to the ground, its shallow root ball drying in the wind. She blinked it away and saw him wave just before a turn in the road blocked their views of each other.

She shivered, and goose bumps—Daddy used to call them goose berries—speckled her bare arms. The Revelationists looked so grim today and she didn't recognize any of them from the social center. She wished they would sing, but they walked as silently as ghosts. She hoped they would sing when they got to Revelations. Then she remembered that this morning the buses had not come from New York City.

For Springer and Margaret the hot, humid weekend was interminable. The town was almost silent; few cars and fewer pedestrians stirred on the streets. The absence of children's calls left the heavy wet air as the only sign that a world existed beyond the bedroom where they had retreated. It was air conditioned there and they watched television and read. Springer wanted to go to his office, but he couldn't leave Margaret alone with the worry. They spoke little about it, but it hung as oppressively as the heat.

At dusk on Sunday the children marched back into Hudson City. Unaccompanied by the Revelationists, seemingly leaderless, they burst singing onto Main Street. The song stopped. They stood in silent, menacing vigil before the Presbyterian Church, frightening the senior citizens' Sunday supper club, then, at some unseen sign, dispersed quietly to their homes, flitting silently, like bats, along the dusk-darkening streets.

Samantha stumbled onto the front porch where Springer and Margaret were waiting anxiously under the guise of seeking an evening breeze. She was glassy-eyed, trembling, and pale, physically exhausted. They hustled her into bed, where she lay quietly for a few moments.

All at once she sat up, casting her eyes about.

"Easy, dear. How do you feel?"

"Wonderful!" Her voice was high-pitched, hysterical. Angry that they had let her get so tired, Springer tried to soothe her. She pulled away. Her eyes sparkled unnaturally.

"Have you heard the news?"

"What news?" asked Margaret. She put the nearest Snoopy dog on the pillow to distract Samantha.

Samantha brushed the toy aside. "Michael is coming."

"Lie down, dear."

Samantha's voice rose. "Michael is coming to Hudson City. He will cleanse our town for Christ."

"Is Christ coming too?" Springer asked acidly.

"He will."

"When's he due?" asked Springer, ignoring Margaret's pressure on his hand.

Samantha seemed unaware of his sarcasm. "When Michael tells him that the time is right."

"Did you have a nice time?" asked Margaret.

The words were so mechanical, so empty, that though they came from Margaret's fear Springer laughed. "Nice time?" He was scared, angry. What the hell had they done to her? "What went on up there?" he asked sharply. Margaret squeezed his hand again. He pulled away. "Samantha? What happened?"

Samantha sagged against the pillows. Life seemed to drain from her face, but her voice stayed strong. "I pledged my soul to Jesus."

"You converted?" whispered Margaret.

"And I pledged my body to His servant, Michael."

The words ripped Springer apart. The idea of his daughter pledging her body to anyone stirred up a violent rage that caused his stomach to twist and his heart to pound. As if a stranger were doing it, he felt his fists clench until his fingernails bit into his palms like steel splinters.

Samantha sat up again. He tried to make her lie down.

"Pray with me," she demanded.

"What?"

"Pray with me," she repeated harshly.

"Pray for what?" asked Springer.

Samantha shut her eyes. "Pray for your souls to be cleansed."

Springer shook her hard. "Snap out of it."

She shoved his hands away. "I promised I would help you see the truth. Pray with me."

"You promised? Who did you promise?"

"We promised Michael. Each child promised to take responsibility for her parents' souls and help them find love. Please pray, Mom. Daddy. Please, quickly, before it's too late."

"You can't take that responsibility," said Springer.

Samantha's eyes were still closed. She shook her head violently. "But I love you."

"I love you, too," said Springer. "But don't let someone tell you how to run my life. Open your eyes, dear." He forced himself to laugh. "Me and my soul worked out a pretty good arrangement a long time ago. We take full responsibility for each other." He waited vainly for a smile.

Samantha's face hardened. Her eyes screwed shut to two tiny lines. She began to chant, "Pray-pray-pray-pray-pray-pray."

"Not like this," said Springer.

"Pray, Mother. Please pray-pray-pray-pray-pray."

Hesitantly, casting a fearful look at Springer, Margaret sat on the edge of the bed and bowed her head.

"Pray," intoned Samantha, swinging her head from side to side. "Pray-pray-pray. Pray to Michael to cleanse your soul." The chant got louder.

Margaret's lips began to move.

Springer shook her. Samantha began to sway. The bed rocked. Margaret caught the rhythm and began to sway with her.

Springer yelled, "Who's Michael? You can't pray to a nut just because he claims he's got a tie line to God."

A chilling shriek burst from Samantha's mouth. "Pray! Pray! PRAY! PRAY! PRAY!"

Springer reached for her. He saw his outstretched fingers going for her mouth and jerked back as if burned. Terrible sounds were coming from her now. He had started from the room to get a needle to put her out when suddenly her voice dropped to a whisper and her eyes took on a distant, glassy look.

"Dear Michael, forgive Daddy. Give me the strength to heal my father and help him transcend his sinful life. He can't help himself, Michael. We can save him. I'm sure we can."

25

A double line of teen-agers stretched across Main Street from storefront to storefront. Forty of them, heads bent low to their task, worked south from the social center wielding push brooms over the sidewalks. From a distance they reminded Springer of the television newsreels of the Chinese proletariat sweeping snow from the streets of Peking.

"Here they come," said Bob Kent. "Talk to you later, Alan. Okay, Tom?"

The white-haired newspaperman readied his camera.

Kent struck a pose on the corner of Grand Street and Main, his eyes fixed on the approaching sweepers. It was a hot, humid morning, four days since the children had come back from Revelations, and calm was settling, at last, over the town.

On Sunday night many families had been shocked by scenes similar to the one that had occurred in Samantha's bedroom. Hysterical teen-agers had pleaded with their parents to give up their sinful lives and pray for salvation. Reactions had varied from outrage to compliance and on Monday morning an anxious crowd had gathered in the streets and stores to commiserate. Matters had gone too far, they agreed, but no one knew what to do about them. Even the sect's strongest supporters seemed worried.

But by Tuesday, the children seemed less fervent, less glassy-eyed, and less inclined to preach. Clearly, said some the effects were wearing off. The children organized th early morning sweep-up patrol on Wednesday. Now Thursday morning, Tom House was recording the event i hopes of garnering another by-line in the *Daily News*. H had titled his story "Revvies Sweep Clean" and asked Ker to pose for a picture with the volunteers.

As they approached, pushing their brooms with vigoro strokes, Kent raised his arms in welcome.

"Morning, kids."

House clicked away with his ancient Nikon. "Move in a little closer, Bob."

"Like this?"

The volunteers swept nearer. Springer pressed into a doorway. One of Joe Preston's kids flicked his broom over his shoes and kept going without a word. He spotted Samantha. She was working mechanically, eyes down. Dicky Lewis was next to her, sweeping like a little machine. Neither took notice of the other. When they did raise their eyes it was to watch the brisk hand signals of the apparent leader of the group, Danny Moser. The boy's eyes, big in his tired, drawn face, darted from side to side, missing nothing.

"Hiya, Danny," Kent called jovially.

"Good morning, sir." He swept up to Kent and started around him. The mayor said, officiously, "Just wanted to tell you kids how much the town appreciates what you're doing to keep it clean."

"Hey, Danny," called House. "Pick up your head, son. Let's have a smile."

Danny flashed the requested smile and resumed sweeping. "Hey, sweetheart," called Springer, but Samantha passed too far away to hear him. He watched them work past the stores to the school, where the volunteer firemen had draped a huge banner over the driveway announcing the town fair on Sunday.

Kent finished thanking Tom House, and after the publisher walked toward his office the mayor turned to Springer. "What were you saying?"

Springer assessed his friend's beaming face. Bob lived for these official moments; now was no time to speak against the Revvies. "Just stopped to say 'Hi.' "

"What do you think of these kids," Kent enthused. "Aren't they something?"

"Marvelous."

"The town never looked so good. You know they're talking about doing a free paint job on everybody's store?"

"Blue?" asked Springer.

Kent didn't notice the sarcasm. "Think that picture might get me a vote or two?"

Springer smiled. "You're such a pol, Bob, you keep forgetting nobody's running against you."

Kent laughed. "As long as I run hard enough no one else will. Tom thinks he might get one of those pictures in the New York papers."

Some early shoppers walked past, a farmer and several city people. Kent lowered his voice. "Tom wanted the pictures. I'm getting in a pitch about vacation property. Nice clean place to summer." He said good morning to the passers-by. Then he turned to Springer. "Damn, I wish that mountain was shaped right for skiing."

Springer was watching the city people. He recognized the red-headed woman whose picnic the Revelationists had attacked. She was attractive and the memory stirred his body. He wondered what her memories were like and what she would think if she knew he had seen it all.

Springer glanced at the mountain. The old asylum was barely visible in the hazy air. Ellen. Was she in there? He turned his attention to Kent. "I'll bet you never thought you'd want your picture in the paper with Danny Moser."

Kent laughed. "That's for sure. What a change in that kid," he marveled. "Behaves himself just like—"

"A machine."

"What?" Kent's smile vanished. "Don't start that again, Alan. They've done wonders with him and the rest of them."

"Sure, Bob."

"They straightened out a lot of screwy kids."

"You still don't get what's going on, do you?"

Kent's face closed. "*You* don't get what's going on. You're making up a whole crazy thing about them that isn't true."

"You wouldn't say that if you'd seen Samantha Sunday night."

"Samantha looks great this morning. She's with friends and she's contributing to the town. Now what the hell is wrong with that? You know that kid was a little screwy herself until recently."

"What?"

"If I were you I'd be grateful to the Revvies for making her happy."

Springer's mouth compressed into a hard line. He glared at his friend, spun on his heel, and walked stiffly to the hospital.

Kent telephoned later that day. "I'm juggling my dignitaries. Just wanted to make sure you and Margaret will be at our supper table at the fair."

Grateful that Kent had the kindness and good sense to end their argument before it festered with time, Springer thanked him with a joke. "Is Isaac, Stern?"

Kent laughed. "Which reminds me. We're going to Saratoga weekend after next, right?"

Each summer the two couples had spent a weekend together at the Saratoga music festival. "Right," said Springer. "Thanks for calling."

"See you Sunday."

Margaret cooked a big breakfast Sunday, which they ate alone. Samantha had left early for sweep-up patrol. She would not accompany them to church, but she had promised to meet them at the fair. Kent had invited the Revelationists, but had received no response, and it seemed as if the children of Hudson City would attend without their religious guides.

The church was about a third full. Attendance had continued to drop since Davies had challenged his parishioners to bring their children back and, this morning of the fair, people who might ordinarily have attended were busy setting up stalls and trucking animals in from the farms.

Davies looked haggard as he mounted the pulpit, but after hurrying through the beginning of the service, he exploded into an impassioned sermon with a vigor that snapped Springer straight up in his pew, concentrating on the tenor tirade.

"False Prophets and Mindless Faith" was Davies' subject. The diminutive minister was hitting back. His voice rose bravely. He pounded the pulpit, which seemed to give him greater courage, and for several minutes his startling energy, his passionate conviction, and his anger transfixed the little congregation.

"Choice!" Davies cried. "Choice is the strength of Protestantism. *Free* choice.

"Protestant Christians *chose* the way of the Lord. By so chosing, they bring to the Lord the best that man has to offer, his talent to reason, to think. That talent, God-given, elevates man above the other animals God has created to share His earth.

"To think, to reason, to choose. A Christian who does less insults the Lord."

Davies glared scornfully at the foyer doors as if daring the Revelationists to enter. Charlie Daniels was on the other side of the double doors, as he had been every Sunday since the last invasion. No one had told him to take the post, but he stood there in the at-ease position, his bull horn dangling from a leather wrist strap, his revolver protected in a special flap holster, his long night stick at his belt.

The minister said, "Protestant men and women choose freely not to sin. They are not brainwashed not to sin. Choice of God is love of God—love freely given, not surrendered upon demand." He looked at his notes, lost his place, and faltered through his next point.

The spell was broken.

The heat intruded and the sounds of cars and trucks and laughing people reminded the congregation that the fair awaited.

Davies plowed on.

Protestantism, the religion of protest, and the belief in the individual's duty to choose God, would resist the authoritarian impulse of mass society, while the pressure that mass society exerted against the individual would drive him back to Protestantism. Armed with his freely chosen faith, the Protestant would resist mass society and save the individual for God.

Springer's interest waned. What had been electrifying turned complex when Davies abandoned passion for sociology. It was stuff better suited to private conversation, and when at last he had done, the congregation rose with grateful sighs to sing the final hymn.

Springer and Margaret strolled leisurely home to change into cooler clothes. Margaret wore a broad-brimmed hat that brought to him a sudden memory of a romantic day they had shared in Saratoga years before. He took her hand as they crossed the street, then walked down the high school's cinder driveway past the red-brick building to the fair behind it.

The fairgrounds were on four acres of open playing fields burned brown by the August sun; goal posts marked the soccer field, bare earth the baseball diamond, and shallow, heel-ground holes marble players' arenas. Nearest the school building, within easy distance of the running water and bathrooms, food stalls, manned by perspiring, beer-drinking volunteer firemen, sold charcoal-cooked hamburgers and hot dogs, steaming buckets of corn, and canned beer from ice-filled washtubs. The firemen's wives, the Ladies Auxiliary, sold cakes, pies, and cookies.

Next to the food area, the Hudson City PTA was selling local handicrafts—needlework blankets, shirts, pillows, corn-husk dolls, carved wooden figures, ornamental house plantings, and decorated rocks. Beyond the smoke from the charcoal fires the church supper society had set up rows of picnic tables for the evening meal.

Dust swirled in the heavy air, kicked up by hundreds of feet trampling the dry grass. Traveling slowly from booth to booth, the spectators, whose numbers grew hourly, waded gingerly through running children and barking dogs.

There were animal stalls in which the 4-H judges were inspecting cows, sheep, and hogs. An adjacent area contained cages of guinea pigs, rabbits, and chickens—starter animals for children not old enough to raise a hoofed creature. Now and then a bull bellowed angrily, letting the assemblage know it would just as soon be spending Sunday beneath a shady tree.

Other judging stands displayed baked goods, preserves, and garden vegetables notable for their shiny skins and enormous size. There was a flower show, a carnival, and a portable carrousel that piped recorded calliope music, a sound that always made Springer sad.

Tourists passing through had swelled the numbers of townspeople, farmers, and vacationers, and by late afternoon nearly a thousand people were milling about.

Springer was watching the hog judging when Margaret sought him out.

"You look pleased," he said, admiring the color in her cheeks.

"They sold four of my paintings at the church booth."

"Beautiful."

"Ten dollars each."

"A steal."

"I'm going to do more for next year. Have you seen Samantha?" She stood on tiptoe and tried to scan the throng.

Springer said, "Last I saw she'd conned poor Dicky

Lewis into throwing baseballs at milk bottles. She had her
eye on another Snoopy."

"Oh, yes, there she is. Oh, Alan, I'm so glad they're not
here."

"The Revelationists?" asked Springer. Instinctively he
glanced above the high school at Spotting Mountain. The
clearing on which the old asylum squatted was bright gold
in the sun.

"This is like it used to be. It's as if they had never
come." She smiled and her eyes crinkled in the shadow of
her sun hat. Touching his nose, she said, "You're getting
sunburned."

"Tired, too. A lot of noise. Want to slip home for an
hour?"

Margaret took his hand. "Showers. And wine."

Twenty minutes later they were stretched next to each
other on their bed. The sounds of the fair were audible
through the open window. A breeze stirred the sheer summer curtains.

"I feel so evil," said Margaret. "We can hear everybody.
It's almost like being watched."

Springer traced her bare back with his fingernails. "Does
that turn you on?"

Margaret turned her head and looked at him shyly.
"Something is."

He kissed her mouth and lay beside her, seeking solace
in familiar places.

Some time later, Bob Kent's amplified voice awakened
them. They dressed quickly and got back to the fair as the
mayor was announcing the winners of the 4-H livestock
contests. By the time the last grinning prize winner had
descended the podium with his blue ribbon, evening was
falling. Kent congratulated the winners, then reminded
everyone that square dancing would follow the supper that
the church ladies had begun to lay out.

With the loudspeakers quiet, a comparative hush enveloped the fairgrounds, and people herded toward the picnic
tables. The sun was lowering in the west, angling down
toward Spotting Mountain. Its rays lanced through the slot
that the high school driveway cut between the building and
some trees. Squinting into the glare, Springer, Margaret,

and Samantha sat with Mary Kent, Sophie Wilkins, and the Lewis family at the mayor's table, while Bob glad-handed his way through the crowds.

Sophie Wilkins sniffed, "He'd rather shake hands than eat."

"Now, Sophie."

"Doesn't he know that they won't serve until he sits down?"

Springer watched with amusement as his friend forged slowly toward their table. He saw hundreds of familiar faces—children he had delivered, adults he had ministered to. He inhaled the cooking odors mingling with the fresh scent of the animal pens. Margaret's hand lay softly in his.

He noticed that Alfie Potter had won a blue ribbon for his prize hog. Alfie won it every year to the consternation of the full-time farmers who insisted that a plumber couldn't know a good hog from a hole in the ground. He had pinned it on his overalls, provoking immediate imitation by every other ribbon holder under the age of sixteen.

Springer gazed at the smiling faces, listened to the unhurried talk and easy laughter, and thought that perhaps it was all right. Maybe nothing important had changed in Hudson City. Change was not new to the mountains. Summer estates, lumbermen, the garnet mines, the railroads, the sanitarium had all left, what seemed in retrospect, small marks. Perhaps the land and the people would absorb the Revelationists as they had absorbed all that had come before them.

Kent reached the table and sat down.

"You look happy," he said.

"I feel good." Springer was about to share his reflections with his friend when he realized that a hush had fallen over the fairgrounds. People were stirring as if a cold breeze had swept the field.

"What's happening?" asked Kent.

Springer turned toward the muffled rumble of marching feet. He stared into the red sun and saw beneath it a long double column of Revelationists descending the driveway. The men and women, separated as usual, rounded the corner of the school building and advanced upon them. He estimated there were at least three hundred of them, maybe more. What did they want? The townspeople exchanged nervous glances as they drew near.

Abruptly the front of the line stopped and they grouped in a big circle twenty feet from the tables. Samantha and Dicky and the other teen-agers waved, called "Hello." The Revelationists waved back, silently. Then they sat on the ground and quickly unwrapped sandwiches, stood again, with the precision of a marching band, and sang:

> "Bread of heaven, on thee we feed,
> "For thy Flesh is meat indeed;
> "Ever may our souls be fed,
> "With this true and living Bread."

"That's a communion song," said Margaret.

"A Revvie takes communion whenever she eats," said Samantha.

The Revelationists sat down again and bowed their heads before they began to eat. The people of Hudson City murmured nervously, until Pete Lewis announced in a loud voice, "See? They just came for a good time like everybody else. Even brought their own food."

The whispers continued. Despite the storekeeper's remark, there was still menace in their sudden arrival. They had not so much joined the festivities as challenged them.

"Okay," Bob Kent announced loudly enough to stimulate those at nearby tables, "let's get organized. I'm going for hot dogs, chicken, and hamburgers. Alan, I hereby deputize you to bring potato salad, corn, and coleslaw. We need soda and beer. How about you, Pete? Okay? Let's go. Everybody else sit tight."

Kent's jovial disregard of the menace was contagious, and he, Springer, and Lewis led a rush to the food tables. They returned, laden, and passed their goods to Mary and Sophie, who distributed them on paper plates. Margaret took charge of the beer and soda, filling the children's glasses and smiling a face at Samantha, who remarked disparagingly upon alcohol.

"Everybody ready?" asked Kent when the plates were full.

Sophie Wilkins shook a drumstick at him. "Will you kindly stop being mayor for five minutes? Pass the salt, Alan . . . Alan?"

Springer was distracted by sudden motion among the Revelationists sitting cross-legged on the grass. Something was happening to them. They seemed agitated. For once their machinelike discipline seemed not to function. They were twisting their heads from side to side and talking excitedly—looking for something, he thought.

Abruptly, like sheep facing the dog, they turned their faces toward the school. Springer looked there too, but it was hard to see. The sun, now blindingly red, barely above the mountain, seemed suspended in the center of the driveway. Shading his eyes, he turned toward Samantha. His daughter was staring into the sun, her face transfixed.

"What is it?" asked Springer.

Samantha did not answer.

Springer reached for Margaret's hand. It felt cold.

The Revelationists stared at the sun.

Something moved in its center. A long shadow touched the tables. A woman screamed.

"Michael!"

26

A giant walked out of the sun. The blazing circle back-lighted his golden hair and tinged his flowing shirt blood-red.

"Michael!" shouted the Revelationists, leaping to their feet.

Michael spread his arms wide and smiled down beatifi-cally from his great height. An enormous bass voice pealed from his lips:

"The Lord will come!"

The Revelationists shrieked, hurled their bodies to the ground, writhed in the dust. Samantha and Dicky ran from their benches and crouched at his feet. Other children fol-lowed, the supper, the fair, the prizes, and their gaping par-ents all forgotten.

Michael threw back his beautiful head and raised his stentorian voice in a hymn only the Revelationists and the children knew. They sang with him, cried the words, shouted the chorus, laughed with eerie joy while their par-ents stared in awe. Their children were strangers. Michael raised his arms and the song was over.

"Fall to your knees and pray."

The Revelationists knelt; the children knelt beside them.

"Raise your faces to heaven," he commanded. "Open your bodies to the Lord."

The Revelationists stared up at the darkening sky and spread their arms submissively. The children mirrored their mentors.

Michael prayed.

His powerful voice blotted out the quiet evening noises and the anxious murmuring of the townspeople. It was rhythmic, sonorous, soothing, compelling. Springer strained to hear the words, detect meaning, but that was impossible. The sound was the power, the constant, omnipresent sound, resonant, vibrant, hypnotic.

Michael walked among his kneeling followers while he prayed, touching their heads. His transparent shirt blew in the light breeze he seemed to have brought with him and his hair shimmered from gold to red as the sun plunged behind the mountain.

Moaning supplicants threw their arms around his massive legs. Gently, he extricated himself and walked on, quivering the mass of bodies as he passed through, trailed by every eye on the fairgrounds. He was, Springer guessed, at least six and a half feet tall. His body was beautifully formed, with the power and graceful musculature of a dancer. His face was as godlike as any Springer had seen, with bold, clean lines as if his strong nose, lean cheeks, and high brow had been sculpted in living granite.

At some unobserved point, Michael had stopped speaking. Amid the kneeling, keening throng, he faced the townspeople and smiled.

Springer shivered, unnerved.

Michael's eyes were piercing, deep, impenetrable black orbs. His power seemed beyond the human.

"Arise!" he told the children. "Bring the news to your mothers and fathers."

They rose with the Revelationists and formed a circle around the picnic tables. When the townspeople were entirely surrounded, their children and the Revelationists began to chant.

"The Lord will come. The Lord will come. The Lord will come. The Lord will come-the-Lord-will-come. . . ."

Springer searched the wall of blank faces, one to another. Where was Samantha? They all looked the same. He had lost sight of her when they moved.

"Where is she?" Margaret whispered, her hand biting into his.

Springer did not know. He spotted Dicky by his glasses and searched the area around him. Nothing. All the while, the chant continued.

"The-Lord-will-come-the-Lord-will-come-the-Lord-will-come. . . ."

They roared louder and louder and always Michael's great voice outstripped theirs, setting the tempo. Now he bellowed, his huge head shaking with the effort. The children's voices, high and innocent, shrieked after him.

Some parents hesitantly approached the wall of faces and found their children only to meet blank, staring eyes that laced through them as if they were invisible.

"The Lord has come-the-Lord-has-come-the-Lord-has-come-the . . ."

Springer caught the change in wording. He craned his neck. Where was she? The noise and the tight circle were oppressive. Pete Lewis and his wife were staring, awe-struck, at Dicky. Sophie Wilkins' lips were pressed tightly together. Mary Kent watched Bob, her face frightened, and Kent looked worried, but alert, as if waiting for a break in the din when he might do something. Margaret still searched for Samantha's face.

Then Buster Crayton, the dairyman who had tried to brave the Revelationists' fence, spotted his daughter, Betsy. He waded into the chanting circle and grabbed her plump arm. Betsy tried to claw free of his calloused hand. Buster slapped her matter-of-factly, the way he might have urged a reluctant cow through a gate. She screamed with terror, as if startled from a nightmare.

In a second a wall of Revelationists surrounded her, forcing Buster to drop her arm. The farmer stumbled back in confusion. He shook his head like a puzzled bull and charged the knot of men who had encircled his daughter. The knot opened, enveloped Buster, and closed.

Buster's son and nephew, a pair of big men in their thir-ties, came to his aid. They threw themselves, punching and kicking, at the Revelationists. The Revelationists fell back, drawing their attackers with them, pulling them into a cres-cent, closing the horns until they disappeared from sight. All the while the chant continued. "The-Lord-has-come-the-Lord-has-come-the-Lord-has-come."

The circle opened.

The farmers were sprawled on the trampled grass, still as corn-husk dolls.

"The-Lord-has-come-the-Lord-has-come-the-Lord-has-come. . . ."

The people at the tables half rose, exclaiming angrily at the sight of their fallen neighbors. Their wives rushed to ward them with frightened faces, but stopped, awed, before they reached their men.

Michael blocked them, his smile easy, his eyes hot. For a long moment he surveyed the citizens of Hudson City. The sun was almost down now. No one spoke and for the time Michael waited it seemed as if no car passed on the street and no bird sang and no insect murmured. Springer sensed with horrible certainty that Michael intended to punish the town for the Craytons' assault.

But when he spoke, it was to his followers.

"We will go home now."

The people at the tables sighed their relief. The Revelationists formed their usual double line, men and women apart. Springer relaxed, glad he had been wrong about Michael's intention.

Michael took up a position at the head of his column. He smiled upon the children of Hudson City.

"Come with us."

And the children of Hudson City filed between the lines of Revelationists and marched away with them.

27

A deep, numb quiet settled over the fairground as the parents of Hudson City gaped at one another in shock, dumbfounded by what had happened. Already the marching column had disappeared around the school. The children were gone.

The Craytons were regaining consciousness even as Springer knelt to their aid. He found them unmarked, but dazed, and told their wives to try to keep them lying still for a few minutes. When he stood up, people were milling around in angry confusion, shouting that they had to get their children back. Margaret grabbed Springer's arm. Her eyes were wild. "What are we going to do?"

Springer said, "Calm down. We'll do something."

"What?" she shrilled. "Alan, please . . ."

Springer felt the hysteria building around him. He held Margaret with both hands and shouted, "Just calm down." Out of the corner of his eye he saw Bob Kent scrambling onto the podium. He turned back to his wife. "Listen. Go home. Please, before this gets out of hand. I'll get Samantha."

"How?" she wailed.

"I'll get her. I promise."

Kent was frantically gesturing to the high school janitor to turn on the sound system. His face was red and tense. The loudspeakers crackled to life.

Springer pushed Margaret toward the driveway. "Go. I'll help Bob and I'll get Samantha."

Margaret started hesitantly, threw him a final pleading glance, and ran.

Kent waved his arms and yelled, "Let's everybody just calm down."

"Where are they taking our kids?" screamed a farmer's wife. The crowd responded with an unsettling roar.

Kent shouted, "We'll take care of this right away," and added, incongruously, "How about everybody sitting down and eating the supper the ladies cooked?"

"What the hell are you talking about?" yelled a truck driver.

"Relax," Kent yelled back, his face purpling in the dying light. "Charlie Daniels and me'll take care of this."

"What the hell are you going to do?" an irate voice shouted. "I'm getting my kids back right now. Anybody wants to come with me can come right along."

That elicited an angry cheer and within moments, despite Kent's pleas, three hundred people surged out of the schoolyard onto Main Street. Springer waved to Kent and, panting with effort, the two men took off, managing to outdistance the mob. "We got to stop this," Kent shouted as he caught up to Springer.

The tail of the Revelationists' column was already turning onto Spotting Mountain Road. The front runners of the townspeople saw them and increased their pace, shouting encouragement to those behind them.

Springer and Kent bolted toward the stores. Behind them the townspeople had spread across the width of Main Street. Their shouts melded into an animal sound, half fear, half pain. Springer saw Margaret watching from their porch. She was huddled against one of the square columns, her face terrified.

Kent was gasping for air by the time they reached the storefronts. He slammed open the police-station door and bellowed for Daniels.

The khaki-clad officer stumbled out of the back room, his face puffy, his eyes confused.

"What's wrong?"

"Get in your car," yelled Kent.

Springer held the door open and glanced anxiously at the approaching mob as Daniels shook his head violently and snapped alert. He brushed past them, muttering, "Nap. On all day."

They were surging abreast of the police car, which was parked at the curb as Springer, Kent, and Daniels slid in from the sidewalk side.

"Cut 'em off," Kent growled. He was still wheezing and Springer worried that the run had been too much for him.

Daniels started the engine, hit the lights and siren simultaneously, and managed to pull ahead before the crowd blocked him. The roof resounded as angry fists pounded the sheet metal, but few people could stand the scream of the siren long enough to impede the car. Daniels drove through the siren-slashed opening into the empty space of Main Street. Two cars, which had come around the bend at the church, had pulled tightly against the curb when their drivers saw the mob. Springer flinched from the siren and watched Daniels. The police officer looked awfully young.

He looked in the mirror and nudged the gas as the leaders moved forward, threateningly. "What happened? Everything was fine when I left."

Kent's struggle to regain his breath kept his explanation brief. "The kids went with the Revvies. The parents want 'em back. We're in the middle."

Daniels took a long look through the rearview mirror. Springer noticed that he was chewing the insides of his lips.

"I don't think I can stop 'em here. They'll walk all over us."

"Let's just keep them apart," said Springer. "The walk up the mountain should cool them down."

Daniels turned onto Spotting Mountain Road. It was dark beneath the overhanging trees. He turned off the siren and switched on his headlights. The beams reached the rear guard of the Revelationists' march.

"What if they haven't cooled down when we get up there?" asked Kent. "They're mighty upset. I mean that son of a bitch took those kids like they were puppets." Kent stared glumly at the roadside. "Another mile," he said. "What the hell are they up to taking the kids like that?"

"What son of a bitch?" asked Daniels.

Springer and Kent explained about Michael.

"Number one?" asked Daniels. "I figured we'd be seeing him one of these days."

"What a mess," said Kent.

Less than two hundred yards separated the groups as they marched up the mountain into the gathering dark. Daniels edged the police car ahead until they were very close to the back of the Revelationists' line. They were spread over the entire width of the narrow, gully-lined road, making it impossible to pass.

"Wish I could stop 'em before they get inside that place."

"We're all that's keeping them apart," cautioned Springer.

He searched vainly for Samantha's slim form, but the children were blocked from sight by a wall of broadshouldered men, a stolid rear guard who climbed the steep road at a steady pace and never looked back.

"Got to hand it to them," said Daniels. "When they do something they do it right. Look at the size of those boys. Anybody who catches up with them will wish they hadn't."

At that moment the pursuers split down the middle and several cars, horns blaring, emerged from their ranks and tried to pass the police car. In a swift motion, Daniels swerved and pulled to a sharp stop, blocking them skillfully. He rolled down his window and addressed the occupants of the lead car, threatening arrests in the morning if they didn't haul ass down the mountain. The men in the car huddled briefly, shouted that Daniels better do something, then pulled onto the shoulder as the mob drew near.

Daniels floored his accelerator and regained his position behind the Revelationists. Kent chuckled dryly. "Nice going, Charlie."

Daniels chewed his lips. "One on one is easy." He glanced apprehensively at Springer, but the doctor was staring ahead into the night. Then Daniels saw what the doctor was looking at.

The blue lights of Revelations had come into view. The marchers quickened their pace, until, when they reached the gates, they were traveling at a dead run. The move caught the townspeople by surprise and the gates were shut again with ample time before they had caught up. Daniels stopped his car on the apron in front of the gates.

"Okay," said Kent. "Alan and I will talk to the bastards. You watch our people."

Daniels got out of the car and faced the mob.

Springer and Kent walked up to the gate. The Revelationists had vanished up the dark driveway. Then floodlights blazed on, bathing both the gate area and the broad, sloping lawn in front of the building in brightness.

The Revelationists and the children were seated, crosslegged, on the lawn, about a hundred yards from the gate. The townspeople drew close, shouting at Kent, the Revelationists, and each other. Daniels raised both hands. They were conspicuously empty.

"Let's just calm down, everybody. The mayor's getting everything under control."

Springer grabbed Daniels' electric bull horn from the back seat of the car and gave it to Kent. Kent turned it on and bellowed, "Michael! Come on down here and let's talk!"

The Revelationists responded with song.

The townspeople swarmed forward, pushing Daniels against his car. Someone near the front of the crowd shouted, "Over the fence. Let's go. We'll get 'em back."

While the Revelationists and the children continued singing, Michael led a contingent of big men to the gate. Those who had shouted for an attack grew quiet. Daniels took advantage of the lull to back into his car and radio the state police. Then he slid out the passenger side, shouldered his way between Kent and Springer, and addressed Michael, who was standing a dozen feet from the gate.

"Let's stop this before it gets worse. Let the kids go."

Michael smiled blandly. But his eyes were intense, glittering in the electric lights.

"The children," he said, "are our guests. They can go anytime they want to."

His speaking voice had the same eerie resonance as when he had prayed and sung. Again, Springer felt moved by his extraordinary power. Charlie Daniels also seemed affected; as if he sensed instinctively that he could not cope with Michael's aura, he turned to the townspeople and ordered them to move back.

Minutes later, sirens howled. Two state police cars split the mob and stopped next to Daniels' car. Four uniformed, helmeted officers leaped out and began to clear a space around the gates, shoving the townspeople out of their way. Three stood guard, their riot sticks held menacingly, while the fourth listened to Daniels' and Kent's account of what had happened, then rapped his stick on the gates and ordered that they be unlocked.

Michael, surrounded by his retinue, stepped a little closer and looked down beneficently at the trooper, who repeated his order.

"Open up!"

Michael smiled. His eyes glowed eerily. When he spoke his voice carried beyond the police to the townspeople, frightened men and women, tired from the climb and bewildered by the troopers' rough tactics.

"The children are our guests. They've come for song and prayer and they will not leave my sanctuary until the prayers are over."

He smiled in response to some angry shouts and added, "You are all welcome to listen from the gates. You'll learn much from your children."

The trooper slapped his stick in his palm. He had the hard face of a man used to command. "I'm giving you a direct police order to open this gate."

"You are no longer in the realm of police power," said Michael. He turned gracefully, his flowing shirt drifting like a cloud, and walked away.

"I'll knock it down and arrest you and every damn one of your bunch," yelled the trooper.

Michael turned again and impaled the man with his awesome eyes. "*You will not.*"

The trooper recoiled, bringing his stick up into a defensive position even though Michael was a dozen feet away and separated from him by the gate. Michael nodded slightly and twenty of his men pressed their bodies against the bars, reinforcing them with a wall of flesh. Springer looked at their blank faces and realized that nothing short of deadly force would budge them from their post. Their minds—or what was left of their minds—were already made up: they would die rather than move. They would die for Michael.

The trooper glared uncertainly.

Up the slope, the children sang, oblivious to the drama on the road.

A barrel-chested little white-haired man in a vested suit shouldered briskly through the mob. The troopers on guard moved to stop him but he gestured impatiently and they fell back in recognition.

"Strunk," said Kent.

"Evening, Mr. Mayor," said the Warington lawyer. "Evening, Officer. Evening, Doctor. Evening, Trooper, how's your wife? All better?"

"Pretty good, Mr. Strunk."

"Wonderful. Now, what's all this? I received a call that my client was besieged. Seems that's so. What are you doing about it?"

"Your client? You mean them, sir?"

"I represent the Revelationists on certain matters. What the hell is going on here? Who are all those people?" He nodded disdainfully at the citizens of Hudson City.

"They're holding the kids," said Kent. "Marched them right out of our fair."

"Holding?" asked Strunk. He peered doubtfully at the singing children.

"They defied my order to open up," said the trooper.

Strunk looked around with elaborate dismay. "Well, *I* sure as hell wouldn't open *my* gates if hundreds of people were stomping around outside. Would you?"

"They defied a police order."

"Well, sure they did. They're afraid. . . . Now look here." Strunk opened his arms and drew Kent and Daniels and the trooper around him. Springer listened over Kent's shoulder. "Those children look like they're having a nice time. There's no crime in progress that I can see. Can you see a crime, Trooper?"

"But—"

"I suggest that rather than storm a group of unarmed citizens who are merely practicing their religious faith, you consider doing something about these people out here. They're in a nasty mood, Trooper."

Springer glanced over the heads of the men guarding the gate. Michael stood behind them, aloof, a faint smile playing over his sensual mouth, and Springer wondered if the sect leader had planned the entire incident. Michael's gaze flickered idly in his direction. Before Springer looked away, he was sure he saw amusement there. It was a game, a ruthless game, to show the town his power.

Strunk listened patiently to Kent, Daniels, and the trooper. Then he said, "Still and all, these people out here pose a greater threat to the peace than a bunch of singing children, Trooper, Mr. Mayor, Constable. Don't you agree?"

"Strunk," Kent said wearily. "It's a lot more than that and you know it."

"Now, now, now," Strunk said soothingly. "I think it would be in all our interests to send these people home or back them up at least, before somebody gets hurt."

"Then what?" snapped Kent. "We can't push them away without doing something about their children."

"Ah!" said Strunk. "A good point. Let me see what I can do."

He walked to the gate and spoke quietly to one of the young men in the human wall. The man remained expressionless, but allowed himself to be moved when one of Michael's retinue squeezed next to him. This second man conferred with Strunk for a moment, then went to Michael. They conferred. The young man returned to the gate and spoke to Strunk. Strunk returned to Kent and the police.

He said, "Michael promises that the religious service will be over at ten o'clock, at which time the children will go home."

Kent looked at his watch. "An hour. Okay, seems reasonable."

Strunk drew an ancient pocket watch from his vest, opened it, and held it to the glare of the police-car headlamps. "An hour," he confirmed. "In the meantime, Trooper, if you would please move those people back or send them home . . ."

"I'll take care of it," said Kent. He took the bull horn and climbed, with Springer's help, onto the hood of Daniels' car and addressed the townspeople.

"The kids are going to do some singing. They'll leave at ten o'clock—about an hour from now. You can either wait across the road or go home. Everything is going to be okay."

There was sullen muttering, but no more shouting. It had been a long day, a long hike up the mountain, and a long vigil in the cold night air. Some of the crowd dispersed, taking rides from the many people who had followed in their cars. Others, parents mostly, huddled in little groups and waited.

Behind the circles of white flood lighting that played over the Revelationists and the children, the blue window lights burned placidly in the stone building.

Springer and Kent stayed at the gate, watching the children and discussing Michael, who was leading the songs and prayers, his bass voice clearly audible, the sturdy framework for all the sounds the children made.

The singing stopped at ten o'clock. The children hugged and kissed the Revelationists and filed down the long driveway. Michael stood by the open gate and blessed them as they went out. Their faces reflecting the awe they felt for him, the children marched silently past their baffled parents.

"We have to get rid of them," said Springer as they watched the tight line move down the dark road to Hudson City.

Kent looked around furtively, as if afraid they'd be overheard. "Well . . . yes, but not everybody's going to want to see them go. And they have money and Strunk and more like him. It'll take some doing."

"We'll start right now," said Springer. "Pass the word to be at tomorrow's board meeting."

28

A sullen crowd jammed into Hudson City's storefront town hall the next night a full hour before the Monday board meeting was scheduled to begin. By the time Bob Kent called for order, several hundred who couldn't get in were shouting loudly for more room. Kent quickly conferred with his board and announced that the meeting would be moved to the high school auditorium.

The crowd cheered, excited by their number, and trooped down the street to the high school, where the women clumped in whispering groups while the men banged open folding chairs on the basketball court. The members of the board set up their own chairs behind a table facing the people and Kent again called the meeting to order.

One of the winched-up baskets cast a netted shadow over the board members. Kent and Ed Stratton looked pleased with the size of the gathering, but Pete Lewis, Ken Moser, Joe Preston, and Gary Spencer gazed apprehensively at the noisily muttering crowd. Springer sat on the aisle seat in the front row, facing the board. Across the aisle sat Wilber Strunk. The Warington lawyer looked nervously alert—an old fox trying to sniff a shifting wind.

The town clerk, an elderly woman named Norah Bone who kept records and registered voters, read the brief minutes of the last meeting in a quavering voice. Forty years before her husband had owned most of the timber worth owning in the county. The usable remnants of that empire were in Moser's hands now, the remainder sold for taxes and covered with worthless second growth.

The crowd fidgeted restlessly while "old business" was discharged.

When Kent called for "new business," Ed Stratton thrust

a pink palm out of the netted shadow. "I want to talk about the Revelationists."

An angry murmur rippled through the room.

"What about them?" Pete Lewis demanded stridently.

"They gotta go!"

The people roared.

Stratton stood up. He was wearing the light glen-plaid suit he'd worn all day at the showroom and it was rumpled. His belly strained his shirt. "There are too damned many of them living up there. They present a clear and present danger to the well-being of Hudson City."

Strunk snapped to attention at the legalistic jargon. He riffled quickly through the papers in his briefcase and extracted a yellow-bound copy of Hudson City's housing code. Springer watched admiringly as the lawyer zeroed in on the appropriate section and was rewarded with a sudden and very brief tightening of his thin lips. Springer knew exactly how Strunk felt. The town had torpedoed his low-income housing plan with that same law.

Stratton picked up his copy of the yellow booklet and turned to the page Springer had marked for him. He brandished the booklet like a club as he spoke. "The housing code of Hudson City requires the town board to rule upon any group living we deem injurious to the well-being of Hudson City."

"They're two miles out of town," Pete Lewis interrupted loudly. "They're not bothering us."

A wrathful, wordless denial rumbled from the audience.

Joe Preston said, "Let's get something straight. The housing code refers to living conditions and doesn't have anything to do with certain things that have gone on recently that might have upset a few people."

Stratton let the audience mutter irately before he answered. "The housing code refers to anything stemming from group living that might cause trouble for the town."

"It's not that broad," said Gary Spencer. He was the youngest man on the board and often deferred to his elders. Preston and Moser nodded emphatically.

Kent used his open palm for a gavel. "I think Fred Zinser can clarify this for us."

Zinser sat at the opposite end of the long table from the town clerk. Neither were voting members. He said, "It's broad. The town wrote itself the legal right to protect itself from group living, which is defined as more than five unrelated people living under the same roof."

Strunk started to raise his hand, but pulled it back down. Unless he was appealing an official ruling, he had no rights in a Hudson City town meeting.

Stratton said, "That's clear. Mr. Mayor, I propose that we invoke the law as it pertains to the old asylum now known as Revelations."

A ragged cheer broke from those members of the audience who could translate Stratton's motion into its actual meaning.

Kent slapped the table for order. "Do I hear a second?"

Pete Lewis vehemently shook his head. Joe Preston and Gary Spencer stared at the table. Ken Moser gazed at the assembled citizenry through rheumy eyes. If Hudson City had a patriarch, it would be Ken Moser, and it was apparent, Springer thought, that the old lumberman regarded an aroused citizenry with extreme distaste.

Kent confirmed the lack of support, then announced, "As a voting member of the board I second the motion." He waited until the cheering had stopped. "The proposition that we limit the number of people allowed to live at Revelations is open to comment from the floor. This is a public meeting and anybody who has something to say about this should say it."

A hundred hands shot up from the seated listeners.

Kent chose at random. "Wally?"

A skinny auto mechanic from Grand's Gas Station stood up. "I don't like what they're doing. They marched my kids off like they was on a leash. We gotta get rid of 'em."

The room rang with applause. Wally ducked his head and sat down.

"Carl," called Kent.

A farmer stood up in the back of the room and mumbled a barely audible agreement with the mechanic's statement. He was followed by another farmer with a booming voice. "They did something to my girl. She's got a look in her eyes like a blind cow."

"Buster Crayton," said Kent.

"They gotta go or it's gonna be them or us," Crayton shouted. "I'm ready to go to war over this."

Springer shivered at the rage released by the thunderous applause. It resonated ominously again and again as one after another of the speakers echoed Crayton's warning. Then Alfie Potter rose to speak. The audience quieted respectfully. The big plumber looked perplexed.

"I'm all mixed up, Bob. My kids went with 'em, too, and it tore my heart the way my Amy acted like I wasn't there. But I just keep thinkin' about that fire down by the tracks. We woulda lost three houses without the new pumper they gave us."

He shrugged his huge shoulders and sat down. No one clapped.

Kent searched the suddenly solemn crowd, hesitated, then called on Matthew Wright. The high school principal's pert wife, Jeannie, patted his leg as he rose.

Gesticulating stiffly, he said, "They're trouble. They are serious trouble. The board should vote them out right away." He swallowed hard and smiled at Jeannie. "And I think the members of the board ought to remember that this is an election year."

Wild applause greeted his reminder. Springer clapped loudly and tried to catch his eye. Matt had shown great courage. Most of the town board members were also on the board of education—Matt's employers.

Wright grinned jerkily. "And you can be sure that Jeannie and I will remember who voted how come November. And if the Revelationists are still here, we're going to see a few changes on the town board."

The audience roared. Wright sat down. Jeannie grabbed his arm and held tight. Springer waved to them. He was sorry that Margaret hadn't come to the meeting, but she had insisted that Samantha needed her now more than ever.

Spencer, Lewis, Moser, and Preston stared at the table. Kent nodded and Ed Stratton confidently popped a fat cigar into his mouth. When the clapping subsided, Pete Lewis raised his hand. "I'd like to say something, Mr. Mayor."

"Go right ahead, Pete."

Lewis straightened his narrow tie and tugged at his limp jacket. "I'd like to speak as a citizen of Hudson City, not just a board member. The money that the Revvies spend here is good for us. Six hundred people need a lot of food, clothes, household goods, materials, gasoline, lumber. Everything you and I buy they have to buy too. And you might be thinking, 'That's fine for you guys who own stores.' But listen to this. I've hired three new salesgirls since the Revvies came. Local girls. Molly Franklin, Betty Peters, and Barbara James. Gary Spencer has four new stock boys. A couple of the Stratton kids, Joe Francis, and Davy Johnson. The same goes for the lumberyard, the gas station, the drugstore, everywhere. The Revvies mean jobs and money for us and we can't afford to lose them."

"Thank you," Kent began. He was cut short.

"I'm not through! What they spend is good and, as far as I'm concerned, what they stand for is good too. My boy, Dicky, has been spending a lot of time with the Revvies. I don't see any damage. He was a good kid before and now he's better. Dicky took me up to Revelations a couple of days ago and I had a nice chat with some of their leaders." Lewis's voice took on a respectful hush. "I even met Michael. He's a heck of a nice guy. . . . You know, I'm a deacon at the church, but I think the Revvies offer something pretty solid to a person who's really looking for God. I'll tell you something, they're making me think twice."

He sat down. Kent thanked him and looked around for raised hands, but Lewis had stunned his listeners. Springer raised his hand. Kent looked as though he wasn't sure Springer was the right man to reply, but there was no one else.

"Dr. Springer."

Springer stood, turned around, and faced the people.

"I'm very happy for Pete Lewis that he doesn't think the Revelationists have hurt his son. . . . I'm envious, too. I have a daughter and I think I'm losing her to the Revelationists."

He waited, gauging the murmured response. This was it, his chance to turn it around and vote them out. Unexpectedly, tears formed in his eyes. He felt himself losing control. It caught their attention. They strained toward him, drawn to his pain.

"I want her back," he said when he could trust his voice. "And I want my town back, my home. I want to send my daughter to school without worrying about what people will do to her mind. I want her to learn to choose her beliefs. I don't want them battered into her. I want her to grow to be a human being, not a machine."

He felt more words pushing up his throat, the headwaters of a torrent of emotion, but instinct told him he had said enough. After a moment of silence, they began clapping. They clapped steadily, not like the earlier explosions but a sad sound, like the fall of rain.

He sat to a roaring in his ears, only dimly conscious of the debate continuing around him, overwhelmed with sadness. Some time later, he recognized a change, the tinny scraping of chairs. He had been sitting with his eyes closed. He opened them. People were shuffling from the gym but the board remained seated. Kent and Stratton looked tense, neither elated nor depressed. Springer snapped alert and listened. He gathered quickly that Kent had called a twenty-minute recess.

"We shouldn't have let them split us like that," old Moser said. "We should stand solid, together."

Kent said, "Sorry, Ken. But the way I read this one, anybody who votes for the Revvies isn't going to be sitting at this table come November."

"It'll blow over," said Moser, rubbing his wrinkled jowls. "People never remember the bad times."

Stratton snorted his disbelief. "The only way they'll forget the Revvies is when they're gone."

"But there's no slate against us," said Moser. "The election was won in the primary last June as usual."

"They'll write us out," said Kent.

"Bob's right," said Gary Spencer. "I sure as heck don't want to lose the business, but we're in trouble if we go against the people on this one."

"We have to vote according to what we believe is right," Lewis said sanctimoniously.

Kent smiled. "I believe it's right to get rid of them. That's how I'm voting."

Preston said, "The bank would hate to lose their account."

"We'll get somebody new up there," Kent said. "Don't you worry."

"Tell that to my superiors," said Preston.

Moser looked up like an old wolf considering a likely way to eat a porcupine. "Maybe we can stall a vote until after the election."

Kent laughed mirthlessly. "No way. What do you think, Alan?"

The others looked surprised that Springer was listening

He rose wearily and approached the table, his heels echoing in the now empty gymnasium.

"I think this is our chance to get our town back. The people know it and they know you know it. You guys have no choice. Vote 'em out."

Lewis's, Preston's, and Moser's faces set in hard, stubborn lines. Springer assessed them grimly.

"I'll give you something else to worry about. If this board votes in favor of the Revelationists, I'll personally organize the write-in opposition."

Moser reddened. "I'll remind you, Dr. Springer, that you are an employee of this town."

Springer felt rash. He whirled on the lumberman. "And I'll remind you that medical men with my administrative experience don't often work in little upstate towns, Mr. Moser. You get rid of me and you can turn your hospital into a sawmill."

"Hey, hey, hey," laughed Kent. "Come on, you guys, let's not get excited." He threw a stubby arm around Springer and reached in vain for Moser, who rubbed his gray eyebrows and angrily stalked toward the door, muttering that he needed some fresh air.

Smiling over Springer's shoulder at the returning people, Kent quietly accused the doctor of being irresponsible. "What the hell is wrong with you? Moser's one of the guys we can turn around. We're not going to get Lewis and Preston, so we can't win without Spencer and Moser."

Sophie Wilkins sat next to Springer after the recess. She noticed Strunk's empty chair. "What happened to the Warington Weasel?"

"Maybe he thinks they've won," said Springer.

"Or lost," Sophie countered cheerfully. "We've got to do something to scare these old buzzards into action."

"What?"

"Wait and see," said Sophie. "It's going to be a long night."

Her prediction was accurate. The hours rolled by as fear and anger drove one person after another to denounce the Revelationists and threaten the town board. The crowd thinned slightly after one o'clock, but still the protest continued and when, at three, Pete Lewis suggested adjourning, the storekeeper was met by a chorus of angry abuse. An exhausted Mrs. Bone surrendered her notepad to Fred Zinser at four, pleading that she needed to sleep before opening her office in the morning. Now, as people drifted from the meeting, those in rear seats moved up to fill the gaps so that by five-thirty the weary board still faced a solid wall of outraged citizens.

Ironically, in the end, it was a Revelationist supporter who finally tipped the issue against the sect. Following a violent condemnation of the board by Buster Crayton's nephew, a white-haired woman rose suddenly, unbidden, with the help of a cane and cried out in a shrill voice:

"They saved my boy!"

People twisted toward the unfamiliar voice.

"Danny's one of them and I'm proud."

Springer was amazed to see her. Danny Moser's alcoholic mother had rarely ventured beyond her scrubby back yard since the night years ago when her husband had beaten her senseless, leaving her a partial invalid, and disappeared. She whined, as Danny had.

"The Revelationists are good people. I'm working real hard so I can join 'em."

A woman near Springer said archly, "What do you expect from someone like that." Her companions murmured agreement. On the social scale of Hudson City, only the shack dwellers were lower than the residents of Spotting Street.

Mrs. Moser glared defiantly at people who had ignored her all her life. She shook her stringy hair and raised her cane in a macabre salute.

"Christ is coming," she cried. "With Michael helping me, I'll be ready when He does. We will cleanse the world!"

It was the slogan that did it. They had heard the words too often in the mouths of their children to let it foul their protest. Bitter shouts sounded about the room. For a second Springer thought they might attack the old woman, but Sophie Wilkins turned the rage in the right direction.

"Vote!" she yelled. "Get rid of them. Vote. Vote."

Springer took up the cry. "Vote."

The rest joined in, turning back to the board, demanding, "Vote, vote, vote, vote, vote, vote, vote, vote, vote!"

They stamped their feet and clapped. The room echoed their chant. The floor shook under their shoes. "Vote, vote, vote."

"Okay, okay," yelled Bob Kent, waving his arms. "We'll vote. Right?" He turned to the board. They nodded. Gradually the room quieted. Acting for Mrs. Bone, Fred Zinser called the roll of the board.

"The question before the board: Do we invoke the section of the housing code, uh, thirty-four, B, banning more than five unrelated people living under the same roof, against the Revelationists who are living at the old asylum. In other words, vote yes to get—to ban them—and no if you want them to stay.

"Kent."

"Yes."

The people cheered.

"Lewis."

"No."

There were boos.

"Moser."

Moser hesitated. "Yes." He glared at the resultant cheers.

"Preston."

"No." The banker stared at the table when they booed.

"Spencer."

There was a hush. Everyone knew Stratton would vote yes, so Spencer's vote was crucial. The young grocer looked embarrassed. He glanced from Moser to Kent.

"Is he ever going to grow up?" muttered Sophie Wilkins.

"Yes," said Spencer.

The clapping and cheering drowned out Stratton's yes.

The gymnasium emptied quickly.

"They'll appeal," said Kent.

"We'll win the appeal," said Zinser. "Don't worry. It's our town." He swept his papers and notes into his briefcase.

Springer stretched luxuriously. He was looking forward to a shower and a couple of hours' sleep. Morning sunshine poured in through the gymnasium's skylight.

"Good night, everybody. Nice going, Sophie."

He walked out on a genial chorus of sleepy good nights.

The streets were empty but for a few late leavers like himself. He had crossed the street and was about to turn up his front walk when he noticed one of the Revelationists' blue station wagons pulling up in front of the town hall. Eight people scrambled out and formed a line in front of the locked door. The station wagon turned around and sped back toward Spotting Mountain Road. Springer glanced up the mountain. The rising sun had already touched Revelations.

A second blue car appeared on Main Street. As it disgorged its occupants at town hall, another car pulled up behind it, and another. Each car turned around and drove back in the direction it had come. The line of blue-clad Revelationists was growing.

Springer started walking toward them, becoming more and more uneasy as a steady stream of blue cars delivered additional Revelationists to the line. When he reached town hall, he saw a long march of them swinging onto Main from Spotting Mountain Road. The marchers tripled the length of the line. And still the cars came.

He looked back. Other people who had left the meeting late were hurrying up Main with worried expressions on their tired faces. The Revelationists wore dungaree jackets over their overalls and their breath clouded in the cold morning that seemed to promise a harsh, early fall. They stood silently, in a single soldier-straight line stretching from town hall back to Spotting Mountain Road—an endless blur of blue reaching as far as Springer could see. Each held a scrap of green paper.

"What is this?" asked Kent, who had hurried up behind him.

"I don't know," Springer answered. "There's Strunk." He pointed toward the black sedan that had rounded the bend at the church and parked opposite the town hall several yards from where Springer and Kent were standing. Wilber Strunk rolled down his window and nodded civilly as Springer approached.

"Good morning, Doctor."

Springer thought he seemed uncomfortable. "What's going on?" he asked.

Strunk said, "They asked me to observe."

"Observe what?"

There was uncertainty in Strunk's clear eyes. "Registration."

"Registration? What are they registering for?"

"To vote."

29

"They can't do it!" shouted Bob Kent.

He, Springer, the town clerk, Fred Zinser, and several members of the elections board clustered inside the town hall. It was five minutes before nine. The panicky debate had been under way for an hour. A breath-fogged window dimly showed the silhouettes of the waiting Revelationists.

"I repeat," said Fred Zinser, wearily rubbing his eyes, "we are talking about voting rights. If we block 'em and lose in court they can sue for damages. Create a real mess."

"Come on, Fred," said Springer. "There must be something we can do. You already said that postal receipts are self-serving documents."

"True. But look at the weight of evidence as a judge would see it. Postal receipts, mail received, documents from their house manager, whoever the hell he is, birth certificates. They're prepared. Strunk is out there and you can be damned sure he's got a judge ready to slap an injunction on us if we try to stop them. We have no choice but to let the board of elections conduct a correct and legal voter registration." He looked at his watch. "You better open the door, Mrs. Bone."

The old woman crossed her arms. "They can rot in hell before I'll register them."

"Mrs. Bone," said Zinser. "You personally can go to jail for depriving citizens of their voting rights."

"Fred's right," said Kent. "You better do as he says."

Springer watched with sick fascination. As Mrs. Bone's Seth Thomas struck nine o'clock, the Revelationists' line shuffled into the little office and up to her desk.

"I am registering to vote," said the pale young woman in the lead.

Mrs. Bone pulled her cardigan sweater tight. "You must be a resident of Hudson City Township."

The woman spoke in a flat monotone. "I have lived here since April second, on which day I mailed a registered letter from the Hudson City Post Office. This is the return receipt. These are letters I have received here. This is my birth certificate and this statement from the house manager of Revelations confirms my date of arrival."

Mrs. Bone's wrinkled lips tightened as she compared the name and date. Slowly, she filled out a voter registration card. "We'll mail you this. You have to send it back to be registered."

Strunk, who was observing from one side, opened his watch. "Mr. Mayor, there are over seven hundred people waiting. Could you do something to expedite the registration?"

"I'm doing the best I can," snapped Mrs. Bone.

Strunk gave her a courtly bow. "Yes, Mrs. Bone, but I'm sure you could use help. Mr. Mayor?"

Kent nodded. He was ashen, the fight gone from him. "I'll get some people over here right away."

Springer went with him to his office and sat quietly while the mayor made the necessary telephone calls. Finally, he slammed down the phone and turned to the doctor. "That goddamned Strunk. This must've been his idea."

"No," said Springer. "I talked to him. He's kind of upset. Didn't know anything about it until they called him this morning."

Kent liked that. "Oh yeah? So they snookered him like they snookered us. I'll be damned." His smile vanished. "What a mess."

A gloomy silence enveloped the two men. The telephone rang. Kent answered.

"Right. You heard right. . . . Oh really? . . . As soon as you do tell me about it. . . . 'Bye."

He hung up. "Stratton. He thinks we have to do something."

Springer nodded. Kent stared blankly at the floor and drummed his desk top while Springer stood up and paced the room. Kent had Scotch-taped his real estate advertisements on the walls. Springer stopped walking and looked out the window. The Revelationists waited impassively.

"Well," he said after a while. "Just what are we going to do?"

"Do?" Kent asked with dull anger. "Do? Don't you

know what this means? They'll vote in their own people. They'll have their own mayor, their own board. They'll run Hudson City as their own private municipality, except it will be public. They'll have their own government." He shook his head in amazement. "Jesus Christ. They'll even have their own police force, all the town jobs, the teachers, the roads, sanitation, even yours, Alan. It'll be their town. They'll do what they want with it."

Springer plodded home, shivering, wearied to the bone by the long bitter night, his stomach sour from too much coffee, his mouth tasting of other people's cigarette smoke. He found Samantha and Margaret huddled at the kitchen table in robes and slippers drinking hot chocolate. Samantha looked quite normal, as if Michael's effect had worn off. They obviously hadn't seen the line from the back of the house and Springer, numbed by the enormity of the Revelationists' victory, hadn't the heart to discuss it.

He kissed the top of Samantha's head and smiled at Margaret, grateful that she had managed to prevent Samantha from descending into another trance like the one they'd endured after the weekend retreat.

"Cocoa?" asked Margaret.

"Wonderful." He sat opposite them. Somehow being together in their kitchen made things seem less bleak. They were lucky, he thought. They could leave Hudson City. A doctor could work anywhere. Margaret would like that. Samantha would adjust.

The old furnace rumbled on in the cellar, sparking a hundred memories. First heat this year. He loved fall, loved the way the house became quieter with the storm windows up and cozy from the wood fires in the hearths.

Samantha pushed a third cup and saucer toward the pot.

Springer smiled his thanks. God, he was tired. Then he saw the apprehensive look in Margaret's eyes and noticed for the first time how tensely she sat and the way her fingers twisted the sleeve of her robe.

"Wasn't he beautiful?" asked Samantha.

Springer casually sipped his chocolate. *Play it straight,* he warned himself. "Michael? Yes. A beautiful man. I never saw anyone quite that handsome."

"Like an angel," Samantha sighed.

"Like a person," Springer suggested gently.

"What was the meeting about?" asked Samantha.

Springer refilled Margaret's cup. Samantha covered her cup with her hand, the way he had taught her to decline more wine.

"The meeting was about what happened to the children, dear."

Samantha smiled innocently. "What happened, Daddy?"

Springer still had difficulty handling her new boldness. "I don't know, dear. You ran after him like . . ."

"Like what, Daddy? Like I was brainwashed?"

"Like nothing I ever saw you do. You and the rest of the children."

She gestured impatiently, a brisk repeat of the way she had refused the cocoa. "Forget them. We're talking about me."

"Samantha," said Margaret.

"What, Mother?"

Her face became fixed, rigid, as if she were digging in, erecting her defenses. Her eyes flickered toward Margaret, then back at Springer, an animal assessing her enemies, gauging where the greater danger lay. They fastened on Springer.

He felt frightened. He knew neither what to say nor where to start. He looked at Margaret. She couldn't help.

"Am I brainwashed?" Samantha repeated shrilly. "Is that what you think of me?"

"I don't know what to think," he replied, alarmed by the paranoia. *Is that what you think of me?*

"Why don't you ever call me by my name, Daddy?"

"What?"

"Why is it always *sweetheart* and *dear* and *angel* and all those other awful, empty endearments? Why don't you call me Samantha?"

"I call you Samantha."

"When?" she asked coldly.

Springer wildly thought back. "Often."

"When?"

"Well, dear—Samantha. I guess I never thought about it. Does it matter?"

"I don't think you talk to *me*, Daddy. You talk to your image of your daughter. What you think I should be. But what do you ever say to me?"

"Say to you? We used to talk about everything."

"You tease me. That's all. That's the only way you can talk, by teasing."

"That's not true."

Springer was confused. Margaret wouldn't meet his eye. He faced his child and nothing he could remember had been harder. He said, "I'm sorry. I didn't know that." It got easier. "I love you and I want you to see that I do. I'll do anything to show you that I love you, Samantha."

She regarded him appraisingly and when, at last, she spoke she said, "It's not your fault, Daddy."

He thrilled to her forgiveness. "Whose fault is it?"

"The Devil."

"Oh, Samantha." The sweet joy turned to gall in his stomach. "Oh, sweetheart, what are you saying?"

"The Devil reigns, Daddy. He makes war and strife everywhere, in every home and family. The world is in chaos."

"Samantha, please . . ."

"Don't worry, Daddy. Christ will come and clear it up. He'll banish the strife and misunderstanding. There will be no more war and hate."

Springer tamped his fury and spoke softly. "Strife and hate have been with us since the beginning of time. And they will remain with us as long as ignorance and superstition control the way people deal with each other."

"Christ will come soon with Michael's help."

Springer knew that if Michael walked in now he would kill the man with his bare hands. He said, quietly, "In the meantime, we would do better to educate people. Teach them to read, to learn, to reason, to study their history. That is the way they'll learn to live together."

"You don't believe that garbage," Samantha said scornfully.

"Our intellect is our only salvation."

"And love," said Margaret. "The love Christ taught is necessary too."

"Of course," said Springer.

"Those are just words to you, Daddy. You don't know what He taught. You don't believe in Christ, or God, or anything but your silly brain."

"Stop that," said Margaret.

"No, let her go on," said Springer. "Let her talk it out."

"That's what Michael's task is," said Samantha. "He has

to convert the nonbelievers like you and cleanse the earth of their evil."

Springer tried a small joke. "Do we have to be cleansed? Nonbelievers have rights, too."

Samantha ignored it. "History is repeating itself."

"How so?" asked Springer.

"Look at the Arabs."

"The Arabs? Where did they come from?"

Her explanation seemed recited, the words oft-practiced. Her eyes ticked back and forth as if she were reading a text on the wall.

"Again the barbarians are at the gates. This time they control the oil supply as once they occupied Jerusalem. A new crusade is demanded—a great missionary effort to convert the Saracen nonbelievers. It will start in America—Christianity's stronghold."

"If I might interrupt," said Springer. "You're mixing Saracens and barbarians and Crusaders and missionaries into a mulligan stew of religious claptrap. You know damned well that the only barbarians the Crusaders ever met were each other."

Samantha sat, hands folded, perfectly polite while he spoke and resumed speaking as soon as he stopped.

"But first America itself must be cleansed. Americans must join hands and march the path of righteousness. Michael will lead the way."

"No," said Springer, relieved to be off brainwashing and into debate. "You're not going to convert two hundred and fifty million literate people to a fundamentalist religion."

"The young," said Samantha, "we who are not as tainted by sin, will show the way."

"Self-righteous bull!" Springer exploded.

He shook off Margaret's restraining hand. "I never heard such sanctimonious, holier-than-thou hypocrisy in my life. *'Not as tainted with sin?'* Good God, Samantha."

"Sin," said Samantha, looking Springer straight in the eye. "Sin. You know what sin is, Daddy. Fornication. Adultery."

"What?" Springer looked at Margaret. She was white-faced, gripping the edge of the table with bunched fingers.

"Sin," Samantha repeated. "You have sinned against God."

"Oh, come on, Samantha."

"And you sinned against Mother and me."

"No," Margaret gasped. "Don't."

The kitchen was suddenly warm and stuffy. Springer wanted to open the door. Samantha stared into his eyes. She said, "You left us alone for your pleasure."

"What do you mean?" Springer whispered. He wanted to see Margaret's face, but he couldn't escape Samantha's gaze.

"Angela," said Samantha.

"She's gone," whispered Margaret. "It's over."

"No," said Samantha. "He got somebody new."

Springer couldn't tear his eyes from his daughter's frozen face, her mask of pain and hate. Terrible sounds noised in Margaret's throat. Samantha patted her arm in a grotesque parody of comfort.

"Don't worry, Mother. Michael promised me she won't bother Daddy anymore."

"What do you mean?" said Springer.

"Michael promised," said Samantha. "She'll be cleansed." She rose slowly from the table, pushing off with her hands like an old woman, and plodded up the stairs.

Margaret covered her face, muffling her sobs. Springer sat for a long time, listening. When he touched her arm, she cried, "How did she know?"

"*You* knew?" asked Springer.

"Oh, Alan. You're such a fool. How could I not know?"

"I'm sorry."

Margaret uncovered her face.

"For getting caught? I'm sorry too, dear. Now I can't pretend anymore."

She withdrew her arm. The motion was neither abrupt nor angry, merely definitive.

"I better go up to her," said Springer.

"You should." She gazed out the bay window and mechanically straightened a curtain.

Springer climbed the back stairs and knocked on Samantha's door. There was no reply. He knocked again and opened the door.

Samantha was kneeling by her bed. He knelt beside her.

"There are certain things you don't . . . understand. When you're older . . ."

He stopped talking when her teary eyes went blank.

She was praying to Michael as he backed out of her room.

30

"I'm really tempted to dump every one of those registration mailers in the garbage," said Sophie Wilkins with a bitter laugh. "Wonder what the louses would do about that?"

"How many are there?" asked Springer. He had caught up on his sleep and now, as he sat commiserating with Sophie and Bob at Rigby's lunch counter, he found himself thinking about the old McGovern campaign, recalling his strategies, the tricks he had learned. An idea was forming in his mind.

"Seven hundred and fifty-four," Kent answered hoarsely. He looked as worn as he had the night of the meeting

"Some more came into the post office this morning," said Sophie. She dabbed disinterestedly at her chocolate sundae.

But Springer was barely listening. "We can beat them," he said suddenly. "We can win the election."

"Like hell we can," snapped Kent. "You heard the numbers. They own this town."

"But they've registered everybody they have," said Springer. "Why don't we? We must have three hundred people in the township who aren't registered."

"He's right," said Sophie.

Kent shook his head. "There's three and a half weeks before final registration for this election. You'd never get enough people in that time."

"I'll goddamn try," Springer snarled, his desperate anger surging into his throat. He had nothing more to lose. No place to go. No one to go with him. The Revelationists had seen to that.

"Take it easy, Alan."

"It's worth a try," Springer insisted. "We could advertise in the paper. Canvass by phone. I'll drive around the farms. People know me out there. You and Sophie could work the town. Maybe Ed Stratton would help. And Reverend Davies."

Guarded interest flickered in Kent's tired eyes. "Maybe."

"It's better than nothing," said Sophie. "Come on, Bob, snap out of it. Alan's right. There's a chance."

Kent stared at his reflection in the smoky mirror. "I guess we could give it a try. . . . I'll ask Tom House to push a registration drive in the paper. But you'll have to get the names off the tax rolls. I'll tell Mrs. Bone it's okay."

"What about you?"

"I've got a meeting with Fred. We've got some options to discuss. Sophie, why don't you talk to Stratton and Davies?"

Sophie went back to the post office and Kent and Springer hurried across the street. A cool north wind ruffled Kent's thin hair, baring his pink scalp. He hunched his shoulders against the chill. They went into the town clerk's file room, where Kent laid out the appropriate records. They were in enormous loose-leaf books with cracked plastic bindings. "You know how these work?"

"How do you think I found all those Democrats for McGovern?"

"Try for a more practical victory this time."

"He would have been better than Nixon."

"So would Mussolini. Good luck."

Springer spent the morning comparing names in the tax rolls to names in the voting rolls. He made a list, with addresses, of those he found in the former but not in the latter. The list totaled eighty-four before he had to quit to open the clinic.

Later that afternoon, after the last of the Revelationists had been registered, he returned to the clerk's office and worked until nine. Light-headed with hunger, his eyes weary, he counted 130 unregistered adult residents of Hudson City Township before exhaustion made him quit.

He marked some forty names of people he knew personally or had treated recently. The rest were relative strangers. Most lived on remote farms. Reaching them was going to take a lot of time.

He telephoned Sophie and told her what he had. She promised to work on the rolls tomorrow. She had convinced Reverend Davies and Ed Stratton to work on the drive. Then Springer called Kent, who sounded even more dispirited than he had earlier. "House won't help," he said glumly. "Doesn't want to get involved."

"I'll talk to him," said Springer. "See you in the morning."

"I have to run down to Albany," said Kent. "Fred thinks we might have a case down there."

"How?"

"It's complicated. He thinks we can lobby for help."

"What about the canvassing?"

"You and Sophie and the others will have to start without me."

Springer wished him luck and hung up. What the hell was wrong with Tom House? He was starving, but Rigby's drugstore was closed, so he stifled his desire to eat and knocked, instead, on the *Sun*'s door until a light came on and Tom House appeared in an old blue robe.

"Did I wake you?" asked Springer.

"Nope," House said cheerfully. "Just finished phoning a story down to the *News*. The Revvies are keeping me hopping."

"May I come in?"

House led him through his darkened office to the back room where he lived. It had one window. A television played at the foot of the bed. There was a half-size refrigerator with a hot plate on top. House indicated that Springer should take the single chair, while he sat on the bed.

Springer wasted no time. "Bob says you don't want to help us."

House preened his hair. It was so white it seemed to glow. He turned off the sound on the television. "I've been doing some research. This is the first time a group like this has taken over a town."

"They haven't done it yet," said Springer.

"Foregone conclusion," said House.

"We can stop them. We're making a list of unregistered voters. Enough to win the election. Reaching them and rousing the others is a publicity battle. We need you, Tom."

House shook his head. "I'm not looking for a battle. I'll sell you any ad space you want for the usual rate, but otherwise the *Sun* is sitting this one out. No endorsements. No editorials. No favorites."

"Are you afraid the Revelationists will retaliate if they win?"

"Nope. The fact of the matter is that Kent and his bunch have been in office too long. We could use some changes."

"Not outsiders."

House shrugged. His eyes drifted toward the silent television images. "I want to keep a clear perspective on this one."

"A clear perspective? . . . Oh." Springer stood up. "I get it, Tom. You're a good, old reporter, aren't you? The New York *Daily News* is glad to have you on the scene as long as you're not part of it. But if you took sides, they'd send another man."

"They'd send a punk kid," House said savagely. "This is my story."

Springer laughed. "Do you think the Revvies will let you send out stories about them when they're running the town? They'll shut you down in a day, Tom."

House stretched toward the television and turned on the sound.

Springer picked his way through the dark front office and slammed the door behind him. The night was cool and the blue lights of Revelations glowed clear and bright on the face of the mountain. A car passed, then a truck. Otherwise the streets were as empty as the sidewalk.

He had paused, debating whether to go home or to the hospital, when he saw the blue light bright against the blackness, swinging slowly back and forth. For a moment its motion mesmerized him. Then, shaking the sensation off, he hurried to investigate. It was in Lewis's General Store, and as he drew nearer he saw that Pete was perched on a ladder in the window, amidst his display of chain saws and rakes, hanging a single blue Christmas light from a hook in the ceiling.

Springer tapped on the glass. Lewis looked at him blankly for a moment, then finished wrapping the wire around the hook. Springer watched, his mind racing, while the storekeeper climbed down the ladder, carried it out of the window, and finally reappeared at the front door. He waited while Lewis locked up. He was astonished when the storekeeper turned around and the streetlight revealed the exhaustion in his face.

"What's the light for?" Springer asked, knowing the answer.

Lewis's tired eyes focused on Springer. His face set in a rigid smile.

"What's the light for?" Springer repeated.

"The Lord will come." Lewis's voice was hoarse.

"What?"

"Christ will come when Michael says it's time. We cleanse the path, we light the way."

"Pete!" Springer said sharply. "Were you up there?"

Lewis's face closed.

"What happened?" yelled Springer.

"I took the training."

"Did you join them?"

Lewis nodded.

"What did they do to you?"

Lewis laughed.

"What?"

Lewis laughed some more. He couldn't stop. Hysteria tinged his voice. He convulsed into a doubled-up crouch. Springer hit his face with his open palm. The laughter stopped.

"What happened?" Springer demanded.

"I saw God," Lewis said and walked away.

For two grueling weeks, Springer crisscrossed the township in his car, pleading with people to register to vote, while Sophie and Reverend Davies canvassed door to door in the town itself and Ed Stratton did follow-up work on the telephone, spurring people to fulfill their promises. Whether out of fear of the Revelationists or from the constancy of the canvassers' demands, people came to town and registered to vote and gradually the rolls expanded—sixty new voters the first week, fifty more the second—and it began to look as if the town might outpoll the sect.

After the town had been thoroughly canvassed, Sophie joined Springer on the road, roaring over the countryside in her red Blazer, pouncing upon farmers and shack dwellers whom Springer had been unable to budge. She was enormously persuasive and soon she was herding to town hall some particularly scruffy types who hadn't been seen in Hudson City in years.

Springer was exhausted. He switched shifts with his intern so he could canvass days, which put him on call at night, and he had been roused at least once a night from the couch in the den where he was sleeping. Margaret had laid down a stern truce. She would cook meals and run the house, but she wanted neither to talk to him nor spend time in the same room with him. Samantha would not talk to him either, though several times when he was on the telephone he caught her watching, her eyes fathomless. Whenever he made overtures, she looked blank and turned away.

Thus he was surprised upon wakening on a Friday morning to find her kneeling uneasily next to his couch. Sunlight, sliced by the den shutters, scored her face with black and white lines.

He spoke first. "Good morning, darling."

She stared. "I love you, Daddy."

"Come here." Aching with gratitude, he pulled her to him. Her body felt very strong. He kissed her hair and rumpled it where it was stubbly short in back.

"I love you too, Samantha. I've missed you." He held her for a while, luxuriating in the physical contact. He had been alone, it seemed, forever.

Samantha spoke against his bare chest. "Daddy?"

"Yes?"

"You must stop resisting Michael."

He pushed her away, the joy crashing inside him. She struggled back. "Daddy, you're wrong. Michael doesn't hate you. But you must stop before it's too late."

"Did he tell you to say that?" Springer recoiled from the animal snarl he heard in his voice.

"God told me," said Samantha. "You've suffered enough for your sin, Daddy. If you accept Michael, God will forgive you, and then I will forgive you."

He almost broke; he would have if he had not seen her eyes. But she was staring through him as if he were clear glass. He sat up wearily, tired before the day had started, and turned his mind to the work at hand. He and Sophie would spend the next two days on the north end of the township. They would hit everyone else on the list by midweek, which would give them another few days for follow-up. He was getting excited. It would work.

The telephone rang. Bob Kent.

"How's Albany?" asked Springer. Kent had stayed to lobby.

"Albany is Albany. How we doing on your end?"

Springer related their progress, then asked when Kent would return.

"Maybe Monday," said Kent. He sounded doubtful.

"Daddy," said Samantha as Springer hung up the telephone.

"What, dear?" he asked absently, tying his robe to pad upstairs through Margaret's room to the shower. He thought it was curious how quickly he was able to harden himself to Samantha. But for the moment she was Michael's instrument and he had first to defeat him before he could help her.

She said, "Mr. Spencer is taking the training."

"What?"

"Michael says he'll be allowed to join."

"Spence?"

"You could too, before it's too late."

Springer recovered quickly. The baby-faced grocer was not a surprise. Like Pete Lewis, he had a lot to lose by alienating the Revelationists. Springer put it from his mind. The merchants were bound to suck up to their best customers.

Still, as he drove out of town and saw the blue light in the IGA window, he thought of something else. Both Lewis and Spencer were very religious men. Few people in Hudson City ever took church more seriously. Two blue lights. He braced himself for more. Preston, perhaps. And possibly Moser, though the old lumberman was probably too independent and too crafty to be cornered.

But that would be it, with the exception of a nut or two. None of the teachers would capitulate. And for the moment the farmers were too busy with harvest to convert to anything. Springer knew. He had been trekking through their fields, cornering them for hasty words in the lee of a hay truck or, mingled with cigarette smoke, leaning against the thick treads of a tractor wheel.

Throughout the day, he thought about Samantha's overture. If Michael had sent her—and he had a strong feeling that he had—it meant that they were afraid that Springer would register enough new voters to defeat the Revelationists in the November election. Springer grinned as he swung into another dirt driveway. Resistance was reassuring. The bastards had noticed.

It was a good day. By dark he had persuaded twenty people to register. He had their telephone numbers so he could call to remind them. Ed Stratton's showroom lights were still on when Springer passed on the state highway. The dealer was at his desk in the corner, on the telephone. He waved, hung up, and unlocked the glass door.

"You too? Sophie just roared by a minute ago. That woman drives like incoming artillery."

"Just finishing," said Springer. "How'd you do today?"

Stratton used his cold cigar to indicate the sheets of yellow legal paper strewn over his desk. "Thirty telephone promises. Most of 'em solid."

"Nice going."

Stratton grinned a rare grin. "There's a lot of people going to be driving new cars, cheap, if they remember the promises I made today."

"We're going to make it," said Springer. He summarized his successes. Stratton wrote calculations on a fresh page.

"We'll make it, but it's going to be close."

"We'll lean on them all week," said Springer. "I'll follow up yours and you follow up mine."

"Where's Kent?"

"Still in Albany. He called this morning."

"What the hell can he do down there on the weekend?"

Springer shrugged. "He said he'd be back Monday."

"That reminds me. Davies called. He says we can address the congregation about registration on Sunday. I told him you'd do it."

"Thank you."

"Now if that's all," said Stratton, "I'm calling it a night."

"Like a drink?" asked Springer.

"No. I gotta go home. It's Roscoe's birthday. Eighteen. Hey, want to see what I got him?"

He walked Springer into the service area. A sleek red Camaro crouched by the door. "Think he'll like it?"

Springer whistled. "If he doesn't I'll take it."

Stratton chuckled. "I raised him strict, but . . . he's my oldest. I always wanted something like this when I was his age. My dad didn't think so. You think it's too much?"

"I think it's great."

Stratton stroked the car's sleek fender. "*I* think it's too much. But I want that kid to know he doesn't have to go anywhere else. . . . You know what I mean?"

"Sure. How's Jackie?"

Stratton shook his big head from side to side. "I don't know. He just kinda sits in his room. Roscoe'll run him around in this. That'll cheer him up. . . . How's Samantha?"

"Not good. She tried to talk me into converting this morning. She said Spence is."

Stratton sneered. "Him and Lewis are a pair of ass-kissers."

The telephone rang and Stratton said, "I'll let you out this door, Springer. See you tomorrow. Don't forget the church thing."

As Springer drove home on Main Street, he passed another blue light. The bank. Preston had gone over. It didn't matter. Votes, not businessmen, were going to beat the Revelationists.

Margaret was up in their room and Samantha was sprawled on the living-room couch reading her book of Revelations. She got up without saying hello and climbed the stairs. Springer turned out the lights in the empty room and went to the den. He was getting into bed when the front doorbell rang. It was Ed Stratton.

"Hi. What's up?"

Stratton shoved through the door and leaned it shut. The lines of his face were sharp with anxiety.

"They took my kids."

"What?"

"Jackie and Roscoe are gone."

"Where did they go?"

"Revelations."

"Are you sure?"

"Of course I'm sure, goddammit. They called me. They put the kids on the phone. They said they wouldn't come home if I didn't stop the registration drive."

Springer felt his mouth gape. "What are you going to do?"

Stratton's face worked. "I told 'em I would."

"Stop?"

"I told Roscoe about the car. He said he didn't want worldly goods. What the fuck have they done to that kid? He doesn't even know what *worldly* means."

"You can't stop, Ed. Don't you realize this means they're scared? They know we'll win."

"I'm stopping, Springer. They got me by the balls."

"But—"

"But nothing. They're smart bastards. I'm sitting this one out. Sorry, Springer." He reached in his jacket and pulled out several folded sheets of yellow paper. "Where's your daughter?"

"Upstairs."

Stratton glanced at the light spilling from the banister. He whispered, "You'll need these. Telephone numbers of everybody I talked to. Good luck."

Springer saw a shadow on the stairs. Instinctively, he slipped the papers in the folds of his robe.

Sophie took the news with characteristic cheerfulness.

"Don't blame Ed, we can finish up on our own."

"It's going to be close."

"I wonder why they didn't try the same thing with Samantha," said Sophie.

"It wouldn't have worked," Springer said grimly. "We . . . we've already broken. I don't think it will change until we get rid of them. . . . *If* we get rid of them."

Sophie patted his arm. "Don't worry. We'll get rid of them. Remember, I don't have any kids. There's nothing they can do to me."

They stopped on a remote crossroads near the northern boundary that afternoon and shared a sandwich and thermos lunch. Comparing notes, they split up the remaining farms and agreed to meet at the same crossroads at dusk. Sophie took the lowland farms, Springer the hill farms.

The sun was setting as he eased down a switchback road on a high ridge overlooking a valley. Far below he saw Sophie's red Blazer racing along a dirt road trailing a dust cloud in the dying light. Quickening his own pace so he wouldn't keep her waiting, he noticed a dark truck parked on the shoulder just beyond the bend she was approaching. If she swung wide—which she was likely to do at her crazy pace, he thought with a smile—she would scare the daylights out of the occupants of the truck.

The truck began moving. It rolled off the shoulder onto the road. Springer waited for it to stop as the driver heard the roar of Sophie's engine, but it kept on very slowly. She was almost at the bend when it finally stopped.

Springer didn't have time to think about what happened next. Sophie rounded the bend, swerving wide. The truck shot across the road, directly in her path. Sophie's car skidded, fishtailed. The rear wheels slid wildly, chasing the front until the car was spinning in crazy, sliding circles. It leaped the shoulder and smashed into a huge tree with a crash that Springer heard a quarter mile away.

He pressed his accelerator to the floor. The last he saw before a hairpin turn blocked his view were flames flickering in the wreck of Sophie's car and the dark truck speeding away. He drove as fast as he was able, heaving his car around the tight bends, careening from side to side of the empty road. Gaining the road she had been on moments later, he skidded to a stop beside the wreck.

The Blazer was bent around the tree like a flattened stovepipe. Sophie lay by the tree, bloodied. Springer took one look at the flames crackling fiercely under the car and ran to pull her away before it exploded.

Her right arm was pinned in the wreckage, crushed between the twisted car and the tree. Springer wrenched the fire extinguisher from his trunk and sprayed the flames. They died fitfully under a heavy blanket of white mist, flaring up under the gas tank while he concentrated on the engine, then rising again under the engine when he returned to the tank. At last they were out and he knelt to examine Sophie.

She was unconscious, her face bloody from numerous small cuts. Her legs and torso showed no serious wounds. The arm. Springer checked it last. Christ. There seemed no space at all between the twisted metal and the mashed tree bark. Her hand and forearm had to be crushed flat. Moving around for a better look, he stumbled over the splinters of her guitar. The twisted strings snatched at his pants. Her arm, her arm.

He needed the ambulance, which meant driving nearly two miles to the nearest house with a telephone. He covered her with blankets to protect her shocked body from the evening chill. But as he got into his car, the flames suddenly reappeared under the wreck.

By the time he had sprayed them out, the extinguisher was nearly empty. He looked up and down the empty road. No cars, no houses, no one to help. Sophie's car might ignite and explode while he drove for aid. He shuddered. He had to free her.

He felt sick. A tongue of red flame decided it for him. He sprayed again, emptying the extinguisher, then quickly maneuvered his car to cast the headlights on Sophie and took stock of his few instruments. A scalpel and a twenty-one blade. A few clamps, not enough. Surgical thread. She seemed in deep shock, which would spare her the pain. Hopefully, with great luck, the shock would hold her blood vessels in spasm so she wouldn't bleed too much. He had no one but himself to tie her bleeders.

But he had no saw. He tore through his bag, searching for a cutting wire, knowing he wouldn't find one. He looked around. What the hell did he have in the car? Nothing, nothing, nothing. Something brushed his leg. The guitar. Quickly he wound the high E, the thinnest string, off its post. He laid it on the blanket next to his scalpel. He fumbled open the twenty-one blade's sterile foil wrapper and clicked it into the scalpel.

His instruments were ready, but he hesitated, looked again up and down the road, prayed for help. The road was dark and empty. The flames crackled a warning. He cut.

The scalpel was widest just below the point where the blade bellied gracefully like the bow of a boat. It launched into blood, cleaving, submerging, sailing between ever-deepening walls of flesh and muscle as Springer encircled Sophie's arm, cutting in layers, searching for the bone.

Sophie's head lolled to her shoulder and her eyes fluttered. "Please don't wake up," Springer murmured. He left a U-shaped bulge in the circle to make a skin flap for the stump. As he cut layer after layer, he followed his course with clamps, shutting the vessels, then looping sutures over the clamps and tightening them around the oozing bleeders before removing the clamps.

Suddenly an artery spurted warm blood on his hands.

"Get the pumper," he muttered to himself, searching the slippery artery with a clamp while he pressed his fingers into Sophie's armpit until the spurting slowed. He clamped the pumper and resumed cutting. By the time he was through the flesh of her heavy arm, the flames were licking high around the gas tank. He felt their warmth on his bent legs.

Protecting his skin with gauze, he wrapped the guitar string around his hands until the taut section between them was a foot long. Then he pressed the wire to the exposed bone of Sophie's forearm and began to cut.

The Blazer exploded with a flash that painted Springer's rearview mirror bright orange. Rolling thunder shook his car as he sped away. Sophie stirred on the seat next to him. He'd put her within reach in case she started bleeding.

"Please don't wake up," he pleaded. "Please don't."

His face was wet. He'd cried the entire time it took to dress her wound and load her into the car. What could he ever say to her?

Miraculously, her eyes opened.

"Easy," whispered Springer, his hand on her shoulder. She tried to sit up. "Don't, Sophie."

He looked down at her. Her eyes were clear. She understood everything that had happened, and knew that he had taken her arm. "It's all right, Alan."

She lay quietly as he raced to the hospital.

She was dead when he got there. Her heart had stopped somewhere along the way.

31

The silent organ seemed an eloquent memorial to Sophie Wilkins, Springer thought as he waited to address the congregation. Silence, Davies had said, and Springer had agreed, would best mark Sophie's space in the church.

Every pew was taken and when Springer had politely congratulated the old minister on the attendance, Davies had replied, "They come when they're afraid."

He kept his voting talk brief and ended with a plea to make sense out of Sophie's death. "She made it her battle. She was confident of victory. It's up to us to fight in her place and prove her right."

He stepped down to his pew on the center aisle. Reverend Davies was thanking him ceremoniously when the congregation stirred nervously to the distant sound of marching feet. Outside, Charlie Daniels' amplified voice crackled tinnily—a faraway cry that ended with chilling abruptness.

The silence that followed was as compelling as a scream. Seconds passed. Minutes.

Slowly, the double doors swung open, pushed, it seemed, by a cold breeze. People in the Revelationists' overalls shuffled tentatively into the church and milled uncertainly in the center aisle. They were expressionless, as if drugged by some substance that dissolved the chemical connections to those parts of their minds which made them human. Some were strangers. Most were citizens of Hudson City, known to everyone in the congregation.

Springer saw Pete Lewis, his eyes as lunatic as they had been the night he claimed he had seen God, and Joe Preston, his jowly face empty, and Gary Spencer, without his boyish smile, and Danny Moser's mother, her stringy hair chopped short. Springer scanned the group, his heart sinking. All the merchants were there. He saw Dwight Rigby and Margy next to him. There was Ken Moser with the fathomless eyes of an old wolf brought to bay. And Stratton, standing as patiently as a steer in a slaughter pen. Suddenly he leaped up.

He saw Ellen Barbar. She was among them, her face curiously devoid of animation. He had been right. The Revelationists had had her all along. But what had they done to her? Her exotic eyes were dull, her hair a sad remnant of the silky black cloud he remembered. He started down the aisle, but before he could reach her the church trembled to the pounding of heavy boots.

The Revelationists stormed in the open doors and raced up the aisles. Within seconds, they crammed the aisles until the congregation was split and surrounded. Springer was caught among them, trapped halfway between his pew and Ellen Barbar, whom he had lost sight of behind a wall of blue-clad shoulders.

Again, an eerie silence settled over the church. Springer swallowed his panic and wormed his way toward Ellen. The congregation, frightened wordless, gaped at the Revelationists in the aisles and strained to glimpse their neighbors who had apparently joined the invaders. Softly, seductively, the Revelationists began to chant.

"Turn to the Lord. Turn to the Lord. Turn to the Lord . . ."

It was a low, moaning chant and the words blended smoothly, one into the other, a flowing sound which seemed to fill all space and time. They began swaying, and as they did, Springer squeezed between their moving bodies until he reached the first group, who were still milling in confusion, neither swaying nor chanting.

"Turn to the Lord turn to the Lord turn to the Lord."

He moved among them, conscious of the wall of swaying Revelationists all around, until he found Ellen Barbar. She looked as if she were in a deep trance, but when he took her arm to try to guide her out of the church, she flinched.

He looked around. The Revelationists were lost in their chant. No one seemed to pay attention to him. He was halfway between the altar and the doors. Again, he took Ellen's arm, and tried to turn her toward the back of the church. She pulled away.

"Ellen," he said sharply. "Snap out of it."

"Let go of my arm." She wrested it away. He grabbed her again.

"What are you doing?"

"Let go of me, I'm turning to God."

"Get off that," Springer shouted, his words carrying above the chant.

She looked at him as if staring through a window. "I only wonder why I waited so long."

"Please," cried Springer. "Before they stop us."

"No one will stop you, Dr. Springer," said the trainer, John. He easily pried Springer's hand from Ellen's arm. "No one is coerced, Doctor. You're free to go."

Springer stared at Ellen. Her face seemed a peaceful mask, as if she had died in her sleep. "What have you done to her?" he asked the trainer.

The trainer's voice cut clearly through the chanting. "We have shown her God. Haven't we, Ellen?"

"Yes," said Ellen. "I hope you find Him too, Alan. Before it's too late."

"Where's Rose?" shouted Springer. "Where's your sister?"

"She never had a sister," said the trainer.

"What?"

"That was just Ellen's why of resisting us. Wasn't it, Ellen?"

"Yes."

"It was hard for you to find God."

"Yes."

"Are you ready to give yourself to Michael?"

"Yes."

"Are you ready to be initiated?"

"Yes."

The trained glanced at Springer, his eyes malevolent, as he asked Ellen the last question.

"Are you sure?"

Terror skipped fleetingly across her face. "Yes."

The chanting stopped abruptly. As one, the Revelationists turned toward the doors and watched with grim expressions. Then they cheered. Clad in a flowing white gown, Michael strode into the church. The Revelationists cleared a narrow lane down the middle of the center aisle. Springer was shoved to one side.

Michael marched forward and ascended the pulpit. He raked Reverend Davies with his awesome eyes. Davies cowered, retreating toward the flower-covered altar. Mi-

chael turned his back on him and gripped the lectern with
both enormous hands.

"REJOICE! THE LORD HAS COME!"

"The Lord has come!" echoed his followers.

"He can save you," shouted Michael. "He can save every
man and woman here as he will save these fresh converts
who await his love so eagerly." His mighty arm leveled at
Ellen and the others who were watching with rapt expressions. "He will save these initiates." His gesture broadened
to include the entire congregation. "And he will save you.
If you let him. *If* you know that the Lord has come. *If* you
turn to him."

"Turn to the Lord!" shouted the Revelationists. "Turn to
the Lord!"

Reverend Davies crept behind Michael, his mouth working fearfully. Several broad-shouldered men blocked his
way. The diminutive minister tried to claw between them,
but they stood still, not noticing.

Michael's voice rose until its power seemed to shake the
church like a mighty wind.

"The day is here! The time is now!"

The Revelationists roared their joy.

"We will cleanse this temple. We will initiate our new
converts within these foul walls. Let them turn to God
when they feel his love." He raised his arms and commanded the congregation, "Let *all* be cleansed and march
with us to God's house."

Great waves of hypnotic sound pealed from his mouth.
Springer's skin prickled. *"God marshals his forces. Michael
leads them to battle. Turn to Michael!"*

A wild, strange moan filled the air. The Revelationists
were attending their leader with a wordless wail that spoke
of utter submission. And throughout the church Springer
saw the faces of men and women he had known his whole
life begin to change before his eyes. They seemed possessed, their souls transported. Fear changed to wonder,
pleasure. Faces scarred by the years of hard times and
dreams lost glowed blankly.

Michael's voice flowed like a thick, soft liquid that
threatened to engulf every human in the church. Now they
all were moaning. Springer felt a sound pass between his
lips. He looked frantically about, seeking detachment. They
all looked the same. Movement attracted his eye. Behind

Michael, unseen by his guard, Reverend Davies crept from the altar and shambled out the back door, his head bowed in shame.

"ARISE!" proclaimed Michael. "ARISE AND PLEDGE YOUR LIFE TO CHRST! ARISE AND TURN TO GOD!"

Ellen Barbar screamed.

"ARISE!" Michael urged.

She pushed up the aisle. Stroking her body, shrieking with her, the Revelationists hurried her toward the altar.

"No!" Springer yelled. He lunged for her passing figure. He had seen her terror and terror was life. He could still save her. . . . But his cry was lost in the screaming. A surging flow of converts bore her from his grasp as dozens of men and woman abandoned the congregation and struggled toward the altar. Like sleepwalkers, they brushed past their neighbors through the double line of moaning Revelationists toward the giant with the golden hair who exhorted them on with wordless sounds.

Springer plunged after Ellen. Fighting to keep his balance, he felt as if he were on the crest of a wave, surging toward destruction on the lunatic tide of Michael's voice. He rammed through the frenzied, shrieking supplicants and seized her arm.

"Run!" he screamed. "Get away!"

Ellen tugged toward the altar.

Holding her tightly, he tried to veer out of the aisle. The Revelationists blocked him with a wall of shoulders. Ellen pulled harder.

"Ellen," he pleaded.

He felt Michael's eyes burning into him.

The Revelationist was watching sardonically, his mouth twisted with derision, his eyes glowing. He made a swift hand signal. Two enormous blond men stepped between Springer and Ellen and broke Springer's grasp with a blow that numbed his wrist.

Ellen slipped away, borne to the altar by a dozen hands. Other hands pawed his body and pushed him forward. Springer wrenched free and struggled toward the door through which Reverend Davies had fled. Looking back, he caught a glimpse of Ellen kneeling at Michael's feet. Michael touched her hair. She screamed and grabbed his legs, thrusting her face into his thighs.

"ARISE! TURN TO MICHAEL!"

Springer slammed the door behind him and staggered into the churchyard and ran until he could no longer hear the seductive moaning.

Gradually his senses returned and he took fierce joy in the cold air on his face, the sound of his shoes scraping the stone path, the spongy softness of the grass.

Reverend Davies was in the cemetery kneeling by his wife's grave, crying. Springer knelt beside the old man and put his arm around his shoulders. As would a child when comforted, Davies sobbed harder. Springer embraced him, rocking him gently until his crying subsided.

After a while the minister pulled away.

"Thank you," he said formally, drawing around him his cloak of reserve. "You were most kind."

He struggled to his feet, his tear-streaked face smooth and rigid as a stone bust.

Shock, Springer thought.

"Did they come forward?" Davies asked.

"Some did."

"I heard a man preach like that once years ago. I presume he died because I never heard of him again and that kind of preaching makes a man immortal. . . . God help us." His voice was curiously detached.

"Mass hysteria," said Springer. He located a low, smooth black headstone and sat on it, drawing his knees up to his chest.

"Mass hysteria," Davies repeated. "The madness of crowds. The grand delusion."

"It can't last," said Springer.

"It can't?" The minister smiled down at Springer. "Grand delusions often last a long, long time. The Crusades spanned several centuries. Hitler convinced the Germans for a decade."

"This craziness will be over in a week," said Springer.

Davies didn't hear him. "But we Christians are the record holders. We've maintained a stance in one form or another for two thousand years."

It was quiet in the graveyard. The oak trees had turned red, the maples yellow. The grass was still bright, bright green. Davies picked up a fallen leaf and inspected its veins in the sun.

Springer looked at him dully. *"You* don't believe in God?"

"Of course I believe in God. I'm one of the deluded. I believe with all my heart and soul, but when I see these Revelationists converting people to their mindless faith I get a new perspective on my own. I see that I'm as trapped in belief as they are. But I still love my God . . . and my belief." Davies drew himself up, some of his dignity regained. "I am a minister of God. Eighty generations of clergy support my ministry. A thousand years ago we died by the Viking sword. Five hundred years later we hid in the forest from King Henry. We led people to this new land. We've built nations, ruled nations, and fled nations. We have been many things to many men. We have survived."

A Revelationist hymn thundered from the church.

"I have another week to get people registered," Springer said doggedly.

Davies smiled. "Are you sure those you've registered will vote your way?"

Springer stared at the nearest headstone. Mary Beth Moser, sixteen, had died in 1887.

> Borne to the Lord on wings of gold,
> Would that Mary had been old.
> Bless the family left behind her,
> Hope, to them, God will be kinder.

He said, "It's madness. It can't last."

"Perhaps," said Davies.

The wind blew dry leaves past their legs. The singing stopped. Davies gazed at his rectory. A model ship sailed the sunlight in the window. He murmured to himself, "I hope they let me keep the house."

32

Springer watched from the shelter of a stone fence pillar while the Revelationists marched singing from the church. Ten abreast, they wheeled up Spotting Mountain Road with Michael in the lead. Midway, the column had formed a tight rectangle inside of which walked fifty converts who had heeded Michael's call. They looked, Springer thought, like the prisoners of a triumphant Roman legion.

Where were the children, he wondered. Why hadn't they come running? The answer hit him with bitter certainty. *The children had stayed home because Michael told them to.*

With sick fascination, he watched the column from the roadside until it disappeared around a bend. Then he walked slowly back. Reverend Davies was still in the cemetery. Through the double church doors, which were flapping in the breeze, he saw that the church was empty.

A nurse ran from the hospital, her uniform startling white.

"Dr. Springer! Doctor!"

Springer crossed Main Street. She was a part-timer, a local, middle-aged woman he barely knew. "What?"

"Thank God we found you. It's Mr. Daniels."

Springer strode smoothly into the hospital, calming her with simple questions. Moments after he had tried to stop the Revelationists from invading the church, Charlie Daniels had staggered into the emergency room, blood streaming over his face, and collapsed. Neither the nurse nor Reggie, the ambulance driver, knew how badly he was hurt, but he still hadn't regained consciousness.

Reggie had him on the emergency table. He was positioning the X-ray machine as Springer came in.

"Thanks," said Springer, shouldering him aside. He bent over Daniels. The officer's khakis were dappled with blood.

In their confusion neither the nurse nor Reggie had removed the electric bull horn which dangled from its wrist strap.

"Take that off."

Reggie pulled it off.

Daniels was breathing shallowly. He looked like a pale, frightened child. Springer sympathized with the panicked nurse; an injured, helpless police officer was a frightening sight.

"Did you call the state police?" asked Springer.

"Mr. Kent took care of it," said Reggie.

"Kent?"

"He's in your office."

Wondering when he had gotten back, Springer turned his attention to Charlie Daniels. His scalp was laid open in several places. Springer did not like the look and feel of the wounds and X rays confirmed his fears.

"Multiple fractures. You're going to have to run him to Saratoga. He needs surgery. I'll get him ready to travel. Take Mel with you. I'll phone ahead."

Ten minutes later, the big ambulance eased onto Main Street and howled south, building gently to tremendous speed.

Springer found Kent in his office. He dropped wearily into his desk chair. "He's bad."

"That's a shame."

"Where are the troopers?"

Kent shrugged. He was sitting on the couch, his legs stretched out, his arms spread wide.

Springer picked up his telephone. "I'll give 'em another yell."

"That's not necessary," said Kent.

Springer stopped dialing, arrested by the casual note in Kent's voice. "What?"

"Let's not worry about the troopers just now. We've got other things to talk about."

Springer cradled the telephone.

"How's the registration drive coming?" asked Kent.

Springer stared at him for a long time. "You didn't go to Albany."

"Sure I did. Me and Fred went down Thursday. A friend

of Michael's got in touch. I drove back up and had an interesting chat with Michael."

"At Revelations?"

Kent smiled affably. "I came around to Michael's way of seeing things. He's right, you know. The world *is* in chaos. We *have* sinned greatly, destroyed the environment, and let the Heathen get the upper hand."

"The Heathen?" Springer asked incredulously.

"The Arabs and the Africans. God's servants are going to have to straighten things out. I got to thinking we ought to put ourselves on the right side before that happens, if you know what I mean."

"Fred agreed?"

Kent frowned. "Fred's been given the opportunity to consider the problem. He'll come around."

Springer stared. *"You?* You *believe* all that?"

A familiar blank look came over Kent's round face.

"Did you convert?" Springer was shouting.

Kent's eyes lanced through him. "Michael trained me personally. I'm a servant of the highest order."

"Bob."

"Michael wants me to stay on as mayor."

"His mayor?"

"He needs experienced men. You really should consider coming over real soon, Alan. Before it's too late."

"You're crazy. You're brainwashed. Bob, you can't—"

Kent stood up. "The parents are going to have a final opportunity to reunite with their children this afternoon. Why don't you go home and talk it over with Samantha?"

Springer pointed a quivering finger at Kent. "I'll stop you. I'll register those voters and I'll stop you."

Kent spoke in monotone. "See to your daughter, Dr. Springer."

33

Main Street was empty.

A cold breeze rustled the leaves in the gutters. Most of them were down, here, and a big sky loomed through the skeletal trees.

At home, Springer found Margaret and Samantha sharing the Revelations pamphlet in front of a crackling fire. He told them what had happened at the church and to Charlie Daniels and what Bob Kent had done. Margaret bowed her head.

Samantha regarded him with empty eyes.

"God has come, Daddy."

A sarcastic laugh died in Springer's throat. "No, darling. God was here all along, but I think He just left."

For a second—an instant that restored all his strength, all his hope—Samantha's eyes lighted at the feeble joke. He grinned at her, fanning the spark.

Heavy boots thudded on the porch. A fist hammered the door. Samantha and Margaret looked as if they had expected the intrusion. Springer's belly clutched when he noticed two overnight bags next to the front door. He crossed the living room in a smooth, quick motion and yanked it open.

Four Revelationists were waiting.

"Samantha Springer," the heavy-set woman in front said sternly.

"I'm here," called Samantha.

They pushed past Springer and grouped in the living room. "Samantha, are you ready to turn to God?"

"I am ready."

"Are your mother and father coming with you?"

Margaret moved behind her and placed her hands on Samantha's shoulders.

"My mother is coming." She turned to Springer. "You can come too, Daddy."

"What for?"

"For training," said the woman.

"I forbid it," snapped Springer.

"Is your father coming, Samantha?" asked the woman.

"I said I forbid it," said Springer.

"Please come, Daddy."

"Neither of you can go there."

Margaret spoke. "Does that mean you won't come with us?"

"What is this?" asked Springer.

The four Revelationists watched him with unblinking eyes—snakes waiting for a rat to make the first move. Samantha took his arm.

"Daddy. Each child was told to bring her parents so Michael can teach them and cleanse their souls." She pulled him to the window and drew the curtain. "See?"

A school bus was parked at the curb. His neighbors were inside with their children, watching from the foggy windows."

"No," said Springer. "You can't do this."

He locked the front door and blocked it with his body.

The Revelationists spread out and stalked him. He swiveled his head trying to anticipate which would attack first.

"Daddy, don't," cried Samantha.

"Please let us go," Margaret said.

A man with a flat, broad face and big hands lunged for him.

"*Don't!*" screamed Samantha. She thrust herself between the Revelationist and her father.

"Samantha!" the woman said sharply.

Samantha froze, backed away. "I'm sorry," she whispered. When she was clear, the man came again at Springer.

"Alan," said Margaret. "You'll just get hurt. We'll go anyway."

"How can you do this?" whispered Springer.

Margaret raised her chin. "Samantha is all I have now. All I ever had."

Springer stood aside.

Margaret and Samantha picked up their bags and

walked out. The Revelationists followed. The last one carefully shut the door. Springer watched from the window as the bus rolled down the empty street and stopped a few houses away. A man, a woman, and a boy got on. Springer strained for a glimpse of Samàntha or Margaret through the reflections in its windows. Only after it had driven out of sight did he wonder how long they would be gone.

He stood by the window a long time. Then he sat by the fire and had a drink. When the embers grew cold he put his coat on and walked to the hospital. Passing Grand Street he saw blue lights in several homes. He saw others in the apartments above the stores. A large one shone in the window of Kent's realty office.

The duty nurse looked worried—like a cat awaiting a thunderstorm. The ward was empty. Reggie and the intern weren't back from Saratoga. The nurse wanted to talk. Springer sent her home.

He went to his office and sat, thinking, until it was dark. Still he sat, neither turning on the lights nor answering the telephones the several times they rang. A small part of his mind told him he shouldn't have sent the nurse home. He checked the duty chart. Her replacement was due at six.

He took Danny Moser's gun from his desk drawer, fished the loose cartridges from paper clips and pencil stubs, and loaded the weapon. Then he walked home, got his car, and drove up Spotting Mountain Road.

He stopped outside the gates of Revelations. The only lights were the blue ones in the windows. He left his headlights on so he could see, and clutching the gun in his coat pocket, rang the bell, and waited, shivering in the cold. It was too dark to see anything beyond the circle of his headlights. He rang the bell again, held it for a full minute. He smelled snow on the wind.

"Yes, Dr. Springer?"

34

Michael stepped out of the darkness, opened the gate, and moved close to Springer. Springer backed away, his feet feeling for purchase on the sloping apron. He wondered why Michael was alone, and why that frightened him.

He said, "I want my daughter."

"Samantha is God's child," said Michael. "My child. She chooses to stay here."

"You've taken everything," said Springer. "Give me my daughter. I beg you. Give her back to me."

"Everything belongs to God," said Michael, looming closer.

With a shudder, Springer raised the gun. "I want my daughter."

Michael's eyes lighted as if he were amused. He came closer, tracking Springer as the doctor backed away. "Give me the gun."

"What do you want?" asked Springer, watching his eyes.

"Give me the gun."

"Why are you doing this? What do you want?"

Michael laughed. "Want? I want nothing. I have everything. All the things *you* want. I have your money and your power and your love and your sex and all your pleasures—everything but your fear."

Springer felt the apron dropping sharply. He was afraid to back away any more. Close behind he heard his car, the engine hissing, the transmission's high whine. Michael's long arm reached for him in a lazy, slow motion. His hands were enormous, the powerful fingers beautifully formed. His eyes sighted over his hand. Springer felt them bore into him, seeking his doubt. Michael's hypnotic voice was insistent.

"Give it to me, Doctor."

The hand was inches from the gun. The fingers spread for the grab.

Springer fired.

The gun cracked sharply and a look of infinite surprise crossed Michael's face. He staggered against the gate post, bright arterial blood spurting from his arm. It fountained in the glare of the headlights and splashed on Springer's hand, as Sophie's had. He was horrified. The taste of insane victory soured in his mouth. He dropped the gun and retreated to the comfort of his craft.

Darting between the giant's massive arms, he guided him down to a sitting position against the stone post. Then he got his bag from the car and wrapped a cloth tourniquet above the wound.

Floodlamps flared on, lighting the building and gateway.

Springer worked frantically to stem the bleeding. The bullet had pierced the artery right above the elbow, somehow missing the bone, and Michael's enormous muscular development made it difficult to squeeze the artery shut. He tried a second tourniquet under the armpit.

Doors were banging open at the asylum. Voices called the alarm. As he struggled with Michael's arm, it occurred to Springer that he had never heard the Revelationists shouting this way before. Confusion, or panic, had broken their discipline, but if Michael noticed the difference it did not seem to trouble him. He watched confidently, a smile on his lips, as Springer fought the pumping blood.

The tourniquet was as tight as he could make it with the penlight he was using as a lever. He looked for a second lever. Michael's cross. Springer ripped it from its chain and inserted the long end in the cloth. He twisted hard and the bleeding stopped.

"We have to get you to the hospital," he muttered, securing the tourniquet by forcing the short arms of the cross under the bandage. The Revelationists were pounding down the driveway carrying blue-shaded lanterns. Springer glanced anxiously at the bobbing lights.

"Don't be afraid," said Michael. "I won't let them hurt you." He raised his arm as if to stop them, but it fell heavily to his lap. Puzzlement glazed his eyes, his leonine head sagged, and, to Springer's horror, he fainted against the stone post.

The front runners were a hundred feet away. They saw Springer crouching over Michael's body. One of them shrieked, "The Devil!"

"He's not dead!" shouted Springer. "Get him to the hospital. Save him."

The rest took up a howling chorus. "The Devil! The Devil!"

A blue light arced through the night and crashed at his feet. Springer leaped into his car and locked the doors. He slammed the gear shift into reverse, but they had already blocked the road behind him. One of them picked up a large rock and flung it. It shattered the back window.

Springer jammed the car into drive and shot up the mountain road, leaving the blue lanterns behind. He drove fast for a mile. When the road ended he swerved onto the gravel lumber track and continued up to the parking area on the high plateau. It was as far as he could take the car. He rolled down his window and listened. The night was still.

His hands were shaking and he felt nauseated. He got out of the car and leaned on the fender, his head roaring. What if they didn't take Michael to the hospital? What if that damned medic tried to handle it? If the artery were severed would he have the brains to bring him in or would he screw around with acupressure? Springer took deep breaths of the cold air. He had to go back.

A light stabbed the darkness. Dozens of blue lanterns were bobbing up the lumber road. They were looking for him. He crouched low and ran from the car, fleeing across the plateau until he had to stop short at the brink of a sheer drop. Trapped. He looked down at the black bowl of the valleys.

Blue lights shone in the old asylum. Below, more blue lights pocked the white cluster that marked the town, and even while he watched more and more blue lights blossomed in the town and out among the farms as new converts signaled their surrender to the Revelationists.

The madness of crowds, Reverend Davies had called it. A grand delusion. Springer could not take much comfort in a phrase. The Revelationists' blue lanterns were drawing near. He heard them shout when they found his car.

They sounded angry.

Dell Bestsellers

REMEMBER IT DOESN'T GROW ON TREES

ENERGY CONSERVATION -
IT'S YOUR CHANCE TO SAVE, AMERICA

Department of Energy, Washington, D.C.

A PUBLIC SERVICE MESSAGE FROM DELL PUBLISHING CO., INC.